Official Guide to Certified SOLIDWORKS Associate Exams: CSWA, CSDA, CSWSA-FEA

SOLIDWORKS 2015 – SOLIDWORKS 2017

An authorized CSWA preparation exam guide with additional information on the CSDA and CSWSA-FEA exams

David C. Planchard
CSWP & SOLIDWORKS Accredited Educator

Publications

SDC Publications
P.O. Box 1334
Mission, KS 66222
913-262-2664
www.SDCpublications.com
Publisher: Stephen Schroff

INTRODUCTION

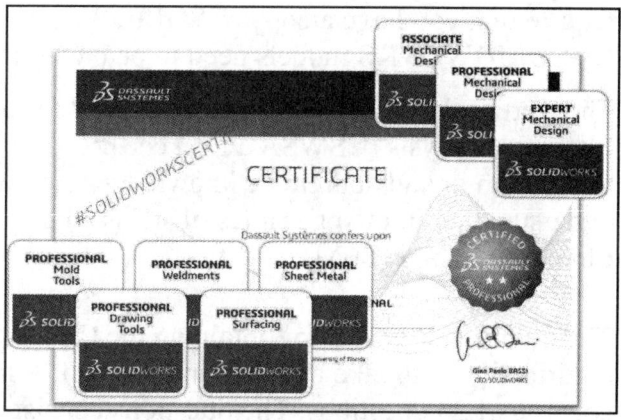

The **Official Guide to Certified SOLIDWORKS Associate Exams: CSWA, CSDA, CSWSA-FEA** is written to assist the SOLIDWORKS user to pass the associate level exams. Information is provided to aid a person to pass the Certified SOLIDWORKS Associate (CSWA), Certified SOLIDWORKS Sustainable Design Associate (CSDA) and the Certified SOLIDWORKS Simulation Associate Finite Element Analysis (CSWSA FEA) exam.

DS SOLIDWORKS Corp. offers various types of certification. Each stage represents increasing levels of expertise in 3D CAD: Certified SOLIDWORKS Associate (CSWA), Certified SOLIDWORKS Professional (CSWP) and Certified SOLIDWORKS Expert (CSWE) along with specialty fields.

The CSWA certification indicates a foundation in and apprentice knowledge of 3D CAD design and engineering practices and principles. The main requirement for obtaining the CSWA certification is to take and pass the two part online proctored exams. This first exam (part 1) is 90 minutes, minimum passing score is 80 with 6 questions. The second exam (part 2) is 90 minutes, minimum passing score is 80 with 8 questions.

Copy the corresponding CSWA Model Folder from the book that matches your release of SOLIDWORKS to your hard drive. Work directly from your hard drive on the tutorials in this book. SOLIDWORKS model files for 2015 - 2017 are provided.

The Certified SOLIDWORKS Sustainable Design Associate (CSDA) certification indicates a foundation in and apprentice knowledge of demonstrating an understanding in the principles of environmental assessment and sustainable design.

The main requirement for obtaining the CSDA certification is to take and pass the online 30 minute exam (minimum of 24 out of 30 points).

The CSDA exam consists of a total of 30 questions in various categories: *Environmental Assessment, Introduction to sustainability* and *Sustainable design*.

Introduction

All questions are in a multiple choice/multi answer format. SOLIDWORKS does not require that you have a copy of SOLIDWORKS Sustainability, or even SOLIDWORKS. No SOLIDWORKS models need to be created for this exam.

The Certified SOLIDWORKS Simulation Associate - Finite Element Analysis (CSWSA-FEA) certification indicates a foundation in and apprentice knowledge of demonstrating an understanding in the principles of stress analysis and the Finite Element Method (FEM).

The main requirement for obtaining the CSWSA-FEA certification is to take and pass the online 120 minute exam which consists of 20 questions. The questions consist of 3 hands-on problems, single answer, multiple choice, yes/no and multiple selection for a total of 100 points. Minimum passing score is 70.

The purpose of this section is not to educate a new or intermediate user on SOLIDWORKS Simulation or Finite Element Analysis theory, but to cover and to inform you on the required understanding types of questions, layout and what to expect when taking the CSWSA-FEA exam.

Copy the corresponding CSWSA FEA Model Folder from the book that matches your release of SOLIDWORKS to your hard drive. Work directly from your hard drive on the tutorials in this book. SOLIDWORKS model files for 2015 - 2017 are provided.

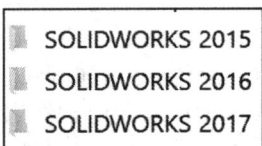

Goals

The primary goal is not only to help you pass the CSWA, CSDA and CSWSA-FEA exams, but also to ensure that you understand and comprehend the concepts and implementation details of the three certification processes.

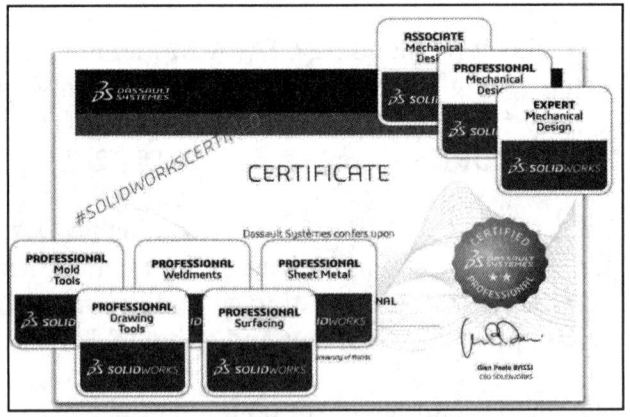

The second goal is to provide the most comprehensive coverage of CSWA, CSDA and CSWSA-FEA exam related topics available, without too much coverage of topics not on the exam.

The third and ultimate goal is to get you from where you are today to the point that you can confidently pass the CSWA, CSDA and the CSWSA-FEA exam.

CSWA Exam Audience

The intended audience for this book trying to take and pass the CSWA exam is anyone with a minimum of 6 - 9 months of SOLIDWORKS experience and basic knowledge of engineering fundamentals and practices. SOLIDWORKS recommends that you review their SOLIDWORKS Tutorials on Parts, Assemblies and Drawings as a prerequisite and have at least 45 hours of classroom time learning SOLIDWORKS or using SOLIDWORKS with basic engineering design principles and practices.

CSDA Exam Audience

The intended audience for this book trying to take and pass the CSDA exam is anyone interested in Sustainable design and life cycle assessment. Although *no hands on usage of SOLIDWORKS* is required for the CSDA certification exam, it is a good idea to review the SOLIDWORKS SustainablityXpress and SOLIDWORKS Sustainability tutorials inside of SOLIDWORKS to better understand the actual workflow.

CSWSA-FEA Exam Audience

The intended audience for this book trying to take and pass the CSWSA-FEA exam is anyone with a minimum of 6 - 9 months of SOLIDWORKS experience and knowledge in the following areas: Engineering Mechanics - Statics, Strength of Materials, Finite Element Method/Finite Element Analysis Theory, Applied concepts in SOLIDWORKS Simulation: namely Static Analysis, Solid, Shell, and Beam elements, Connections and Applying loads and boundary conditions and interpreting results.

The purpose of this section in the book is NOT to educate a new or intermediate user on SOLIDWORKS Simulation, but to cover and to inform you on the required understanding types of questions, layout and what to expect when taking the CSWSA-FEA exam.

About the Author

David Planchard is the founder of D&M Education LLC. Before starting D&M Education, he spent over 27 years in industry and academia holding various engineering, marketing, and teaching positions. He holds five U.S. patents. He has published and authored numerous papers on Machine Design, Product Design, Mechanics of Materials, and Solid Modeling. He is an active member of the SOLIDWORKS Users Group and the American Society of Engineering Education (ASEE). David holds a BSME, MSM with the following professional certifications: CCAI, CCNP, CSDA, CSWSA-FEA, CSWP, CSWP-DRWT and SOLIDWORKS Accredited Educator. David is a SOLIDWORKS Solution Partner, an Adjunct Faculty member and the SAE advisor at Worcester Polytechnic Institute in the Mechanical Engineering department. In 2012, David's senior Major Qualifying Project team (senior capstone) won first place in the Mechanical Engineering department at WPI. In 2014, 2015 and 2016 David's senior Major Qualifying Project team won the Provost award in Mechanical Engineering for design excellence.

David Planchard is the author of the following books:

- **SOLIDWORKS® 2017 Reference Guide with video instruction**, 2016, 2015, 2014, 2013, 2012, 2011, 2010, 2009 and 2008

- **Engineering Design with SOLIDWORKS® 2017 and video instruction**, 2016, 2015, 2014, 2013, 2012, 2011, 2010, 2009, 2008, 2007, 2006, 2005, 2004, and 2003

- **Engineering Graphics with SOLIDWORKS® 2017 and video instruction**, 2016, 2015, 2014, 2013, 2012, 2011, 2010

- **SOLIDWORKS® 2017 in 5 Hours with video instruction**, 2016, 2015, 2014

- **SOLIDWORKS® 2017 Tutorial with video instruction**, 2016, 2015, 2014, 2013, 2012, 2011, 2010, 2009, 2008, 2007, 2006, 2005, 2004, and 2003

- **Drawing and Detailing with SOLIDWORKS® 2014**, 2012, 2010, 2009, 2008, 2007, 2006, 2005, 2004, 2003, and 2002

- **Official Certified SOLIDWORKS® Professional (CSWP) Certification Guide with video instruction, Version 4: 2015 - 2017**, Version 3: 2012 - 2014, Version 2: 2012 - 2013, Version 1: 2010 - 2011

- **Official Guide to Certified SOLIDWORKS® Associate Exams: CSWA, CSDA, CSWSA-FEA Version 3: 2015 - 2017**, Version 2: 2012 - 2015, Version 1: 2012 – 2013

- **Assembly Modeling with SOLIDWORKS® 2012**, 2010, 2008, 2006, 2005-2004, 2003 and 2001Plus

Acknowledgements

Writing this book was a substantial effort that would not have been possible without the help and support of my loving family and of my professional colleagues. I would like to thank Professor John M. Sullivan Jr., Professor Jack Hall and the community of scholars at Worcester Polytechnic Institute who have enhanced my life, my knowledge and helped to shape the approach and content to this text.

I am greatly indebted to my colleagues from Dassault Systèmes SOLIDWORKS Corporation for their help and continuous support: Avelino Rochino and Mike Puckett.

Thanks also to Professor Richard L. Roberts of Wentworth Institute of Technology, Professor Dennis Hance of Wright State University, Professor Jason Durfess of Eastern Washington University and Professor Aaron Schellenberg of Brigham Young University - Idaho who provided vision and invaluable suggestions.

Contact the Author

We realize that keeping software application books current is imperative to our customers. We value the hundreds of professors, students, designers, and engineers that have provided us input to enhance the book. Please contact me directly with any comments, questions or suggestions on this book or any of our other SOLIDWORKS books at dplanchard@msn.com or planchard@wpi.edu.

Note to Instructors

Please visit the publisher's website **www.SDCpublications.com** for classroom support materials (.ppt presentations, labs and more) and the Instructor's Guide with model solutions and tips that support the usage of this text in a classroom environment.

Trademarks, Disclaimer and Copyrighted Material

SOLIDWORKS®, eDrawings®, SOLIDWORKS Simulation®, SOLIDWORKS Flow Simulation, and SOLIDWORKS Sustainability are a registered trademark of Dassault Systèmes SOLIDWORKS Corporation in the United States and other countries; certain images of the models in this publication courtesy of Dassault Systèmes SOLIDWORKS Corporation.

Microsoft Windows®, Microsoft Office® and its family of products are registered trademarks of the Microsoft Corporation. Other software applications and parts described in this book are trademarks or registered trademarks of their respective owners.

The publisher and the author make no representations or warranties with respect to the accuracy or completeness of the contents of this work and specifically disclaim all warranties, including without limitation warranties of fitness for a particular purpose. No warranty may be created or extended by sales or promotional materials. Dimensions of parts are modified for illustration purposes. Every effort is made to provide an accurate text. The authors and the manufacturers shall not be held liable for any parts, components, assemblies or drawings developed or designed with this book or any responsibility for inaccuracies that appear in the book. Web and company information was valid at the time of this printing.

The Y14 ASME Engineering Drawing and Related Documentation Publications utilized in this text are as follows: ASME Y14.1 1995, ASME Y14.2M-1992 (R1998), ASME Y14.3M-1994 (R1999), ASME Y14.41-2003, ASME Y14.5-1982, ASME Y14.5-1999, and ASME B4.2. Note: By permission of The American Society of Mechanical Engineers, Codes and Standards, New York, NY, USA. All rights reserved.

Additional information references the American Welding Society, AWS 2.4:1997 Standard Symbols for Welding, Braising, and Non-Destructive Examinations, Miami, Florida, USA.

Introduction

References

- SOLIDWORKS Help Topics and What's New, SOLIDWORKS Corporation, 2017.

- Beers & Johnson, <u>Vector Mechanics for Engineers</u>, 6th ed. McGraw Hill, Boston, MA.

- Jensen & Helsel, <u>Engineering Drawing and Design</u>, Glencoe, 1990.

- Lockhart & Johnson, <u>Engineering Design Communications</u>, Addison Wesley, 1999.

- Walker, James, <u>Machining Fundamentals</u>, Goodheart Wilcox, 1999.

- 80/20 Product Manual, 80/20, Inc., Columbia City, IN, 2012.

- Ticona Designing with Plastics - The Fundamentals, Summit, NJ, 2009.

- SMC Corporation of America, Product Manuals, Indiana, USA, 2012.

- Emerson-EPT Bearing Product Manuals and Gear Product Manuals, Emerson Power Transmission Corporation, Ithaca, NY, 2009.

- Emhart - A Black and Decker Company, On-line catalog, Hartford, CT, 2012.

Redeem your code on the inside cover of the book. Download the corresponding model folders from the book that matches your release of SOLIDWORKS to your hard drive. Work directly from your hard drive on the tutorials in this book.

SOLIDWORKS 2015
SOLIDWORKS 2016
SOLIDWORKS 2017

SOLIDWORKS 2017 >

Name

Bracket SOLIDWORKS 2017
CSDA Model Folder 2017
CSWA FEA Model Folder 2017
CSWA Model Folder 2017

TABLE OF CONTENTS

About the Book

You will find a wealth of information in this book. The book is written for new and intermediate users. The following conventions are used throughout this book:

- The term document refers to a SOLIDWORKS part, drawing or assembly file.

- The list of items across the top of the SOLIDWORKS interface is the Menu bar menu or the Menu bar toolbar. Each item in the Menu bar has a pull-down menu. When you need to select a series of commands from these menus, the following format is used: Click **Insert**, **Reference Geometry**, **Plane** from the Menu bar. The Plane PropertyManager is displayed.

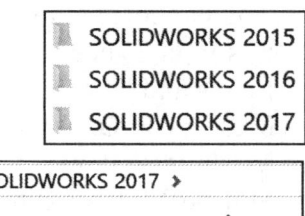

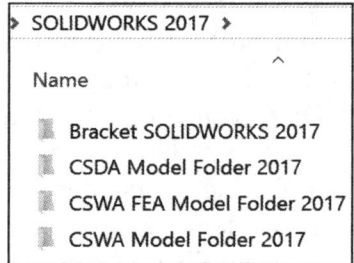

- The book is organized into chapters. Each chapter is focused on a specific certification category. Use the model files in the book for the chapter exercises.

- Copy the corresponding model folders that match your release of SOLIDWORKS to your hard drive. Work directly from your hard drive on the tutorials in the book. SOLIDWORKS model files for 2015 - 2017 are provided.

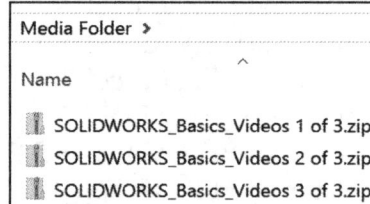

- The ANSI overall drafting standard and Third Angle projection is used as the default setting in this text. IPS (inch, pound, second) and MMGS (millimeter, gram, second) unit systems are used.

Chapter 1

Overview of SOLIDWORKS® and the User Interface

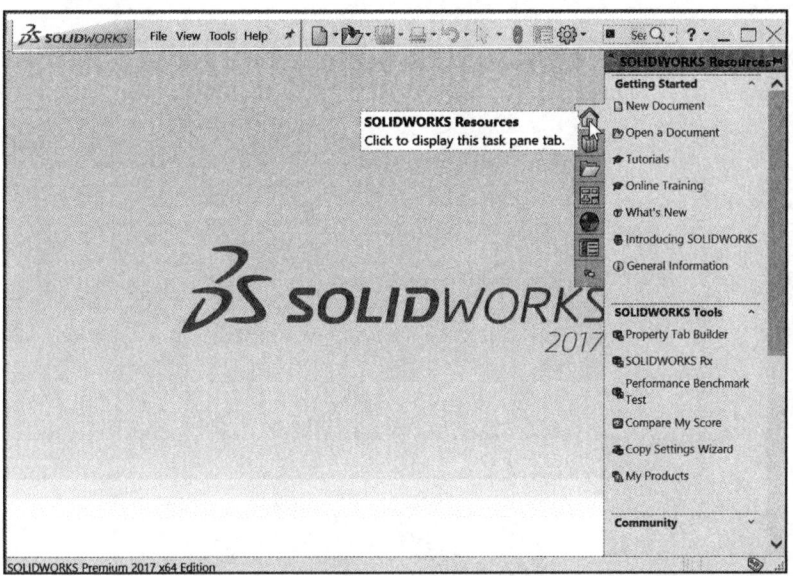

Below are the desired outcomes and usage competencies based on the completion of Chapter 1.

Desired Outcomes:	Usage Competencies:
• A comprehensive understanding of the SOLIDWORKS® 2017 User Interface (UI) and CommandManager.	• Ability to establish a SOLIDWORKS session. • Aptitude to utilize the following items: *Menu bar toolbar, Menu bar menu, Drop-down menus, Context toolbars, Consolidated drop-down toolbars, System feedback icons, Confirmation Corner, Heads-up View toolbar, Document Properties and more.* • Open a new and existing SOLIDWORKS part. • Knowledge to zoom, rotate and maneuver a three button mouse in the SOLIDWORKS Graphics window.

Notes:

CHAPTER 1: OVERVIEW OF SOLIDWORKS AND THE USER INTERFACE

Overview

SOLIDWORKS is a design software application used to model and create 2D and 3D sketches, 3D parts and assemblies and 2D drawings. Over the years, the SOLIDWORKS UI has changed, but will not affect the experienced user during the exam.

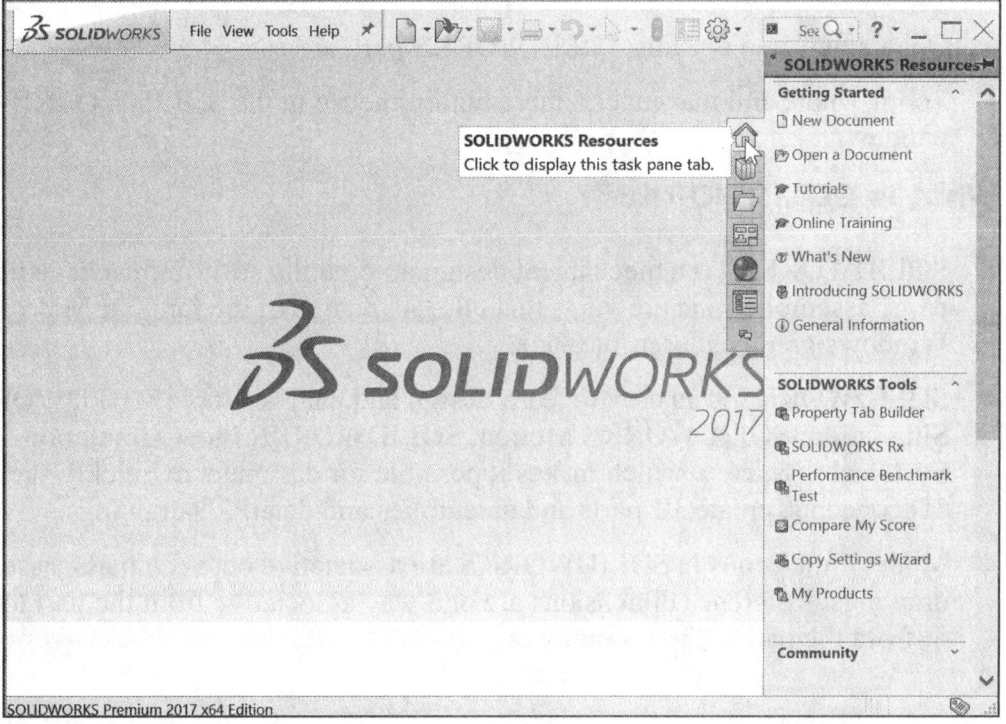

Chapter 1 covers the SOLIDWORKS 2017 User Interface and CommandManager. The following items are addressed: Menu bar toolbar, Menu bar menu, Context toolbars, Drop-down menus, Consolidated drop-down toolbars, Confirmation Corner, System feedback icons, Heads-up View toolbar and more.

Redeem your code on the inside cover of the book. Download the corresponding Model folder which matches your release of SOLIDWORKS.

View the provided videos and models to enhance the user experience. Work directly from your hard drive on the tutorials in this book.

SOLIDWORKS 2015
SOLIDWORKS 2016
SOLIDWORKS 2017

Chapter Objective

Provide a comprehensive understanding of the SOLIDWORKS default User Interface and CommandManager: Menu bar toolbar, Menu bar menu, Drop-down menu, Right-click Pop-up menus, Context toolbars/menus, Fly-out tool button, System feedback icons, Confirmation Corner, Heads-up View toolbar and more.

On the completion of this chapter, you will be able to:

- Establish a SOLIDWORKS session.

- Comprehend the SOLIDWORKS User Interface.

- Recognize the default Reference Planes in the FeatureManager.

- Utilize SOLIDWORKS Help and SOLIDWORKS Tutorials.

- Open a new and existing SOLIDWORKS part.

- Zoom, rotate and maneuver a three button mouse in the SOLIDWORKS Graphics window.

What is SOLIDWORKS®?

- SOLIDWORKS® is a mechanical design automation software package used to build parts, assemblies and drawings that take advantage of the familiar Microsoft® Windows graphical user interface.

- SOLIDWORKS is an easy to learn design and analysis tool (SOLIDWORKS Simulation, SOLIDWORKS Motion, SOLIDWORKS Flow Simulation, Sustainability, etc.), which makes it possible for designers to quickly sketch 2D and 3D concepts, create 3D parts and assemblies and detail 2D drawings.

- Model dimensions in SOLIDWORKS are associative between parts, assemblies and drawings. Reference dimensions are one-way associative from the part to the drawing or from the part to the assembly.

Start a SOLIDWORKS Session

Start a SOLIDWORKS session and familiarize yourself with the SOLIDWORKS User Interface. As you read and perform the tasks in this chapter, you will obtain a sense of how to use the book and the structure. Actual input commands or required actions in the chapter are displayed in bold.

The book does not cover starting a SOLIDWORKS session in detail for the first time. A default SOLIDWORKS installation presents you with several options. For additional information, visit http://www.SOLIDWORKS.com.

Redeem your code on the inside cover of the book. View the provided videos and models to enhance the user experience with this chapter.

Activity: Start a SOLIDWORKS Session

Start a SOLIDWORKS session.

1) Click **Start** on the Windows Taskbar.

2) Click **All Programs**.

3) Click the **SOLIDWORKS** folder.

4) Click **SOLIDWORKS** application. The SOLIDWORKS program window opens. Note: Do not open a document at this time.

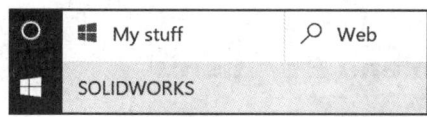

If available, double-click the SOLIDWORKS icon on your desktop to start a SOLIDWORKS session.

Read the Tip of the Day dialog box.

If you do not see this screen, click the SOLIDWORKS Resources 🏠 icon on the right side of the Graphics window located in the Task Pane.

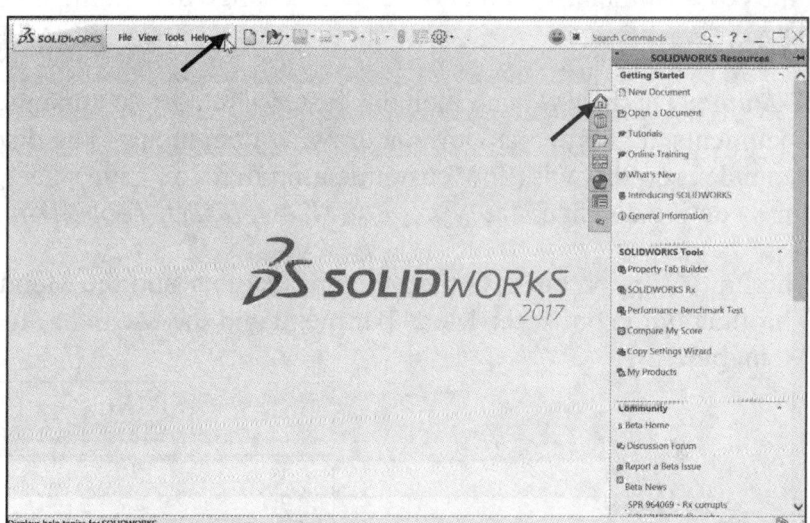

5) **Hover** the mouse pointer over the SOLIDWORKS icon as illustrated.

6) **Pin** the Menu Bar toolbar. View your options.

Menu Bar toolbar

The SOLIDWORKS (UI) is designed to
make maximum use of the Graphics
window. The Menu Bar toolbar contains a set of the most
frequently used tool buttons from the Standard toolbar.

The available default tools are:

- **New** ⬜ - Creates a new document; **Open** 🗁 - Opens an existing document;
  Save 💾 - Saves an active document; **Print** 🖨 - Prints an active document; **Undo** ↺
  - Reverses the last action; **Select** ⬚ - Selects Sketch entities, components and more;
  Rebuild 🔘 - Rebuilds the active part, assembly or drawing; **File Properties** 🗒 -
  Shows the summary information on the active document; and **Options** ⚙ - Changes
  system options and Add-Ins for SOLIDWORKS.

Menu Bar menu

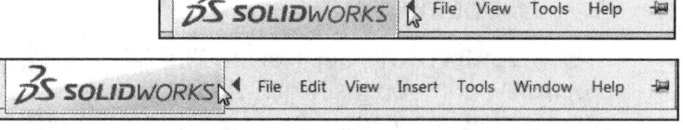

Click SOLIDWORKS in the Menu
Bar toolbar to display the Menu
Bar menu. SOLIDWORKS
provides a context-sensitive menu structure. The menu titles remain the same for all three
types of documents, but the menu items change depending on which type of document is
active.

Example: The Insert menu includes features in part documents, mates in assembly
documents, and drawing views in drawing documents. The display of the menu is also
dependent on the workflow customization that you have selected. The default menu items
for an active document are *File*, *Edit*, *View*, *Insert*, *Tools*, *Window*, *Help* and *Pin*.

The Pin ⚲ option displays the Menu bar toolbar and the Menu bar menu as illustrated.
Throughout the book, the Menu bar menu and the Menu bar toolbar are referred to as the
Menu bar.

Drop-down menu

SOLIDWORKS takes advantage of the familiar Microsoft® Windows user interface. Communicate with SOLIDWORKS through drop-down menus, Context sensitive toolbars, Consolidated toolbars or the CommandManager tabs.

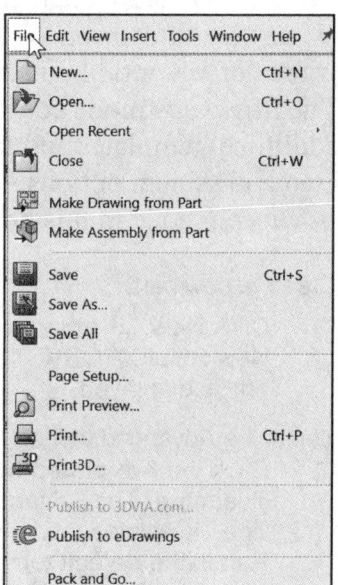

A command is an instruction that informs SOLIDWORKS to perform a task.

To close a SOLIDWORKS drop-down menu, press the Esc key. You can also click any other part of the SOLIDWORKS Graphics window or click another drop-down menu.

Create a New Part Document

In the next section create a new part document.

Activity: Create a new Part Document

A part is a 3D model, which consists of features. What are features?

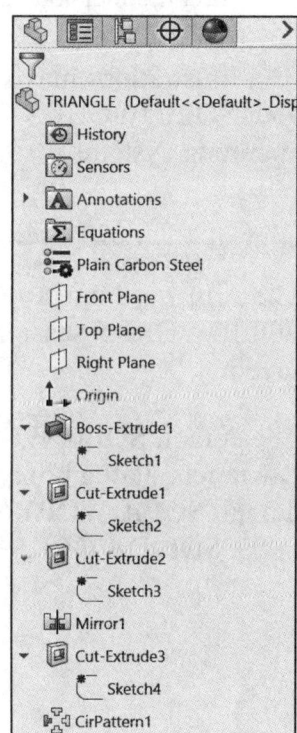

- Features are geometry building blocks.

- Most features either add or remove material.

- Some features do not affect material (Cosmetic Thread).

- Features are created either from 2D or 3D sketched profiles or from edges and faces of existing geometry.

- Features are an individual shape that, combined with other features, make up a part or assembly. Some features, such as bosses and cuts, originate as sketches. Other features, such as shells and fillets, modify a feature's geometry.

- Features are displayed in the FeatureManager as illustrated (Boss-Extrude1, Cut-Extrude1, Cut-Extrude2, Mirror1, Cut-Extrude3 and CirPattern1).

The first sketch of a part is called the Base Sketch. The Base sketch is the foundation for the 3D model. In this book, we focus on 2D sketches and 3D features.

There are two modes in the New
SOLIDWORKS Document dialog box:
Novice and *Advanced*. The *Novice* option
is the default option with three templates.
The *Advanced* mode contains access to
additional templates and tabs that you
create in system options. Use the
Advanced mode in this book.

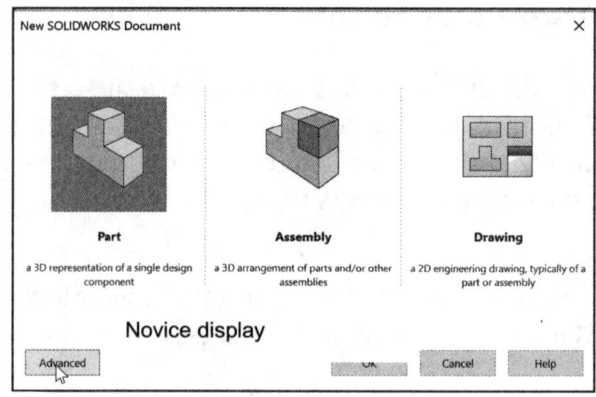

Create a new part.

7) Click **New** ⬜ from the Menu bar. The
New SOLIDWORKS Document dialog
box is displayed.

Select the Advanced mode.

8) Click the **Advanced** button as
illustrated. The Advanced mode is set.
The Templates tab is the default tab.
Part is the default template from the
New SOLIDWORKS Document dialog
box.

9) Click **OK** from the New SOLIDWORKS
Document dialog box.

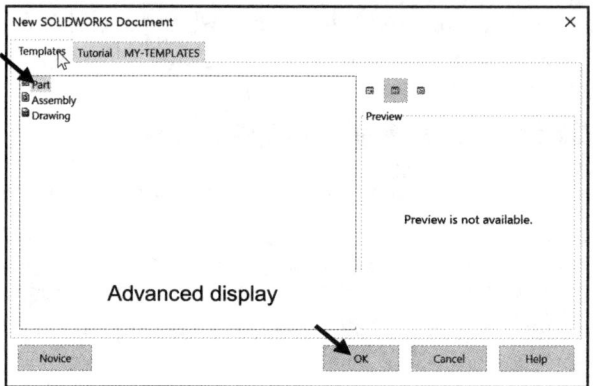

🔅 Illustrations may vary depending on
your SOLIDWORKS version and
operating system.

The Advanced mode remains selected for all new documents in the current
SOLIDWORKS session. When you exit SOLIDWORKS, the Advanced mode setting is
saved.

The default SOLIDWORKS installation contains two tabs in the New SOLIDWORKS
Document dialog box: *Templates* and *Tutorial*. The *Templates* tab corresponds to the
default SOLIDWORKS templates. The *Tutorial* tab corresponds to the templates utilized
in the SOLIDWORKS Tutorials.

Part1 is displayed in the FeatureManager and is the name of the document. Part1 is the default part window name. The Menu bar, CommandManager, FeatureManager, Heads-up View toolbar, SOLIDWORKS Resources, SOLIDWORKS Search, Task Pane and the Origin are displayed in the Graphics window.

The Part Origin ↳ is displayed in blue in the center of the Graphics window. The Origin represents the intersection of the three default reference planes: *Front Plane*, *Top Plane* and *Right Plane*. The positive X-axis is horizontal and points to the right of the Origin in the Front view. The positive Y-axis is vertical and points upward in the Front view. The FeatureManager contains a list of features, reference geometry, and settings utilized in the part.

🔆 Edit the document units directly from the Graphics window as illustrated.

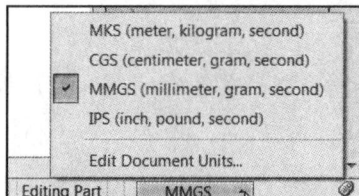

🔆 Grid/Snaps are deactivated in the Graphics window for improved modeling clarity.

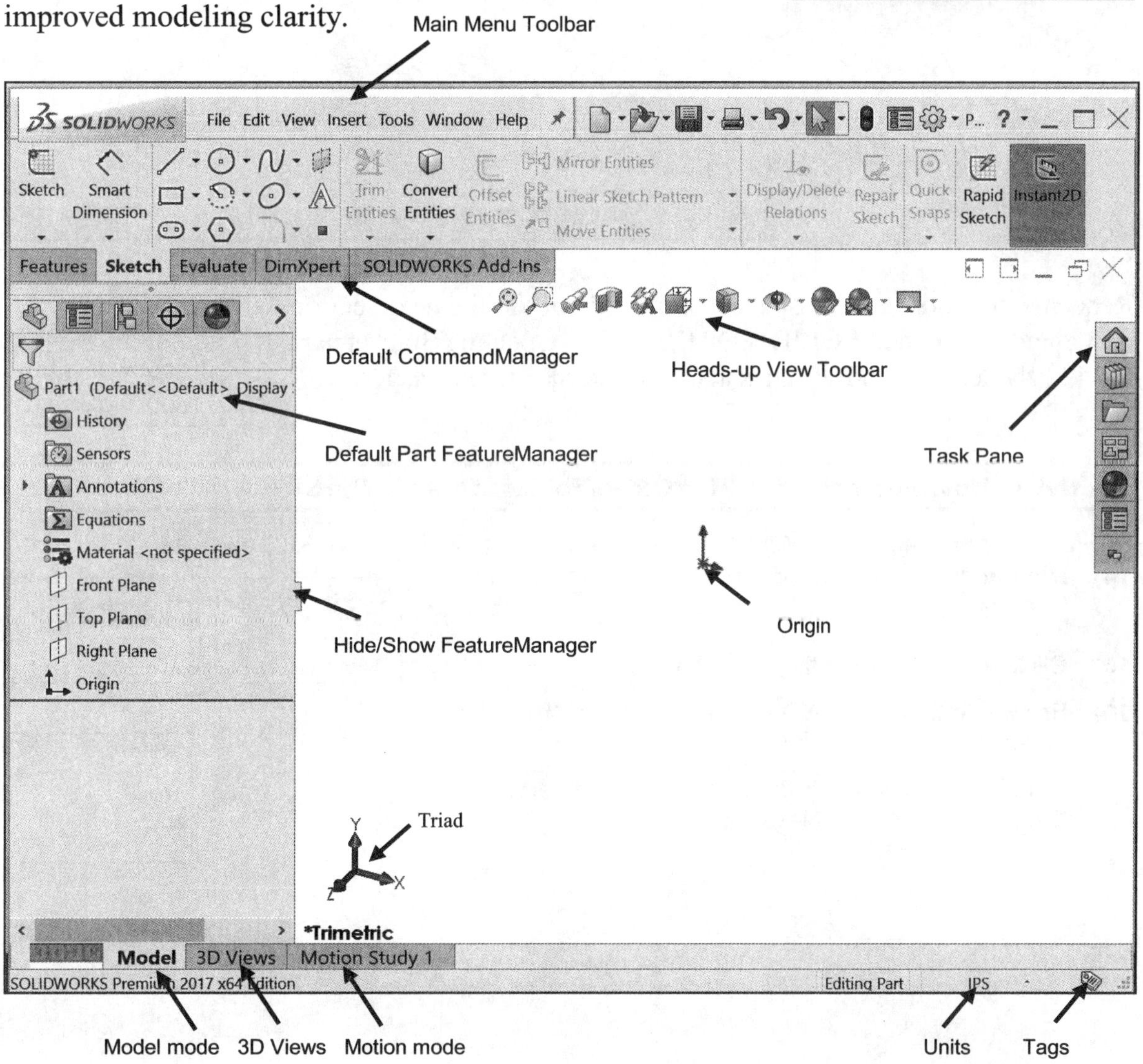

Main Menu Toolbar

Default CommandManager

Heads-up View Toolbar

Default Part FeatureManager

Task Pane

Hide/Show FeatureManager

Origin

Triad

Model mode   3D Views   Motion mode

Units   Tags

View the Default Sketch Planes.

10) Click the **Front Plane** from the FeatureManager.

11) Click the **Top Plane** from the FeatureManager.

12) Click the **Right Plane** from the FeatureManager.

13) Click the **Origin** from the FeatureManager. The Origin is the intersection of the Front, Top and Right Planes.

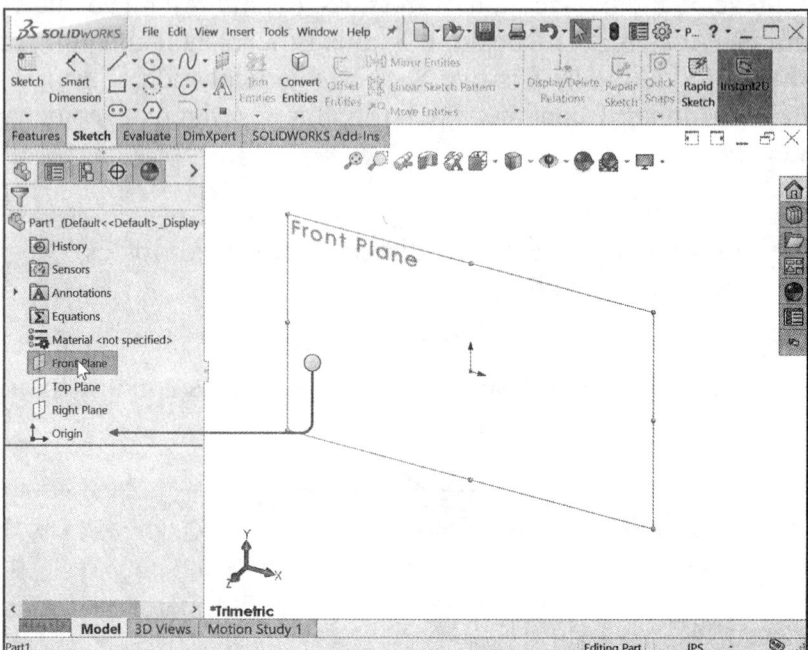

Redeem your code on the inside cover of the book. In the next section, download the needed SOLIDWORKS folder. Open the Bracket part. Review the features and sketches in the Bracket FeatureManager.

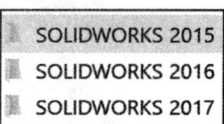

SOLIDWORKS 2015
SOLIDWORKS 2016
SOLIDWORKS 2017

Activity: Download the SOLIDWORKS folder. Open a Part.

Download the needed SOLIDWORKS folder. Open an existing SOLIDWORKS part.

14) **Download** the needed SOLIDWORKS folder to your local hard drive.

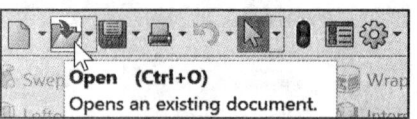

Open (Ctrl+O)
Opens an existing document.

15) Click **Open** from the Menu bar menu.

16) Browse to the **SOLIDWORKS-MODELS 201#\Bracket** folder.

17) Double-click the **Bracket** part. The Bracket part is displayed in the Graphics window.

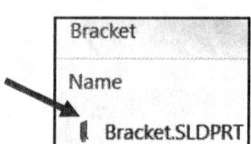

Bracket

Name

Bracket.SLDPRT

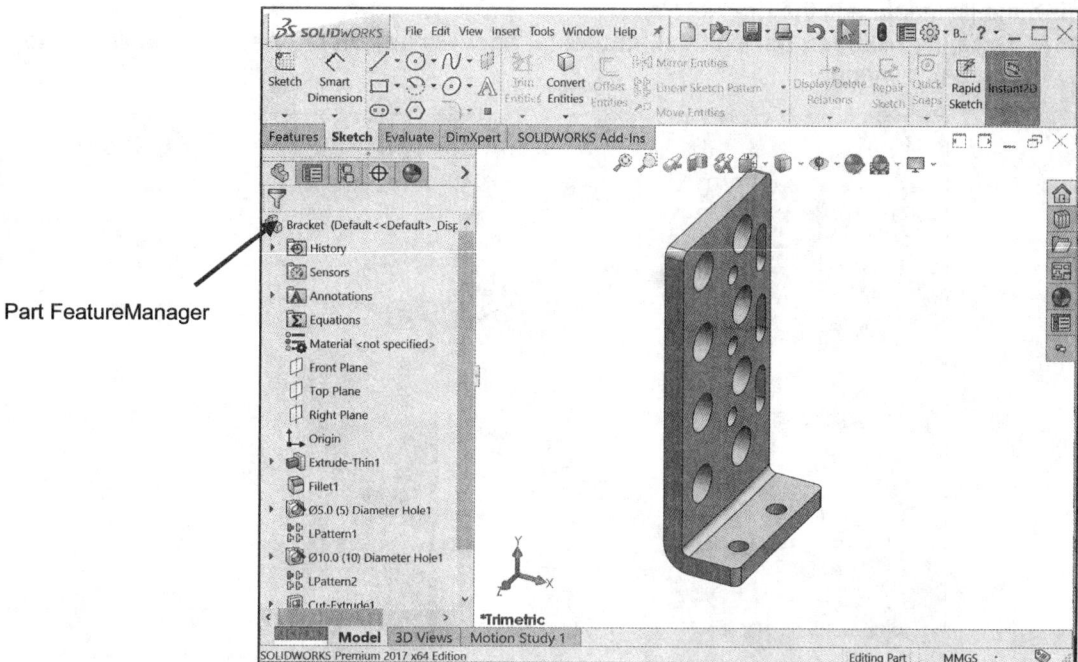

Part FeatureManager

The FeatureManager design tree is located on the left side of the SOLIDWORKS Graphics window. The FeatureManager provides a summarized view of the active part, assembly, or drawing document. The tree displays the details on how the part, assembly or drawing document was created.

Use the FeatureManager rollback bar to temporarily roll back to an earlier state, to absorbed features, roll forward, roll to previous, or roll to the end of the FeatureManager design tree. You can add new features or edit existing features while the model is in the rolled-back state. You can save models with the rollback bar placed anywhere.

In the next section, review the features in the Bracket FeatureManager using the Rollback bar.

Activity: Use the FeatureManager Rollback Bar

Apply the FeatureManager Rollback Bar. Revert to an earlier state in the model.

18) Place the **mouse pointer** over the rollback bar in the FeatureManager design tree as illustrated. The pointer changes to a hand 🖐. Note the provided information on the feature. This is called Dynamic Reference Visualization.

19) Drag the **rollback bar** up the FeatureManager design tree until it is above the features you want rolled back, in this case Diameter Hole1.

20) **Release** the mouse button.

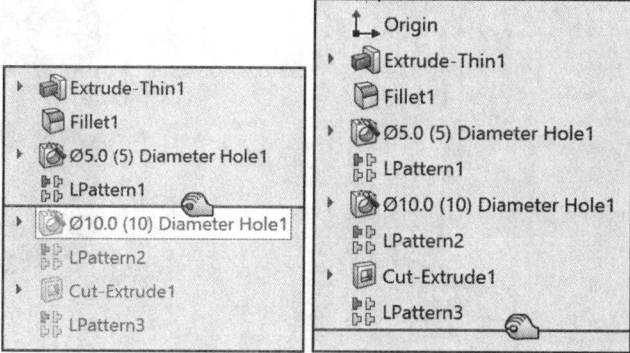

View the first feature in the Bracket Part.

21) Drag the **rollback bar** up the FeatureManager above Fillet1. View the results in the Graphics window.

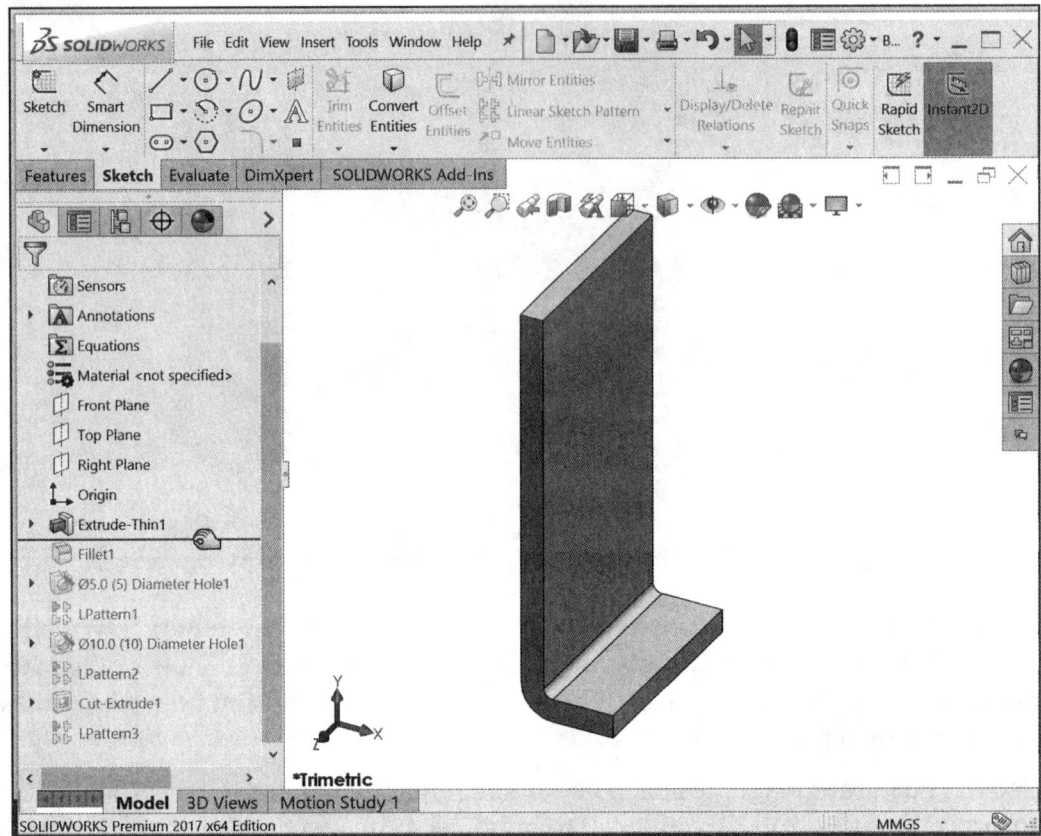

Return to the original Bracket Part FeatureManager.

22) Right-click **Extrude-Thin1** in the FeatureManager. The Pop-up Context toolbar is displayed.

23) Click **Roll to End**. View the results in the Graphics window.

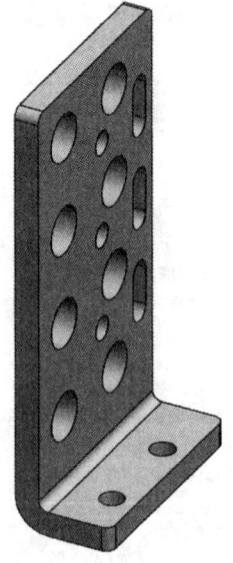

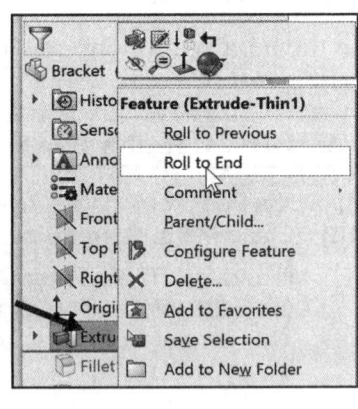

Heads-up View toolbar

SOLIDWORKS provides the user with numerous view options. One of the most useful tools is the Heads-up View toolbar displayed in the Graphics window when a document is active.

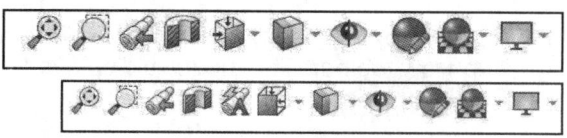

🔆 Dynamic Annotation Views 🖎: Only available with SOLIDWORKS MBD (Model Based Definition). Provides the ability to control how annotations are displayed when you rotate models.

In the next section, apply the following tools: Zoom to Fit, Zoom to Area, Zoom out, Rotate and select various view orientations from the Heads-up View toolbar.

Activity: Utilize the Heads-up View toolbar

Zoom to Fit the model in the Graphics window.

24) Click the **Zoom to Fit** 🔎 icon. The tool fits the model to the Graphics window.

Zoom to Area on the model in the Graphics window.

25) Click the **Zoom to Area** 🔎 icon. The Zoom to Area 🔎 icon is displayed.

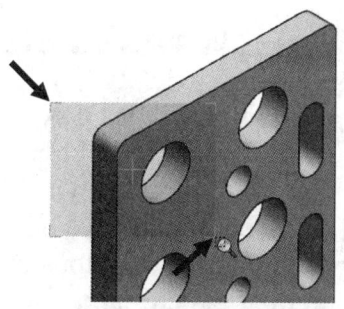

Zoom in on the top left hole.

26) **Window-select** the top left corner as illustrated. View the results.

De-select the Zoom to Area tool.

27) Click the **Zoom to Area** 🔎 icon.

Fit the model to the Graphics window.

28) Press the **f** key.

Rotate the model.

29) Hold the **middle mouse button** down. Drag **upward** ↻, **downward** ↻, to the **left** ↻ and to the **right** ↻ to rotate the model in the Graphics window.

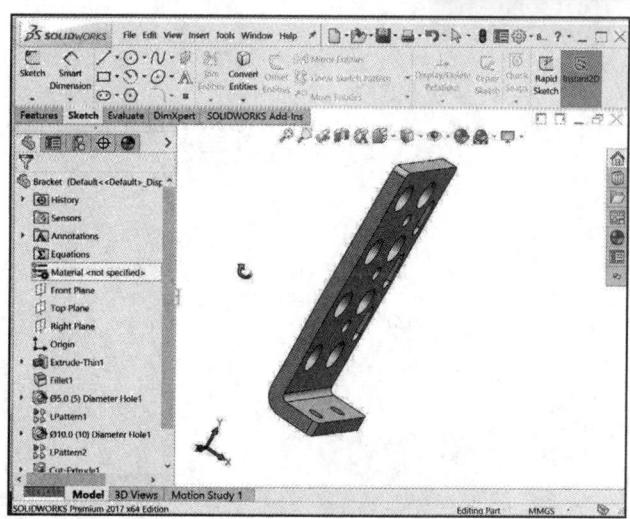

Display a few Standard Views.

30) Click **inside** the Graphics window.

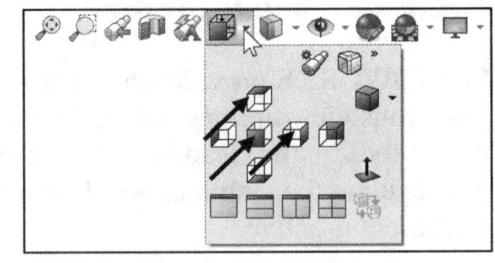

31) Click **Front** from the drop-down Heads-up view toolbar. The model is displayed in the Front view.

32) Click **Right** from the drop-down Heads-up view toolbar. The model is displayed in the Right view.

33) Click **Top** from the drop-down Heads-up view toolbar. The model is displayed in the Top view.

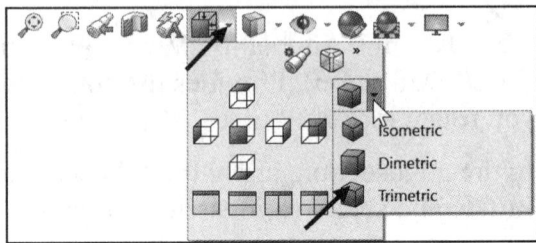

Display a Trimetric view of the Bracket model.

34) Click **Trimetric** from the drop-down Heads-up view toolbar as illustrated. Note your options. View the results in the Graphics window.

SOLIDWORKS Help

Help in SOLIDWORKS is context-sensitive and in HTML format. Help is accessed in many ways, including Help buttons in all dialog boxes and PropertyManager (or press F1) and Help ⑦ tool on the Standard toolbar for SOLIDWORKS Help.

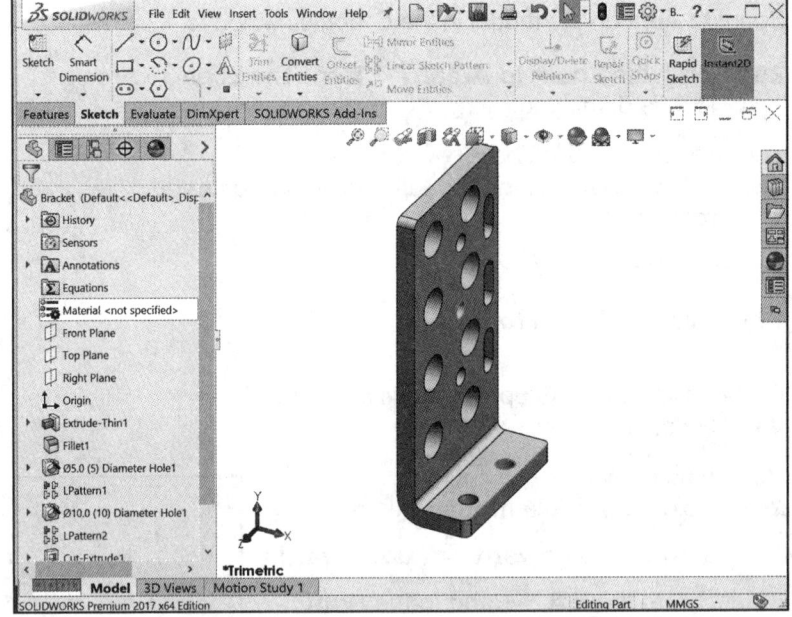

35) Click **Help** from the Menu bar.

36) Click **SOLIDWORKS Help**. The SOLIDWORKS Help Home Page is displayed by default. View your options.

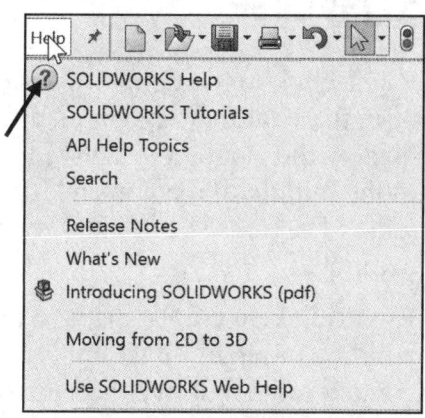

💡 SOLIDWORKS Web Help is active by default under Help in the Main menu.

Close Help. Return to the SOLIDWORKS Graphics window.

37) **Close** ☒ SOLIDWORKS Home.

SOLIDWORKS Tutorials

Display and explore the SOLIDWORKS tutorials.

38) Click **Help** from the Menu bar.

39) Click **SOLIDWORKS Tutorials**. The SOLIDWORKS Tutorials are displayed. The SOLIDWORKS Tutorials are presented by category.

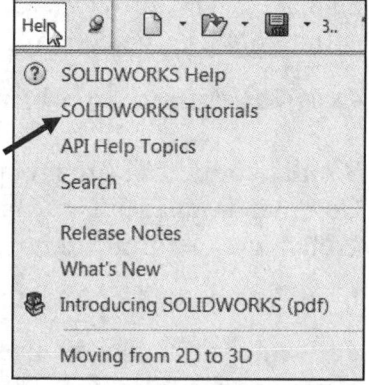

40) Click the **Getting Started** category. The Getting Started category provides three 30 minute lessons on parts, assemblies, and drawings.

In the next section, close all models, tutorials and view the additional User Interface tools.

Activity: Close all Tutorials and Models

Close all SOLIDWORKS Tutorials and models.

41) **Close** ☒ SOLIDWORKS Tutorials.

42) Click **Window**, **Close All** from the Menu bar menu.

SOLIDWORKS Icon Style

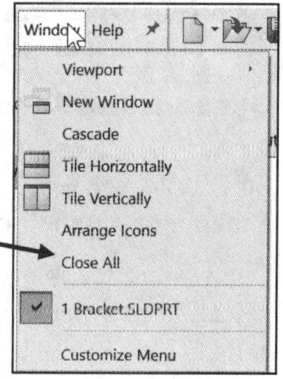

SOLIDWORKS provides a new icon style. It allows vector-based scaling for superior support of high resolution, high pixel density displays. The new icon style standardized the perspective of icons. It also, removes non-essential details and emphasizes primary elements. Consistent visual styling applies to all icons.

Additional User Interface Tools

The book utilizes additional areas of the SOLIDWORKS User Interface. Explore an overview of these tools in the next section.

Right-click

Right-click in the Graphics window on a model, or in the FeatureManager on a feature or sketch to display the Context-sensitive toolbar. If you are in the middle of a command, this toolbar displays a list of options specifically related to that command.

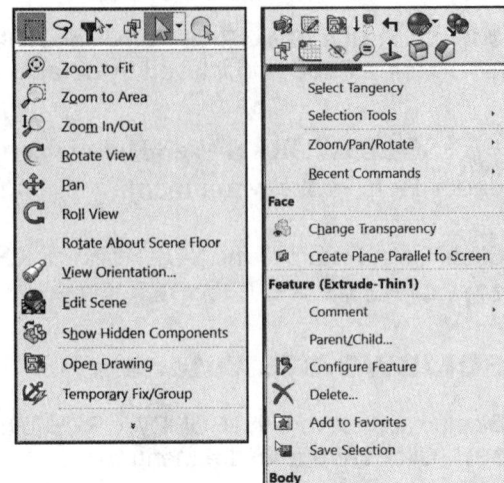

Right-click an empty space in the Graphics window of a part or assembly, and a selection context toolbar above the shortcut menu is displayed. This provides easy access to the most commonly used selection tools.

Consolidated toolbar

Similar commands are grouped together in the CommandManager. For example, variations of the Rectangle sketch tool are grouped in a single fly-out button as illustrated.

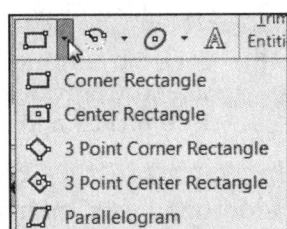

If you select the Consolidated toolbar button without expanding:

For some commands such as Sketch, the most commonly used command is performed. This command is the first listed and the command shown on the button.

For commands such as rectangle, where you may want to repeatedly create the same variant of the rectangle, the last used command is performed. This is the highlighted command when the Consolidated toolbar is expanded.

System feedback icon

SOLIDWORKS provides system feedback by attaching a symbol to the mouse pointer cursor.

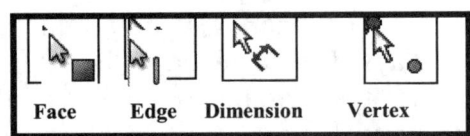

The system feedback symbol indicates what you are selecting or what the system is expecting you to select.

As you move the mouse pointer across your model, system feedback is displayed in the form of a symbol, riding next to the cursor as illustrated. This is a valuable feature in SOLIDWORKS.

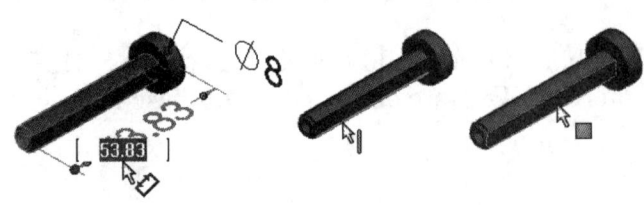

Confirmation Corner

When numerous SOLIDWORKS commands are active, a symbol or a set of symbols are displayed in the upper right hand corner of the Graphics window. This area is called the Confirmation Corner.

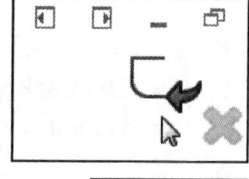

When a sketch is active, the confirmation corner box displays two symbols. The first symbol is the sketch tool icon. The second symbol is a large red X. These two symbols supply a visual reminder that you are in an active sketch. Click the sketch symbol icon to exit the sketch and to save any changes that you made.

When other commands are active, the confirmation corner box provides a green check mark and a large red X. Use the green check mark to execute the current command. Use the large red X to cancel the command.

Confirm changes you make in sketches and tools by using the D keyboard shortcut to move the OK and Cancel buttons to the pointer location in the Graphics window.

Heads-up View toolbar

SOLIDWORKS provides the user with numerous view options from the Standard Views, View and Heads-up View toolbar.

The Heads-up View toolbar is a transparent toolbar that is displayed in the Graphics window when a document is active.

You can hide, move or modify the Heads-up View toolbar. To modify the Heads-up View toolbar, right-click on a tool and select or deselect the tools that you want to display.

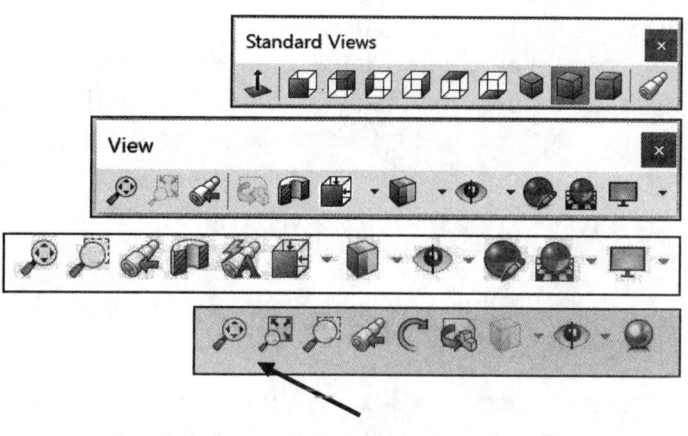

For a drawing document

The following views are available: Note that the available views are document dependent.

- *Zoom to Fit* : Zooms the model to fit the Graphics window.

- *Zoom to Area* : Zooms to the areas you select with a bounding box.

- *Previous View* : Displays the previous view.

- *Section View* : Displays a cutaway of a part or assembly, using one or more cross section planes.

- *Dynamic Annotation Views* : Only available with SOLIDWORKS MBD. Provides the ability to control how annotations are displayed when you rotate models.

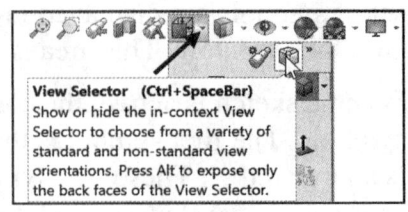

The Orientation dialog has an option to display a view cube (in-context View Selector) with a live model preview. This helps the user to understand how each standard view orientates the model. With the view cube, you can access additional standard views. The views are easy to understand and they can be accessed simply by selecting a face on the cube.

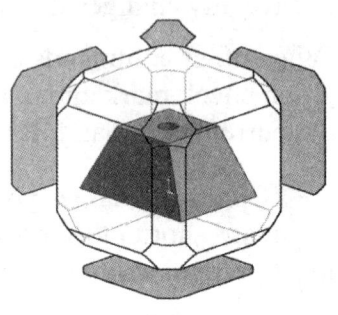

To activate the Orientation dialog box, press (Ctrl + spacebar) or click the View Orientation icon from the Heads up View toolbar. The active model is displayed in the View Selector in an Isometric orientation (default view).

As you hover over the buttons in the Orientation dialog box, the corresponding faces dynamically highlight in the View Selector. Select a view in the View Selector or click the view from the Orientation dialog box. The Orientation dialog box closes and the model rotates to the selected view.

Press **Ctrl + spacebar** to activate the View Selector.

Press the **spacebar** to activate the Orientation dialog box.

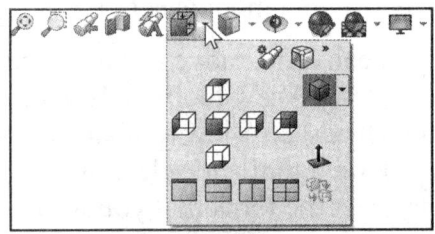

- *View Orientation box* : Provides the ability to select a view orientation or the number of viewports. The available options are *Top, Left, Front, Right, Back, Bottom, Single view, Two view - Horizontal, Two view - Vertical, Four view*. Click the drop-down arrow to access Axonometric views: Isometric, Dimetric and Trimetric.

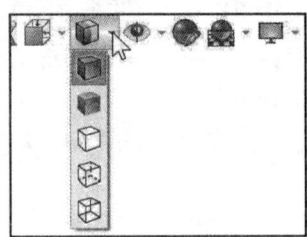

- *Display Style* : Provides the ability to display the style for the active view. The available options are *Wireframe, Hidden Lines Visible, Hidden Lines Removed, Shaded, Shaded With Edges*.

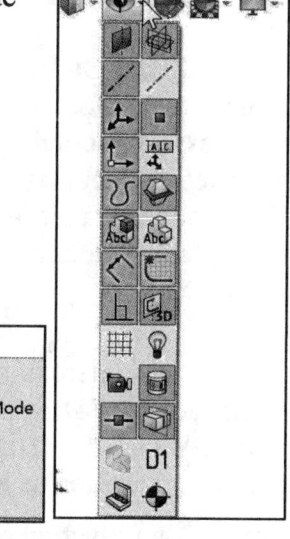

- *Hide/Show Items* 👁 ⌄: Provides the ability to select items to hide or show in the Graphics window. The available items are document dependent. Note the View Center of Mass ✚ icon.

- *Edit Appearance* 🔵: Provides the ability to edit the appearance of entities of the model.

- *Apply Scene* 🔵 ⌄: Provides the ability to apply a scene to an active part or assembly document. View the available options.

- *View Setting* 🖥 ⌄: Provides the ability to select the following settings: *RealView Graphics*, *Shadows In Shaded Mode*, *Ambient Occlusion*, *Perspective* and *Cartoon*.

🖥	
RealView Graphics	
Shadows In Shaded Mode	
Ambient Occlusion	
Perspective	
Cartoon	

- *Rotate view* ↻ : Provides the ability to rotate a drawing view. Input Drawing view angle and select the ability to update and rotate center marks with view.

- *3D Drawing View* 🔲: Provides the ability to dynamically manipulate the drawing view in 3D to make a selection.

🔆 To display a grid for a part, click Options ⚙, Document Properties tab. Click Grid/Snaps, check the Display grid box.

🔆 Add a custom view to the Heads-up View toolbar. Press the space key. The Orientation dialog box is displayed. Click the New View 🔭 tool. The Name View dialog box is displayed. Enter a new named view. Click OK.

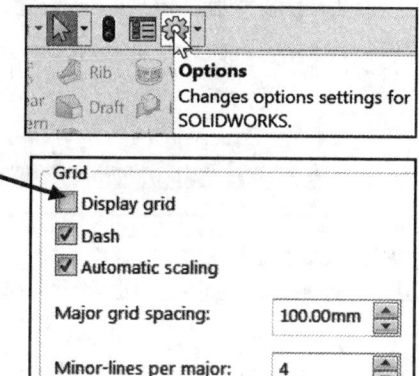

Options
Changes options settings for SOLIDWORKS.

Grid
☐ Display grid
☑ Dash
☑ Automatic scaling

Major grid spacing: 100.00mm

Minor-lines per major: 4

Snap points per minor: 1

Go To System Snaps

SOLIDWORKS CommandManager

The SOLIDWORKS CommandManager is a Context-sensitive toolbar that automatically updates based on the toolbar you want to access. By default, it has toolbars embedded in it based on your active document type. When you click a tab below the CommandManager, it updates to display that toolbar. For example, if you click the Sketch tab, the Sketch toolbar is displayed.

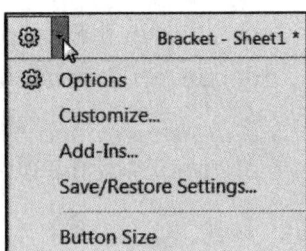

For commercial users, SOLIDWORKS Model Based Definition (MBD) is a separate application. For education users, SOLIDWORKS MBD is included in the SOLIDWORKS Education Edition as an Add In.

Below is an illustrated CommandManager for a default Part document.

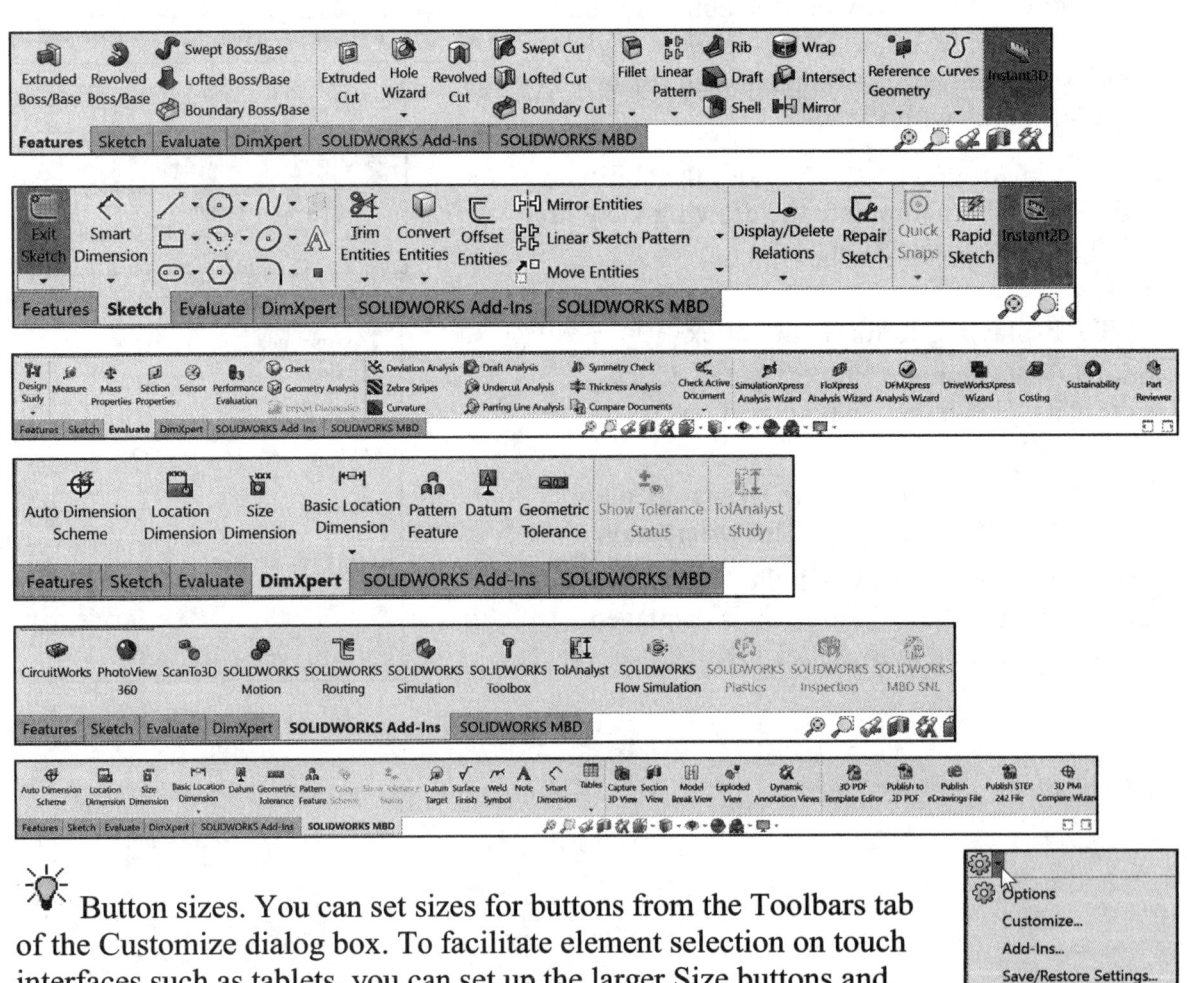

Button sizes. You can set sizes for buttons from the Toolbars tab of the Customize dialog box. To facilitate element selection on touch interfaces such as tablets, you can set up the larger Size buttons and text from the Options menu (Standard toolbar).

The SOLIDWORKS CommandManager is a Context-sensitive toolbar that automatically updates based on the toolbar you want to access. By default, it has toolbars embedded in it based on your active document type.

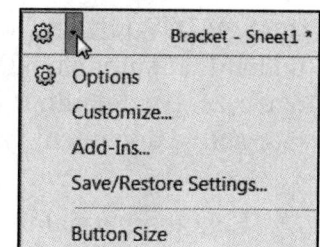

For commercial users, SOLIDWORKS Model Based Definition (MBD) is a separate application. For education users, SOLIDWORKS MBD is included in the SOLIDWORKS Education Edition as an Add In.

Below is an illustrated CommandManager for a default Drawing document.

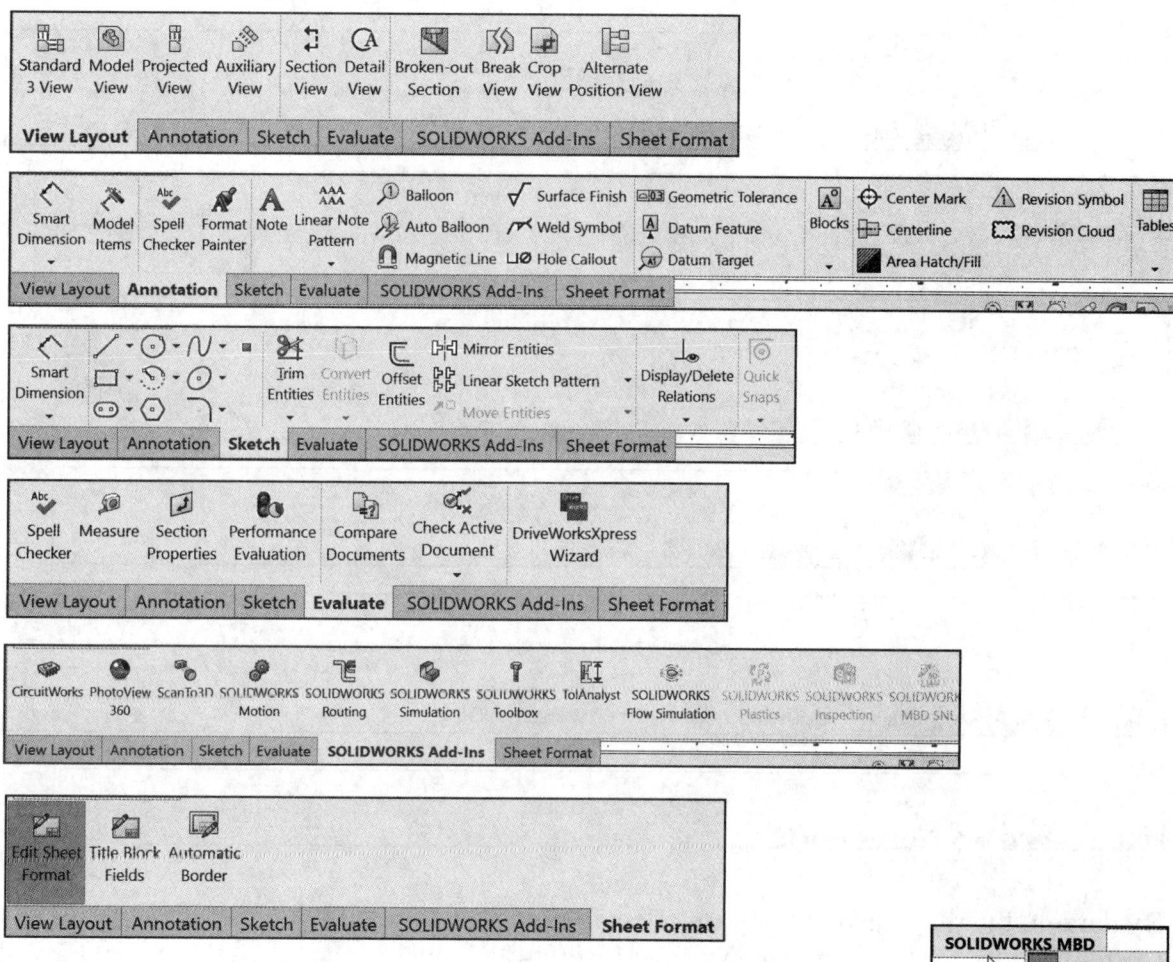

To add a custom tab to your CommandManager, right-click on a tab and click Customize CommandManager from the drop-down menu. The Customize dialog box is displayed. You can also select to add a blank tab as illustrated and populate it with custom tools from the Customize dialog box.

The SOLIDWORKS CommandManager is a Context-sensitive toolbar that automatically updates based on the toolbar you want to access. By default, it has toolbars embedded in it based on your active document type.

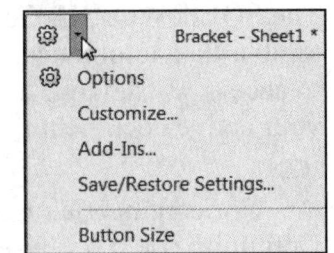

For commercial users, SOLIDWORKS Model Based Definition (MBD) is a separate application. For education users, SOLIDWORKS MBD is included in the SOLIDWORKS Education Edition as an Add In.

Below is an illustrated CommandManager for a default Assembly document.

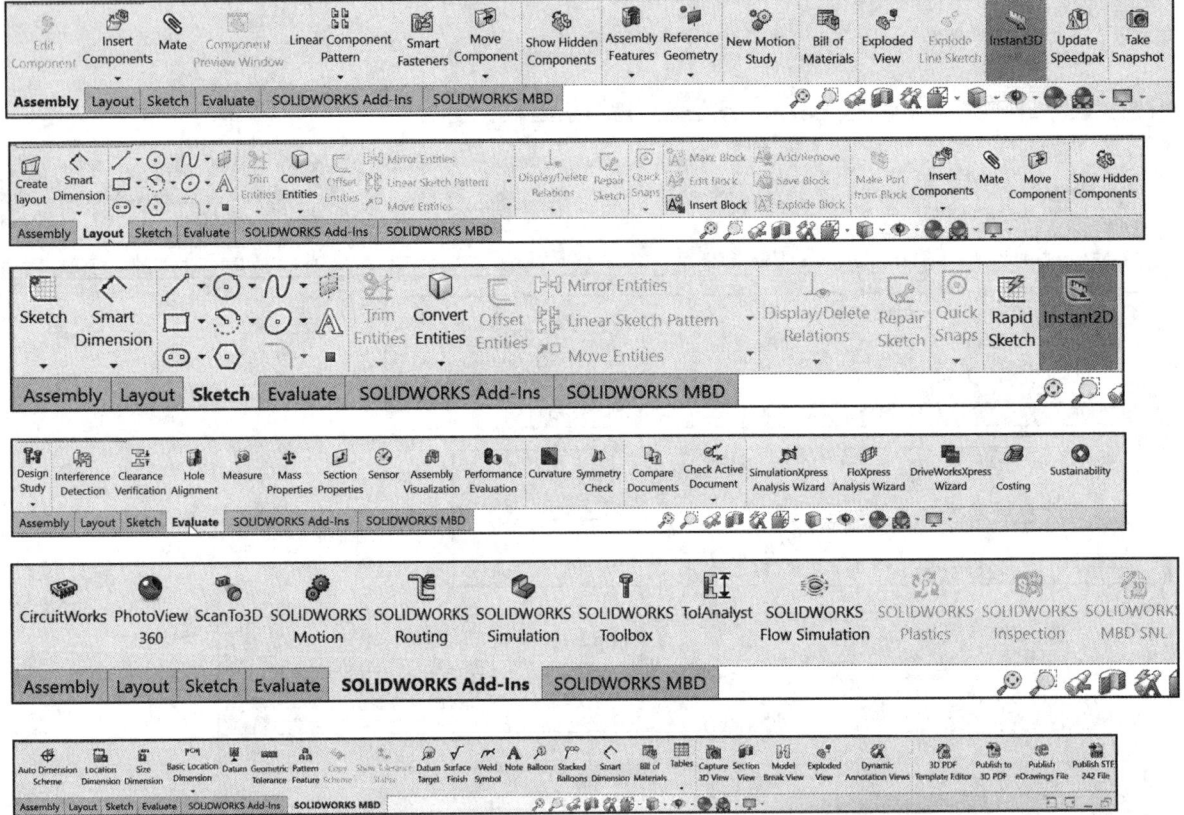

By default, the illustrated options are selected in the Customize box for the CommandManager. Right-click on an existing tab and click Customize CommandManager to view your options.

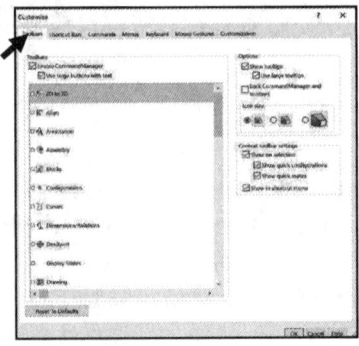

Float the CommandManager. Drag the Features, Sketch or any CommandManager tab. Drag the CommandManager anywhere on or outside the SOLIDWORKS window.

To dock the CommandManager, perform one of the following:

While dragging the CommandManager in the SOLIDWORKS window, move the pointer over a docking icon - ▲ Dock above , ◀ Dock left , ▶ Dock right and click the needed command.

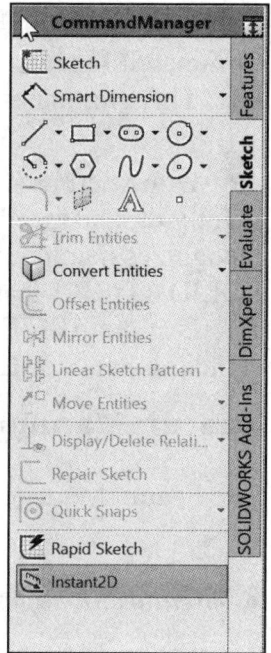

Double-click the floating CommandManager to revert the CommandManager to the last docking position.

Screen shots in the book were made using SOLIDWORKS 2017 SP0 running Windows® 10.

💡 An updated color scheme for certain icons makes the SOLIDWORKS application more accessible to people with color blindness. Icons in the active PropertyManager use blue to indicate what you must select on the screen: faces, edges and so on.

Selection Enhancements

Right-click an empty space in the Graphics window of a part or assembly; a selection context toolbar above the shortcut menu provides easy access to the most commonly used selection tools.

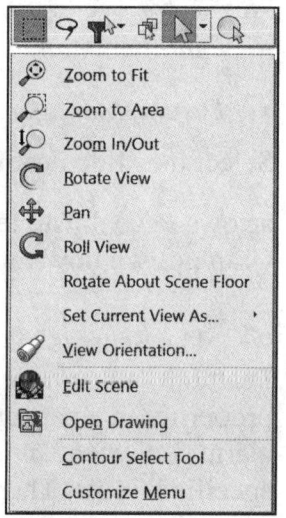

- **Box Selection** ⬚. Provides the ability to select entities in parts, assemblies, and drawings by dragging a selection box with the pointer.

- **Lasso Selection** ℘. Provides the ability to select entities by drawing a lasso around the entities.

- **Selection Filters** 🖙. Displays a list of selection filter commands.

- **Select Other** 🗗. Displays the Select Other dialog box.

- **Select** ⬧. Displays a list of selection commands.

- **Magnified Selection** 🔍. Displays the magnifying glass, which gives you a magnified view of a section of a model.

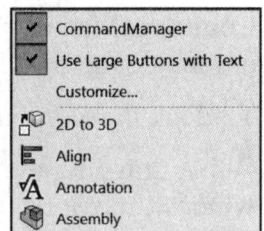

⚡ Save space in the CommandManager: right-click in the CommandManager and un-check the Use Large Buttons with Text box. This eliminates the text associated with the tool.

⚡ DimXpert provides the ability to graphically check if the model is fully dimensioned and toleranced. DimXpert automatically recognizes manufacturing features. Manufacturing features are not SOLIDWORKS features. Manufacturing features are defined in 1.1.12 of the ASME Y14.5M-1994 Dimensioning and Tolerancing standard. See SOLIDWORKS Help for additional information.

FeatureManager Design Tree

The FeatureManager consists of five default tabs:

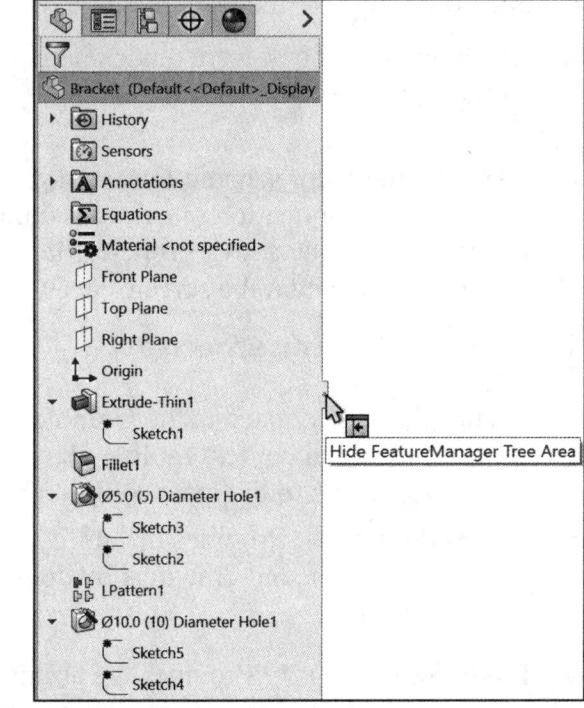

- *FeatureManager design tree* 🔷 tab.

- *PropertyManager* 📑 tab.

- *ConfigurationManager* 🔁 tab.

- *DimXpertManager* ⊕ tab.

- *DisplayManager* ⬤ tab.

Select the Hide FeatureManager Tree Area arrows 🔹 as illustrated to enlarge the Graphics window for modeling.

⚡ The Sensors tool 🔲 located in the FeatureManager monitors selected properties in a part or assembly and alerts you when values deviate from the specified limits. There are five sensor types: Simulation Data, Mass properties, Dimensions, Measurement and Costing Data.

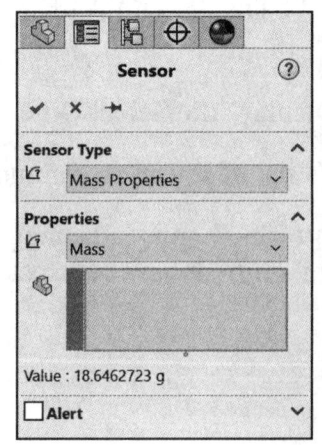

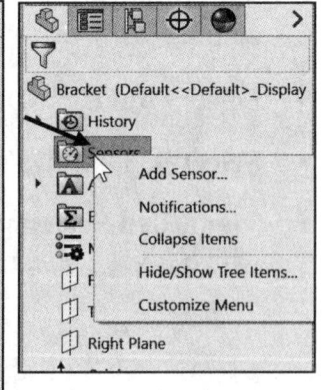

Various commands provide the ability to control what is displayed in the FeatureManager design tree:

1. Show or Hide FeatureManager items.

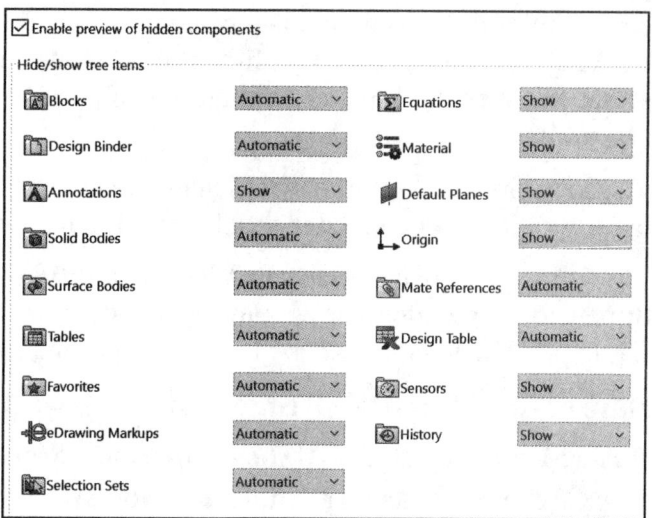

Click **Options** ⚙ from the Menu bar. Click **FeatureManager** from the System Options tab. **Customize** your FeatureManager from the Hide/Show Tree Items dialog box.

2. Filter the FeatureManager design tree. Enter information in the filter field. You can filter by *Type of features*, *Feature names*, *Sketches*, *Folders*, *Mates*, *User-defined tags* and *Custom properties*.

Tags are keywords you can add to a SOLIDWORKS document to make them easier to filter and to search. The Tags 🏷 icon is located in the bottom right corner of the Graphics window.

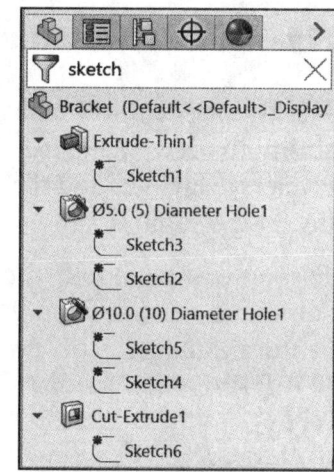

Collapse all items in the FeatureManager, **right-click** and select **Collapse items**, or press the **Shift** + **C** keys.

The FeatureManager design tree and the Graphics window are dynamically linked. Select sketches, features, drawing views, and construction geometry in either pane.

Split the FeatureManager design tree and either display two FeatureManager instances, or combine the FeatureManager design tree with the ConfigurationManager or PropertyManager.

Move between the FeatureManager design tree, PropertyManager, ConfigurationManager and DimXpertManager by selecting the tabs at the top of the menu.

Split line

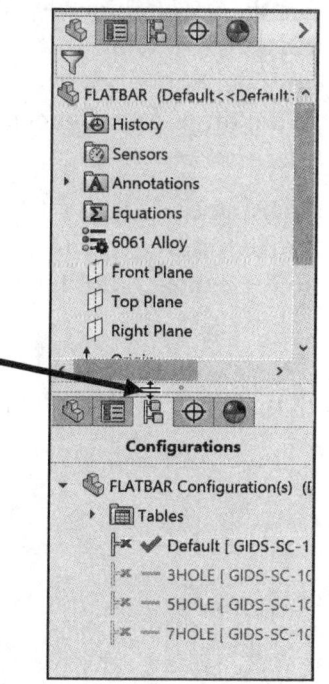

The ConfigurationManager is located to the right of the FeatureManager. Use the ConfigurationManager to create, select and view multiple configurations of parts and assemblies.

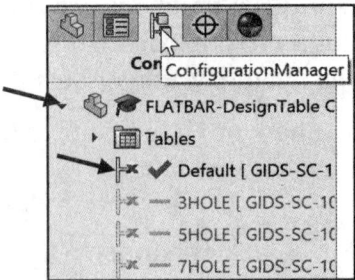

The icons in the ConfigurationManager denote whether the configuration was created manually or with a design table.

The DimXpertManager tab provides the ability to insert dimensions and tolerances manually or automatically. The DimXpertManager provides the following selections: **Auto Dimension Scheme** ⬦, **Basic Location Dimension** ⊢▭⊣, **Basic Size Dimension** ▭ **Show Tolerance Status** ±⊙, **Copy Scheme** ⬦ and **TolAnalyst Study** ⎂.

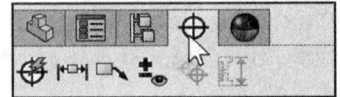

Fly-out FeatureManager

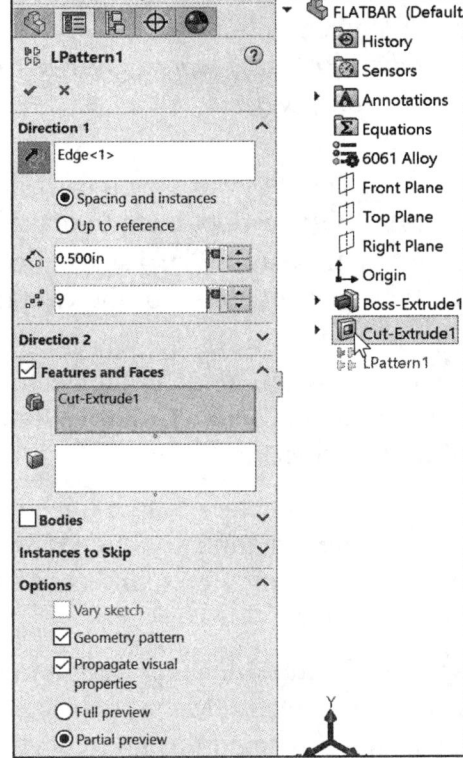

The fly-out FeatureManager design tree provides the ability to view and select items in the PropertyManager and the FeatureManager design tree at the same time.

Throughout the book, you will select commands and command options from the drop-down menu, fly-out FeatureManager, Context toolbar or from a SOLIDWORKS toolbar.

💡 Another method for accessing a command is to use the accelerator key. Accelerator keys are special key strokes, which activate the drop-down menu options. Some commands in the menu bar and items in the drop-down menus have an underlined character.

Pressing the Alt or Ctrl key followed by the corresponding key to the underlined character activates that command or option.

💡 Illustrations may vary depending on your SOLIDWORKS version and operating system.

Task Pane

The Task Pane is displayed when a SOLIDWORKS session starts. The Task Pane can be displayed in the following states: *visible or hidden, expanded or collapsed, pinned or unpinned, docked or floating.*

The Task Pane contains the following default tabs:

- *SOLIDWORKS Resources* 🏠.

- *Design Library* 📦.

- *File Explorer* 📂.

- *View Palette* ▥.

- *Appearances, Scenes and Decals* ●.

- *Custom Properties* ▤.

- *SOLIDWORKS Forum* 💬.

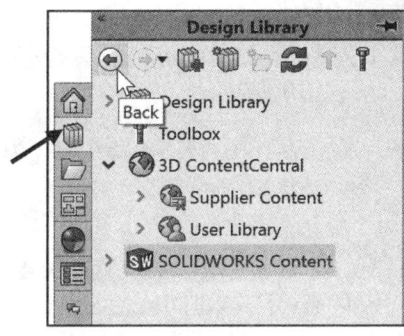

💡 Additional tabs are displayed with Add-Ins.

Use the **Back** and **Forward** buttons in the Design Library tab and the Appearances, Scenes, and Decals tab of the Task Pane to navigate in folders.

SOLIDWORKS Resources

The basic SOLIDWORKS Resources 🏠 menu displays the following default selections:

- *Getting Started.*

- *SOLIDWORKS Tools.*

- *Community.*

- *Online Resources.*

- *Subscription Services.*

- *Tip of the Day.*

Other user interfaces are available during the initial software installation selection: *Machine Design, Mold Design* or *Consumer Products Design.*

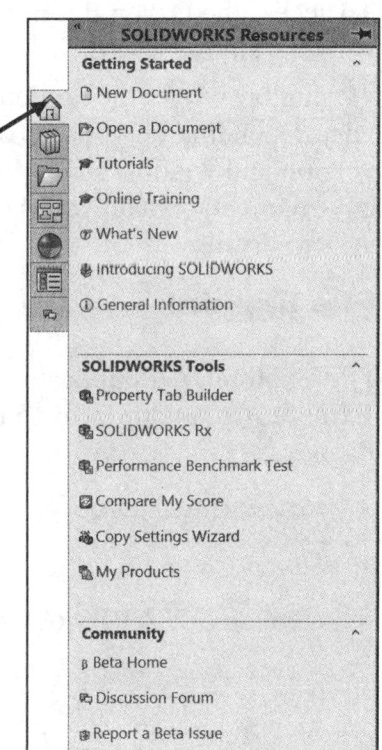

Design Library

The Design Library 🗄 contains reusable parts, assemblies, and other elements including library features.

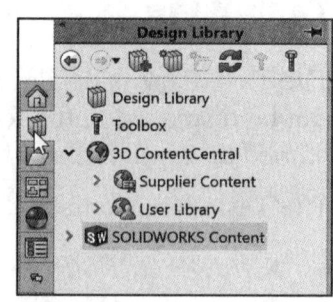

The Design Library tab contains four default selections. Each default selection contains additional sub categories.

These are the default selections:

- *Design Library.*

- *Toolbox.*

- *3D ContentCentral (Internet access required).*

- *SOLIDWORKS Content (Internet access required).*

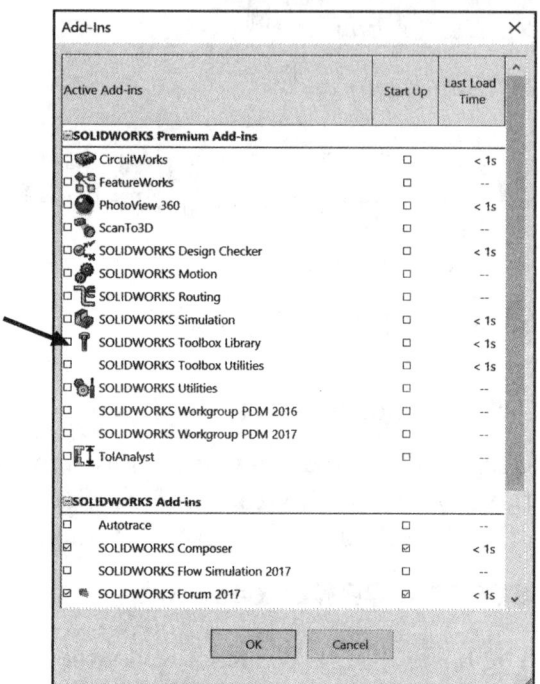

🔅 Activate the SOLIDWORKS Toolbox. Click Tools, Add-Ins.., from the Main menu. Check the SOLIDWORKS Toolbox Library from the Add-ins dialog box or click SOLIDWORKS Toolbox from the SOLIDWORKS Add-Ins tab.

To access the Design Library folders in a non-network environment, click Add File Location 🗄 and browse to the needed path. Paths may vary depending on your SOLIDWORKS version and window setup. In a network environment, contact your IT department for system details.

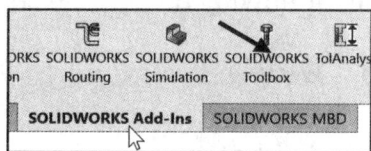

File Explorer

File Explorer 🗁 duplicates Windows Explorer from your local computer and displays:

- *Resent Documents.*

- *Directories.*

- *Open in SOLIDWORKS and Desktop folders.*

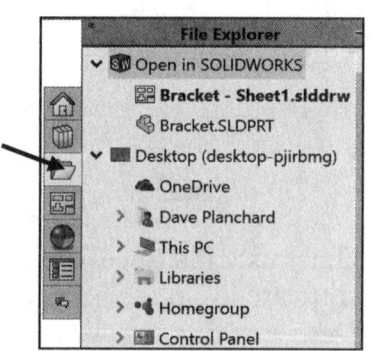

Search

The SOLIDWORKS Search box is displayed in the upper right corner of the SOLIDWORKS Graphics window (Menu Bar toolbar). Enter the text or key words to search.

New search modes have been added to SOLIDWORKS Search as illustrated.

View Palette

The View Palette 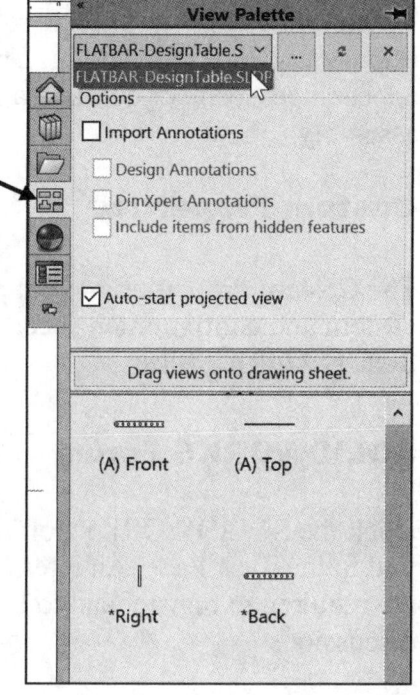 tool located in the Task Pane provides the ability to insert drawing views of an active document, or click the Browse button to locate the desired document.

Click and drag the view from the View Palette into an active drawing sheet to create a drawing view.

☀️ The selected model is FLATBAR in the illustration.

Appearances, Scenes and Decals

Appearances, Scenes and Decals ● provide a simplified way to display models in a photo-realistic setting using a library of Appearances, Scenes, and Decals.

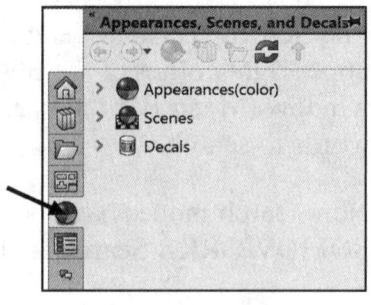

An appearance defines the visual properties of a model, including color and texture. Appearances do not affect physical properties, which are defined by materials.

Scenes provide a visual backdrop behind a model. In SOLIDWORKS they provide reflections on the model. PhotoView 360 is an Add-in. Drag and drop a selected appearance, scene or decal on a feature, surface, part or assembly.

Custom Properties

The Custom Properties 🗐 tool provides the ability to enter custom and configuration specific properties directly into SOLIDWORKS files.

SOLIDWORKS Forum

Click the SOLIDWORKS Forum 🗪 icon to search directly within the Task Pane. An internet connection is required. You are required to register and to login for postings and discussions.

User Interface for Scaling High Resolution Screens

The SOLIDWORKS software supports high-resolution, high-pixel density displays. All aspects of the user interface respond to the Microsoft Windows® display scaling setting.

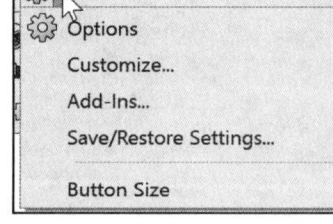

In dialog boxes, PropertyManagers, and the FeatureManager design tree, the SOLIDWORKS software uses your display scaling setting to display buttons and icons at an appropriate size. Icons that are associated with text are scaled to a size appropriate for the text. In addition, for toolbars, you can display Small, Medium, or Large buttons. Click the **Options drop-down arrow** from the Standard Menu bar, and click Button size to size the icons.

Motion Study tab

Motion Studies are graphical simulations of motion for an assembly. Access the MotionManager from the Motion Study tab. The Motion Study tab is located in the bottom left corner of the Graphics window.

Incorporate visual properties such as lighting and camera perspective. Click the Motion Study tab to view the MotionManager. Click the Model tab to return to the FeatureManager design tree.

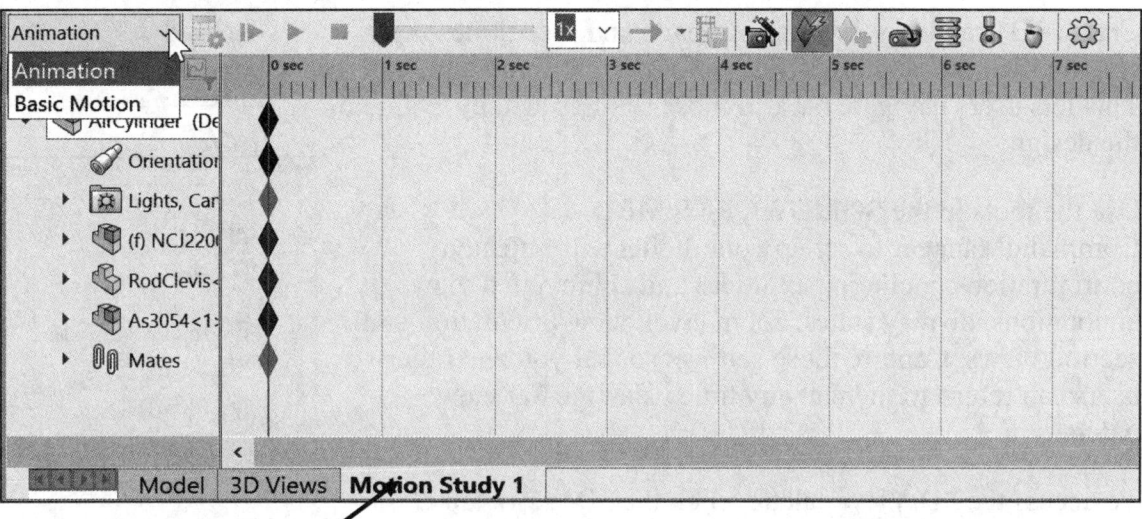

The MotionManager displays a timeline-based interface and provides the following selections from the drop-down menu as illustrated:

- *Animation:* Apply Animation to animate the motion of an assembly. Add a motor and insert positions of assembly components at various times using set key points. Use the Animation option to create animations for motion that do **not** require accounting for mass or gravity.

- *Basic Motion:* Apply Basic Motion for approximating the effects of motors, springs, collisions and gravity on assemblies. Basic Motion takes mass into account in calculating motion. Basic Motion computation is relatively fast, so you can use this for creating presentation animations using physics-based simulations. Use the Basic Motion option to create simulations of motion that account for mass, collisions or gravity.

If the Motion Study tab is not displayed in the Graphics window, click **View**, **MotionManager** from the Menu bar.

3D Views tab

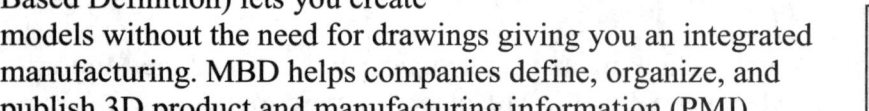

SOLIDWORKS MBD (Model Based Definition) lets you create models without the need for drawings giving you an integrated manufacturing. MBD helps companies define, organize, and publish 3D product and manufacturing information (PMI), including 3D model data in industry standard file formats.

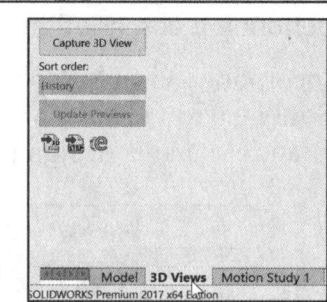

Create 3D drawing views of your parts and assemblies that contain the model settings needed for review and manufacturing. This lets users navigate back to those settings as they evaluate the design.

Use the tools in the SOLIDWORKS MBD CommandManager to set up your model with selected configurations, including explodes and abbreviated views, annotations, display states, zoom level, view orientation and section views. Capture those settings so that you and other users can return to them at any time using the 3D view palette.

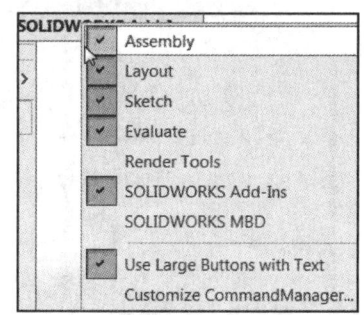

To access the 3D View palette, click the 3DViews tab at the bottom of the SOLIDWORKS window or the SOLIDWORKS MBD tab in the CommandManager. The Capture 3D View button opens the Capture 3D View PropertyManager, where you specify the 3D view name, and the configuration, display state and annotation view to capture. See SOLIDWORKS help for additional information.

Dynamic Reference Visualization

Dynamic Reference Visualization provides the ability to view the parent relationships between items in the FeatureManager design tree. When you hover over a feature with references in the FeatureManager design tree, arrows display showing the relationships. If a reference cannot be shown because a feature is not expanded, the arrow points to the feature that contains the reference and the actual reference appears in a text box to the right of the arrow. Use Dynamic reference visualization for a part, assembly and ever mates.

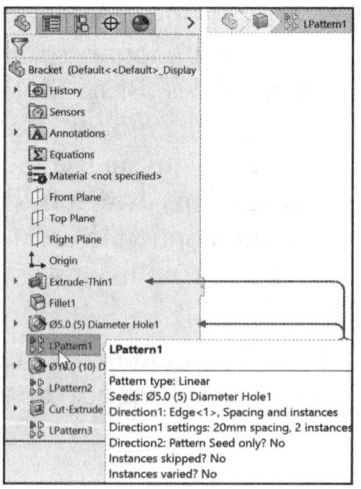

Use Dynamic reference visualization for a part, assembly and ever mates. To display the Dynamic Reference Visualization, click **View** ➤ **User Interface** ➤ **Dynamic Reference Visualization** from the Main menu bar.

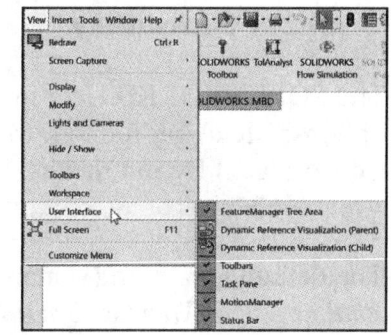

Mouse Movements

A mouse typically has two buttons: a primary button (usually the left button) and a secondary button (usually the right button). Most mice also include a scroll wheel between the buttons to help you scroll through documents and to Zoom in, Zoom out and rotate models in SOLIDWORKS. It is highly recommended that you use a mouse with at least a Primary, Scroll and Secondary button.

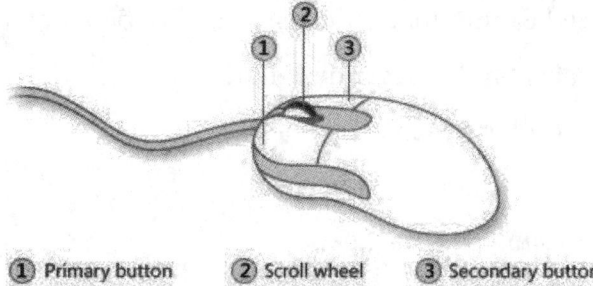

Single-click

To click an item, point to the item on the screen, and then press and release the primary button (usually the left button). Clicking is most often used to select (mark) an item or open a menu. This is sometimes called single-clicking or left-clicking.

Double-click

To double-click an item, point to the item on the screen, and then click twice quickly. If the two clicks are spaced too far apart, they might be interpreted as two individual clicks rather than as one double-click. Double-clicking is most often used to open items on your desktop. For example, you can start a program or open a folder by double-clicking its icon on the desktop.

Right-click

To right-click an item, point to the item on the screen, and then press and release the secondary button (usually the right button). Right-clicking an item usually displays a list of things you can do with the item. Right-click in the open Graphics window or on a command in SOLIDWORKS, and additional pop-up context is displayed.

Scroll wheel

Use the scroll wheel to zoom-in or to zoom-out of the Graphics window in SOLIDWORKS. To zoom-in, roll the wheel backward (toward you). To zoom-out, roll the wheel forward (away from you).

Chapter Summary

The SOLIDWORKS User Interface and CommandManager consist of the following main options: Menu bar toolbar, Menu bar menu, Drop-down menus, Context toolbars, Consolidated fly-out menus, System feedback icons, Confirmation Corner and Heads-up View toolbar.

The default CommandManager Part tabs control the display of the *Features*, *Sketch*, *Evaluate*, *DimXpert* and *SOLIDWORKS Add-Ins* toolbars.

The FeatureManager consists of five default tabs:

- FeatureManager design tree.
- PropertyManager.
- ConfigurationManager.
- DimXpertManager.
- DisplayManager.

You learned about creating a new SOLIDWORKS part and opening an existing SOLIDWORKS part along with using the Rollback bar to view the sketches and features.

You learned about SOLIDWORKS Help, SOLIDWORKS Tutorials and basic mouse movements to manipulate your SOLIDWORKS model.

CSWA Introduction and Drafting Competencies is the next chapter. There are three questions - multiple choice - 5 points each in this category.

Copy the Model Folders from the book which corresponds to your release of SOLIDWORKS. Work directly from the hard drive on the tutorials in this book.

SOLIDWORKS 2017
SOLIDWORKS 2016
SOLIDWORKS 2015

CHAPTER 2 - CSWA INTRODUCTION AND DRAFTING COMPETENCIES

Introduction

DS SOLIDWORKS Corp. offers various types of certification. Each stage represents increasing levels of expertise in 3D CAD: Certified SOLIDWORKS Associate CSWA, Certified SOLIDWORKS Professional CSWP and Certified SOLIDWORKS Expert CSWE along with specialty fields.

The CSWA certification indicates a foundation in and apprentice knowledge of 3D CAD design and engineering practices and principles. The main requirement for obtaining the CSWA certification is to take and pass the two part on-line proctored exams. This first exam (part 1) is 90 minutes, minimum passing score is 80, with 6 questions. The second exam (part 2) is 90 minutes, minimum passing score is 80 with 8 questions.

The CSWA exam consists of 14 questions in the following five categories and subject areas:

- *Drafting Competencies*: (Three questions - multiple choice - 5 points each).

    - Questions on general drawing views: Projected, Section, Break, Crop, Detail, Alternate Position, etc.

Drafting Competencies - To create drawing view 'B' it is necessary to select drawing view 'A' and insert which SolidWorks view type?

- *Basic Part Creation and Modification*: (Two questions - one multiple choice/one single answer - 15 points each).

    - Sketch Planes:

        - Front, Top, Right.

    - 2D Sketching:

Basic Part (Hydraulic Cylinder Half) - Step 1
Build this part in SolidWorks.
(Save part after each question in a different file in case it must be reviewed)

Unit system: MMGS (millimeter, gram, second)
Decimal places: 2
Part origin: Arbitrary
All holes through all unless shown otherwise.
Material: Aluminium 1060 Alloy

Screen shots from an exam

- Geometric Relations and Dimensioning.

- Extruded Boss/Base Feature.

- Extruded Cut feature.

- Modification of Basic part.

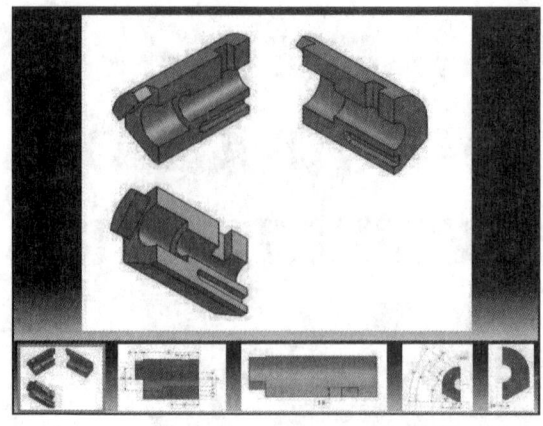

💡 In the *Basic Part Creation and Modification* category, there is a dimension modification question based on the first (multiple choice) question. You should be within 1% of the multiple choice answer before you go on to the modification single answer section.

- *Intermediate Part Creation and Modification;* (Two questions - one multiple choice/one single answer - 15 points each).

  - Sketch Planes:

    - Front, Top, Right.

  - 2D Sketching:

    - Geometric Relations and Dimensioning.

  - Extruded Boss/Base Feature.

  - Extruded Cut Feature.

  - Revolved Boss/Base Feature.

  - Mirror and Fillet Feature.

  - Circular and Linear Pattern Feature.

  - Plane Feature.

  - Modification of Intermediate Part:

    - Sketch, Feature, Pattern, etc.

  - Modification of Intermediate part.

💡 In the *Intermediate Part Creation and Modification* category, there are two dimension modification questions based on the first (multiple choice) question. You should be within 1% of the multiple choice answer before you go on to the modification single answer section.

Intermediate Part (Wheel) - Step 1
Build this part in SolidWorks.
(Save part after each question in a different file in case it must be reviewed)

Unit system: MMGS (millimeter, gram, second)
Decimal places: 2
Part origin: Arbitrary
All holes through all unless shown otherwise.
Material: Aluminium 1060 Alloy

A = 134.00
B = 890.00

Note: All geometry is symmetrical about the plane represented by the line labeled F"" in the M-M Section View.

What is the overall mass of the part (grams)?

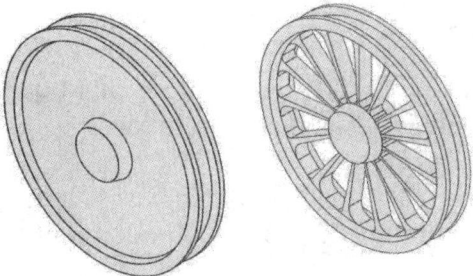

Hint: If you don't find an option within 1% of your answer please re-check your model(s).

Screen shots from an exam

- *Advanced Part Creation and Modification; (Three questions - one multiple choice/two single answers – 15 points each).*

  - Sketch Planes:

    - Front, Top, Right, Face, Created Plane etc.

    - 2D Sketching or 3D Sketching.

  - Sketch Tools:

    - Offset Entities, Convert Entitles, etc.

  - Extruded Boss/Base Feature.

  - Extruded Cut Feature.

  - Revolved Boss/Base Feature.

  - Mirror and Fillet Feature.

  - Circular and Linear Pattern Feature.

  - Shell Feature.

  - Plane Feature.

  - More Difficult Geometry Modifications.

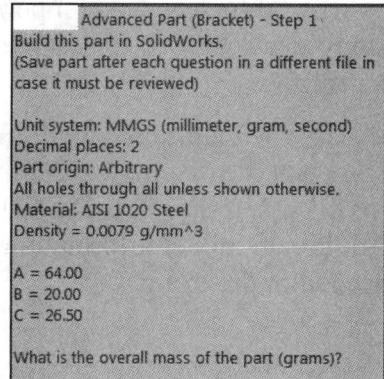

Advanced Part (Bracket) - Step 1
Build this part in SolidWorks.
(Save part after each question in a different file in case it must be reviewed)

Unit system: MMGS (millimeter, gram, second)
Decimal places: 2
Part origin: Arbitrary
All holes through all unless shown otherwise.
Material: AISI 1020 Steel
Density = 0.0079 g/mm^3

A = 64.00
B = 20.00
C = 26.50

What is the overall mass of the part (grams)?

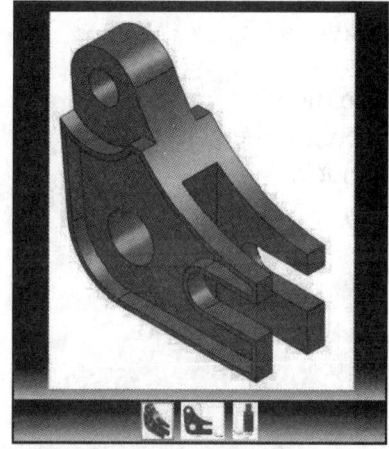

Hint: If you don't find an option within 1% of your answer please re-check your model(s).

In the *Advanced Part Creation and Modification* category, there are two dimension modification questions based on the first (multiple choice) question. You should be within 1% of the multiple choice answer before you go on to the modification single answer section.

- *Assembly Creation and Modification; (Two different assemblies - four questions - two multiple choice/two single answers - 30 points each).*

  - Insert the first (fixed) component.

  - Insert all needed components.

  - Standard Mates.

  - Modification of key parameters in the assembly.

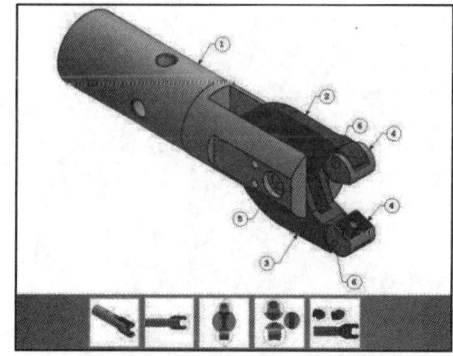

Screen shots from an exam

In the *Assembly Creation and Modification* category, expect to see five to seven components. There are two dimension modification questions based on the first (multiple choice) question. You should be within 1% of the multiple choice answer before you go on to the modification single answer section.

Download the needed components in a zip folder during the exam to create the assembly.

Do not use feature recognition when you open the downloaded components for the assembly. This is a timed exam. Additional model information is not needed in the exam.

Illustrations may vary depending on your SOLIDWORKS version and system setup.

Use the view indicator to increase or decrease the active model in the view window.

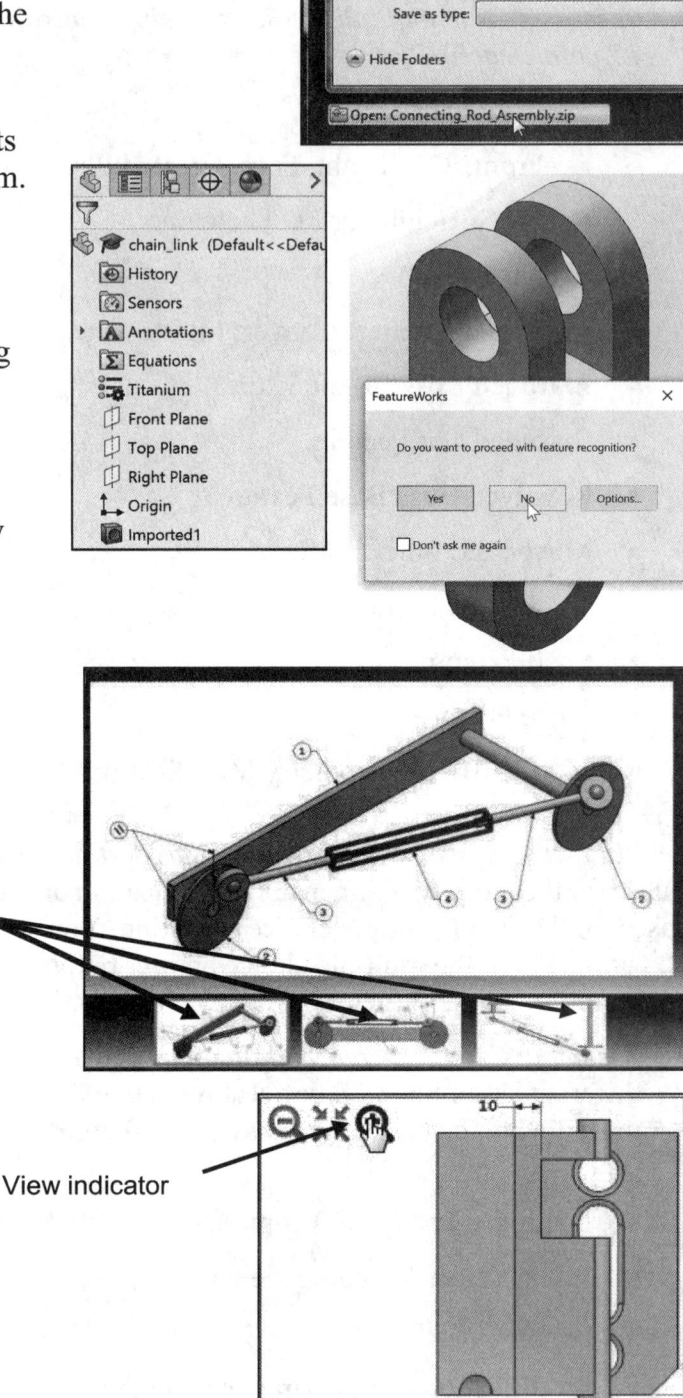

View indications

View indicator

Screen shots from an exam

This first exam (part 1) is 90 minutes, minimum passing score is 80, with 6 questions. The second exam (part 2) is 90 minutes, minimum passing score is 80 with 8 questions.

You are allowed to answer the questions in any order you prefer. Use the Summary Screen during the CSWA exam to view the list of all questions you have or have not answered.

During the exam, use the control keys at the bottom of the screen to:

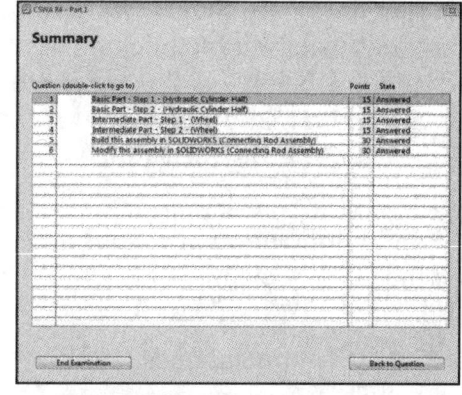

- *Show the Previous Question.*

- *Reset the Question.*

- *Show the Summary Screen.*

- *Move to the Next Question.*

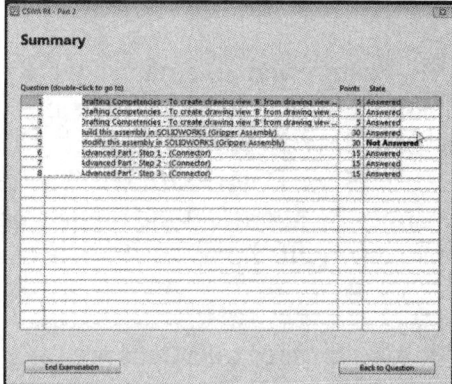

When you are finished, press the End Examination button. The tester will ask you if you want to end the test. Click Yes.

If there are any unanswered questions, the tester will provide a warning message as illustrated.

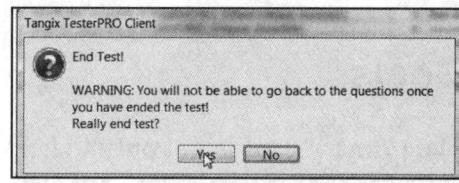

☀ If you do not pass the certification exam, you will need to wait 30 days until you can retake each part of the exam.

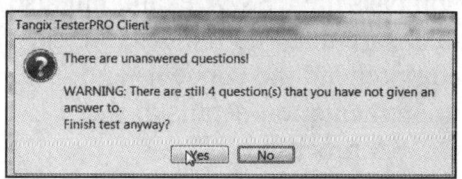

Use the clock in the tester to view the amount of time that you used and the amount of time that is left in the exam.

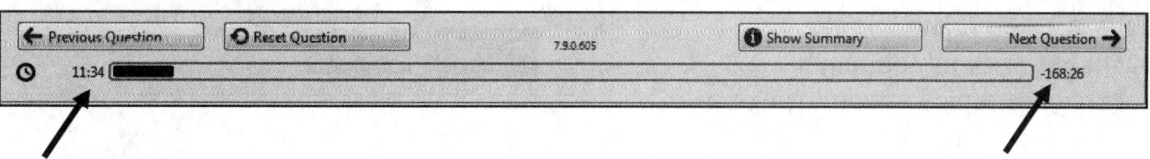

Screen shots from the exam

During the exam, SOLIDWORKS provides the ability to click on a detail view below (as illustrated) to obtain additional details and dimensions during the exam.

💡 No Simulation questions are on the CSWA exam.

💡 No Sheetmetal questions are on the CSWA exam.

💡 FeatureManager names were changed through various revisions of SOLIDWORKS. Example: Extrude1 vs. Boss-Extrude1. These changes do not affect the models or answers in this book.

💡 No Surface questions are on the CSWA exam.

Goals

The primary goal is not only to help you pass the CSWA exam, but also to ensure that you understand and comprehend the concepts and implementation details of the CSWA process.

The second goal is to provide the most comprehensive coverage of CSWA exam related topics available, without too much coverage of topics not on the exam.

The third and ultimate goal is to get you from where you are today to the point that you can confidently pass the CSWA exam.

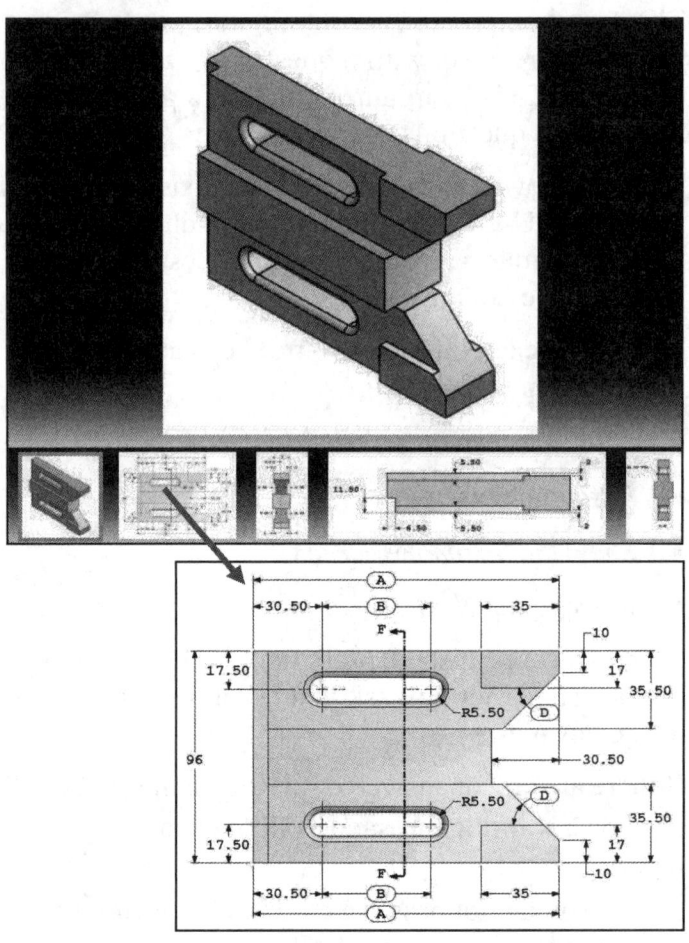

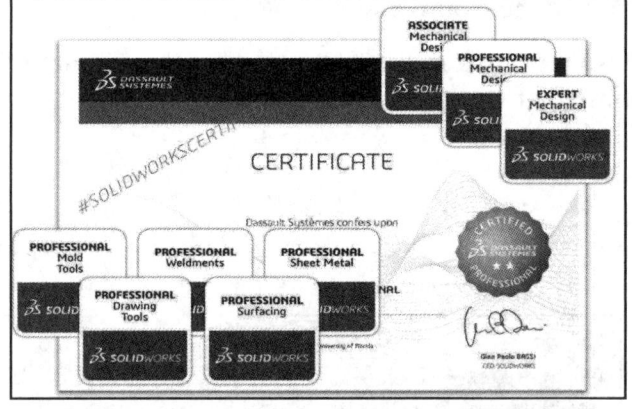

Objectives

Drafting Competencies is one of the five categories *(Drafting Competencies, Basic Part Creation and Modification, Intermediate Part Creation and Modification, Advance Part Creation and Modification and Assembly Creation and Modification)* on the CSWA exam.

There are three questions (total) on the CSWA exam in the *Drafting Competencies* category. Each question is worth five (5) points. Drafting Competency questions are addressed in part 2 of the CSWA exam.

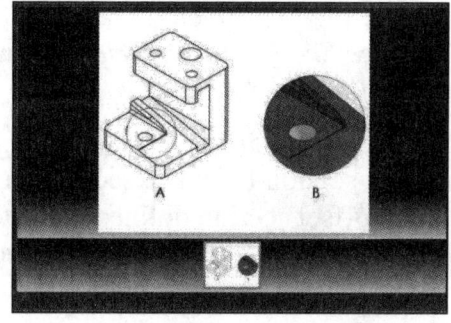

The three questions are in a multiple choice single answer format. You are allowed to answer the questions in any order you prefer. Use the Summary Screen during the exam to view the list of all questions you have or have not answered.

Screen shot from the exam

In the *Drafting Competencies* category of the exam, you are **not required** to create or perform an analysis on a part, assembly, or drawing but you are required to have general drafting/drawing knowledge and understanding of various drawing view methods.

On the completion of the chapter, you will be able to:

- Identify the procedure to create a named drawing view: Projected view, Section view, Break view, Crop view, Detail, Alternate Position view, etc.

SOLIDWORKS 2017
SOLIDWORKS 2016
SOLIDWORKS 2015

In the *Basic Part Creation and Modification, Intermediate Part Creation and Modification, Advanced Part Creation and Modification and Assembly Creation and Modification* categories, you are required to read and interpret various types of drawing views and understand various types of drawing annotations.

All SOLIDWORKS models for the next few chapters (initial and final) are provided in the SOLIDWORKS CSWA Model Folder. Download the SOLIDWORKS CSWA Model Folder.

SOLIDWORKS CSWA Model Folder

Name

Chapter 7
Chapter 7 Final Solutions
Chapter 8
Chapter 8 Final Solutions
Chapter 9
Chapter 9 Final Solutions
Chapter 10
Chapter 10 Final Solutions

Procedure to Create a Named Drawing view

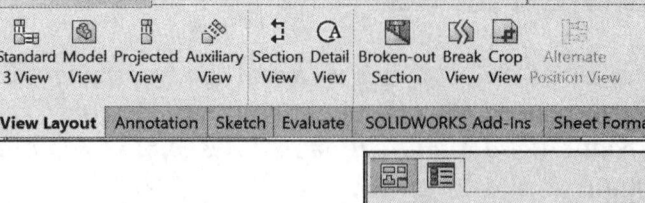

You need the ability to identify the procedure to create a named drawing view: *Standard 3 View, Model View, Projected View, Auxiliary View, Section View, Aligned Section View, Detail View, Broken-out Section, Break, Crop View and Alternate Position View.*

Create a Section view in a drawing by cutting the parent view with a section line. The section view can be a straight cut section or an offset section defined by a stepped section line. The section line can also include concentric arcs.

Create an Aligned section view in a drawing through a model, or portion of a model, that is aligned with a selected section line segment. The Aligned Section view is similar to a Section View, but the section line for an aligned section comprises two or more lines connected at an angle.

Create a Detail view in a drawing to show a portion of a view, usually at an enlarged scale. This detail may be of an orthographic view, a non-planar (isometric) view, a section view, a crop view, an exploded assembly view, or another detail view.

🔅 Crop any drawing view except a Detail view, a view from which a Detail view has been created, or an Exploded view. To create a Crop view, sketch a closed profile such as a circle or spline. The view outside the closed profile disappears as illustrated.

🔅 Create a Detail view in a drawing to display a portion of a view, usually at an enlarged scale. This detail may be of an orthographic view, a non-planar (isometric) view, a Section view, a Crop view, an Exploded assembly view, or another Detail view.

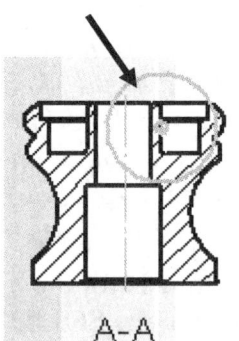

A-A

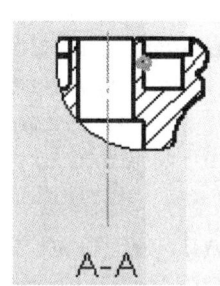

A-A

Tutorial: Drawing Named Procedure 2-1

Identify the drawing name view and understand the procedure to create the name view.

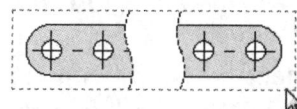

1. **View** the illustrated drawing views. The top drawing view is a Break view. The Break view is created by adding a break line to a selected view.

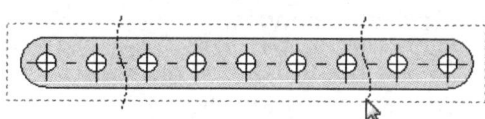

Broken views make it possible to display the drawing view in a larger scale on a smaller size drawing sheet. Reference dimensions and model dimensions associated with the broken area reflect the actual model values.

In views with multiple breaks, the Break line style must be the same.

Tutorial: Drawing Named Procedure 2-2

Identify the drawing name view and understand the procedure to create the name view.

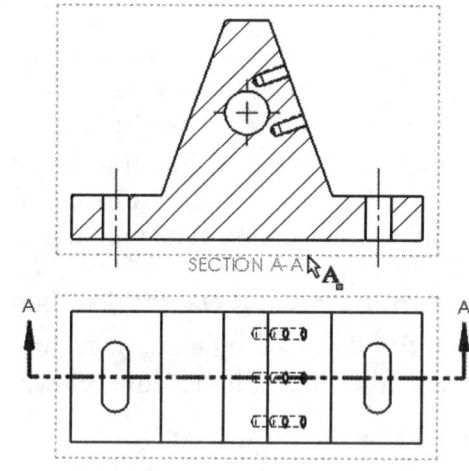

1. **View** the illustrated drawing views. The right drawing view is a Section View. The Section view is created by cutting the parent view with a cutting section line.

Create a Section view in a drawing by cutting the parent view with a section line. The section view can be a straight cut section or an offset section defined by a stepped section line. The section line can also include Concentric arcs.

Tutorial: Drawing Named Procedure 2-3

Identify the drawing name view and understand the procedure to create the name view.

1. **View** the illustrated drawing views. The view to the right is an Auxilary view of the Front view. Select a reference edge to create an Auxiliary view as illustrated.

An Auxiliary view is similar to a Projected view, but it is unfolded normal to a reference edge in an existing view.

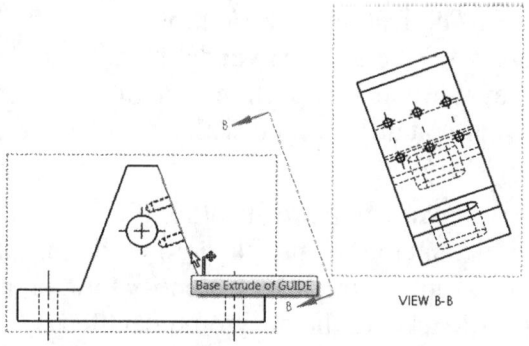

Tutorial: Drawing Named Procedure 2-4

Identify the drawing name view and understand the procedure to create the name view.

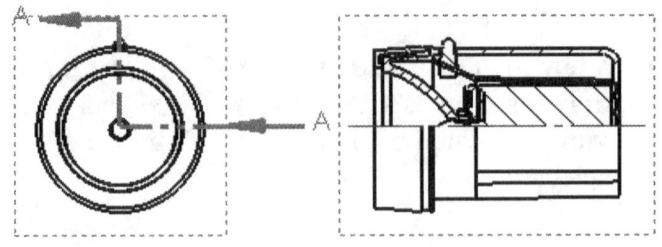

1. **View** the illustrated drawing views. The right drawing view is an Aligned half Section view of the view to the left. The Section view is created by using two lines connected at an angle. Create an Aligned half Section view in a drawing through a model, or portion of a model, that is aligned with a selected section line segment.

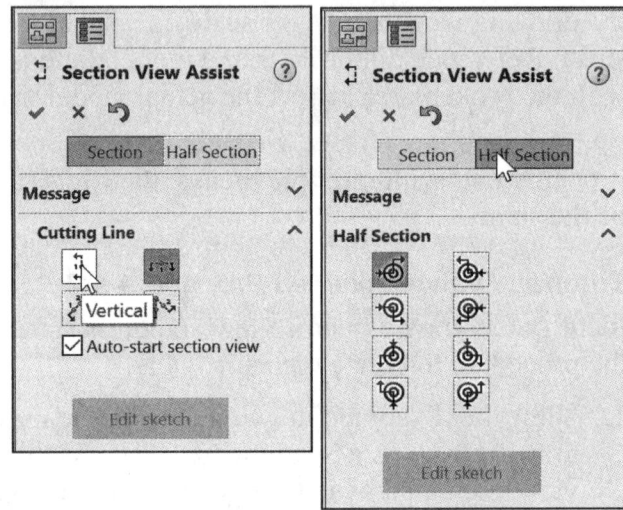

💡 The Aligned Section view is very similar to a Section View, with the exception that the section line for an aligned half section is comprised of two or more lines connected at an angle.

Tutorial: Drawing Named Procedure 2-5

Identify the drawing name view and understand the procedure to create the name view.

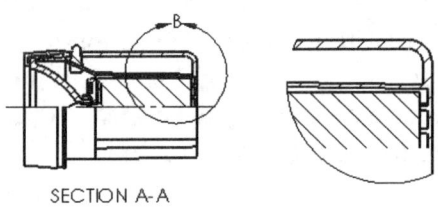

1. **View** the illustrated drawing views. The left drawing view is a Detail view of the Section view. The Detail view is created by sketching a circle with the Circle Sketch tool. Click and drag for the location.

💡 The Detail view ⃝A tool provides the ability to add a Detail view to display a portion of a view, usually at an enlarged scale.

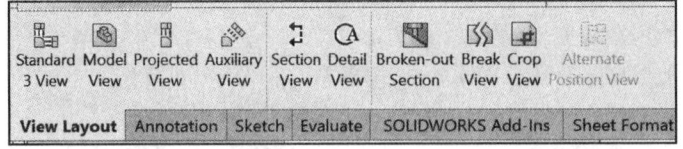

💡 To create a profile other than a circle, sketch the profile before clicking the Detail view tool. Using a sketch entity tool, create a closed profile around the area to be detailed.

Tutorial: Drawing Named Procedure 2-6

Identify the drawing name view and understand the procedure to create the name view.

1. **View** the illustrated drawing views. The right drawing view is a Broken-out Section view. The Broken-out Section View is part of an existing drawing view, not a separate view. Create the Broken-out Section view with a closed profile, usually by using the Spline Sketch tool. Material is removed to a specified depth to expose inner details.

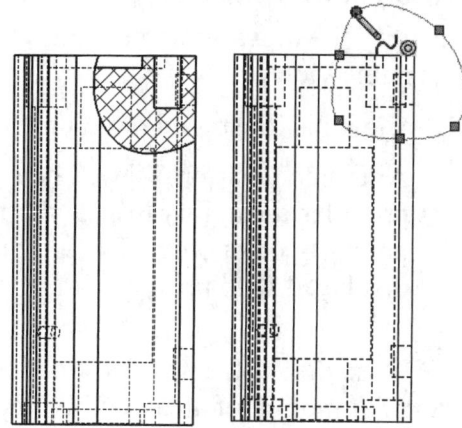

Tutorial: Drawing Named Procedure 2-7

Identify the drawing name view and understand the procedure to create the name view.

1. **View** the illustrated drawing view. The top drawing view is a Crop view. The Crop view is created by a closed sketch profile such as a circle, or spline as illustrated.

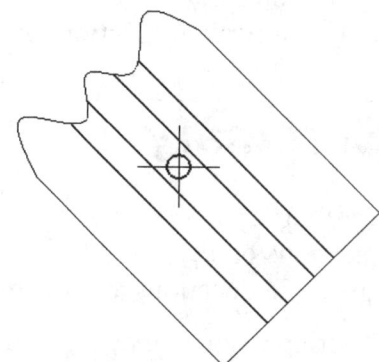

The Crop View provides the ability to crop an existing drawing view. You cannot use the Crop tool on a Detail view, a view from which a Detail view has been created, or an Exploded view.

Use the Crop tool to save steps. Example: instead of creating a Section View and then a Detail view, then hiding the unnecessary Section view, use the Crop tool to crop the Section view directly.

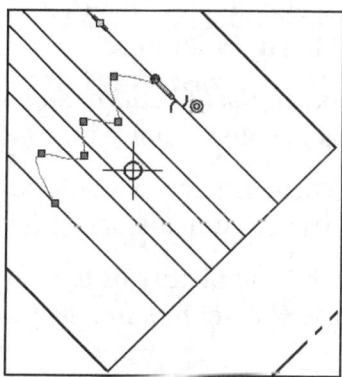

In the exam, you are allowed to answer the questions in any order. Use the Summary Screen during the exam to view the list of all questions you have or have not answered.

Tutorial: Drawing Named Procedure 2-8

Identify the drawing name view and understand the procedure to create the name view.

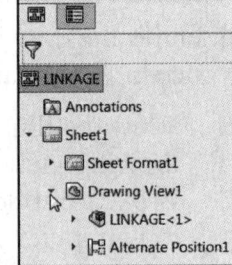

1. **View** the illustrated drawing view. The drawing view is an

   Alternate Position View. The Alternate Position view tool 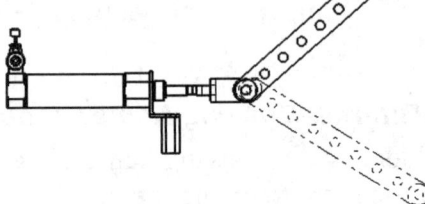 provides the ability to superimpose an existing drawing view precisely on another. The alternate position is displayed with phantom lines.

💡 Use the Alternate Position view to display the range of motion of an assembly. You can dimension between the primary view and the Alternate Position view. You cannot use the Alternate Position view tool with Broken, Section, or Detail views.

Summary

Drafting Competencies is one of the five categories on the CSWA exam. There are three questions on the CSWA exam in this category. Each question is worth five (5) points. The three questions are in a multiple choice single answer format.

Drafting Competency questions are addressed in part 2 of the CSWA exam.

Spend no more than 10 minutes on each question in this category. This is a timed exam. Manage your time.

Basic Part Creation and Modification and *Intermediate Part Creation and Modification* is the next chapter in this book.

This chapter covers the knowledge to create and modify models for these categories from detailed dimensioned illustrations.

The complexity of the models along with the features progressively increases throughout the chapter to simulate the final types of model that could be provided on the exam.

💡 Screen shots in the book were made using SOLIDWORKS 2016 SP2 and SOLIDWORKS 2017 SP0 running Windows® 10.

Questions

1. Identify the illustrated Drawing view.

- A: Projected

- B: Alternative Position

- C: Extended

- D: Aligned Section

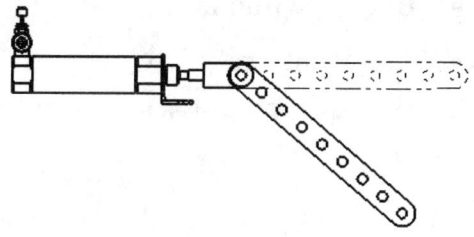

2. Identify the illustrated Drawing view.

- A: Crop

- B: Break

- C: Broken-out Section

- D: Aligned Section

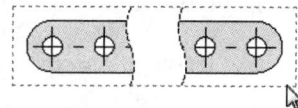

3. Identify the illustrated Drawing view.

- A: Section

- B: Crop

- C: Broken-out Section

- D: Aligned Section

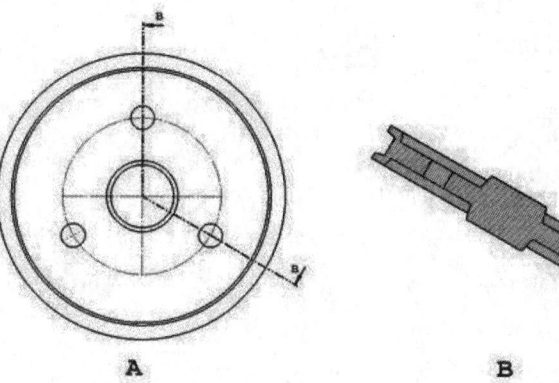

4. Identify the view procedure. To create the following view, you need to insert a:

- A: Rectangle Sketch tool

- B: Closed Profile: Spline

- C: Open Profile: Circle

- D: None of the above

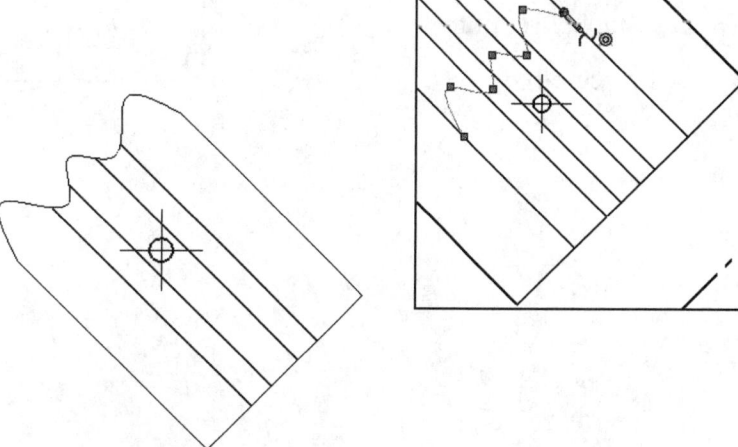

5. Identify the view procedure. To create the following view, you need to insert a:

- A: Open Spline
- B: Closed Spline
- C: 3 Point Arc
- D: None of the above

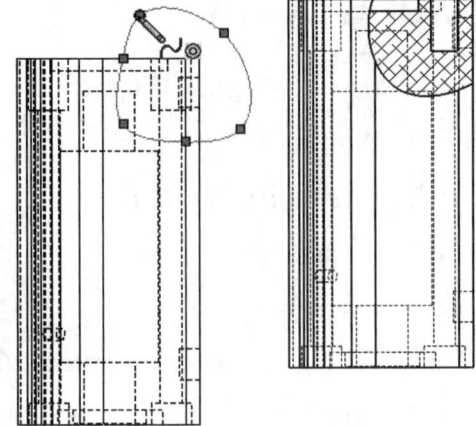

6. Identify the illustrated view type.

- A: Crop
- B: Section
- C: Projected
- D: Detail

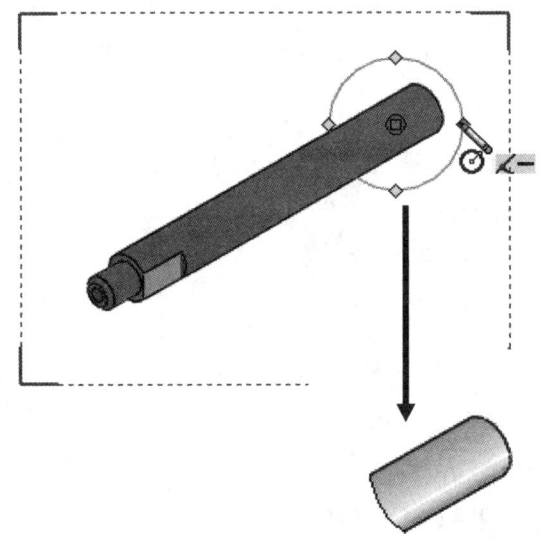

7. To create View B from Drawing View A insert which view type?

- A: Crop
- B: Section
- C: Aligned Section
- D: Projected

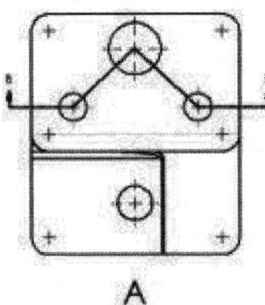

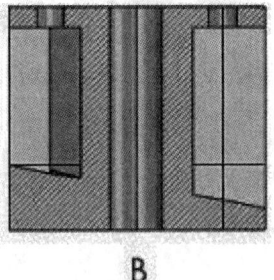

A   B

8. To create View B it is necessary to sketch a closed spline on View A and insert which View type?

- A: Broken out Section

- B: Detail

- C: Section

- D: Projected

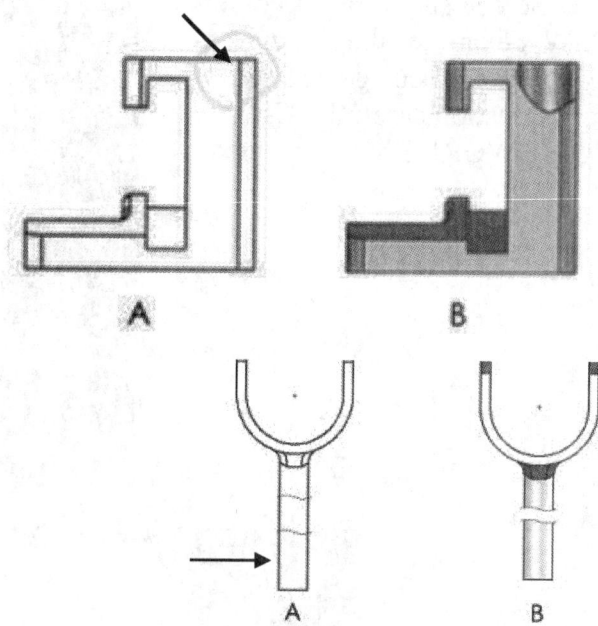

9. To create View B it is necessary to sketch a closed spline on View A and insert which View type?

- A: Horizontal Break

- B: Detail

- C: Section

- D: Broken out Section

Screen shots from an older CSWA exam for the *Drafting Competencies* category. Read each question carefully. Use SOLIDWORKS help if needed.

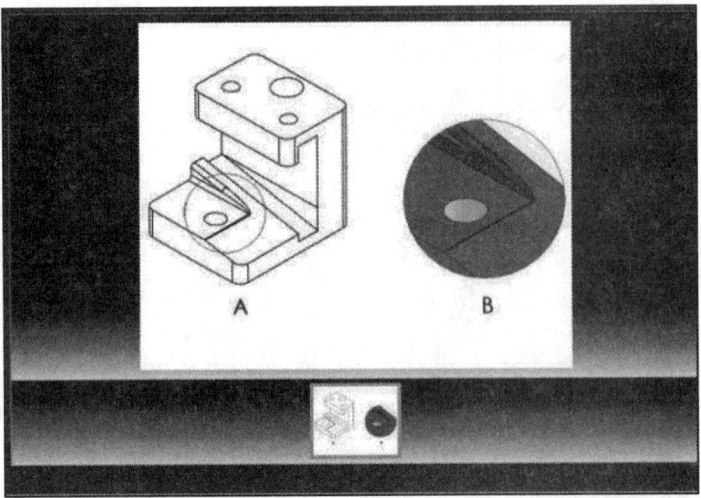

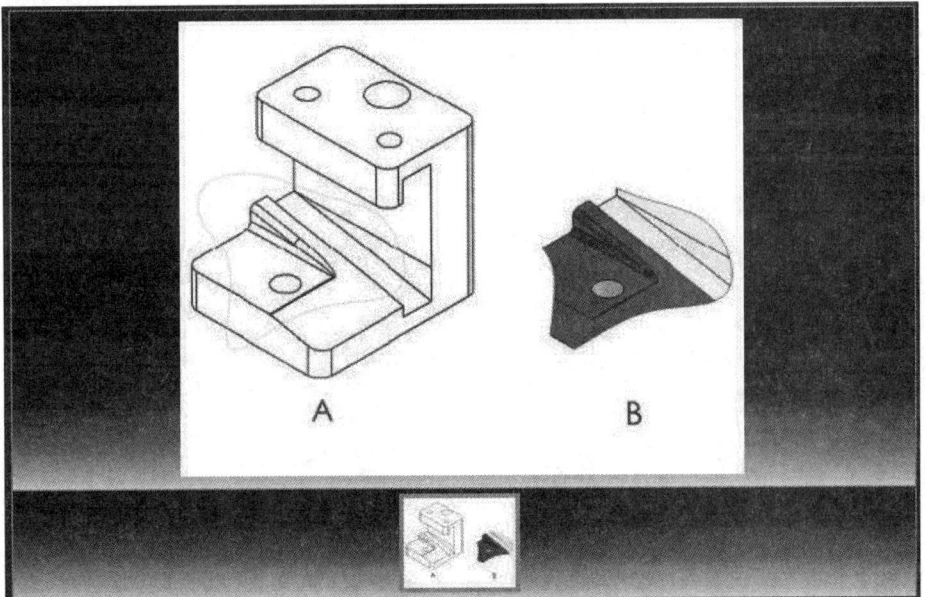

Zoom in on the part or view if needed.

Alternative Position View:

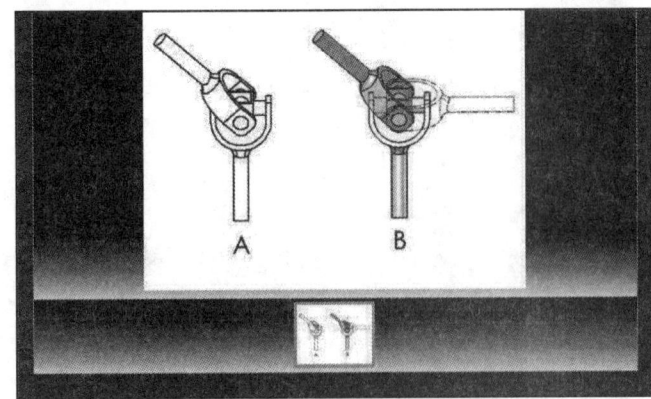

⚡ Screen shots from an older CSWA exam for the *Drafting Competencies* category. Read each question carefully. Use SOLIDWORKS help if needed.

Broken out Section View:

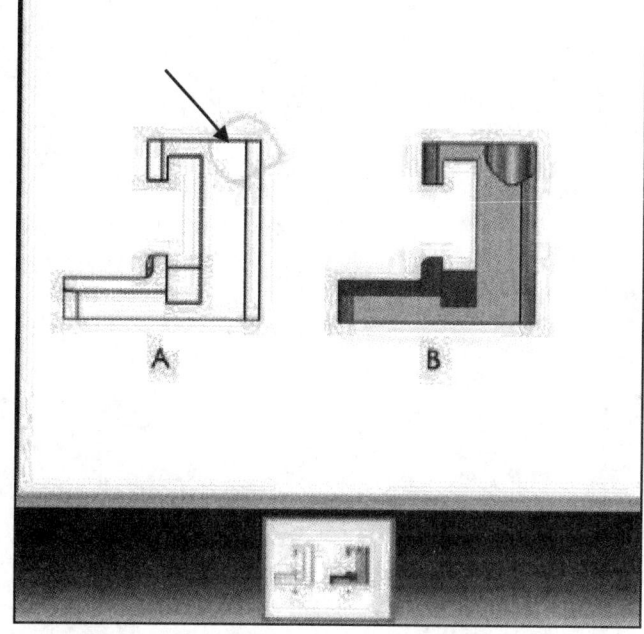

Section View:

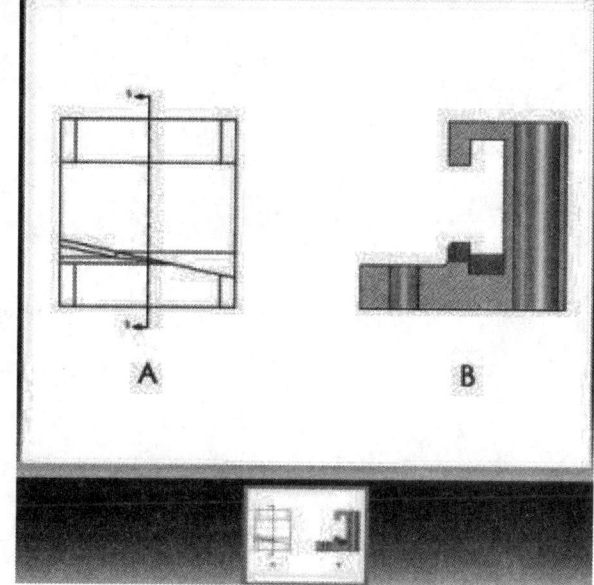

Notes:

CHAPTER 3 - BASIC PART AND INTERMEDIATE PART CREATION AND MODIFICATION

Objectives

Basic Part Creation and Modification and Intermediate Part Creation and Modification are two of the five categories on the CSWA exam. This chapter covers the knowledge to create and modify models in these categories from detailed dimensioned illustrations.

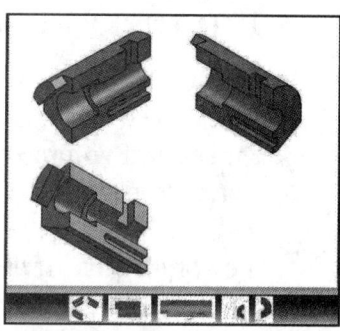

The main difference between the *Basic Part Creation and Modification* category and the *Intermediate Part Creation and Modification* or the *Advance Part Creation and Modification* category is the complexity of the sketches and the number of dimensions and geometric relations along with an increase in the number of features.

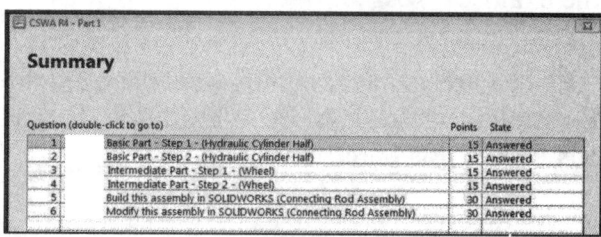

There are two questions on the CSWA exam (part 1) in the *Basic Part Creation and Modification* category and two questions in the *Intermediate Part Creation and Modification* category.

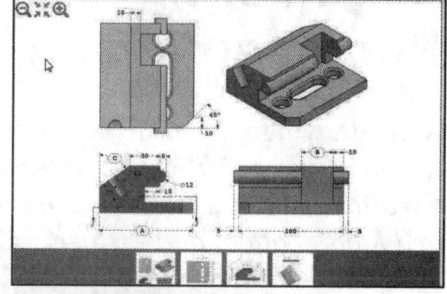

The first question is in a multiple choice single answer format. You should be within 1% of the multiple choice answer before you move on to the modification single answer section (fill in the blank format).

Each question is worth fifteen (15) points for a total of thirty (30) points. You are required to build a model with six or more features and to answer a question either on the overall mass, volume, or the location of the Center of mass for the created model relative to the default part Origin location. You are then requested to modify the part and answer a fill in the blank format question.

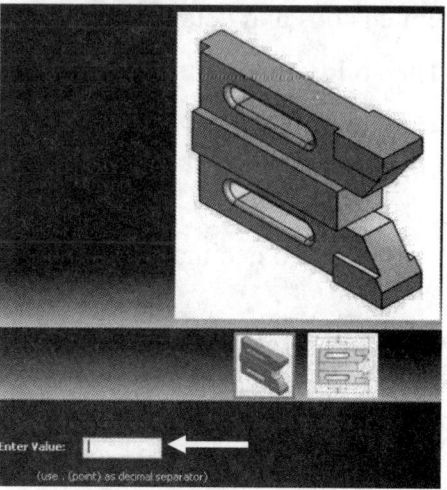

Screen shots from an exam

On the completion of the chapter, you will be able to:

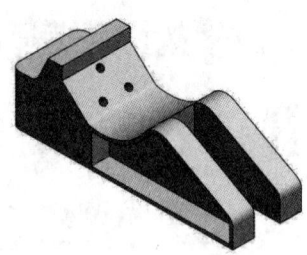

- Read and understand an Engineering document used in the CSWA exam:

  - Identify the Sketch plane, part Origin location, part dimensions, geometric relations, and design intent of the sketch and feature.

- Build a part from a detailed dimensioned illustration using the following SOLIDWORKS tools and features:

  - 2D & 3D sketch tools, Extruded Boss/Base, Extruded Cut, Fillet, Mirror, Revolved Base, Chamfer, Reference geometry, Plane, Axis, Calculate the overall mass and volume of the created part, and Locate the Center of mass for the created part relative to the Origin.

The complexity of the models along with the features progressively increases throughout this chapter to simulate the final types of models that would be provided on the exam.

FeatureManager names were changed through various revisions of SOLIDWORKS. Example: Extrude1 vs. Boss-Extrude1. These changes do not affect the models or answers in this book.

Engineering Documentation Practices

A 2D drawing view is displayed in the *Basic Part Creation and Modification, Intermediate Part Creation and Modification, Advance Part Creation and Modification, and Assembly Creation and Modification* categories of the CSWA exam to clarify dimensions and details.

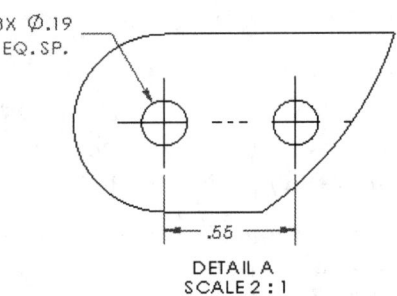

The ability to interpret a 2D drawing view is required.

- Example 1: *8X Ø.19 EQ. SP.* Eight holes with a .19in. diameter are required that are equally (.55in.) spaced.

- Example 2: *R2.50 TYP.* Typical radius of 2.50. The dimension has a two decimal place precision.

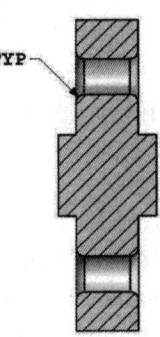

- Example 3: 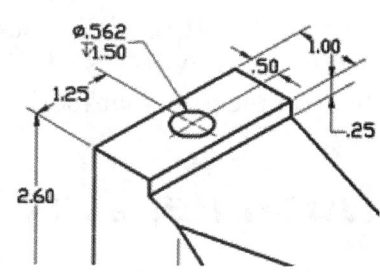. The Depth/Deep ⊽ symbol with a 1.50 dimension associated with the hole. The hole Ø.562 has a three decimal place precision.

- Example 4: *A+40*. A is provided to you on the CSWA exam. A + 40mm.

🔅 N is a Detail view of the M-M Section view.

- Example 5: *ØB*. Diameter of B. B is provided to you on the exam.

- Example 6: ⓘ. Parallelism.

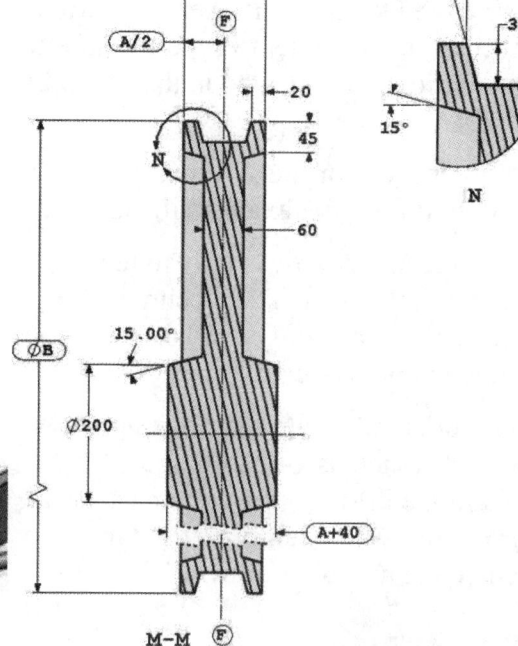

- Example 7: ⊗ The faces are coincident.

During the exam, each question will display an information table on the left side of the screen and drawing information on the right. Read the provided information and apply it to the drawing. Various values are provided on each question.

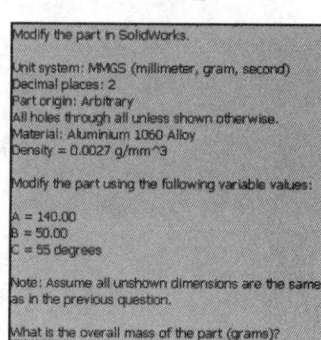

🔅 If you don't find your answer (within 1%) in the multiple choice single answer format section - recheck your solid model for precision and accuracy.

Modify the part in SolidWorks.

Unit system: MMGS (millimeter, gram, second)
Decimal places: 2
Part origin: Arbitrary
All holes through all unless shown otherwise.
Material: Aluminium 1050 Alloy
Density = 0.0027 g/mm^3

Modify the part using the following variable values:

A = 140.00
B = 50.00
C = 55 degrees

Note: Assume all unshown dimensions are the same as in the previous question.

What is the overall mass of the part (grams)?

All SOLIDWORKS models for the next few chapters (initial and final) are provided in the SOLIDWORKS CSWA Model Folder. Download the SOLIDWORKS CSWA Model Folder to your local hard drive.

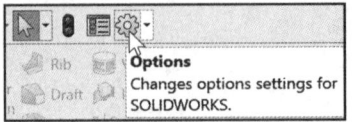

Document Properties

You need the ability to identify the procedure to select system units and precision of a SOLIDWORKS model using the Document Properties section. Access the Document Properties tab from the Options tool located in the Menu bar toolbar.

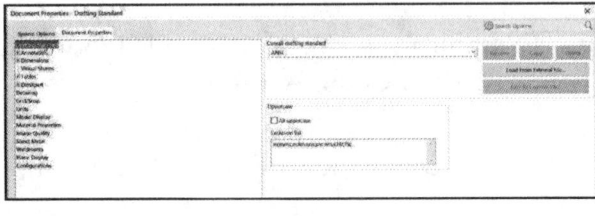

Set precision for the selected unit system during the exam as illustrated.

Document properties apply to the current document. The Document Properties tab is only available when a document is open.

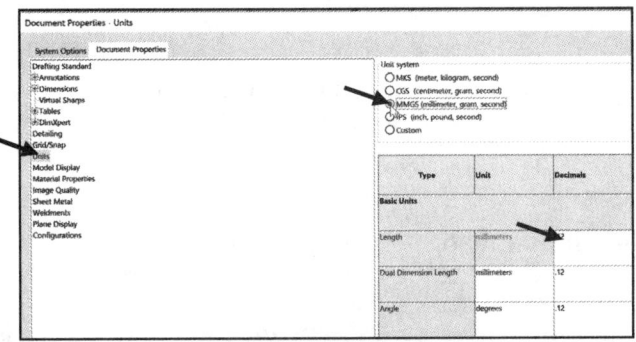

New documents get their document settings (such as Units, Image Quality, etc.) from the document properties of the template used to create the model or drawing.

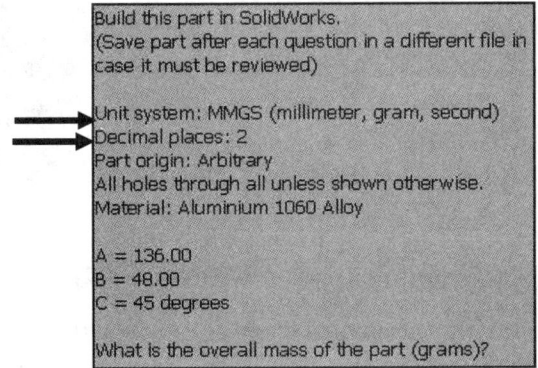

Screen shot from the exam

Build a Basic Part from a detailed illustration

Tutorial: Volume/Center of Mass 3-1

Build this model in SOLIDWORKS. Calculate the volume of the part and locate the Center of mass with the provided information.

1. **Create** a new part in SOLIDWORKS.

2. **Build** the illustrated dimensioned model. The model displays all edges on perpendicular planes. Think about the steps to build the model. Insert two features: Extruded Base (Boss-Extrude1) and Extruded Cut (Cut-Extrude1). The part Origin is located in the front left corner of the model. Think about your Base Sketch plane. Keep your Base Sketch simple.

3. **Set** the document properties for the model.

4. Create **Sketch1**. Select the Front Plane as the Sketch plane. Sketch1 is the Base sketch. Sketch1 is the profile for the Extruded Base (Boss-Extrude1) feature. Insert the required geometric relations and dimensions.

5. Create the **Extruded Base** feature. Boss-Extrude1 is the Base feature. Blind is the default End Condition in Direction 1. Depth = 2.25in. Identify the extrude direction to maintain the location of the Origin.

6. Create **Sketch2**. Select the Top right face as the Sketch plane for the second feature. Sketch a square. Sketch2 is the profile for the Extruded Cut feature. Insert the required geometric relations and dimensions.

7. Create the **Extruded Cut** feature. Select Through All for End Condition in Direction 1.

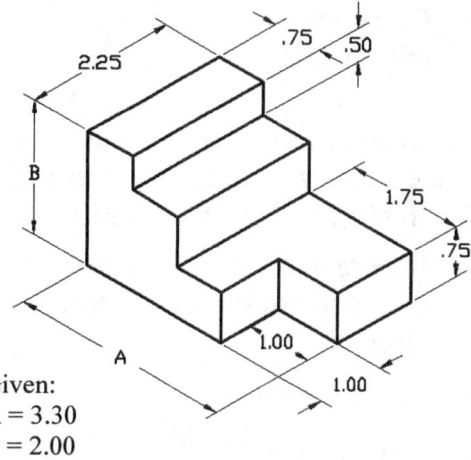

Given:
A = 3.30
B = 2.00
Material: 2014 Alloy
Density = .101 lb/in^3
Units: IPS
Decimal places = 2

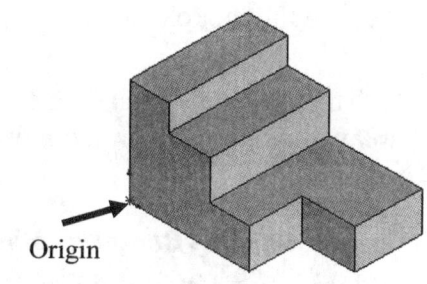

Origin

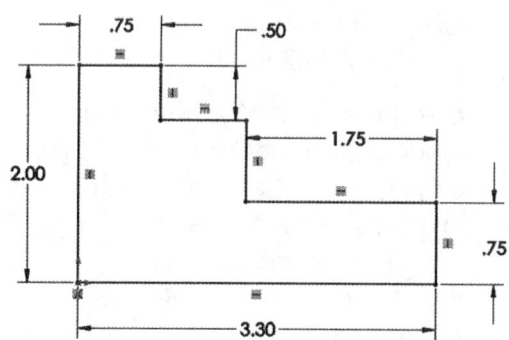

8. **Assign** 2014 Alloy material to the part. Material is required to locate the Center of mass.

9. **Calculate** the volume. The volume = 8.28 cubic inches.

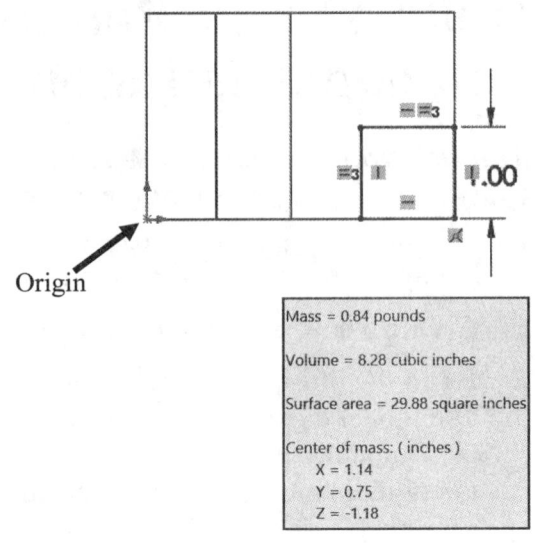

Origin

There are numerous ways to build the models in this chapter. A goal is to display different design intents and techniques.

10. **Locate** the Center of mass. The location of the Center of mass is derived from the part Origin.

- X: 1.14 inches

- Y: 0.75 inches

- Z: -1.18 inches

11. **Save** the part and name it Volume-Center of mass 3-1.

12. **Close** the model.

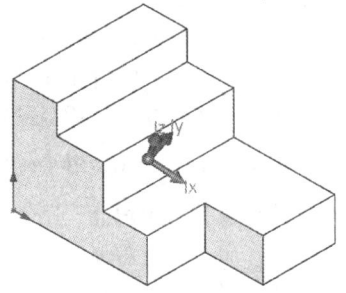

Mass = 0.84 pounds

Volume = 8.28 cubic inches

Surface area = 29.88 square inches

Center of mass: (inches)
    X = 1.14
    Y = 0.75
    Z = -1.18

The principal axes and Center of mass are displayed graphically on the model in the Graphics window.

Tutorial: Volume/Center of Mass 3-2

Build this model in SOLIDWORKS. Calculate the volume of the part and locate the Center of mass with the provided information.

1. **Create** a new part in SOLIDWORKS.

2. **Build** the illustrated dimensioned model. The model displays all edges on perpendicular planes. Think about the steps that are required to build this model. Remember, there are numerous ways to create the models in this chapter.

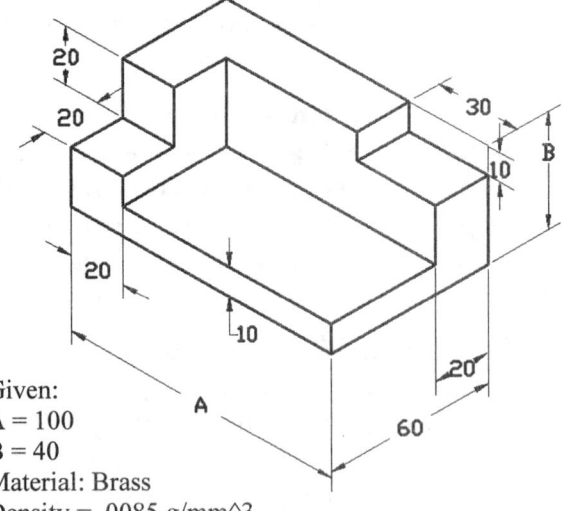

Given:
A = 100
B = 40
Material: Brass
Density = .0085 g/mm^3
Units: MMGS

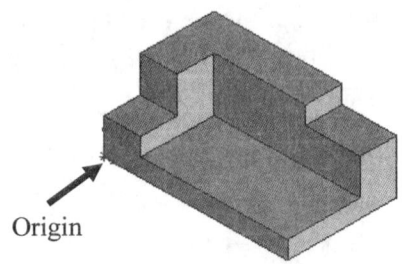

Origin

The CSWA exam is timed. Work efficiently.

View the provided Part FeatureManagers. Both FeatureManagers create the same illustrated model. In Option1, there are four sketches and four features (Extruded Base and three Extruded Cuts) that are used to build the model.

In Option2, there are three sketches and three features (Extruded Boss/Base) that are used to build the model. Which FeatureManager is better? In a timed exam, optimize your time and use the least amount of features through mirror, pattern, symmetry, etc.

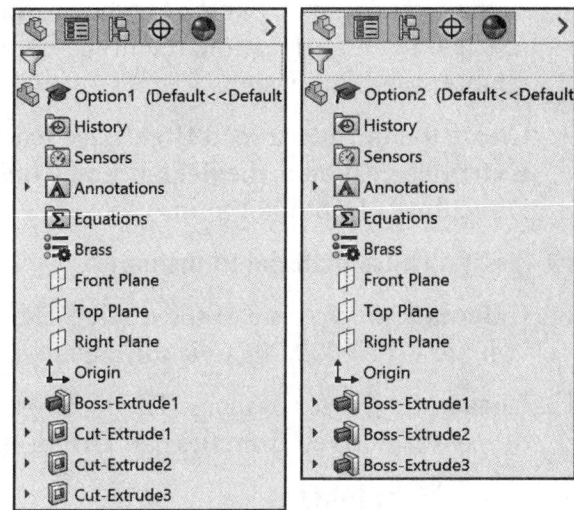

Use Centerlines to create symmetrical sketch elements and revolved features, or as construction geometry.

Create the model using the Option2 Part FeatureManager.

3. **Set** the document properties for the model. Create **Sketch1**. Select the Top Plane as the Sketch plane. Sketch a rectangle. Insert the required dimensions.

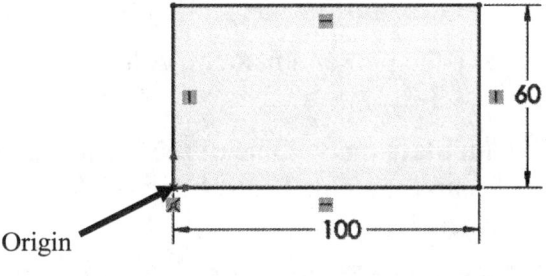

4. Create the **Extruded Base** feature. Boss-Extrude1 is the Base feature. Blind is the default End Condition in Direction 1. Depth = 10mm.

5. Create **Sketch2**. Select the back face of Boss-Extrude1.

6. Select **Normal To** view. Sketch2 is the profile for the second Extruded Boss/Base feature. Insert the required geometric relations and dimensions as illustrated.

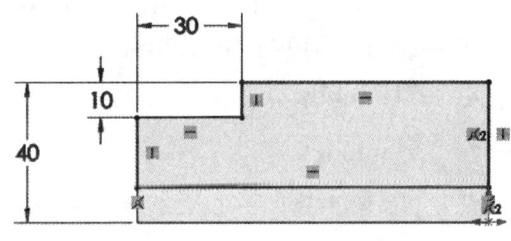

7. Create the second Extruded Boss/Base feature (**Boss-Extrude2**). Blind is the default End Condition in Direction 1. Depth = 20mm. Note the direction of the extrude towards the front of the model.

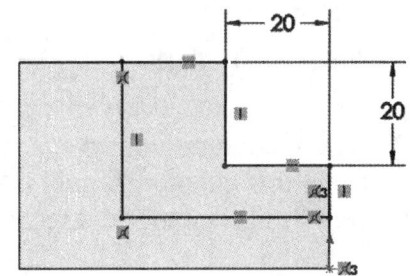

8. Create **Sketch3**. Select the left face of Boss-Extrude1 as the Sketch plane. Sketch3 is the profile for the third Extrude feature. Insert the required geometric relations and dimensions.

9. Create the third Extruded Boss/Base feature (**Boss-Extrude3**). Blind is the default End Condition in Direction 1. Depth = 20mm.

10. **Assign** Brass material to the part.

11. **Calculate** the volume of the model. The volume = 130,000.00 cubic millimeters.

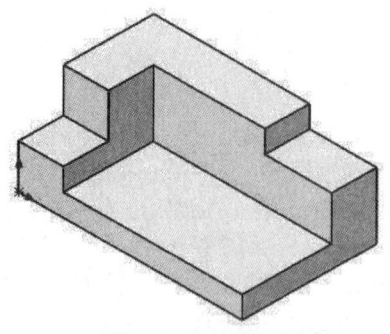

12. **Locate** the Center of mass. The location of the Center of mass is derived from the part Origin.

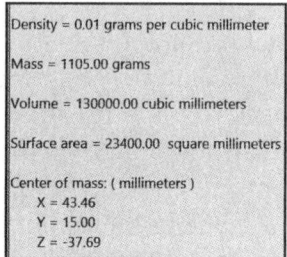

- X: 43.46 millimeters

- Y: 15.00 millimeters

- Z: -37.69 millimeters

13. **Save** the part and name it Volume-Center of mass 3-2.

14. **Calculate** the volume of the model using the IPS unit system. The volume = 7.93 cubic inches.

Origin

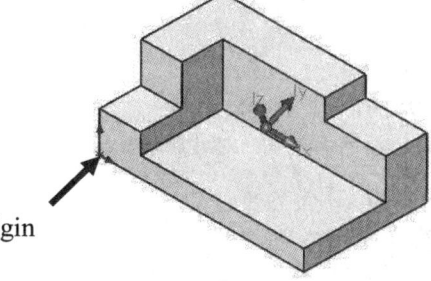

15. **Locate** the Center of mass using the IPS unit system. The location of the Center of mass is derived from the part Origin.

- X: 1.71 inches

- Y: 0.59 inches

- Z: -1.48 inches

16. **Save** the part and name it Volume-Center of mass 3-2-IPS.

17. **Close** the model.

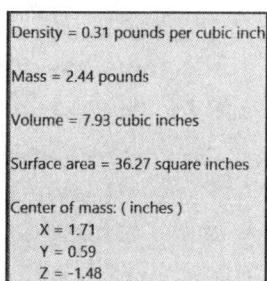

☼ There are numerous ways to create the models in this chapter. A goal is to display different design intents and techniques.

☼ All SW models (initial and final) are provided. Copy the folders and model files to your local hard drive.

Tutorial: Mass-Volume 3-3

Build this model in SOLIDWORKS. Calculate the overall mass of the illustrated model with the provided information.

1. **Create** a new part in SOLIDWORKS.

2. **Build** the illustrated model. The model displays all edges on perpendicular planes. Think about the steps required to build the model. Apply the Mirror Sketch tool to the Base sketch. Insert an Extruded Base (Boss-Extrude1) and Extruded-Cut (Cut-Extrude1) feature.

3. **Set** the document properties for the model.

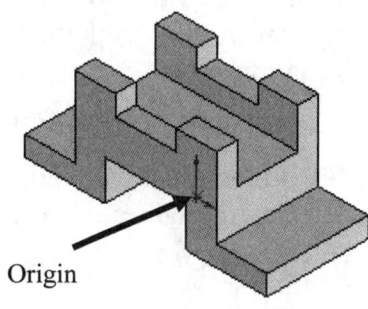

Given:
A = 50, B = 50, C = 120
Material: 6061 Alloy
Density = .0027 g/mm^3
Units: MMGS

💡 To activate the Mirror Sketch tool, click **Tools, Sketch Tools, Mirror** from the Menu bar menu. The Mirror PropertyManager is displayed.

4. Create **Sketch1**. Select the Front Plane as the Sketch plane. Apply the Mirror Sketch tool. Select the construction geometry to mirror about as illustrated. Select the Entities to mirror. Insert the required geometric relations and dimensions.

💡 Construction geometry is ignored when the sketch is used to create a feature. Construction geometry uses the same line style as centerlines.

💡 When you create a new part or assembly, the three default Planes (Front, Right and Top) are aligned with specific views. The Plane you select for the Base sketch determines the orientation of the part.

Origin

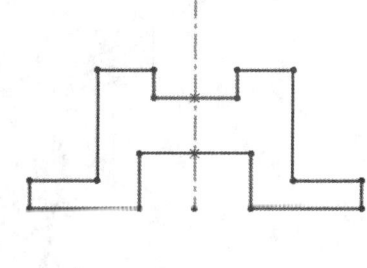

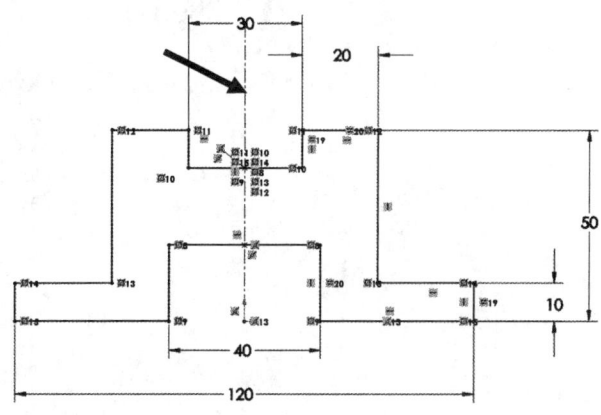

Extrude1 feature. Boss-Extrude1 is ...re. Apply the Mid Plane End Condition ...n 1 for symmetry. Depth = 50mm.

...e **Sketch2**. Select the right face for the Sketch ...ane. Sketch2 is the profile for the Extruded Cut feature. Insert the required geometric relations and dimensions. Apply construction geometry.

7. Create the **Extruded Cut** feature. Through All is the selected End Condition in Direction 1.

8. **Assign** 6061 Alloy material to the part.

9. **Calculate** the overall mass. The overall mass = 302.40 grams.

10. **Save** the part and name it Mass-Volume 3-3.

11. **Close** the model.

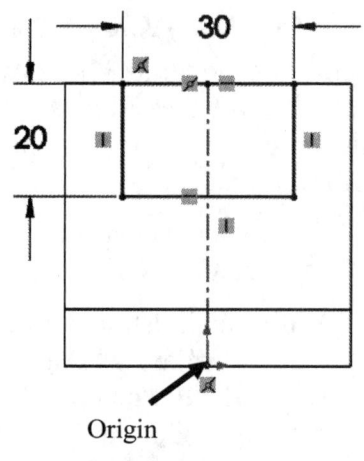

Origin

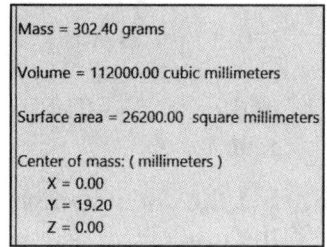

Mass = 302.40 grams

Volume = 112000.00 cubic millimeters

Surface area = 26200.00 square millimeters

Center of mass: (millimeters)
  X = 0.00
  Y = 19.20
  Z = 0.00

Tutorial: Mass-Volume 3-4

Build this model in SOLIDWORKS. Calculate the volume of the part and locate the Center of mass with the provided information.

1. **Create** a new part in SOLIDWORKS.

2. **Build** the illustrated model. The model displays all edges on perpendicular planes.

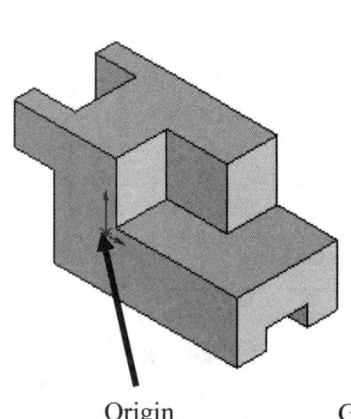

Origin

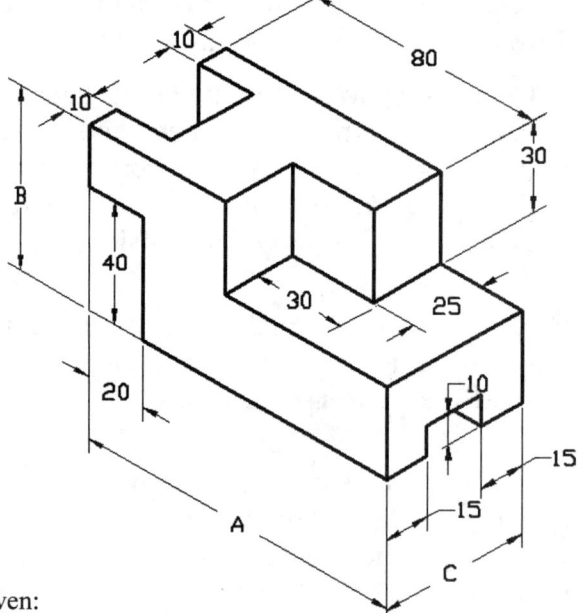

Given:
A = 110, B = 60, C = 50
Material: Nylon 6/10
Density = .0014 g/mm^3
Units: MMGS

View the provided Part FeatureManagers. Both FeatureManagers create the same model. In Option4, there are three sketches and three features that are used to build the model.

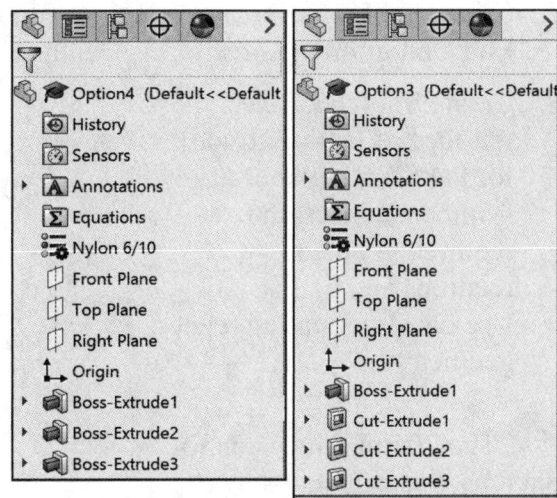

In Option3, there are four sketches and four features that are used to build the model. Which FeatureManager is better? In a timed exam, optimize your design time and use the least amount of features. Use the Option4 FeatureManager in this tutorial. As an exercise, build the model using the Option3 FeatureManager.

3. **Set** the document properties for the model.

4. Create **Sketch1**. Select the Right Plane as the Sketch plane. Sketch1 is the Base sketch. Apply the Mirror Entities Sketch tool. Select the construction geometry to mirror about as illustrated. Select the Entities to mirror. Insert the required geometric relations and dimensions.

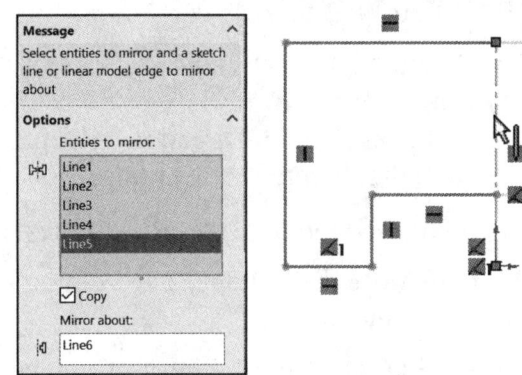

5. Create the **Boss-Extrude1** feature. Boss-Extrude1 is the Base feature. Blind is the default End Condition in Direction 1. Depth = (A - 20mm) = 90mm. Note the direction of the extrude feature.

6. Create **Sketch2**. Select the Top face of Boss-Extrude1 for the Sketch plane. Sketch2 is the profile for the second Extruded Boss/Base feature (Boss-Extrude2). Insert the required geometric relations and dimensions.

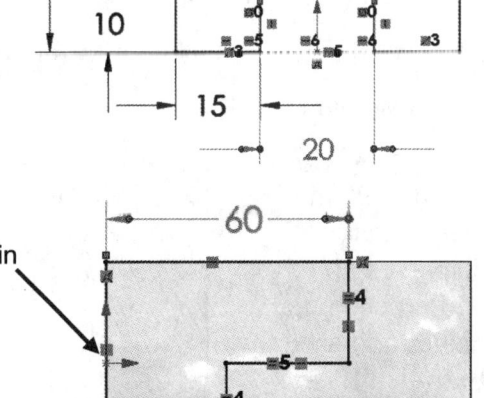

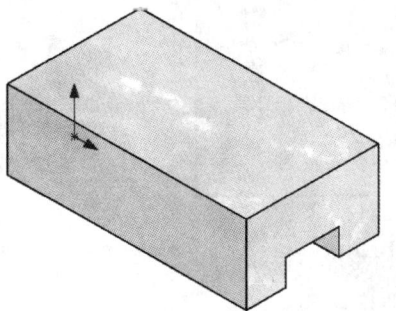

7. Create the **Boss-Extrude2** feature. Blind is the default End Condition in Direction 1. Depth = 30mm.

8. Create **Sketch3**. Select the left face of Boss-Extrude1 for the Sketch plane. Apply symmetry. Insert the required geometric relations and dimensions. Use construction reference geometry.

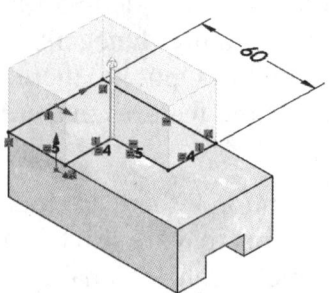

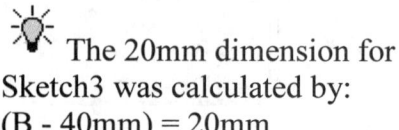 The 20mm dimension for Sketch3 was calculated by: (B - 40mm) = 20mm.

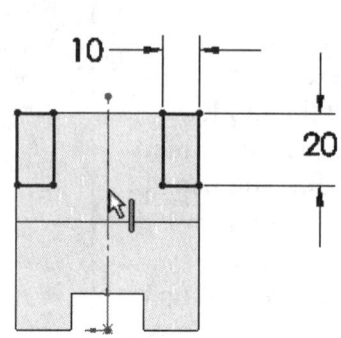

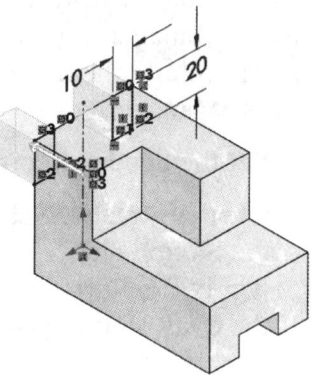

9. Create the **Boss-Extrude3** feature. Blind is the default End Condition in Direction 1. Depth = 20mm. Note the direction of Extrude3.

10. **Assign** Nylon 6/10 material to the part.

11. **Calculate** the volume. The volume = 192,500.00 cubic millimeters.

12. **Locate** the Center of mass. The location of the Center of mass is derived from the part Origin.

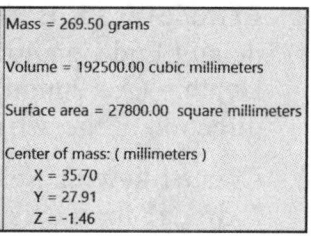

Mass = 269.50 grams

Volume = 192500.00 cubic millimeters

Surface area = 27800.00 square millimeters

Center of mass: (millimeters)
  X = 35.70
  Y = 27.91
  Z = -1.46

- X: 35.70 millimeters

- Y: 27.91 millimeters

- Z: -1.46 millimeters

13. **Save** the part and name it Mass-Volume 3-4.

14. **Close** the model.

In the previous section, the models that you created displayed all edges on Perpendicular planes and used the Extruded Base, Extruded Boss, or the Extruded Cut feature from the Features toolbar.

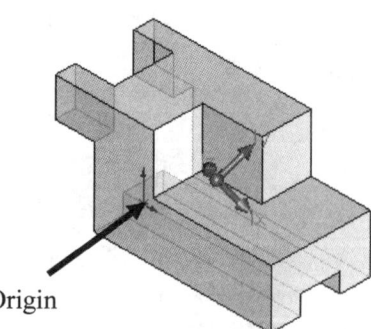

Origin

In the next section, build models where all edges are not located on Perpendicular planes.

First, let's review a simple 2D Sketch for an Extruded Cut feature.

Tutorial: Simple Cut 3-1

1. **Create** a new part in SOLIDWORKS.

2. **Build** the illustrated model. Start with a 60mm x 60mm x 100mm block. System units = MMGS. Decimal place = 2. Note the location of the part Origin.

3. Create **Sketch1**. Select the Front Plane as the Sketch plane. Sketch a square as illustrated. Insert the required dimension. The part Origin is located in the bottom left corner of the sketch.

4. Create the **Extruded Base (Boss-Extrude1)** feature. Apply the Mid Plane End Condition in Direction 1. Depth = 100mm.

5. Create **Sketch2**. Select the front face as the Sketch plane. Apply the Line Sketch tool. Sketch a diagonal line. Select the front right vertical midpoint as illustrated.

6. Create the **Extruded Cut (Cut-Extrude1)** feature. Through All for End Condition in Direction 1 and Direction 2 is selected by default.

7. **Save** the part and name it Simple-Cut 3-1. View the FeatureManager.

8. **Close** the model.

Screen shots in the book were made using SOLIDWORKS 2016 SP2 and SOLIDWORKS 2017 SP0 running Windows® 10.

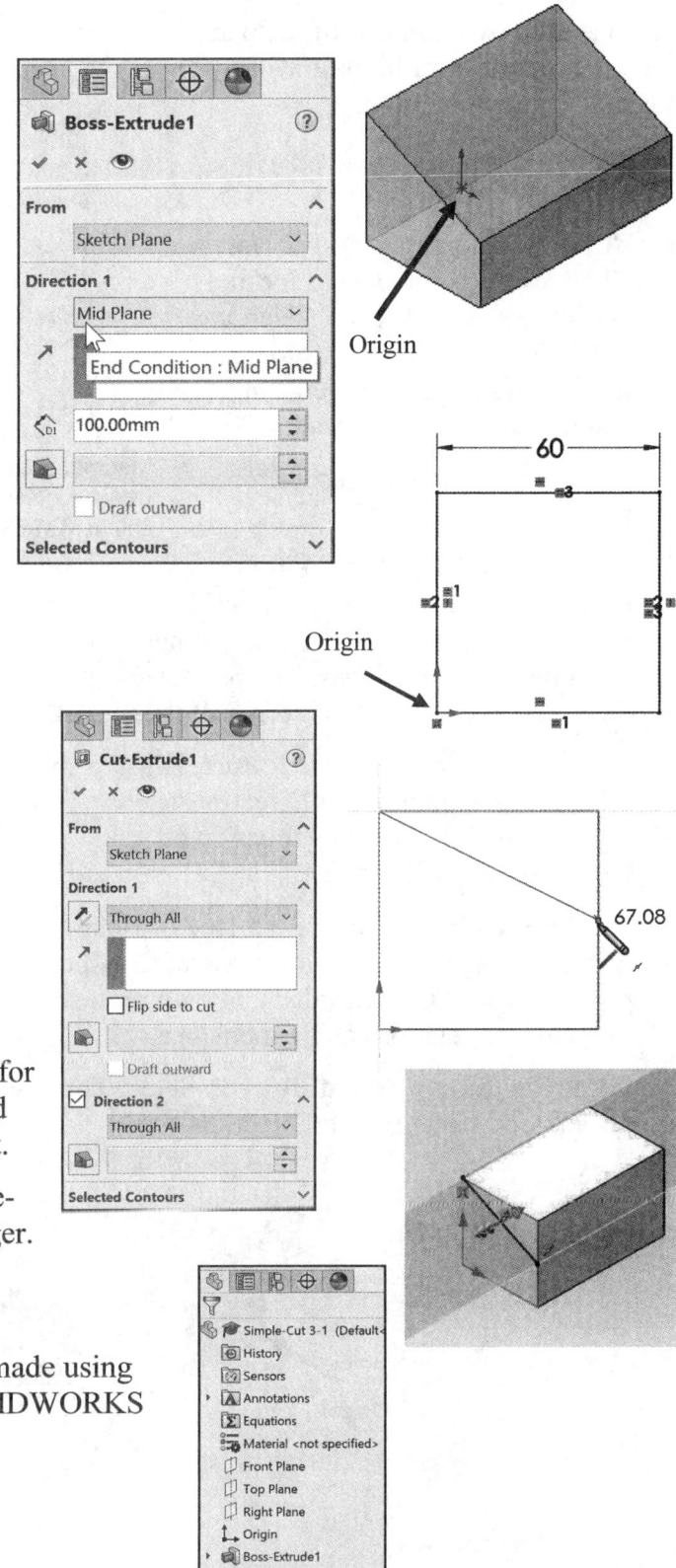

Tutorial: Mass-Volume 3-5

Build this model in SOLIDWORKS. Calculate the overall mass of the part and locate the Center of mass with the provided information.

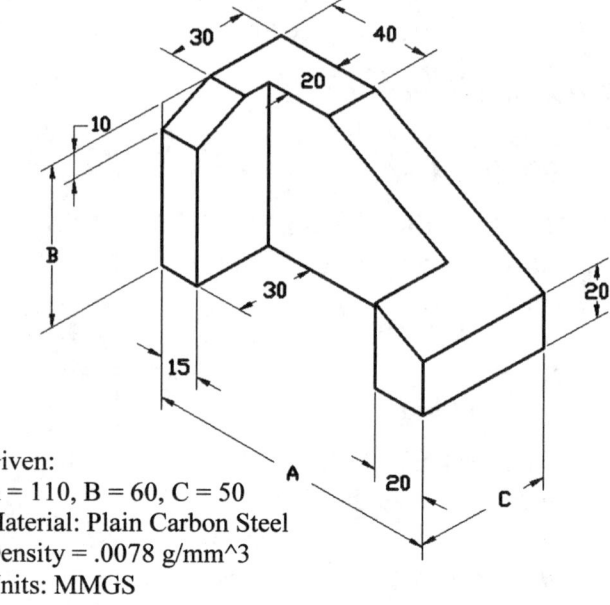

1. **Create** a new part in SOLIDWORKS.

2. **Build** the illustrated model. Not all edges of the model are located on Perpendicular planes. Insert an Extruded Base (Boss-Extrude1) feature and three Extruded Cut features to build the model.

Given:
A = 110, B = 60, C = 50
Material: Plain Carbon Steel
Density = .0078 g/mm^3
Units: MMGS

3. **Set** the document properties for the model.

4. Create **Sketch1**. Select the Front Plane as the Sketch plane. Sketch a rectangle. Insert the required geometric relations and dimensions. The part Origin is located in the left bottom corner of the model.

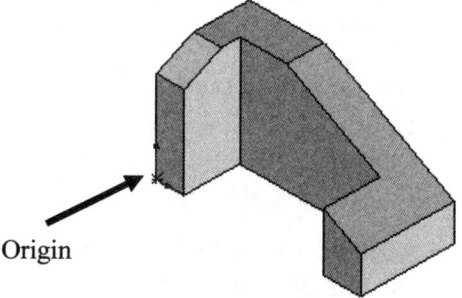

Origin

5. Create the **Extruded Base** feature. Blind is the default End Condition in Direction 1. Depth = 50mm. Note the direction of Extrude1.

6. Create **Sketch2**. Select the top face of Boss-Extrude1 for the Sketch plane. Sketch2 is the profile for the first Extruded Cut feature. Insert the required relations and dimensions.

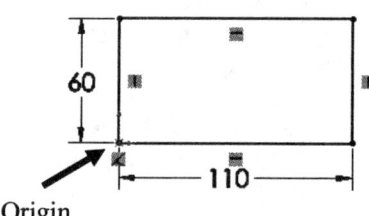

Origin

7. Create the **Extruded Cut** feature. Select Through All for End Condition in Direction 1.

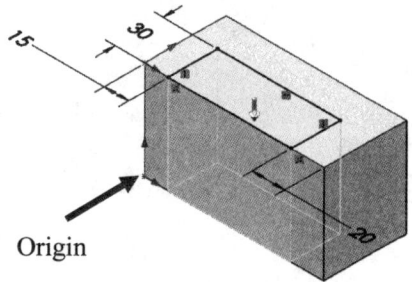

Origin

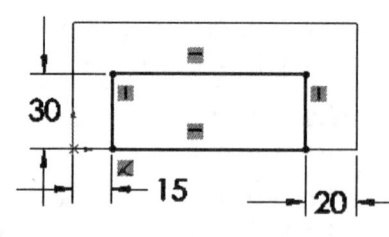

8. Create **Sketch3**. Select the back face of Boss-Extrude1 as the Sketch plane. Sketch a diagonal line. Insert the required geometric relations and dimensions.

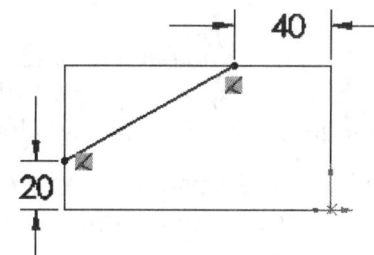

9. Create the second **Extruded Cut** feature. Through All for End Condition in Direction 1 and Direction 2 is selected by default. Note the direction of the extrude feature.

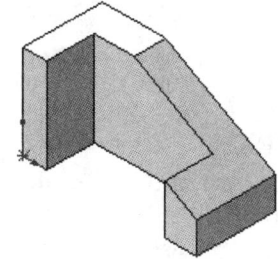

10. Create **Sketch4**. Select the left face of Boss-Extrude1 as the Sketch plane. Sketch a diagonal line. Insert the required geometric relations and dimensions.

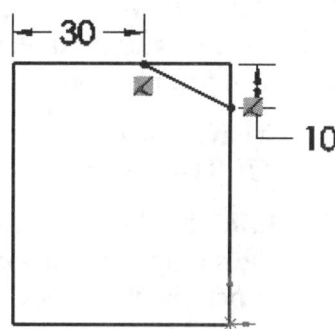

11. Create the third **Extruded Cut** feature. Through All for End Condition in Direction 1 and Direction 2 is selected by default.

12. **Assign** Plain Carbon Steel material to the part.

13. **Calculate** the overall mass. The overall mass = 1130.44 grams.

14. **Locate** the Center of mass. The location of the Center of mass is derived from the part Origin.

- X: 45.24 millimeters

- Y: 24.70 millimeters

- Z: -33.03 millimeters

Density = 0.01 grams per cubic millimeter

Mass = 1130.44 grams

Volume = 144928.57 cubic millimeters

Surface area = 23631.77 square millimeters

Center of mass: (millimeters)
X = 45.24
Y = 24.70
Z = -33.03

In this category an exam question could read: Build this model. Locate the Center of mass with respect to the part Origin.

- A: X = 45.24 millimeters, Y = 24.70 millimeters, Z − -33.03 millimeters

- B: X = 54.24 millimeters, Y = 42.70 millimeters, Z = 33.03 millimeters

- C: X = 49.24 millimeters, Y = -37.70 millimeters, Z = 38.03 millimeters

- D: X = 44.44 millimeters, Y = -24.70 millimeters, Z = -39.03 millimeters

The correct answer is A.

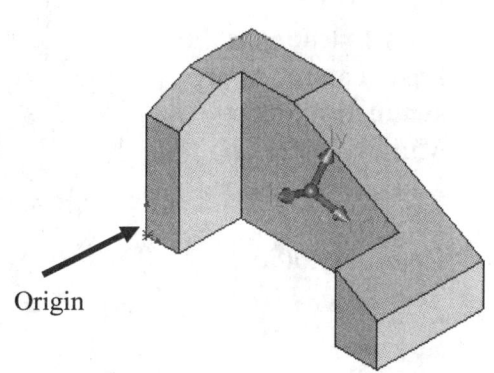

Origin

The principal axes and Center of mass are displayed graphically on the model in the Graphics window.

15. **Save** the part and name it Mass-Volume 3-5.

16. **Close** the model.

Tutorial: Mass-Volume 3-6

Build this model in SOLIDWORKS. Calculate the overall mass of the part and locate the Center of mass with the provided information.

1. **Create** a new part in SOLIDWORKS.

2. **Build** the illustrated model. Not all edges of the model are located on Perpendicular planes. Think about the steps required to build the model. Insert two features: Extruded Base (Boss-Extrude1) and Extruded Cut (Cut-Extrude1).

3. **Set** the document properties for the model.

4. Create **Sketch1**. Select the Right Plane as the Sketch plane. Apply construction geometry. Insert the required geometric relations and dimensions.

5. Create the **Extruded Base** feature. Boss-Extrude1 is the Base feature. Apply symmetry. Select Mid Plane as the End Condition in Direction 1. Depth = 3.00in.

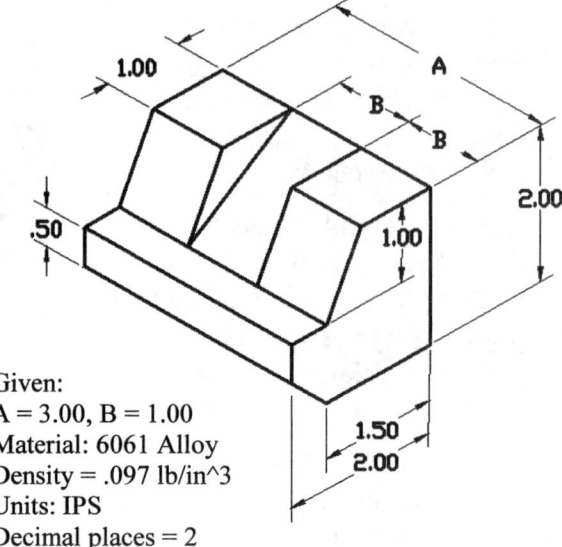

Given:
A = 3.00, B = 1.00
Material: 6061 Alloy
Density = .097 lb/in^3
Units: IPS
Decimal places = 2

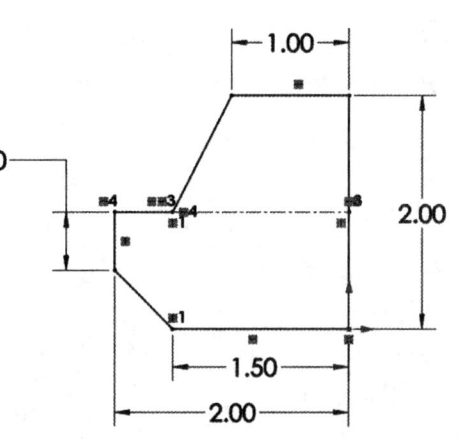

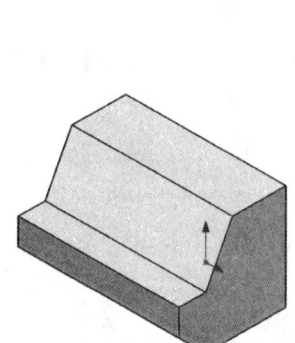

Origin

6. Create **Sketch2**. Select the Right Plane as the Sketch plane. Select the Line Sketch tool. Insert the required geometric relations. Sketch2 is the profile for the Extruded Cut feature.

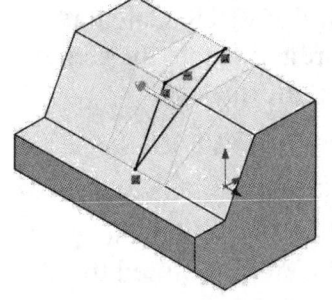
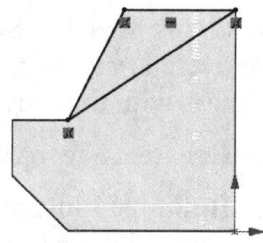
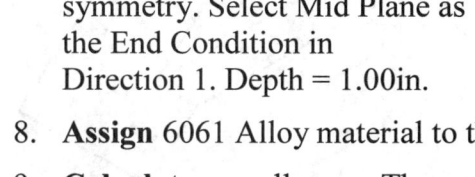

7. Create the **Extruded Cut (Cut-Extrude1)** feature. Apply symmetry. Select Mid Plane as the End Condition in Direction 1. Depth = 1.00in.

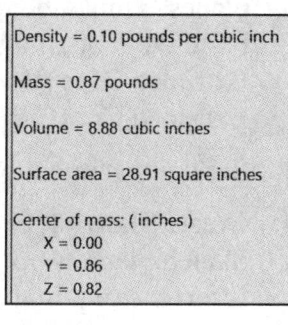

Density = 0.10 pounds per cubic inch

Mass = 0.87 pounds

Volume = 8.88 cubic inches

Surface area = 28.91 square inches

Center of mass: (inches)
   X = 0.00
   Y = 0.86
   Z = 0.82

8. **Assign** 6061 Alloy material to the part.

9. **Calculate** overall mass. The overall mass = 0.87 pounds.

10. **Locate** the Center of mass. The location of the Center of mass is derived from the part Origin.

- X: 0.00 inches

- Y: 0.86 inches

- Z: 0.82 inches

In this category an exam question could read: Build this model. Locate the Center of mass with respect to the part Origin.

- A: X = 0.10 inches, Y = -0.86 inches, Z = -0.82 inches

- B: X = 0.00 inches, Y = 0.86 inches, Z = 0.82 inches

- C: X = 0.15 inches, Y = -0.96 inches, Z = -0.02 inches

- D: X = 1.00 inches, Y = -0.89 inches, Z = -1.82 inches

The correct answer is B.

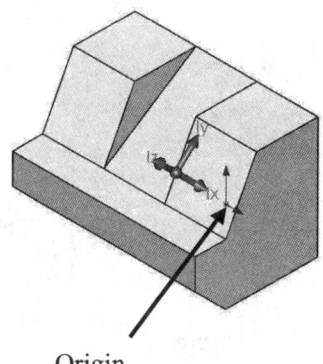

Origin

11. **Save** the part and name it Mass-Volume 3-6.

12. **Close** the model.

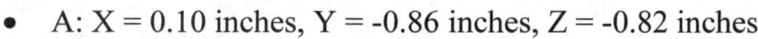

As an exercise, modify the Mass-Volume 3-6 part using the MMGS unit system. Assign Nickel as the material. Calculate the overall mass. The overall mass of the part = 1236.20 grams. Save the part and name it Mass-Volume 3-6-MMGS.

Tutorial: Mass-Volume 3-7

Build this model in SOLIDWORKS. Calculate the overall mass of the part and locate the Center of mass with the provided information.

1. **Create** a new part in SOLIDWORKS.

2. **Build** the illustrated model. Not all edges of the model are located on Perpendicular planes. Think about the steps required to build the model. Insert two features: Extruded Base (Boss-Extrude1) and Extruded Cut (Cut-Extrude1).

3. **Set** the document properties for the model.

4. Create **Sketch1**. Select the Right Plane as the Sketch plane. Apply the Line Sketch tool. Insert the required geometric relations and dimensions. The location of the Origin is in the left lower corner of the sketch.

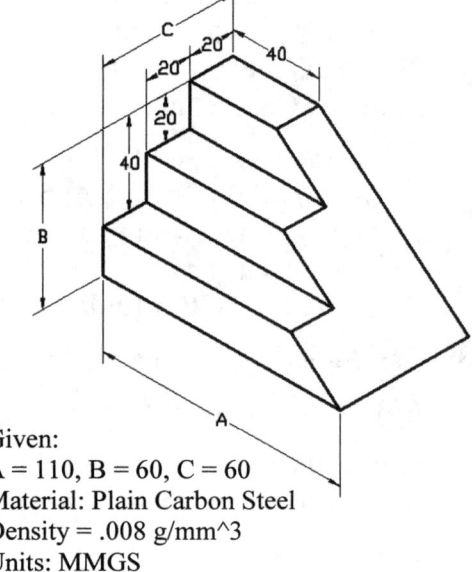

Given:
A = 110, B = 60, C = 60
Material: Plain Carbon Steel
Density = .008 g/mm^3
Units: MMGS

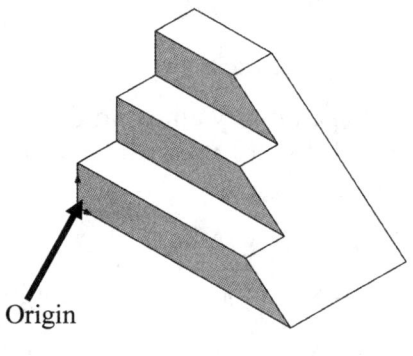

5. Create the **Extruded Base** feature. Boss-Extrude1 is the Base feature. Blind is the default End Condition in Direction 1. Depth = 110mm.

6. Create **Sketch2**. Select the Front Plane as the Sketch plane. Sketch a diagonal line. Complete the sketch. Sketch2 is the profile for the Extruded Cut feature.

7. Create the **Extruded Cut** feature. Through All for End Condition in Direction 1 and Direction 2 is selected by default.

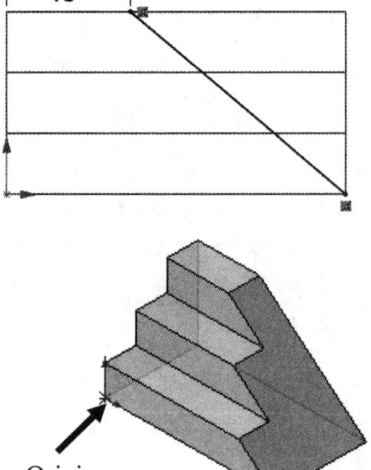

8. **Assign** Plain Carbon Steel material to the part.

9. **Calculate** overall mass. The mass = 1549.60 grams.

10. **Locate** the Center of mass. The location of the Center of mass is derived from the part Origin.

- X: 43.49 millimeters

- Y: 19.73 millimeters

- Z: -35.10 millimeters

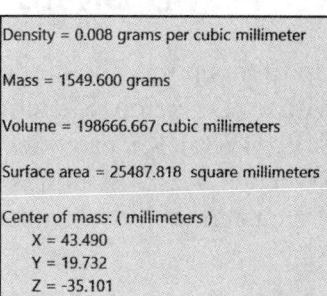

Density = 0.008 grams per cubic millimeter

Mass = 1549.600 grams

Volume = 198666.667 cubic millimeters

Surface area = 25487.818 square millimeters

Center of mass: (millimeters)
   X = 43.490
   Y = 19.732
   Z = -35.101

11. **Save** the part and name it Mass-Volume 3-7.

12. **Close** the model.

In this category an exam question could read: Build this model. Locate the Center of mass with respect to the part Origin.

- A: X = -43.99 millimeters, Y = 29.73 millimeters, Z = -38.10 millimeters

- B: X = -44.49 millimeters, Y = -19.73 millimeters, Z = 35.10 millimeters

- C: X = 43.49 millimeters, Y = 19.73 millimeters, Z = -35.10 millimeters

- D: X = -1.00 millimeters, Y = 49.73 millimeters, Z = -35.10 millimeters

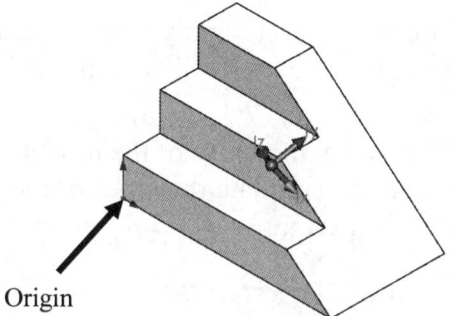

Origin

The correct answer is C.

As an exercise, locate the Center of mass using the IPS unit system, and re-assign copper material. Re-calculate the Center of mass location, with respect to the part Origin. Save the part and name it Mass-Volume 3-7-IPS.

- X: 1.71 inches

- Y: 0.78 inches

- Z: -1.38 inches

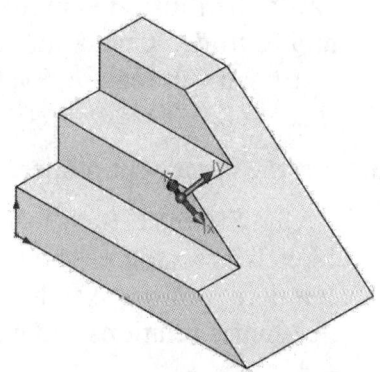

Density = 0.32 pounds per cubic inch

Mass = 3.90 pounds

Volume = 12.12 cubic inches

Surface area = 39.51 square inches

Center of mass: (inches)
   X = 1.71
   Y = 0.78
   Z = -1.38

2D vs. 3D Sketching

Up to this point, the models that you created in this chapter started with a 2D Sketch. Sketches are the foundation for creating features. SOLIDWORKS provides the ability to create either 2D or 3D Sketches. A 2D Sketch is limited to a flat 2D Sketch plane. A 3D sketch can include 3D elements.

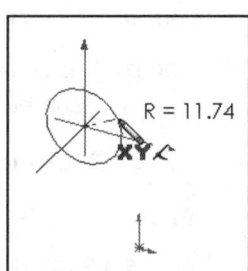

🔆 As you create a 3D Sketch, the entities in the sketch exist in 3D space. They are not related to a specific Sketch plane as they are in a 2D Sketch.

You may need to apply a 3D Sketch in the CSWA exam. Below is an example of a 3D Sketch to create a Cut-Extrude feature.

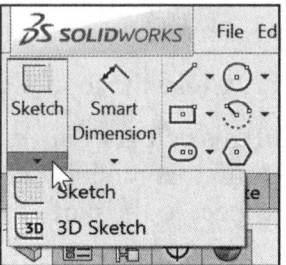

🔆 The complexity of the models increases throughout this chapter to simulate the types of models that are provided on the CSWA exam.

Tutorial 3DSketch 3-1

1. **Create** a new part in SOLIDWORKS.

2. **Build** the illustrated model. Insert two features: Extruded Base and Extruded Cut. Apply the 3D Sketch tool to create the Extruded Cut feature. System units = MMGS. Decimal place = 2.

3. **Set** the document properties for the model.

4. Create **Sketch1**. Select the Front Plane as the Sketch plane. Sketch a rectangle. The part Origin is located in the bottom left corner of the sketch. Insert the illustrated geometric relations and dimensions.

5. Create the **Extruded Base (Boss-Extrude1)** feature. Apply symmetry. Select the Mid Plane End Condition in Direction 1. Depth = 100.00mm.

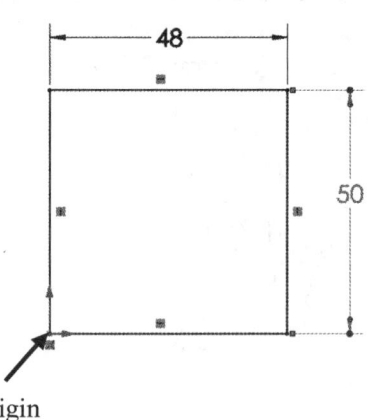

Origin

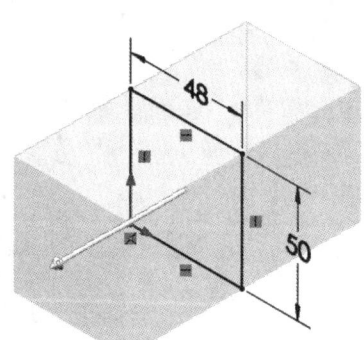

Origin

💡 Click **3D Sketch** from the Sketch toolbar. Select the proper Sketch tool.

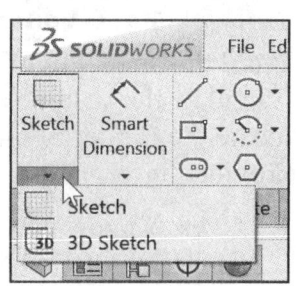

6. Create **3DSketch1**. Apply the Line Sketch tool. 3DSketch1 is a four point sketch as illustrated. 3DSketch1 is the profile for Extruded Cut feature.

7. Create the **Extruded Cut (Cut-Extrude1)** feature. Select the front right vertical edge as illustrated to remove the material. Edge<1> is displayed in the Direction of Extrusion box.

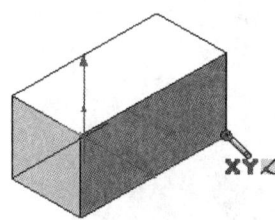
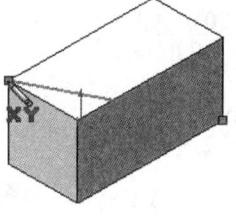
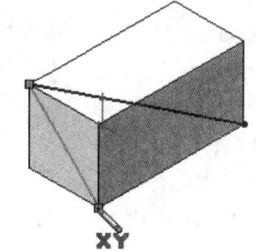
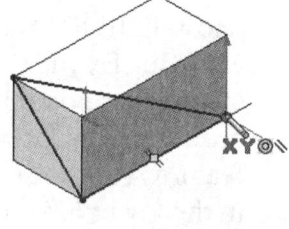

8. **Save** the part and name it 3DSketch 3-1.

9. **Close** the model.

💡 You can either select the front right vertical edge or the Top face to remove the required material in this tutorial.

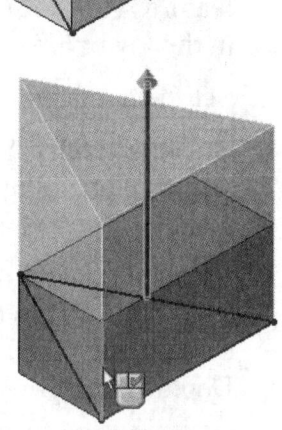

Use any of the following tools to create 3D Sketches: Lines, Circles, Rectangles, Arcs, Splines, and Points.

Most relations that are available in 2D Sketching are available in 3D sketching. The exceptions are:

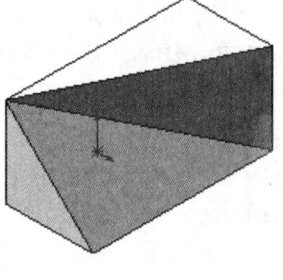
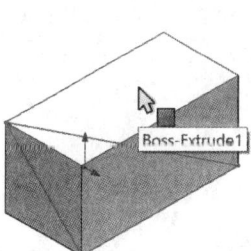

- *Symmetry*

- *Patterns*

- *Offset*

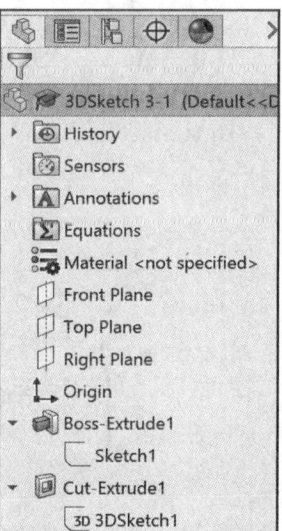

Tutorial: Mass-Volume 3-8

Build this model in SOLIDWORKS. Calculate the volume of the part and locate the Center of mass with the provided information.

1. **Create** a new part in SOLIDWORKS.

2. **Build** the illustrated model. Not all edges of the model are located on Perpendicular planes. Insert two features: Extruded Base (Boss-Extrude1) and Extruded Cut (Cut-Extrude1). Apply a closed four point 3D sketch as the profile for the Extruded Cut feature. The part Origin is located in the lower left front corner of the model.

3. **Set** the document properties for the model.

4. Create **Sketch1**. Select the Right Plane as the Sketch plane. Sketch a square. Insert the required geometric relations and dimension.

5. Create the **Extruded Base** feature. Boss-Extrude1 is the Base feature. Blind is the default End Condition in Direction 1. Depth = 4.00in.

6. Create **3DSketch1**. Apply the Line Sketch tool. Create a closed five point 3D sketch as illustrated. 3DSketch1 is the profile for the Extruded Cut feature. Insert the required dimensions.

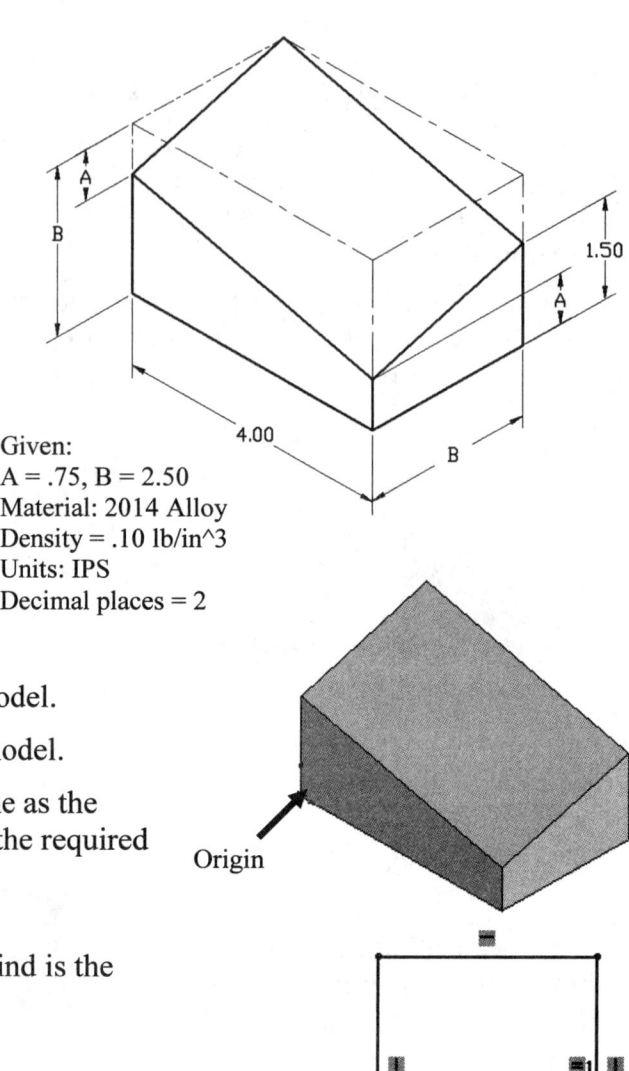

Given:
A = .75, B = 2.50
Material: 2014 Alloy
Density = .10 lb/in^3
Units: IPS
Decimal places = 2

Origin

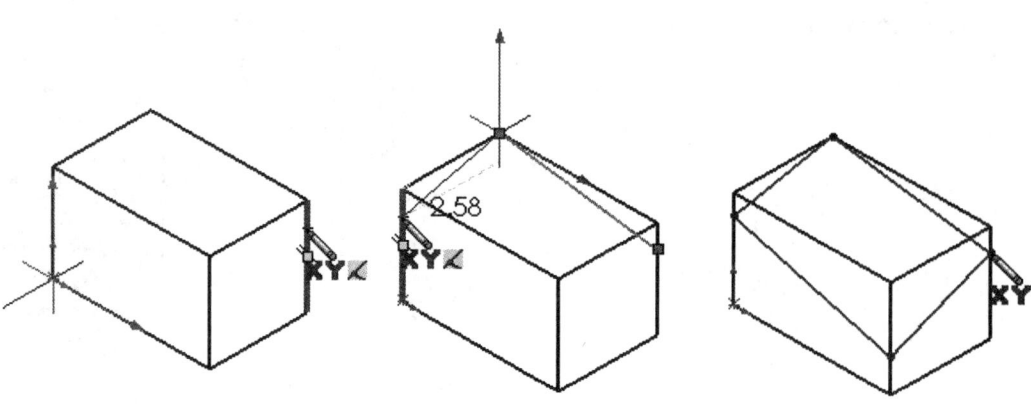

7. Create the **Extruded Cut** feature. Select the front right vertical edge as illustrated. Select Through All for End Condition in Direction 1. Note the direction of the extrude feature.

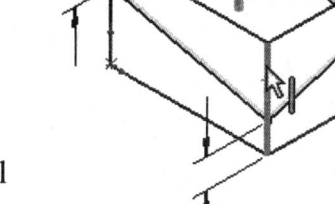
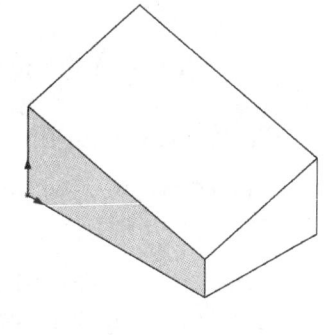

8. **Assign** the defined material to the part.

9. **Calculate** the volume. The volume = 16.25 cubic inches.

Density = 0.10 pounds per cubic inch

Mass = 1.64 pounds

Volume = 16.25 cubic inches

Surface area = 41.86 square inches

Center of mass: (inches)
    X = 1.79
    Y = 0.85
    Z = -1.35

10. **Locate** the Center of mass. The location of the Center of mass is derived from the part Origin.

- X = 1.79 inches

- Y = 0.85 inches

- Z = -1.35 inches

In this category an exam question could read: Build this model. What is the volume of the part?

- A: 18.88 cubic inches

- B: 19.55 cubic inches

- C: 17.99 cubic inches

- D: 16.25 cubic inches

The correct answer is D.

View the triad location of the Center of mass for the part.

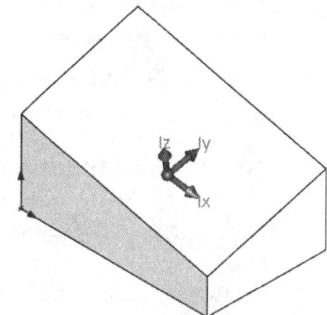

11. **Save** the part and name it Mass-Volume 3-8.

12. **Close** the model.

As an exercise, calculate the overall mass of the part using the MMGS unit system, and re-assign Nickel as the material. The overall mass of the part = 2263.46 grams. Save the part and name it Mass-Volume 3-8-MMGS.

Density = 0.01 grams per cubic millimeter

Mass = 2263.46 grams

Volume = 266289.79 cubic millimeters

Surface area = 27006.69 square millimeters

Center of mass: (millimeters)
    X = 45.59
    Y = 21.66
    Z = -34.19

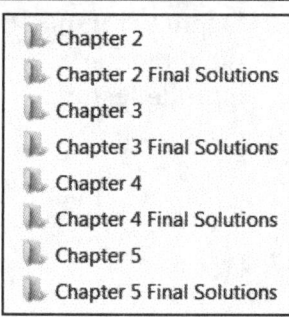

Chapter 2
Chapter 2 Final Solutions
Chapter 3
Chapter 3 Final Solutions
Chapter 4
Chapter 4 Final Solutions
Chapter 5
Chapter 5 Final Solutions

Screen shots in the book were made using SOLIDWORKS 2016 SP2 and SOLIDWORKS 2017 SP0 running Windows® 10.

Tutorial: Mass-Volume 3-9

Build this model in SOLIDWORKS. Calculate the overall mass of the part and locate the Center of mass with the provided information.

1. **Create** a new part in SOLIDWORKS.

2. **Build** the illustrated model. Insert five sketches and five features to build the model: Extruded Base, three Extruded Cut features and a Mirror feature.

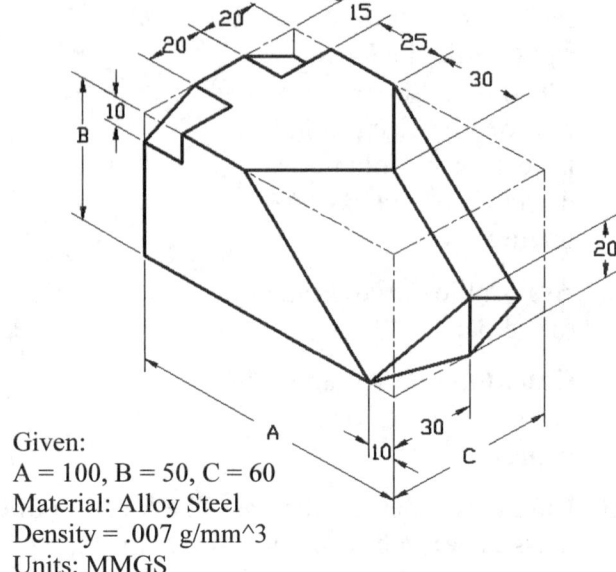

Given:
A = 100, B = 50, C = 60
Material: Alloy Steel
Density = .007 g/mm^3
Units: MMGS

There are numerous ways to build the models in this chapter. A goal is to display different design intents and techniques.

3. **Set** the document properties for the model.

4. Create **Sketch1**. Select the Front Plane as the Sketch plane. Sketch a rectangle. Insert the required dimensions. The part Origin is located in the lower left corner of the sketch.

Origin

5. Create the **Extruded Base (Boss-Extrude1)** feature. Apply symmetry. Select the Mid Plane End Condition for Direction 1. Depth = 60mm.

6. Create **Sketch2**. Select the left face of Boss-Extrude1 as the Sketch plane. Insert the required geometric relations and dimensions.

7. Create the first **Extruded Cut** feature. Blind is the default End Condition in Direction 1.

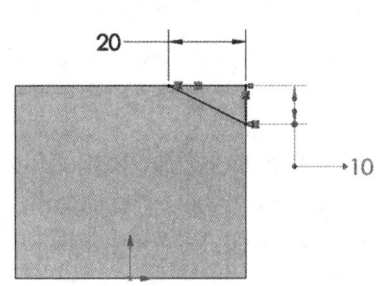

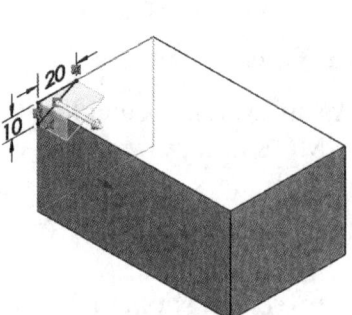

8. Depth = 15mm. Note the direction of the extrude feature.

9. Create **Sketch3**. Select the bottom face of Boss-Extrude1 for the Sketch plane. Insert the required geometric relations and dimension.

10. Create the second **Extruded Cut** feature. Blind is the default End Condition in Direction 1. Depth = 20mm.

11. Create **Sketch4**. Select Front Plane as the Sketch plane. Sketch a diagonal line. Sketch4 is the direction of extrusion for the third Extruded Cut feature. Insert the required dimension.

12. Create **Sketch5**. Select the top face of Boss-Extrude1 as the Sketch plane. Sketch5 is the sketch profile for the third Extruded Cut feature. Apply construction geometry. Insert the required geometric relations and dimensions.

13. Create the third **Extruded Cut** feature. Select Through All for End Condition in Direction 1.

14. Select **Sketch4** in the Graphics window for Direction of Extrusion. Line1@Sketch4 is displayed in the Cut-Extrude PropertyManager.

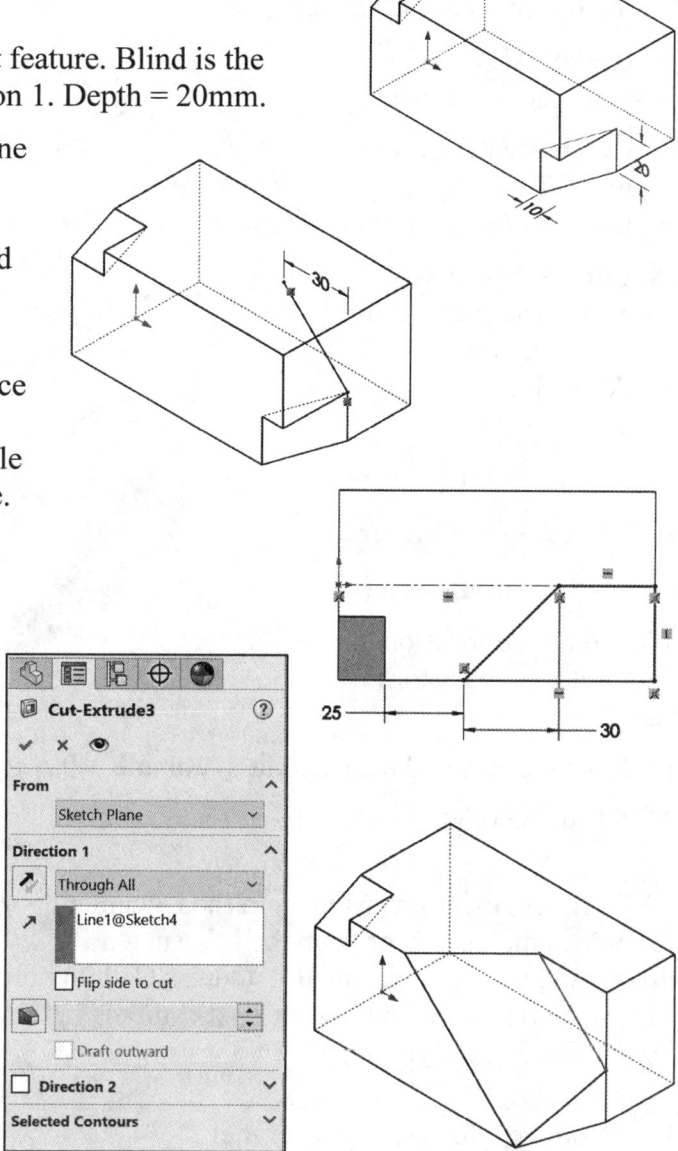

15. Create the **Mirror** feature. Mirror the three Extruded Cut features about the Front Plane. Use the fly-out FeatureManager.

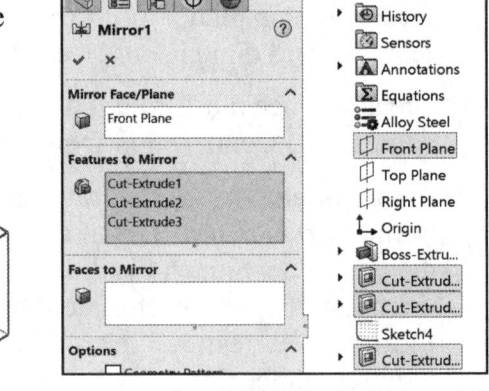

16. **Assign** Alloy Steel material to the part.

17. **Calculate** the overall mass. The overall mass = 1794.10 grams.

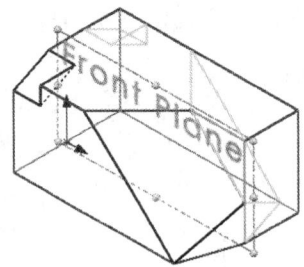

18. **Locate** the Center of mass. The location of the Center of mass is derived from the part Origin.

- X = 41.17 millimeters

- Y = 22.38 millimeters

- Z = 0.00 millimeters

View the triad location of the Center of mass for the part.

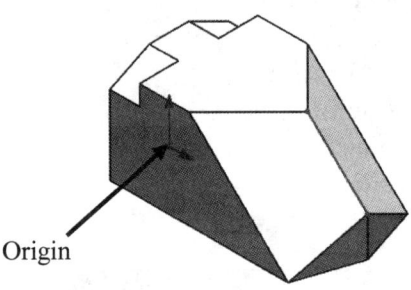

Origin

Mass = 1794.10 grams

Volume = 233000.00 cubic millimeters

Surface area = 23060.20 square millimeters

Center of mass: (millimeters)
   X = 41.17
   Y = 22.38
   Z = 0.00

19. **Save** the part and name it Mass-Volume 3-9.

20. **Close** the model.

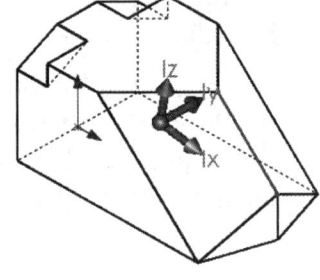

💡 Set document precision from the Document Properties dialog box or from the Dimension PropertyManager. You can also address Callout value, Tolerance type, and Dimension Text symbols in the Dimension PropertyManager.

💡 You are allowed to answer the questions in any order you prefer. Use the Summary Screen during the CSWA exam to view the list of all questions you have or have not answered.

💡 There are no Surfacing or Boundary feature questions on the CSWA exam.

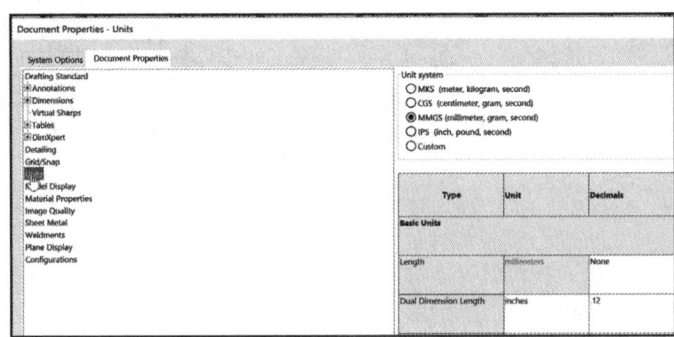

Callout Value

A Callout value is a value that you select in a SOLIDWORKS document. Click a dimension in the Graphics window, the selected dimension is displayed in blue and the Dimension PropertyManager is displayed.

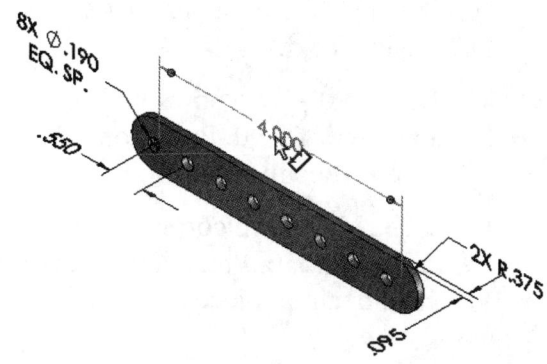

A Callout value is available for dimensions with multiple values in the callout.

Tolerance Type

A Tolerance type is selected from the available drop down list in the Dimension PropertyManager. The list is dynamic. A few examples of Tolerance type display are listed below:

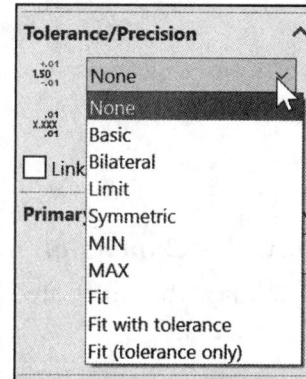

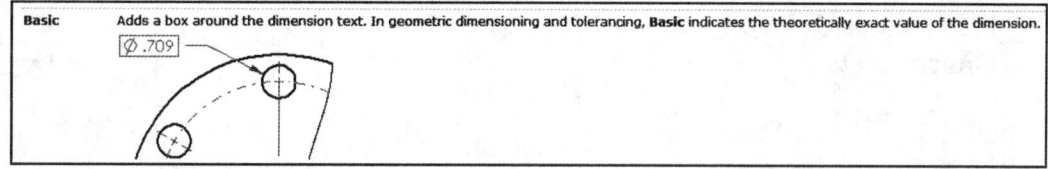

Basic — Adds a box around the dimension text. In geometric dimensioning and tolerancing, **Basic** indicates the theoretically exact value of the dimension.

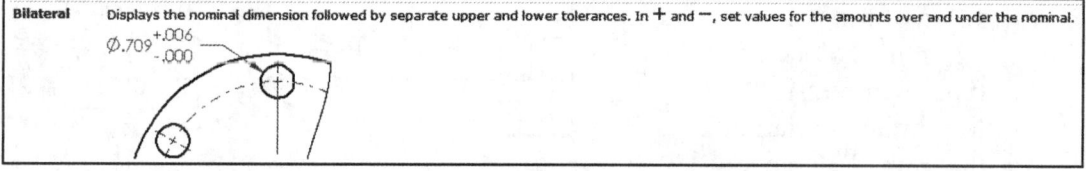

Bilateral — Displays the nominal dimension followed by separate upper and lower tolerances. In + and −, set values for the amounts over and under the nominal.

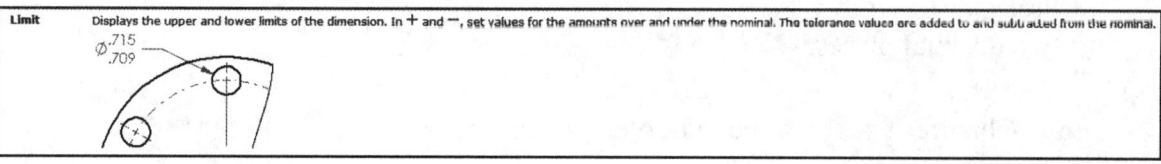

Limit — Displays the upper and lower limits of the dimension. In + and −, set values for the amounts over and under the nominal. The tolerance values are added to and subtracted from the nominal.

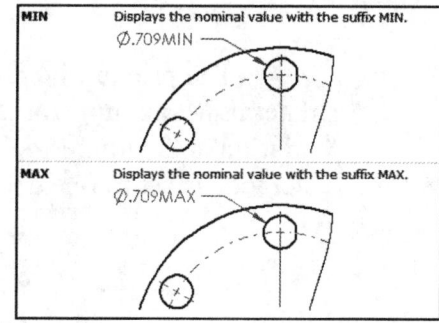

MIN — Displays the nominal value with the suffix MIN.

MAX — Displays the nominal value with the suffix MAX.

Tutorial: Dimension text 3-1

1. **View** the illustrated model.

2. **Review** the Tolerance, Precision, and Dimension Text.

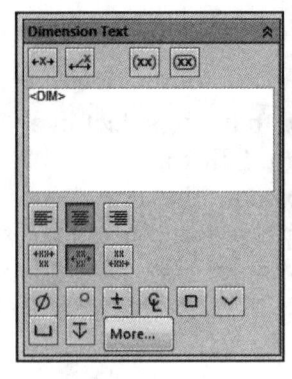
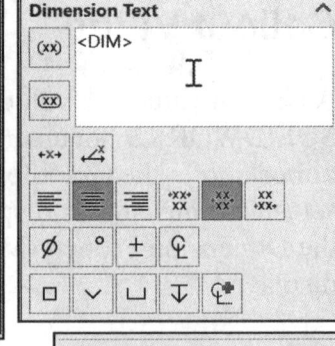

a. 2X Ø.190 - Two holes with a diameter of .190. Precision is set to three decimal places.

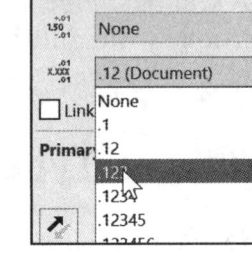

b. 2X R.250 - Two corners with a radius of .250. Precision is set to three decimal places.

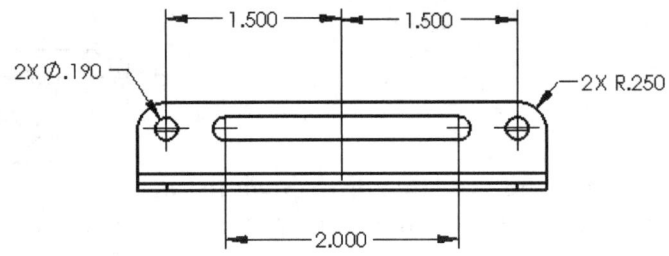

Tutorial: Dimension text 3-2

1. **View** the illustrated model.

2. **Review** the Tolerance, Precision, and Dimension text.

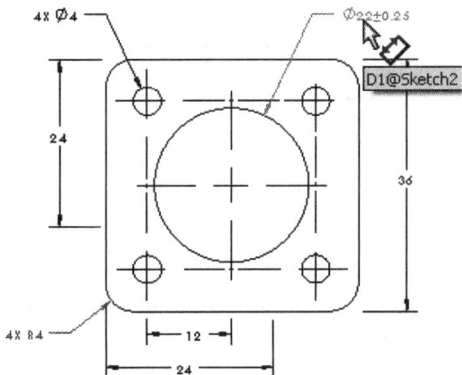
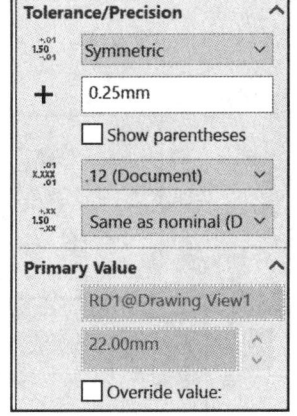

a. Ø 22±0.25 - The primary diameter value of the hole = 22.0mm. Tolerance type: Symmetric. Maximum Variation 0.25mm. Tolerance / Precision is set to two decimal places.

For a Chamfer feature, a second Tolerance/Precision is available.

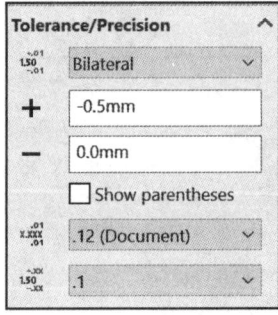

b. $36 {}^{0}_{-0.5}$ - The primary height = 36mm. Tolerance type: Bilateral. Maximum Variation is 0.0mm. Minimum Variation = -0.5mm. Precision is set to two decimal places. Tolerance is set to one decimal place.

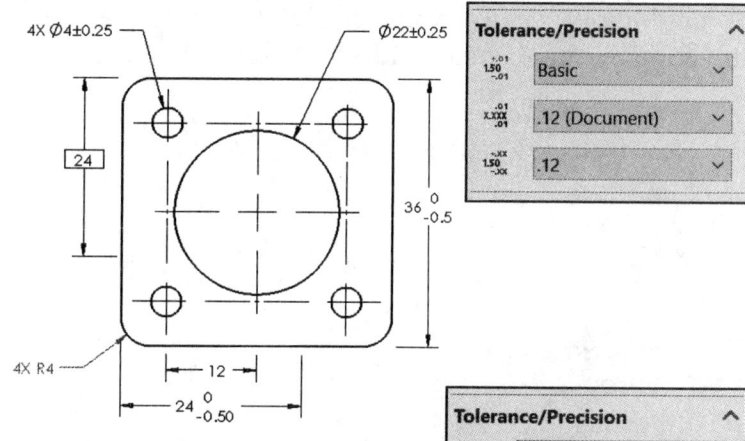

🔅 Trailing zeroes are removed according to the ANSI Y.14.5 standard.

c. ⌴24⌴ - The primary value = 24mm. Tolerance type: Basic. Tolerance / Precision is set to two decimal places.

d. 4X Ø 4±0.25 - Four holes with a primary diameter value = 4mm. Tolerance type: Symmetric. Maximum Variation = 0.25mm. Precision/Tolerance is set to two decimal places.

Tutorial: Dimension text 3-3

1. **View** the illustrated model.

2. **Review** the Tolerance and Precision.

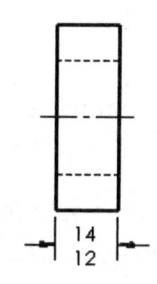
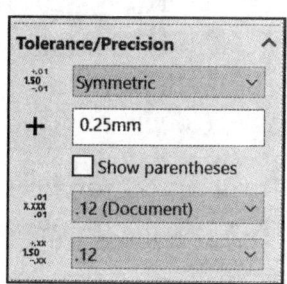

a. ¹⁴₁₂ - The primary value = 12mm. Tolerance type: Limit. Maximum Variation = 2mm. Minimum Variation = 0mm. Tolerance/Precision is set to none.

Dimension Text Symbols

Dimension Text symbols are displayed in the Dimension PropertyManager. The Dimension Text box provides eight commonly used symbols and a more button to access the Symbol Library. The eight displayed symbols in the Dimension Text box from left to right are: Diameter, Degree, Plus/Minus, Centerline, Square, Countersink, Counterbore and Depth/Deep.

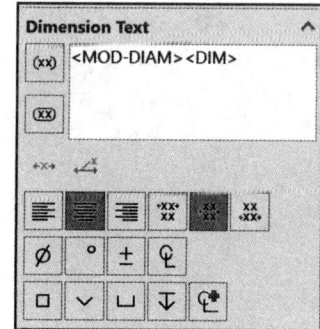
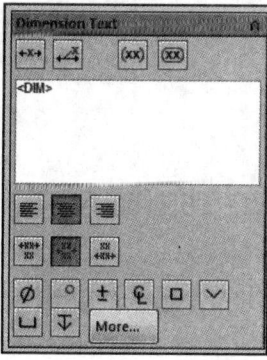

Review each symbol in the Dimension Text box and in the
Symbol library. You are required to understand the meaning
of various symbols in a SOLIDWORKS document.

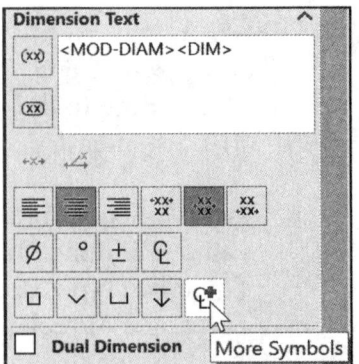

Tutorial: Dimension Text symbols 3-1

1. **View** the illustrated model.

2. **Review** the Dimension Text and document symbols.

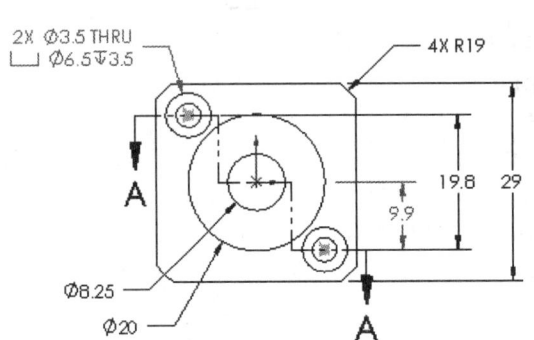

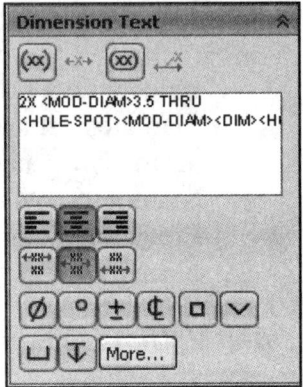

a. 2X Ø3.5 THRU
⊔ Ø6.5⩛3.5
- Two holes with a primary
diameter value = 3.5mm, Cbore Ø6.5 with a
depth of 3.5.

Tutorial: Dimension Text symbols 3-2

1. **View** the illustrated model.

2. **Review** the Dimension Text and document symbols.

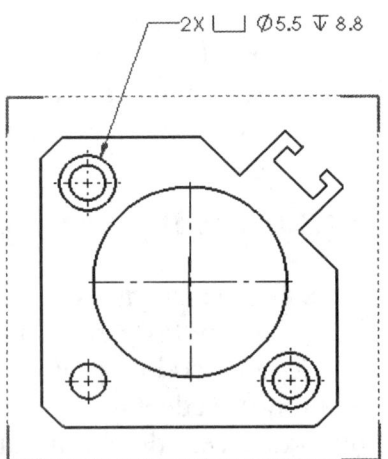

a. 2X ⊔ Ø5.5 ⩛ 8.8 - Two Cbores with a primary
diameter value = 5.5mm with a depth of 8.8.

Build Additional Basic Parts

Tutorial: Mass-Volume 3-10

Build this model in SOLIDWORKS. Calculate the overall mass of the part and locate the Center of mass with the provided information.

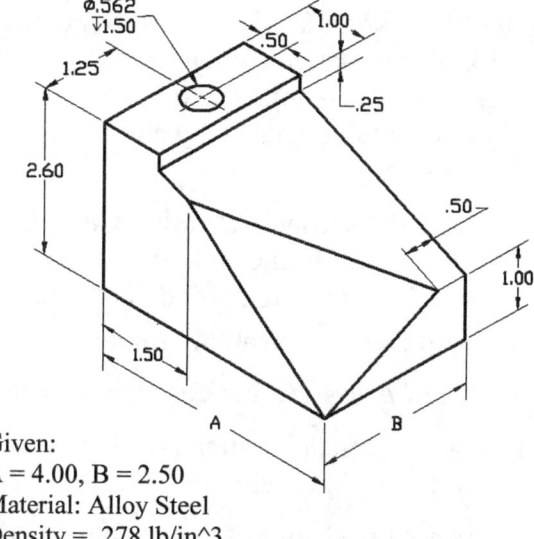

1. **Create** a new part in SOLIDWORKS.

2. **Build** the illustrated model. Note the Depth/Deep ⊥ symbol with a 1.50 dimension associated with the hole. The hole Ø.562 has a three decimal place precision. Insert three features: Extruded Base (Boss-Extrude1) and two Extruded Cuts. Insert a 3D sketch for the first Extruded Cut feature.

Given:
A = 4.00, B = 2.50
Material: Alloy Steel
Density = .278 lb/in^3
Units: IPS
Decimal places = 2

💡 There are numerous ways to build the models in this chapter. A goal is to display different design intents and techniques.

3. **Set** the document properties for the model.

4. Create **Sketch1**. Select the Front Plane as the Sketch plane. The part Origin is located in the lower left corner of the sketch. Insert the required geometric relations and dimensions.

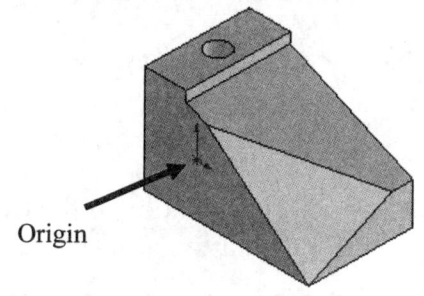

5. Create the **Extruded Base (Boss-Extrude1)** feature. Apply symmetry. Select the Mid Plane End Condition in Direction 1. Depth = 2.50in.

6. Create **3DSketch1**. Apply the Line Sketch tool. Create a closed four point 3D sketch. 3DSketch1 is the profile for the first Extruded Cut feature. Insert the required dimensions.

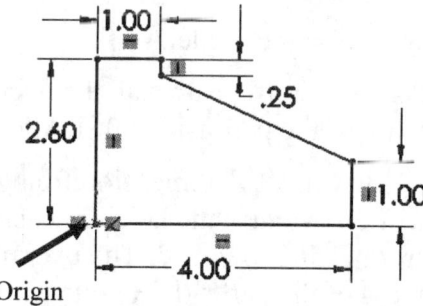

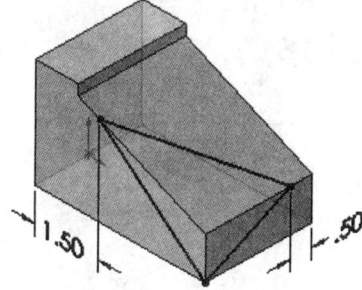

7. Create the first **Extruded Cut** feature. Blind is the default End Condition. Select the top face as illustrated to be removed. Note the direction of the extrude feature.

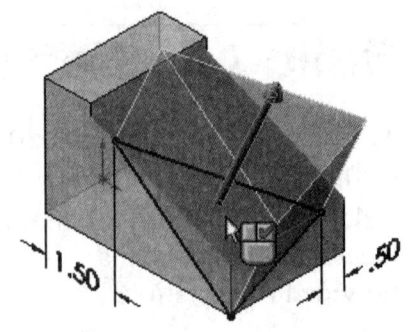

8. Create **Sketch2**. Select the top flat face of Boss-Extrude1. Sketch a circle. Insert the required geometric relations and dimensions. The hole diameter Ø.562 has a three decimal place precision.

9. Create the second **Extruded Cut** feature. Blind is the default End Condition. Depth = 1.50in. Note: For the exam, you do not need to insert the Depth/Deep ▼ symbol or note.

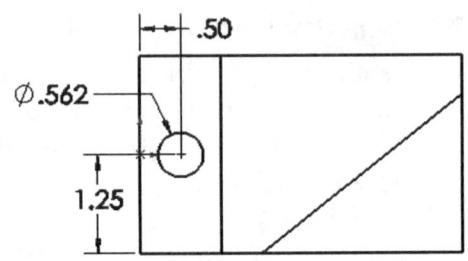

10. **Assign** Alloy Steel material to the part.

11. **Calculate** the overall mass. The overall mass = 4.97 pounds.

12. **Locate** the Center of mass. The location of the Center of mass is derived from the part Origin.

- X: 1.63 inches

- Y: 1.01 inches

- Z: -0.04 inches

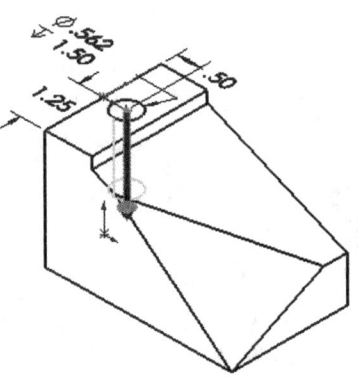

Density = 0.28 pounds per cubic inch
Mass = 4.97 pounds
Volume = 17.86 cubic inches
Surface area = 46.77 square inches
Center of mass: (inches)
　X = 1.63
　Y = 1.01
　Z = -0.04

View the triad location of the Center of mass for the part.

13. **Save** the part and name it Mass-Volume 3-10.

14. **Close** the model.

As an exercise, calculate the overall mass of the part using 6061 Alloy.

Modify the "A" dimension from 4.00 to 4.50. Modify the hole dimension from Ø.562 to Ø.575. The overall mass of the part = 1.93 pounds.

Save the part and name it Mass-Volume 3-10A.

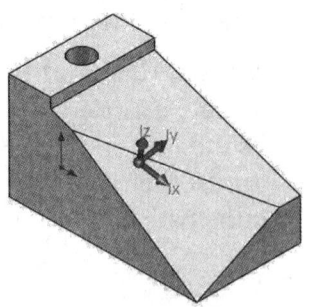

Density = 0.10 pounds per cubic inch
Mass = 1.93 pounds
Volume = 19.77 cubic inches
Surface area = 50.66 square inches
Center of mass: (inches)
　X = 1.83
　Y = 0.99
　Z = -0.04

Tutorial: Mass-Volume 3-11

Build this model in SOLIDWORKS. Calculate the overall mass of the part and locate the Center of mass with the provided information.

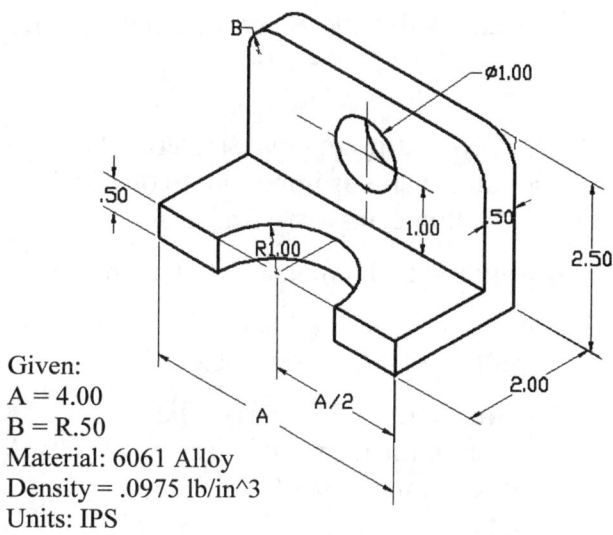

1. **Create** a new part in SOLIDWORKS.

2. **Build** the illustrated model. Think about the required steps to build this part. Insert four features: Extruded Base, two Extruded Cuts, and a Fillet.

Given:
A = 4.00
B = R.50
Material: 6061 Alloy
Density = .0975 lb/in^3
Units: IPS
Decimal places = 2

💡 There are numerous ways to build the models in this chapter. A goal is to display different design intents and techniques.

3. **Set** the document properties for the model.

4. Create **Sketch1**. Select the Right Plane as the Sketch plane. The part Origin is located in the lower left corner of the sketch. Insert the required geometric relations and dimensions.

5. Create the **Extruded Base (Boss-Extrude1)** feature. Apply symmetry. Select the Mid Plane End Condition for Direction 1. Depth = 4.00in.

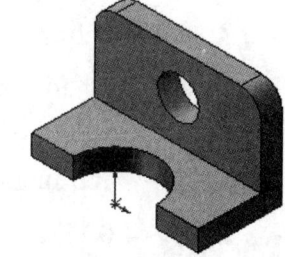

6. Create **Sketch2**. Select the top flat face of Boss-Extrude1 as the Sketch plane. Sketch a circle. The center of the circle is located at the part Origin. Insert the required dimension.

7. Create the first **Extruded Cut** feature. Select Through All for End Condition in Direction 1.

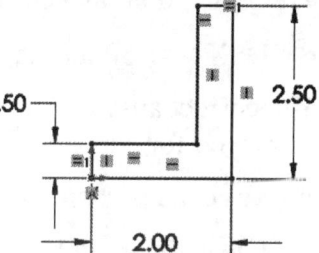

8. Create **Sketch3**. Select the front vertical face of Extrude1 as the Sketch plane. Sketch a circle. Insert the required geometric relations and dimensions.

9. Create the second **Extruded Cut** feature. Select Through All for End Condition in Direction 1.

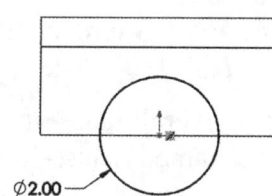

10. Create the **Fillet** feature. Constant radius is selected by default. Fillet the top two edges as illustrated. Radius = .50in.

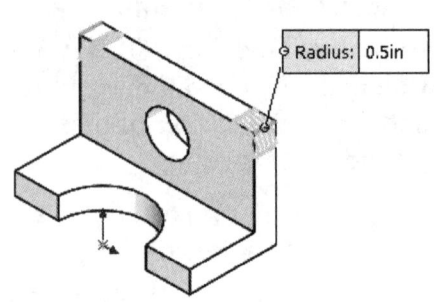

 A Fillet feature removes material. Selecting the correct radius value is important to obtain the correct mass and volume answer in the exam.

11. **Assign** the defined material to the part.

12. **Calculate** the overall mass. The overall mass = 0.66 pounds.

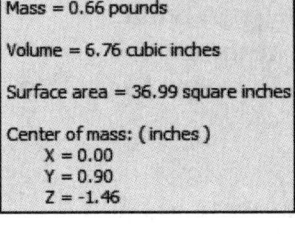

Mass = 0.66 pounds

Volume = 6.76 cubic inches

Surface area = 36.99 square inches

Center of mass: (inches)
   X = 0.00
   Y = 0.90
   Z = -1.46

13. **Locate** the Center of mass. The location of the Center of mass is derived from the part Origin.

- X: 0.00 inches

- Y: 0.90 inches

- Z: -1.46 inches

In this category an exam question could read: Build this model. Locate the Center of mass relative to the part Origin.

- A: X = -2.63 inches, Y = 4.01 inches, Z = -0.04 inches

- B: X = 4.00 inches, Y = 1.90 inches, Z = -1.64 inches

- C: X = 0.00 inches, Y = 0.90 inches, Z = -1.46 inches

- D: X = -1.69 inches, Y = 1.00 inches, Z = 0.10 inches

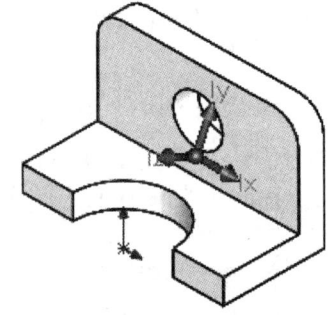

The correct answer is C. Note: Tangent edges and Origin is displayed for educational purposes.

14. **Save** the part and name it Mass-Volume 3-11.

15. **Close** the model.

As an exercise, calculate the overall mass of the part using the MMGS unit system, and assign 2014 Alloy material to the part.

The overall mass of the part = 310.17 grams. Save the part and name it Mass-Volume 3-11-MMGS.

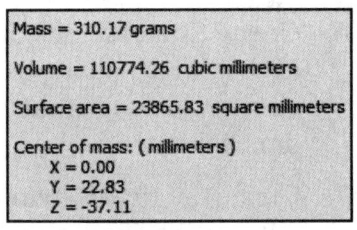

Mass = 310.17 grams

Volume = 110774.26 cubic millimeters

Surface area = 23865.83 square millimeters

Center of mass: (millimeters)
   X = 0.00
   Y = 22.83
   Z = -37.11

 You are allowed to answer the questions in any order you prefer. Use the Summary Screen during the CSWA exam to view the list of all questions you have or have not answered.

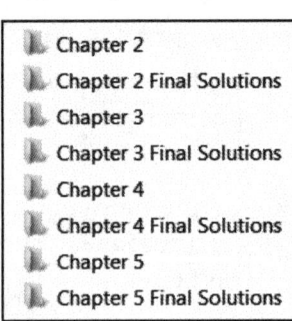

- Chapter 2
- Chapter 2 Final Solutions
- Chapter 3
- Chapter 3 Final Solutions
- Chapter 4
- Chapter 4 Final Solutions
- Chapter 5
- Chapter 5 Final Solutions

Tutorial: Mass-Volume 3-12

Build this model in SOLIDWORKS. Calculate the overall mass of the part and locate the Center of mass with the provided information.

1. **Create** a new part in SOLIDWORKS.

2. **Build** the illustrated model. Insert two features: Extruded Base (Boss-Extrude1) and Extruded Boss (Boss-Extrude2).

3. **Set** the document properties for the model.

4. Create **Sketch1**. Select the Top Plane as the Sketch plane. Apply the Centerline Sketch tool. Locate the part Origin at the center of the sketch. Insert the required geometric relations and dimensions. Note: This is a good case to use the Slot Sketch tool!

5. Create the **Extruded Base (Boss-Extrude1)** feature. Blind is the default End Condition. Depth = 14mm.

6. Create **Sketch2**. Select the Right Plane as the Sketch plane. Insert the required geometric relations and dimensions.

7. Create the **Extruded Boss (Boss-Extrude2)** feature. Apply symmetry. Select the Mid Plane End Condition. Depth = 40mm.

8. **Assign** the defined material to the part.

9. **Calculate** the overall mass. The overall mass = 1605.29 grams.

10. **Locate** the Center of mass. The location of the Center of mass is derived from the part Origin.

- X: 0.00 millimeters

- Y: 19.79 millimeters

- Z: 0.00 millimeters

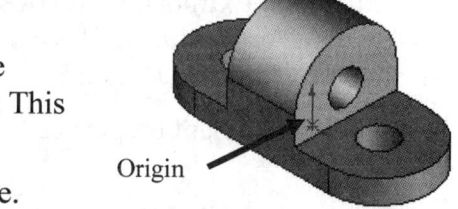

Given:
A = 40, B = 20
All Thru Holes
Material: Copper
Density = .0089 g/mm^3
Units: MMGS

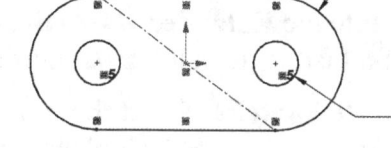

Origin

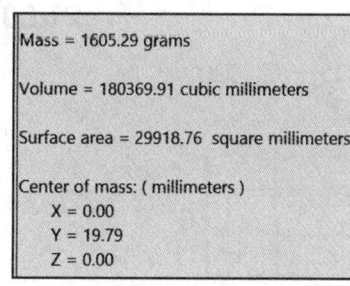

Mass = 1605.29 grams

Volume = 180369.91 cubic millimeters

Surface area = 29918.76 square millimeters

Center of mass: (millimeters)
    X = 0.00
    Y = 19.79
    Z = 0.00

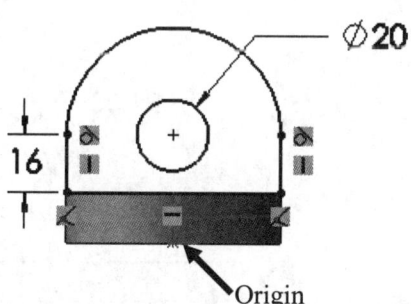

Origin

11. **Save** the part and name it Mass-Volume 3-12.

12. **Close** the model.

☀ There are numerous ways to build the models in this chapter. Optimize your time. The CSWA is a timed exam.

Tutorial: Mass-Volume 3-13

Build this model in SOLIDWORKS. Calculate the volume of the part and locate the Center of mass with the provided information.

1. **Create** a new part in SOLIDWORKS.

2. **Build** the illustrated model. Insert three features: Extruded Base (Boss-Extrude1), Extruded Boss (Boss-Extrude2) and Mirror. Three holes are displayed with an Ø1.00in.

3. **Set** the document properties for the model.

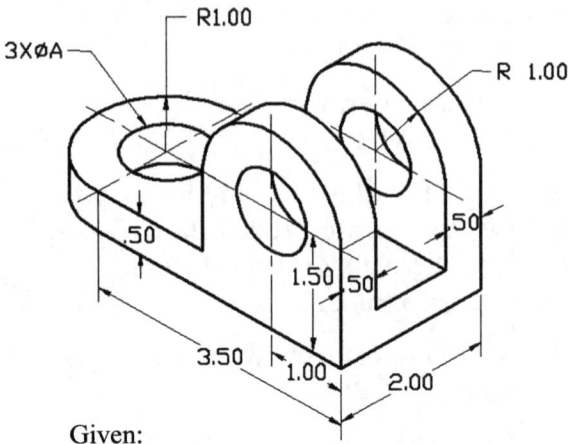

Given:
A = Ø1.00
All Thru Holes
Material: Brass
Density = .307 lb/in^3
Units: IPS
Decimal places = 2

4. Create **Sketch1**. Select the Top Plane as the Sketch plane. Apply the Tangent Arc and Line Sketch tool. Insert the required geometric relations and dimensions. Note the location of the Origin.

5. Create the **Extruded Base (Boss-Extrude1)** feature. Blind is the default End Condition. Depth = .50in.

6. Create **Sketch2**. Select the front vertical face of Extrude1 as the Sketch plane. Insert the required geometric relations and dimensions.

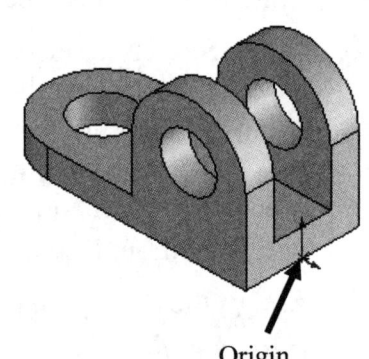

Origin

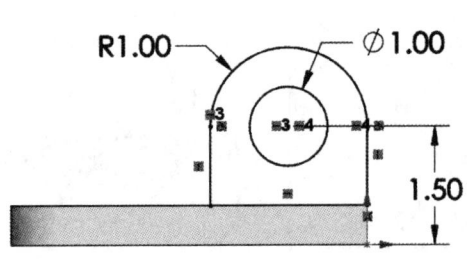

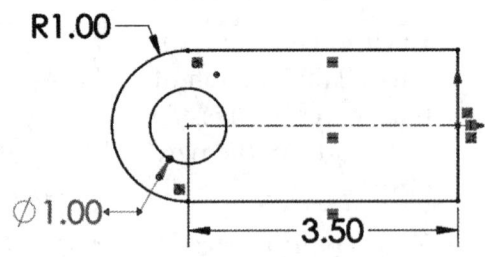

7. Create the **Extruded Boss (Boss-Extrude2)** feature. Blind is the default End Condition in Direction 1. Depth = .50in. Note the direction of the extrude.

8. Create the **Mirror** feature. Apply Symmetry. Mirror Boss-Extrude2 about the Front Plane.

9. **Assign** the defined material to the part.

10. **Calculate** the volume. The volume = 6.68 cubic inches.

11. **Locate** the Center of mass. The location of the Center of mass is derived from the part Origin.

- X: -1.59 inches

- Y: 0.72 inches

- Z: 0.00 inches

In this category an exam question could read: Build this model. What is the volume of the model?

- A = 6.19 cubic inches

- B = 7.79 cubic inches

- C = 7.87 cubic inches

- D = 6.68 cubic inches

The correct answer is D.

View the triad location of the Center of mass for the part.

12. **Save** the part and name it Mass-Volume 3-13.

13. **Close** the model.

As an exercise, calculate the overall mass of the part using the IPS unit system, and assign Copper material to the part. Modify the hole diameters from 1.00in to 1.125in.

The overall mass of the part = 2.05 pounds. Save the part and name it Mass-Volume 3-13A.

This book is designed to expose the new user to many tools, techniques and procedures. It may not always use the most direct tool or process.

Density = 0.31 pounds per cubic inch

Mass = 2.05 pounds

Volume = 6.68 cubic inches

Surface area = 40.64 square inches

Center of mass: (inches)
    X = -1.59
    Y = 0.72
    Z = 0.00

Density = 0.32 pounds per cubic inch

Mass = 2.05 pounds

Volume = 6.37 cubic inches

Surface area = 39.97 square inches

Center of mass: (inches)
    X = -1.58
    Y = 0.70
    Z = 0.00

Tutorial: Mass-Volume 3-14

Build this model in SOLIDWORKS. Calculate the overall mass of the part and locate the Center of mass with the provided information.

1. **Create** a new part in SOLIDWORKS.

2. **Build** the illustrated model. Insert a Revolved Base feature and Extruded Cut feature to build this part.

3. **Set** the document properties for the model.

4. Create **Sketch1**. Select the Front Plane as the Sketch plane. Apply the Centerline Sketch tool for the Revolve1 feature. Insert the required geometric relations and dimensions. Sketch1 is the profile for the Revolve1 feature.

5. Create the **Revolved Base** feature. The default angle is 360deg. Select the centerline for the Axis of Revolution.

🔅 A Revolve feature adds or removes material by revolving one or more profiles around a centerline.

6. Create **Sketch2**. Select the right large circular face of Revolve1 as the Sketch plane. Apply reference construction geometry. Use the Convert Entities and Trim Sketch tools. Insert the required geometric relations and dimensions.

🔅 You could also use the 3 Point Arc Sketch tool instead of the Convert Entities and Trim Sketch tools to create Sketch2.

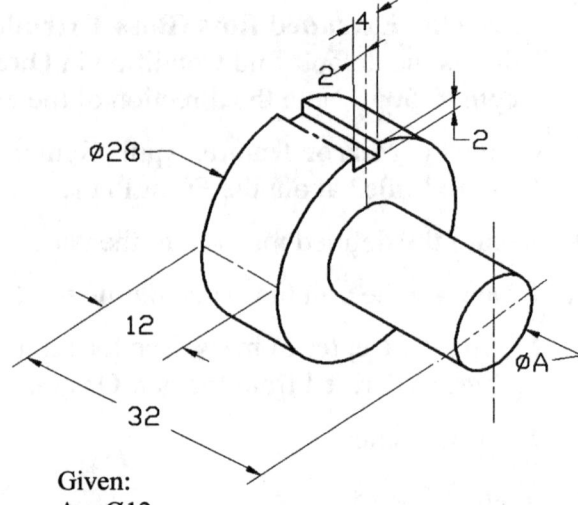

Given:
A = Ø12
Material: Cast Alloy Steel
Density = .0073 g/mm^3
Units: MMGS

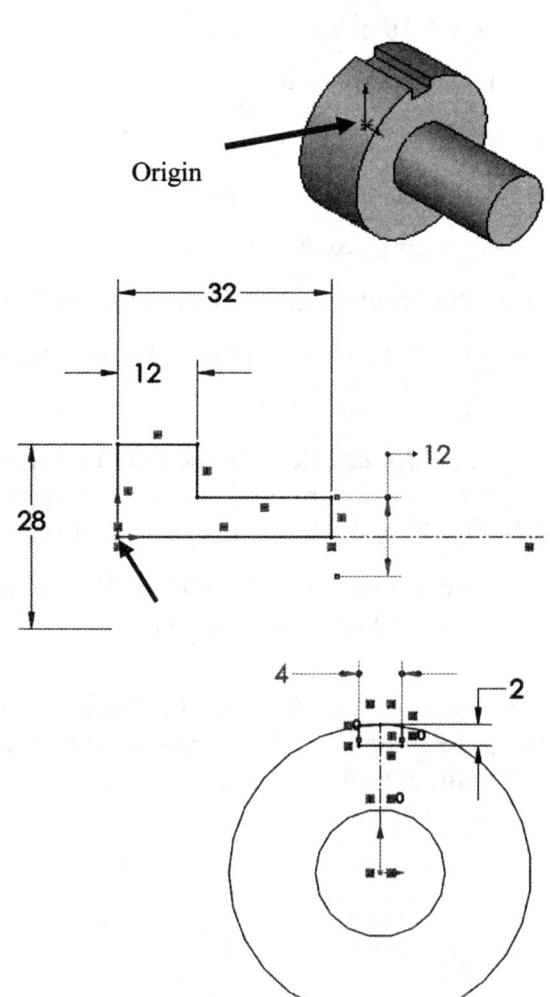

Origin

7. Create the **Extruded Cut** feature. Select Through All for End Condition in Direction 1.

8. **Assign** the defined material to the part.

9. **Calculate** the overall mass. The overall mass = 69.77 grams.

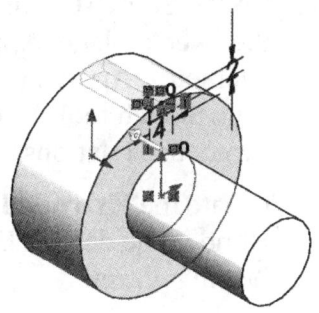

10. **Locate** the Center of mass. The location of the Center of mass is derived from the part Origin.

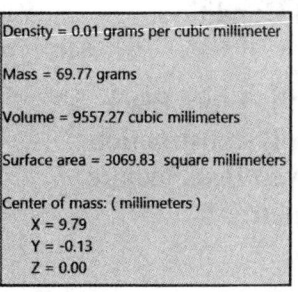

Density = 0.01 grams per cubic millimeter

Mass = 69.77 grams

Volume = 9557.27 cubic millimeters

Surface area = 3069.83 square millimeters

Center of mass: (millimeters)
X = 9.79
Y = -0.13
Z = 0.00

- X = 9.79 millimeters
- Y = -0.13 millimeters
- Z = 0.00 millimeters

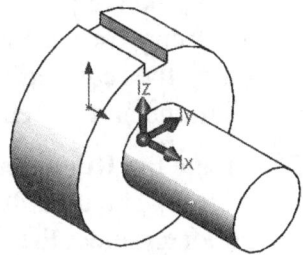

11. **Save** the part and name it Mass-Volume 3-14.

12. **Close** the model.

Tutorial: Mass-Volume 3-15

Build this model in SOLIDWORKS. Calculate the overall mass of the part and locate the Center of mass with the provided information.

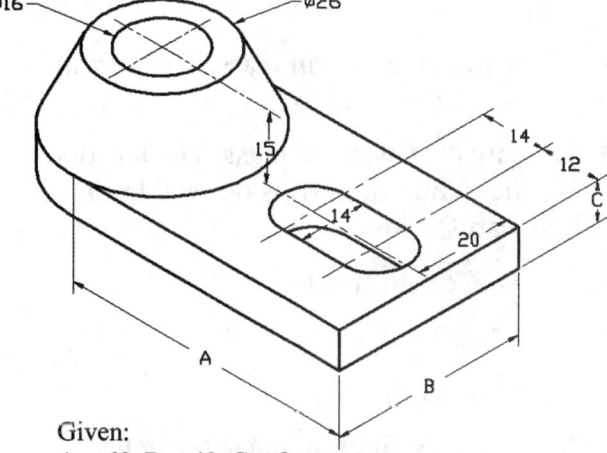

1. **Create** a new part in SOLIDWORKS.

2. **Build** the illustrated model. Insert two features: Extruded Base (Boss-Extrude1) and Revolved Boss.

3. **Set** the document properties for the model.

🔆 Tangent edges and Origin are displayed for educational purposes.

Given:
A = 60, B = 40, C = 8
Material: Cast Alloy Steel
Density = .0073 g/mm^3
Units: MMGS

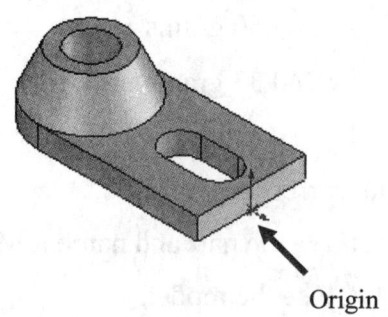

Origin

4. Create **Sketch1**. Select the Top Plane as the Sketch plane. Apply construction geometry. Apply the Tangent Arc and Line Sketch tool. Insert the required geometric relations and dimensions.

5. Create the **Extruded Base** feature. Blind is the default End Condition. Depth = 8mm.

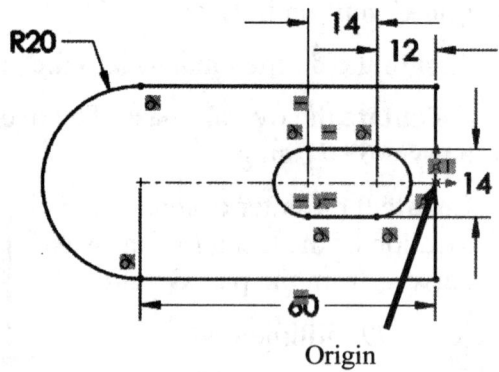

Origin

6. Create **Sketch2**. Select the Front Plane as the Sketch plane. Apply construction geometry for the Revolved Boss feature. Insert the required geometric relations and dimension.

7. Create the **Revolved Boss** feature. The default angle is 360deg. Select the centerline for Axis of Revolution.

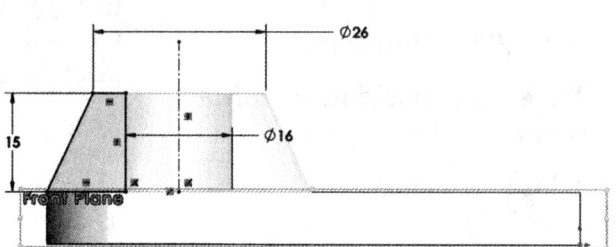

8. **Assign** the defined material to the part.

9. **Calculate** the overall mass. The overall mass = 229.46 grams.

Mass = 229.46 grams

Volume = 31433.02 cubic millimeters

Surface area = 9459.63 square millimeters

Center of mass: (millimeters)
  X = -46.68
  Y = 7.23
  Z = 0.00

10. **Locate** the Center of mass. The location of the Center of mass is derived from the part Origin.

- X = -46.68 millimeters

- Y = 7.23 millimeters

- Z = 0.00 millimeters

In this category an exam question could read: Build this model. What is the overall mass of the part?

- A: 229.46 grams

- B: 249.50 grams

- C: 240.33 grams

- D: 120.34 grams

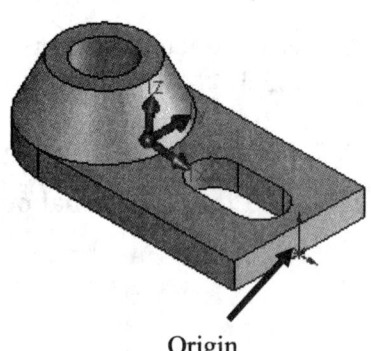

Origin

The correct answer is A.

11. **Save** the part and name it Mass-Volume 3-15.

12. **Close** the model.

Tutorial: Mass-Volume 3-16

Build this model in SOLIDWORKS. Calculate the overall mass of the part and locate the Center of mass with the provided information.

1. **Create** a new part in SOLIDWORKS.

2. **Build** the illustrated model. Insert three features: Extruded Base, Extruded Cut and Circular Pattern. There are eight holes Ø14mm equally spaces on an Ø56mm bolt circle. The center hole = Ø22mm.

3. **Set** the document properties for the model.

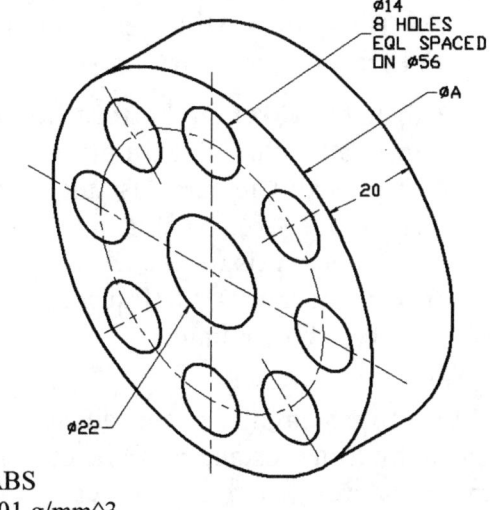

Given:
A = Ø80
Material: ABS
Density: .001 g/mm^3
Units: MMGS

4. Create **Sketch1**. Select the Front Plane as the Sketch plane. Sketch two circles. The part Origin is located in the center of the sketch. Insert the required geometric relations and dimensions.

5. Create the **Extruded Base (Boss-Extrude1)** feature. Blind is the default End Condition. Depth = 20mm.

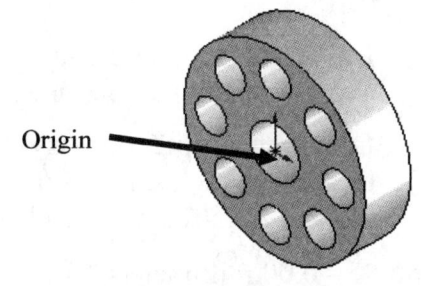

6. Create **Sketch2**. Select the front face as the Sketch plane. Apply construction geometry to locate the seed feature for the Circular Pattern. Insert the required geometric relations and dimensions.

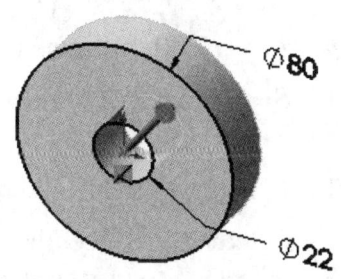

💡 Apply construction reference geometry to assist in creating the sketch entities and geometry that are incorporated into the part. Construction reference geometry is ignored when the sketch is used to create a feature. Construction reference geometry uses the same line style as centerlines.

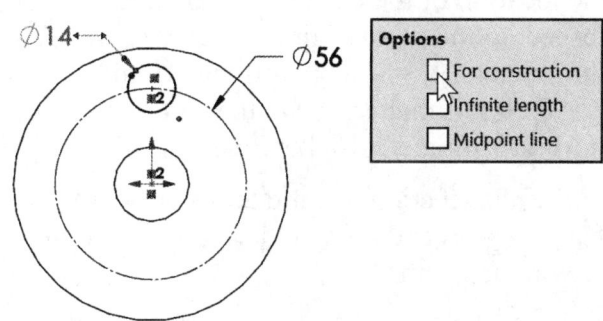

7. Create the **Extruded Cut** feature. Select Through All for End Condition in Direction 1.

8. Create the **Circular Pattern** feature. Create a Circular Pattern of the Cut-Extrude1 feature. Use the View, Temporary Axes command to select the Pattern Axis for the CirPattern1 feature. Instances = 8. Equal spacing is selected by default.

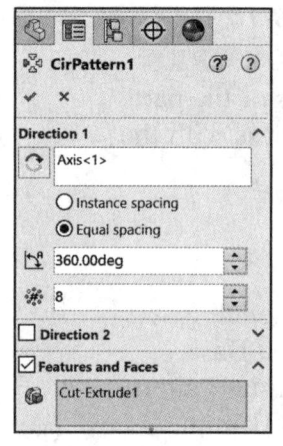

Apply a circular pattern feature to create multiple instances of one or more features that you can space uniformly about an axis.

9. **Assign** the defined material to the part.

10. **Calculate** the overall mass. The overall mass = 69.66 grams.

11. **Locate** the Center of mass. The location of the Center of mass is derived from the part Origin.

- X = 0.00 millimeters

- Y = 0.00 millimeters

- Z = -10.00 millimeters

12. **Save** the part and name it Mass-Volume 3-16.

13. **Close** the model.

As an exercise, select the Top Plane for the Sketch plane to create Sketch1. Recalculate the location of the Center of mass with respect to the part Origin: X = 0.00 millimeters, Y = -10.00 millimeters and Z = 0.00 millimeters. Save the part and name it Mass-Volume 3-16-TopPlane.

In the next section, the models represent the feature types and complexity that you would see on the exam.

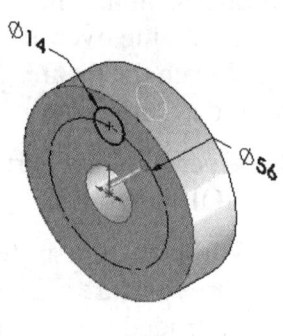

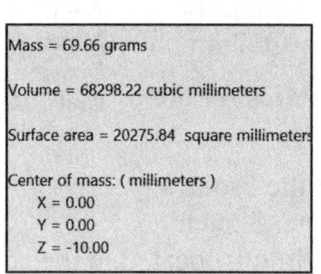

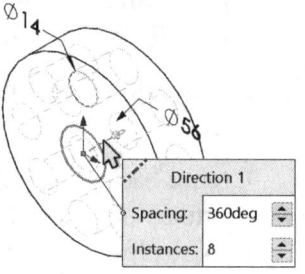

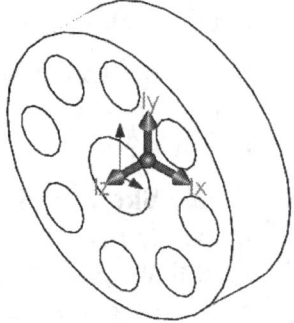

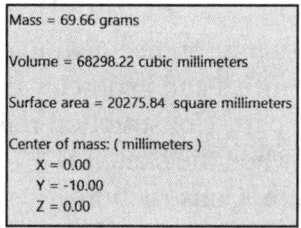

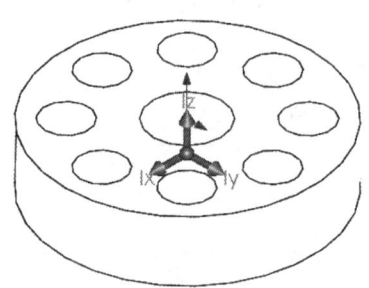

Tutorial: Basic/Intermediate Part 3-1

Build this model in SOLIDWORKS. Calculate the overall mass of the part and locate the Center of mass with the provided information.

1. **Create** a new part in SOLIDWORKS.

2. **Build** the illustrated model. Think about the various features that create the model. Insert seven features to build this model: Extruded Base, Extruded Cut, Extruded Boss, Fillet, second Extruded Cut, Mirror and a second Fillet. Apply symmetry. Create the left half of the model first, and then apply the Mirror feature.

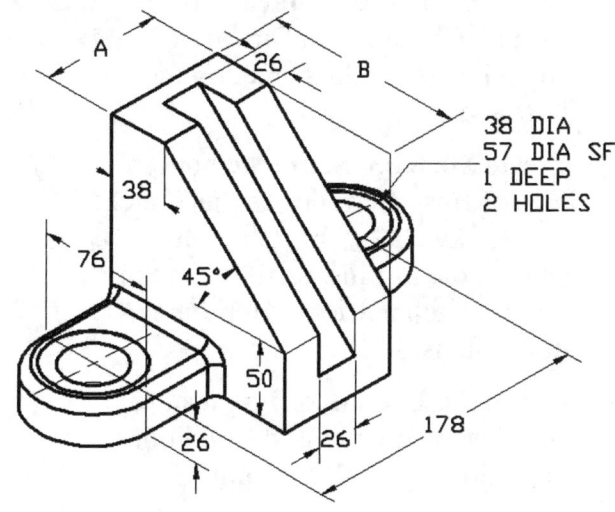

Given:
A = 76, B = 127
Material: 2014 Alloy
Density: .0028 g/mm^3
Units: MMGS
ALL ROUNDS EQUAL 6MM

🔆 There are numerous ways to build the models in this chapter. The goal is to display different design intents and techniques.

3. **Set** the document properties for the model.

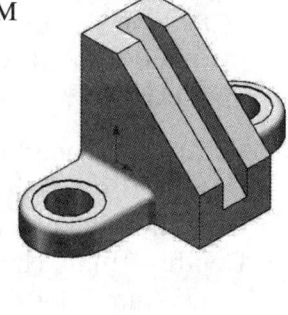

4. Create **Sketch1**. Select the Front Plane as the Sketch plane. Create the main body of the part. The part Origin is located in the bottom left corner of the sketch. Insert the required geometric relations and dimensions.

5. Create the **Extruded Base** feature. Boss-Extrude1 is the Base feature. Select Mid Plane for End Condition in Direction 1. Depth = 76mm.

6. Create **Sketch2**. Select the top flat face of Extrude1 as the Sketch plane. Create the top cut on the Base feature. Apply construction geometry. Insert the required geometric relations and dimensions.

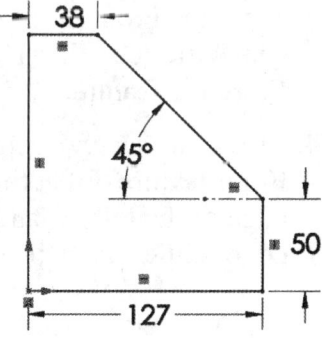

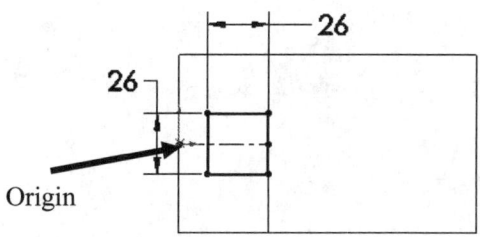

7. Create the first **Extruded Cut** feature. Select Through All for End Condition in Direction 1. Select the illustrated angled edge for the Direction of Extrusion.

8. Create **Sketch3**. Select the bottom face of Boss-Extrude1 as the Sketch plane. Sketch the first tab with a single hole as illustrated. Insert the required geometric relations and dimensions.

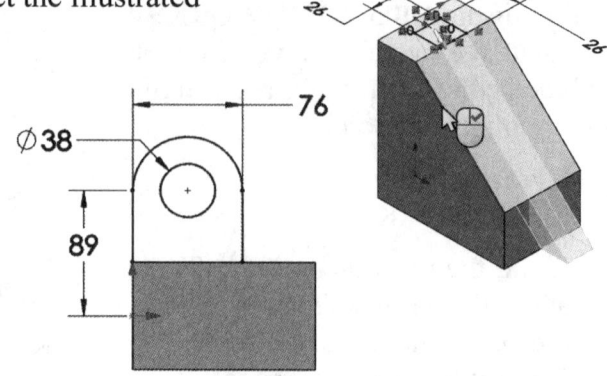

9. Create the **Extruded Boss** feature. Blind is the default End Condition in Direction 1. Depth = 26mm.

10. Create the first **Fillet** feature. Fillet the top edge of the left tab. Radius = 6mm. Constant Size fillet is selected by default.

11. Create **Sketch4**. Select the top face of Extrude3 as the Sketch plane. Sketch a circle. Insert the required dimension.

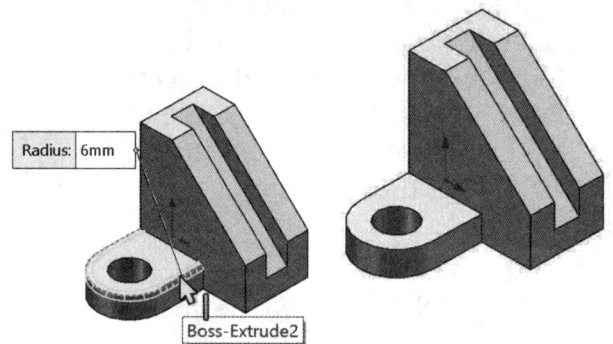

12. Create the second **Extruded Cut** feature. Blind is the default End Condition in Direction 1. Depth = 1mm. The model displayed an Ø57mm Spot Face hole with a 1mm depth.

13. Create the **Mirror** feature. Mirror about the Front Plane. Mirror the Cut-Extrude2, Fillet1, and Boss-Extrude2 feature.

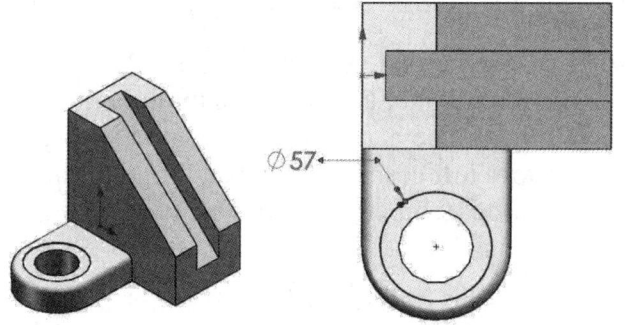

14. Create the second Constant Size **Fillet** feature. Fillet the top inside edge of the left tab and the top inside edge of the right tab. Radius = 6mm.

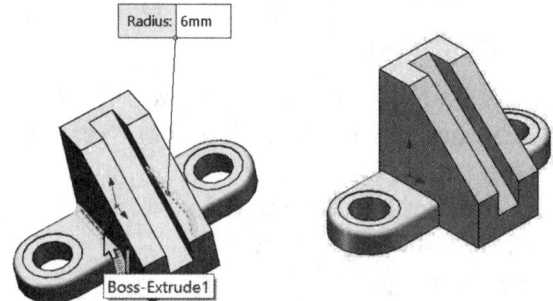

15. **Assign** the defined material to the part.

16. **Calculate** the overall mass of the part. The overall mass = 3437.29 grams.

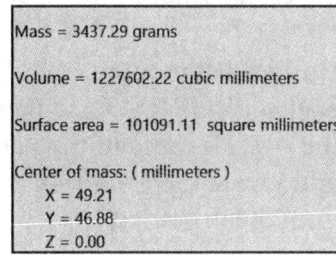

17. **Locate** the Center of mass. The location of the Center of mass is derived from the part Origin.

- X = 49.21 millimeters

- Y = 46.88 millimeters

- Z = 0.00 millimeters

18. **Save** the part and name it Part-Modeling 3-1.

19. **Close** the model.

In this category, an exam question could read: Build this model. What is the overall mass of the part?

- A: 3944.44 grams

- B: 4334.29 grams

- C: 3437.29 grams

- D: 2345.69 grams

The correct answer is C.

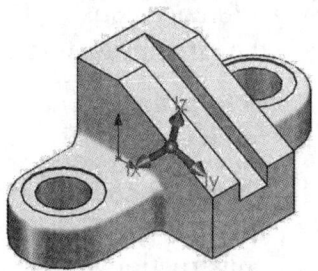

As an exercise, modify all ALL ROUNDS from 6mm to 8mm. Modify the material from 2014 Alloy to 6061 Alloy.

Modify the Sketch1 angle from 45deg to 30deg. Modify the Extrude3 depth from 26mm to 36mm. Recalculate the location of the Center of mass with respect to the part Origin.

- X = 49.76 millimeters

- Y = 34.28 millimeters

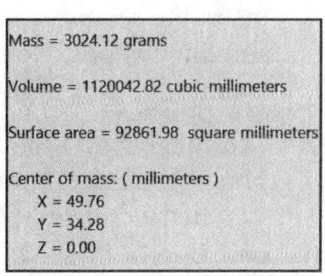

- Z = 0.00 millimeters

20. **Save** the part and name it Part-Modeling 3-1-Modify.

Tangent edges and Origin is displayed for educational purposes.

When you create a new part or assembly, the three default Planes (Front, Right and Top) are aligned with specific views. The Plane you select for the Base sketch determines the orientation of the part.

Tutorial: Basic/Intermediate Part 3-2

Build this model in SOLIDWORKS. Calculate the overall mass of the part and locate the Center of mass with the provided information.

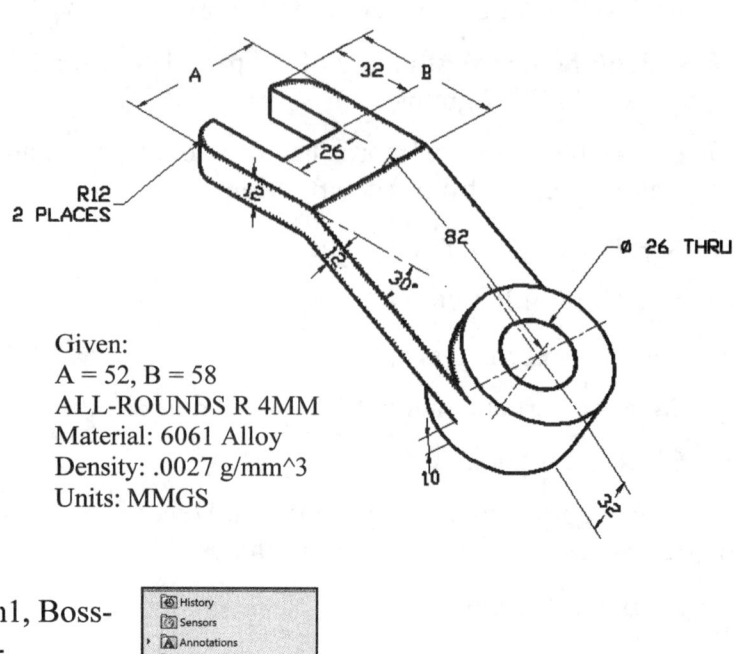

Given:
A = 52, B = 58
ALL-ROUNDS R 4MM
Material: 6061 Alloy
Density: .0027 g/mm^3
Units: MMGS

1. **Create** a new part in SOLIDWORKS.

2. **Build** the illustrated model. Think about the various features that create the part. Insert seven features and a plane to build this part: Extruded-Thin1, Boss-Extrude1, Cut-Extrude1, Cut-Extrude2 and three Fillets. Apply reference construction planes to build the circular features.

3. **Set** the document properties for the model.

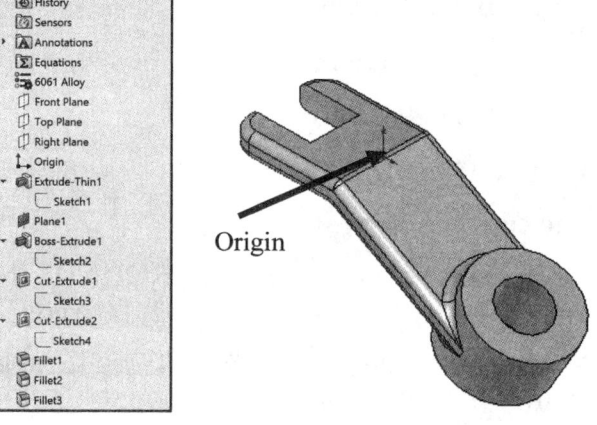

Origin

4. Create **Sketch1**. Select the Front Plane as the Sketch plane. Apply construction geometry as the reference line for the 30deg angle. Insert the required geometric relations and dimensions. Note the location of the Origin.

5. Create the **Extrude-Thin1** feature. This is the Base feature. Apply symmetry. Select Mid Plane for End Condition in Direction 1 to maintain the location of the Origin. Depth = 52mm. Thickness = 12mm.

🔆 Use the Thin Feature option to control the extrude thickness, not the Depth.

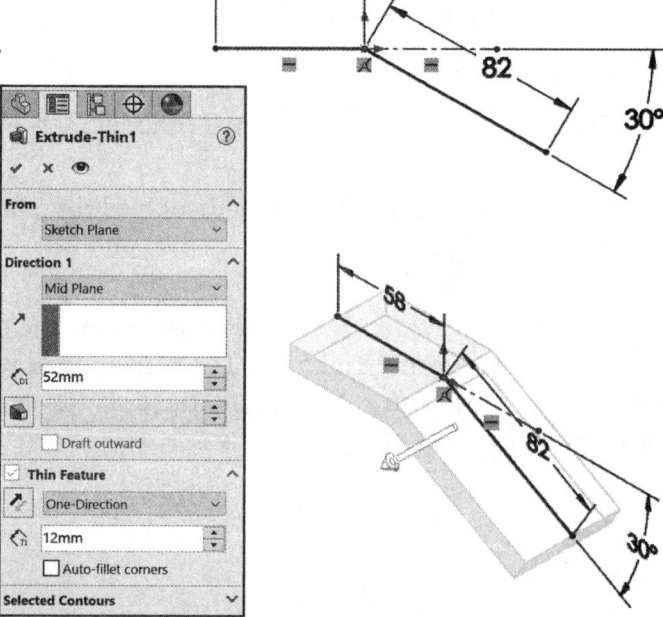

6. Create **Plane1**. Plane1 is the Sketch plane for the Extruded Boss (Boss-Extrude1) feature. Select the midpoint and the top face as illustrated. Plane1 is located in the middle of the top and bottom faces. Select Parallel Plane at Point for option.

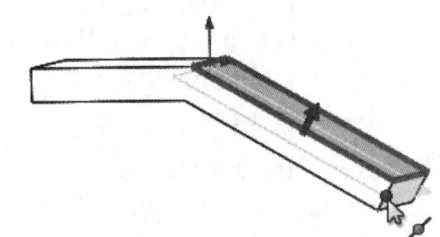

💡 Plane1 uses the Depth dimension of 32mm.

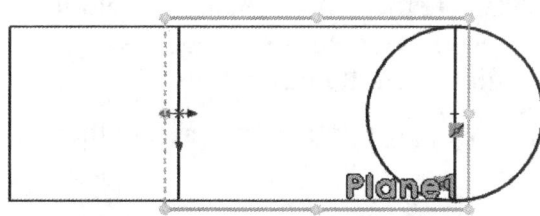

7. Create **Sketch2**. Select Plane1 as the Sketch plane. Use the Normal To view tool. Sketch a circle to create the Extruded Boss feature. Insert the required geometric relations.

💡 The Normal To view tool rotates and zooms the model to the view orientation normal to the selected plane, planar face, or feature.

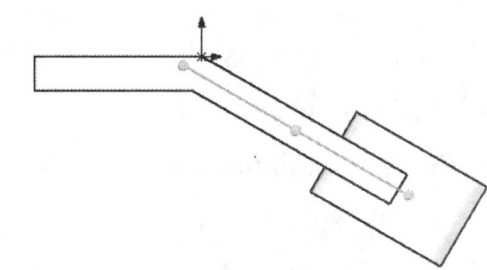

8. Create the **Extruded Boss** feature. Apply Symmetry. Select Mid Plane for End Condition in Direction 1. Depth = 32mm.

9. Create **Sketch3**. Select the top circular face of Boss-Extrude1 as the Sketch plane. Sketch a circle. Insert the required geometric relation and dimension.

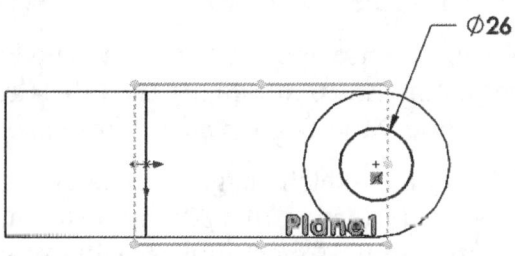

💡 There are numerous ways to create the models in this chapter. A goal is to display different design intents and techniques.

10. Create the first **Extruded Cut** feature. Select Through All for End Condition in Direction 1.

11. Create **Sketch4**. Select the top face of Extrude-Thin1 as the Sketch plane. Apply construction geometry. Insert the required geometric relations and dimensions.

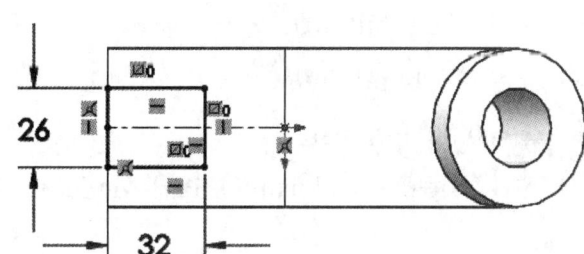

12. Create the second **Extruded Cut** feature. Select Through All for End Condition in Direction 1.

13. Create the **Fillet1** feature. Fillet the left and right edges of Extrude-Thin1 as illustrated. Radius = 12mm.

14. Create the **Fillet2** feature. Fillet the top and bottom edges of Extrude-Thin1 as illustrated. Radius = 4mm.

15. Create the **Fillet3** feature. Fillet the rest of the model, six edges as illustrated. Radius = 4mm.

16. **Assign** the defined material to the part.

17. **Calculate** the overall mass of the part. The overall mass = 300.65 grams.

18. **Locate** the Center of mass. The location of the Center of mass is derived from the part Origin.

- X: 34.26 millimeters

- Y: -29.38 millimeters

- Z: 0.00 millimeters

19. **Save** the part and name it Part-Modeling 3-2.

20. **Close** the model.

As an exercise, modify the Fillet2 and Fillet3 radius from 4mm to 2mm. Modify the Fillet1 radius from 12m to 10mm. Modify the material from 6061 Alloy to ABS.

Modify the Sketch1 angle from 30deg to 45deg. Modify the Extrude depth from 32mm to 38mm. Recalculate the location of the Center of mass with respect to the part Origin.

- X = 27.62 millimeters

- Y = -40.44 millimeters

- Z = 0.00 millimeters

21. **Save** the part and name it Part-Modeling 3-2-Modify.

In the exam, you are allowed to answer the questions in any order. Use the Summary Screen during the exam to view the list of all questions you have or have not answered.

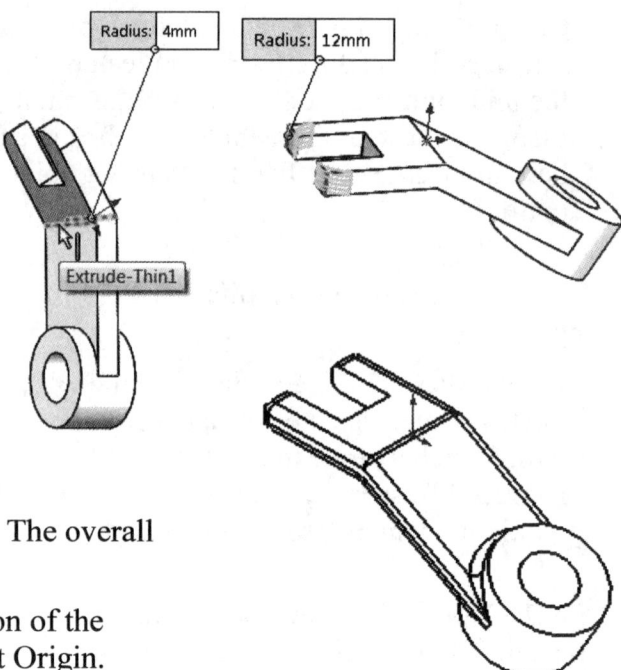

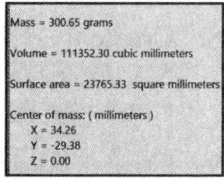

Mass = 300.65 grams

Volume = 111352.30 cubic millimeters

Surface area = 23765.33 square millimeters

Center of mass: (millimeters)
X = 34.26
Y = -29.38
Z = 0.00

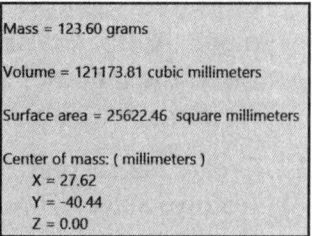

Mass = 123.60 grams

Volume = 121173.81 cubic millimeters

Surface area = 25622.46 square millimeters

Center of mass: (millimeters)
X = 27.62
Y = -40.44
Z = 0.00

Tutorial: Basic/Intermediate Part 3-3

Build this model in SOLIDWORKS. Calculate the volume of the part and locate the Center of mass with the provided information.

1. **Create** a new part in SOLIDWORKS.

2. **Build** the illustrated model. Think about the various features that create this model. Insert five features and a plane to build this part: Extruded Base, two Extruded Bosses, Extruded Cut and a Rib. Insert a reference plane to create the Boss-Extrude2 feature.

3. **Set** the document properties for the model.

4. Create **Sketch1**. Select the Top Plane as the Sketch plane. Sketch a rectangle. Apply two construction lines for an Intersection relation. Use the horizontal construction line as the Plane1 reference. Insert the required relations and dimensions.

5. Create the **Extruded Base** feature. Blind is the default End Condition in Direction 1. Depth = 1.00in. Note the extrude direction is downward.

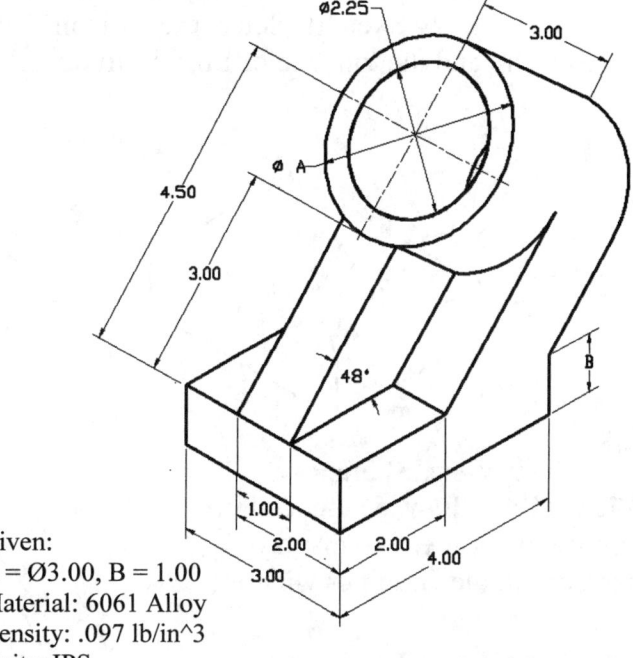

Given:
A = Ø3.00, B = 1.00
Material: 6061 Alloy
Density: .097 lb/in^3
Units: IPS
Decimal places = 2

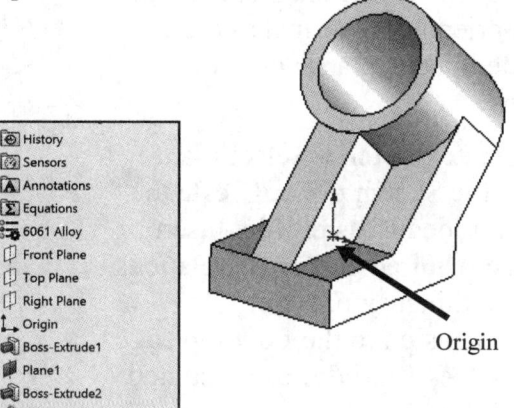

Origin

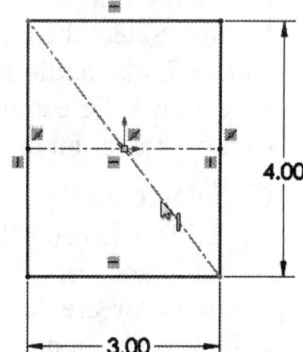

🔆 Create planes to aid in the modeling for the exam. Use planes to sketch, to create a section view, for a neutral plane in a draft feature, and so on.

🔆 The created plane is displayed 5% larger than the geometry on which the plane is created, or 5% larger than the bounding box. This helps reduce selection problems when planes are created directly on faces or from orthogonal geometry.

6. Create **Plane1**. Plane1 is the Sketch plane for the Extruded Boss feature. Show Sketch1. Select the horizontal construction line in Sketch1 and the top face of Boss-Extrude1. Angle = 48deg.

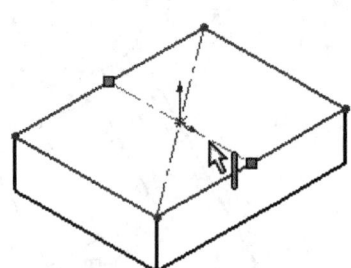

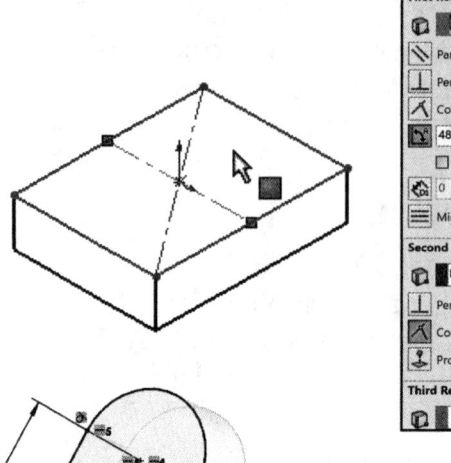

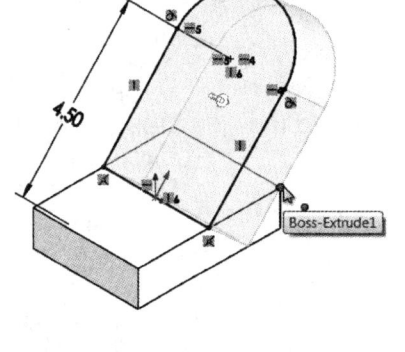

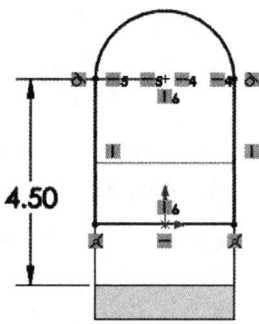

💡 Click **View, Sketches** or **View, Hide/Show, Sketches** from the Menu bar menu to displayed sketches in the Graphics window.

💡 The Normal To view tool rotates and zooms the model to the view orientation normal to the selected plane, planar face, or feature.

7. Create **Sketch2**. Select Plane1 as the Sketch plane. Create the Extruded Boss profile. Insert the required geometric relations and dimension. Note: Dimension to the front top edge of Boss-Extrude1 as illustrated.

8. Create the first **Extruded Boss** feature. Select the Up To Vertex End Condition in Direction 1. Select the back top right vertex point as illustrated.

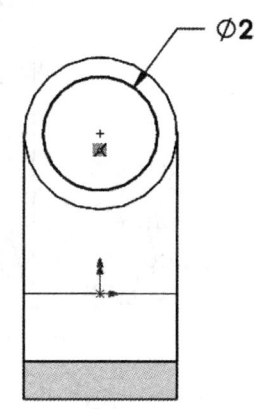

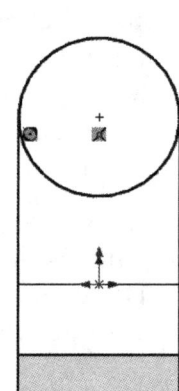

9. Create **Sketch3**. Select the back angled face of Boss-Extrude2 as the Sketch plane. Sketch a circle. Insert the required geometric relations. Create the third **Extruded Boss** feature. Blind is the default End Condition in Direction 1. Depth = 3.00in.

10. Create **Sketch4**. Select the front face of Boss-Extrude3 as the Sketch plane. Sketch a circle. Sketch4 is the profile for the Extruded Cut feature. Insert the required geometric relation and dimension.

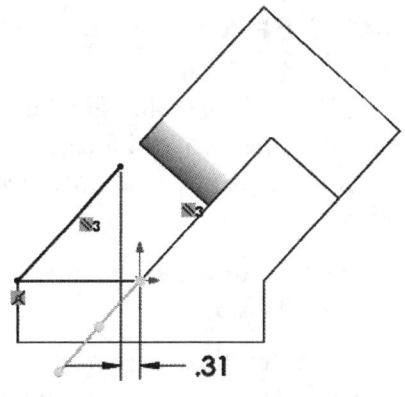

☀️ The part Origin is displayed in blue.

11. Create the **Extruded Cut** feature. Select Through All for End Condition in Direction 1.

12. Create **Sketch5**. Select the Right Plane as the Sketch plane. Insert a Parallel relation to partially define Sketch5. Sketch5 is the profile for the Rib feature. Sketch5 does not need to be fully defined. Sketch5 locates the end conditions based on existing geometry.

13. Create the **Rib** feature. Thickness = 1.00in.

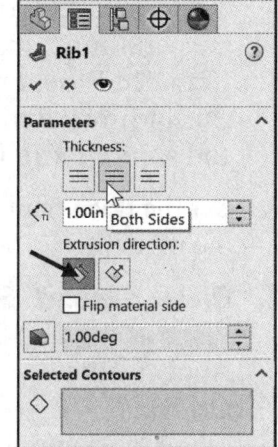

☀️ The Rib feature is a special type of extruded feature created from open or closed sketched contours. The Rib feature adds material of a specified thickness in a specified direction between the contour and an existing part. You can create a rib feature using single or multiple sketches.

14. **Assign** 6061 Alloy material to the part.

15. **Calculate** the volume. The volume = 30.65 cubic inches.

16. **Locate** the Center of mass. The location of the Center of mass is derived from the part Origin.

Mass = 2.99 pounds

Volume = 30.65 cubic inches

Surface area = 100.96 square inches

Center of mass: (inches)
X = 0.00
Y = 0.73
Z = -0.86

- X: 0.00 inches

- Y: 0.73 inches

- Z: -0.86 inches

17. **Save** the part and name it Part-Modeling 3-3.

18. **Close** the model.

As an exercise, modify the Rib1 feature from 1.00in to 1.25in. Modify the Extrude depth from 3.00in to 3.25in. Modify the material from 6061 Alloy to Copper.

Modify the Plane1 angle from 48deg to 30deg. Recalculate the volume of the part. The new volume = 26.94 cubic inches.

19. **Save** the part and name it Part-Modeling 3-3-Modify.

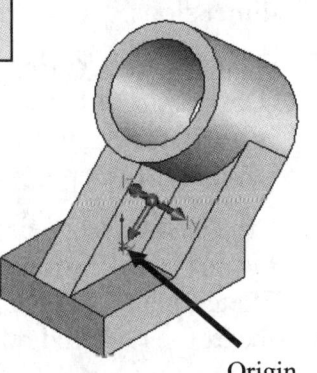

Origin

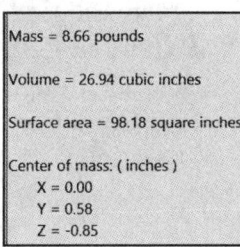

Mass = 8.66 pounds

Volume = 26.94 cubic inches

Surface area = 98.18 square inches

Center of mass: (inches)
X = 0.00
Y = 0.58
Z = -0.85

Tutorial: Basic/Intermediate Part 3-4

Build this model in SOLIDWORKS. Calculate the volume of the part and locate the Center of mass with the provided information.

1. **Create** a new part in SOLIDWORKS.

2. **Build** the illustrated model. Apply symmetry. Think about the various features that create the part. Insert six features: Extruded Base, two Extruded Cuts, Mirror, Extruded Boss, and a third Extruded Cut.

3. **Set** the document properties for the model.

4. Create **Sketch1**. Select the Top Plane as the Sketch plane. Apply symmetry. The part Origin is located in the center of the rectangle. Insert the required relations and dimensions.

5. Create the **Extruded Base** (Boss-Extrude1) feature. Blind is the default End Condition in Direction 1. Depth = .50in.

6. Create **Sketch2**. Select the top face of Boss-Extrude1 for the Sketch plane. Sketch a circle. Insert the required relations and dimensions.

7. Create the first **Extruded Cut** feature. Select Through All as End Condition in Direction1.

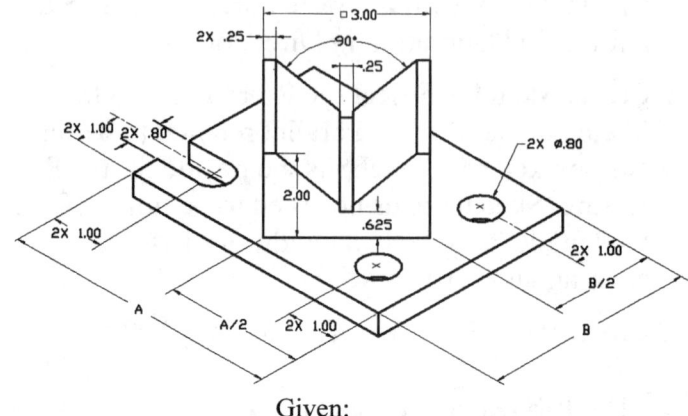

Given:
A = 6.00, B = 4.50
Material: 2014 Alloy
Plate thickness = .50
Units: IPS
Decimal places = 2

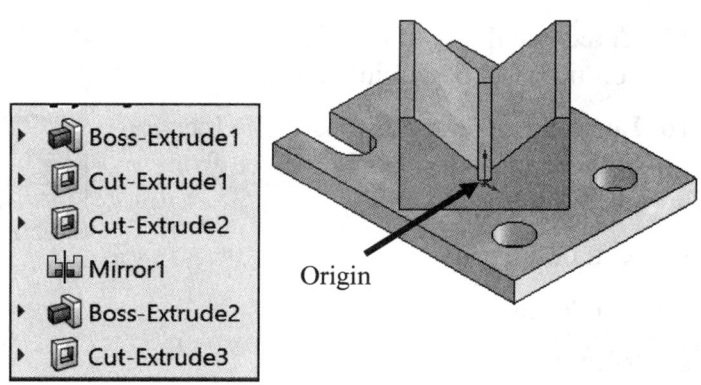

Origin

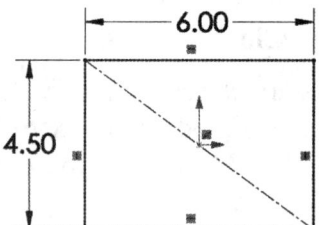

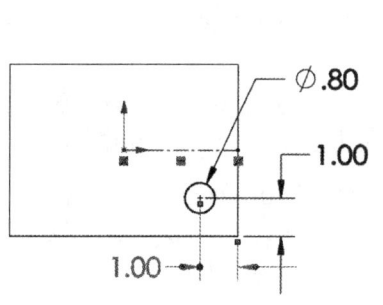

8. Create **Sketch3**. Select the top face of Boss-Extrude1 for the Sketch plane. Insert the required geometric relations and dimensions.

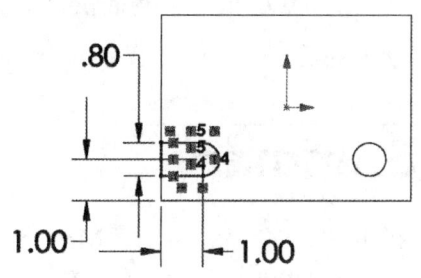

💡 Click **View, Temporary** axes to view the part temporary axes in the Graphics window.

9. Create the second **Extruded Cut** feature. Select Through All as End Condition in Direction1.

10. Create the **Mirror** feature. Mirror the two Extruded Cut features about the Front Plane.

11. Create **Sketch4**. Select the top face of Boss-Extrude1 as the Sketch plane. Apply construction geometry to center the sketch. Insert the required relations and dimensions.

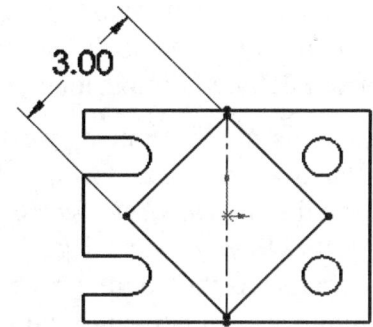

12. Create the **Extruded Boss** feature. Blind is the default End Condition in Direction 1. Depth = 2.00in.

13. Create **Sketch5**. Select the front face of Boss-Extrude as illustrated for the Sketch plane. Sketch5 is the profile for the third Extruded Cut feature. Apply construction geometry. Insert the required dimensions and relations.

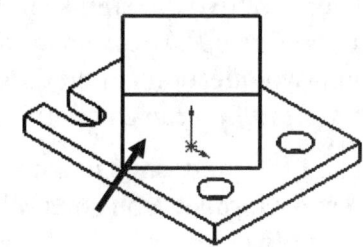

14. Create the third **Extruded Cut** feature. Through All is selected for End Condition in Direction 1 and Direction 2.

15. **Assign** 2014 Alloy material to the part.

16. **Calculate** the volume of the part. The volume = 25.12 cubic inches.

17. **Locate** the Center of mass. The location of the Center of mass is derived from the part Origin.

- X: 0.06 inches

- Y: 0.80 inches

- Z: 0.00 inches

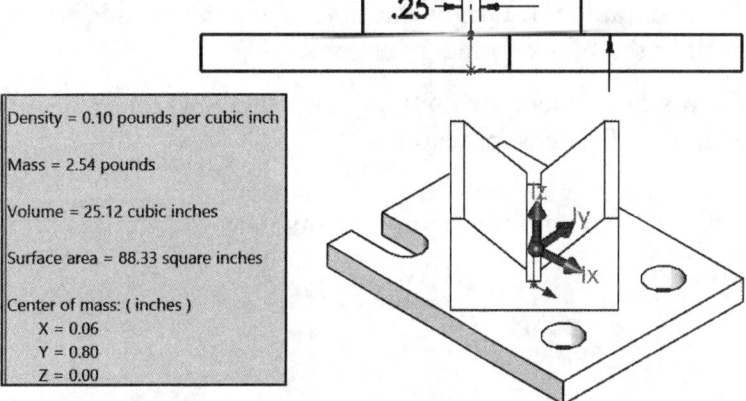

Density = 0.10 pounds per cubic inch

Mass = 2.54 pounds

Volume = 25.12 cubic inches

Surface area = 88.33 square inches

Center of mass: (inches)
  X = 0.06
  Y = 0.80
  Z = 0.00

18. **Save** the part and name it Part-Modeling 3-4.

19. **Close** the model.

Summary

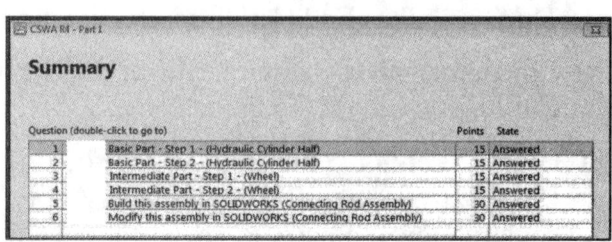

Basic Part Creation and Modification and Intermediate Part Creation and Modification are two of the five categories on the CSWA exam. This chapter covers the knowledge to create and modify models in these categories from detailed dimensioned illustrations.

The main difference between the *Basic Part Creation and Modification* category and the *Intermediate Part Creation and Modification* or the *Advance Part Creation and Modification* category is the complexity of the sketches and the number of dimensions and geometric relations along with an increase in the number of features.

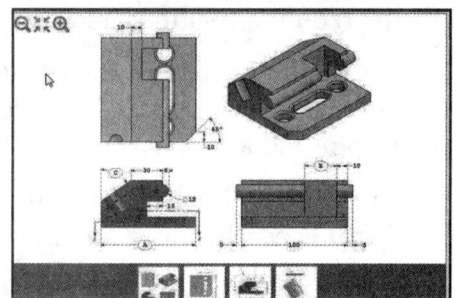

There are two questions on the CSWA exam (part 1) in the *Basic Part Creation and Modification* category and two questions in the *Intermediate Part Creation and Modification* category.

The first question is in a multiple choice single answer format. You should be within 1% of the multiple choice answer before you move on to the modification single answer section, (fill in the blank format).

Each question is worth fifteen (15) points for a total of thirty (30) points. You are required to build a model with six or more features and to answer a question either on the overall mass, volume, or the location of the Center of mass for the created model relative to the default part Origin location. You are then requested to modify the part and answer a fill in the blank format question.

At this time, there are no modeling questions on the exam that require you to use Sheet Metal, Loft or Swept features.

☀ There are no Surfacing or Boundary feature questions on the CSWA exam.

Questions

1. In Tutorial, Volume/Center of mass 3-2 you built the model using the FeatureManager that had three features vs. four features in the FeatureManager.

Calculate the overall mass of the part, volume, and locate the Center of mass with the provided information using the Option1 FeatureManager.

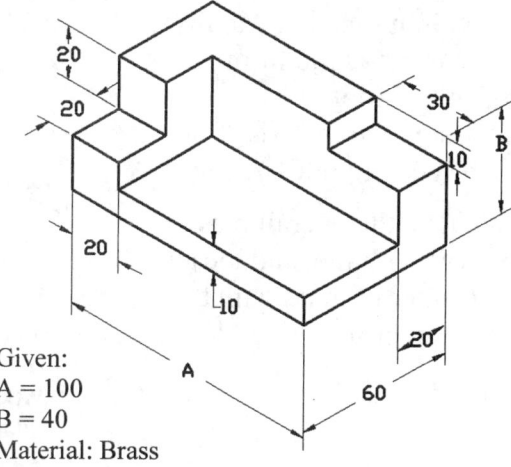

Given:
A = 100
B = 40
Material: Brass
Density = .0085 g/mm^3
Units: MMGS

2. In Tutorial, Mass/Volume 3-4 you built the model using the FeatureManager that had three features vs. four features.

Calculate the overall mass of the part, volume, and locate the Center of mass with the provided information using the Option3 FeatureManager.

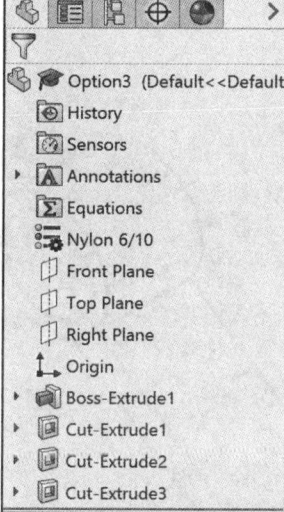

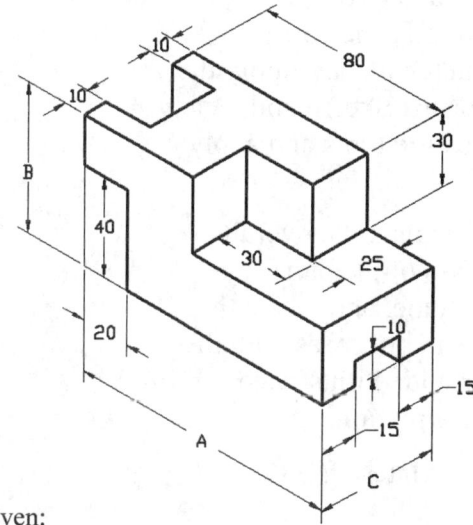

Given:
A = 110, B = 60, C = 50
Material: Nylon 6/10
Density = .0014 g/mm^3
Units: MMGS

3. In Tutorial, Basic/Intermediate 3-4 you built the illustrated model. Modify the plate thickness from .50in to .25in. Modify the Sketch5 angle from 90deg to 75deg. Re-assign the material from 2014 Alloy to 6061 Alloy.

Calculate the overall mass of the part, volume, and locate the Center of mass with the provided information.

Given:
A = 6.00, B = 4.50
Material: 2014 Alloy
Plate thickness = .50
Units: IPS
Decimal places = 2

4. Build this model: Set document properties. Identify the correct Sketch planes, apply the correct Sketch and Feature tools and apply material.

Calculate the overall mass of the part, volume, and locate the Center of mass with the provided illustrated information.

- Material: 6061 Alloy

- Units: MMGS

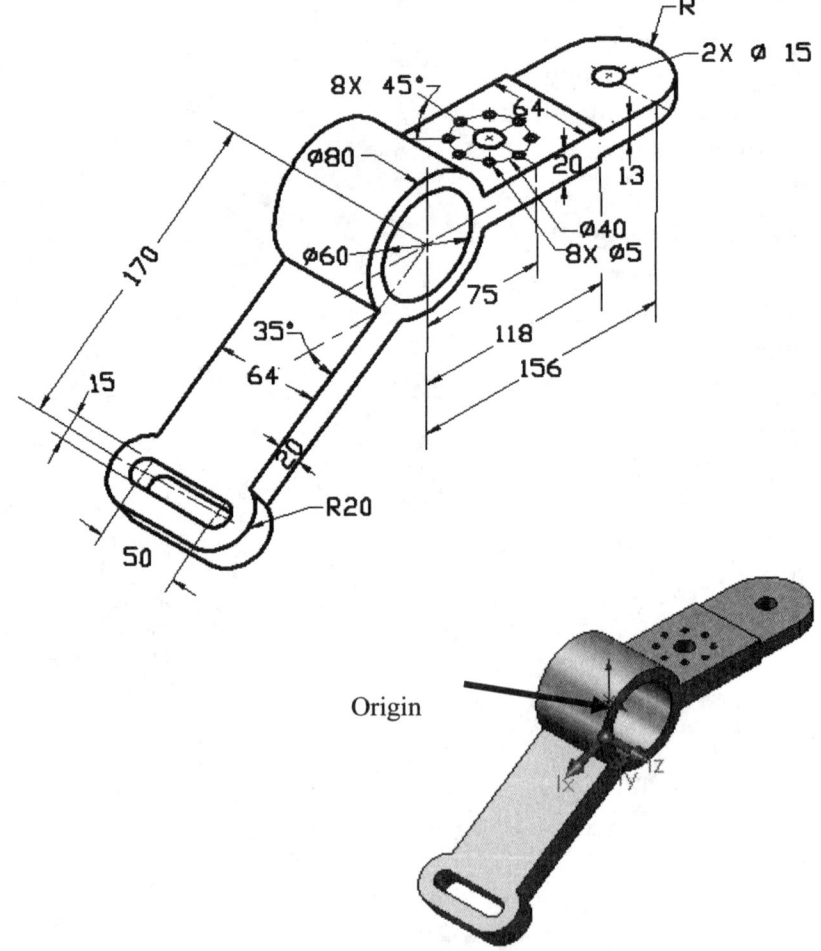

5. Build this model. Set document properties and identify the correct Sketch planes. Apply the correct Sketch and Feature tools, and apply material.

Calculate the overall mass of the part, volume, and locate the Center of mass with the provided information.

- Material: 6061 Alloy

- Units: MMGS

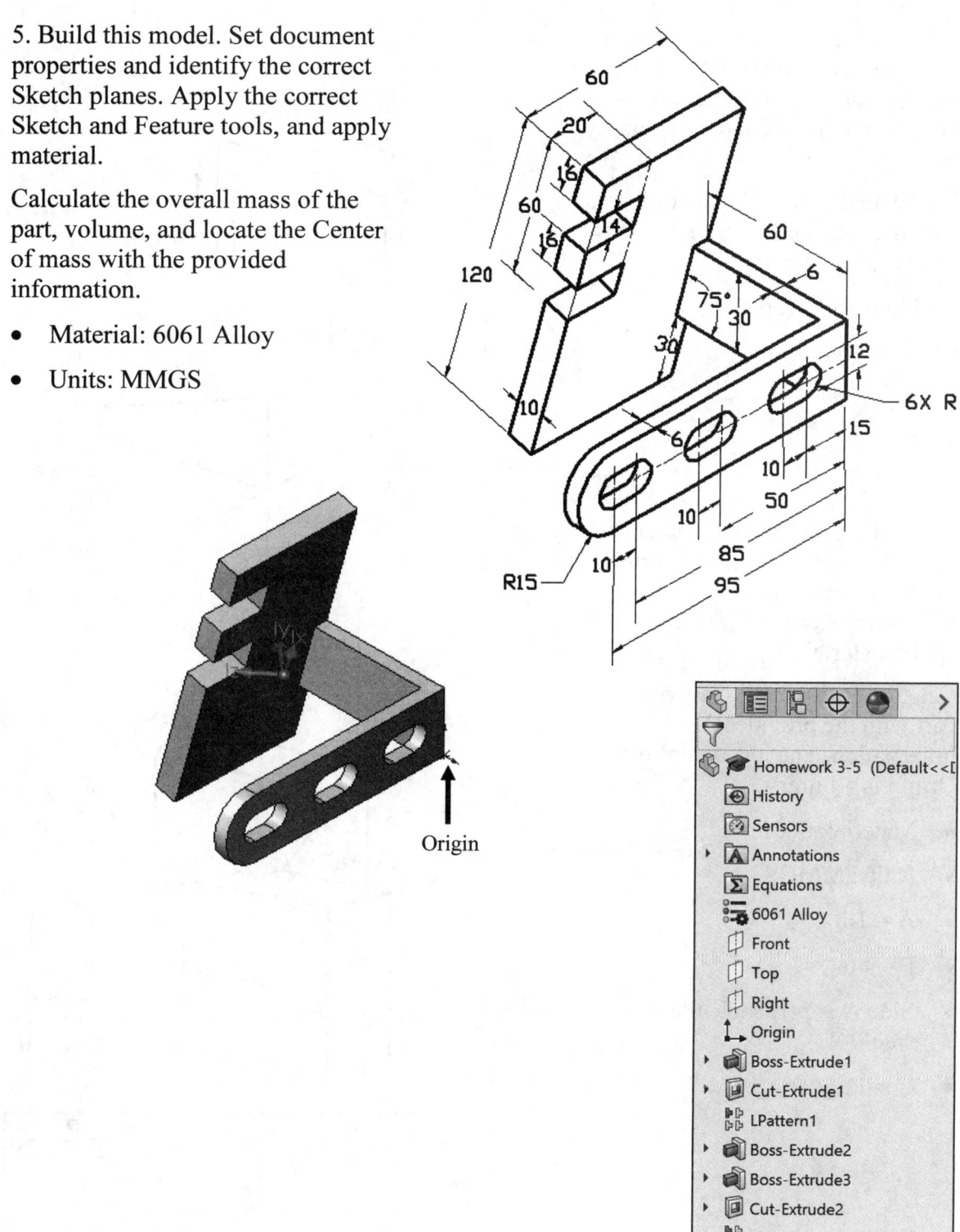

Origin

6. Build this model. Set document properties and identify the correct Sketch planes. Apply the correct Sketch and Feature tools, and apply material.

Calculate the overall mass of the part with the provided information. Note: The Origin is arbitrary.

- Material: Copper
- Units: MMGS
- A = 100
- B = 80

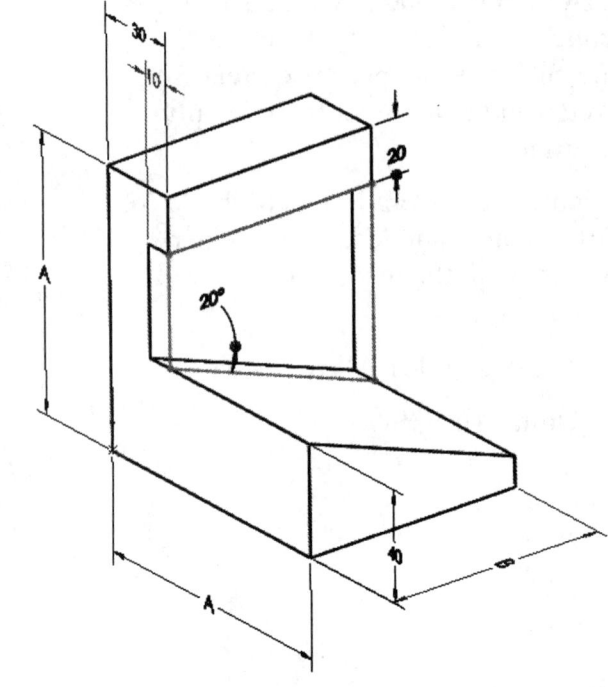

7. Build this model. Set document properties and identify the correct Sketch planes. Apply the correct Sketch and Feature tools, and apply material.

Calculate the overall mass of the part with the provided information. The location of the Origin is arbitrary.

- Material: 6061
- Units: MMGS
- A = 16
- B = 40
- Side A is perpendicular to side B
- C = 18

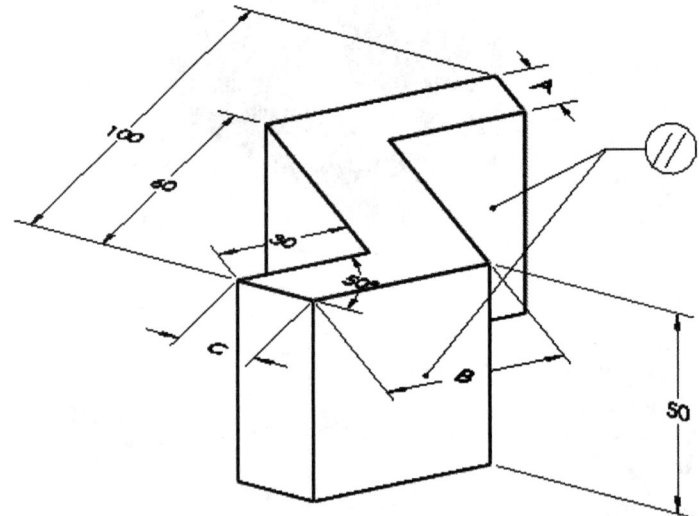

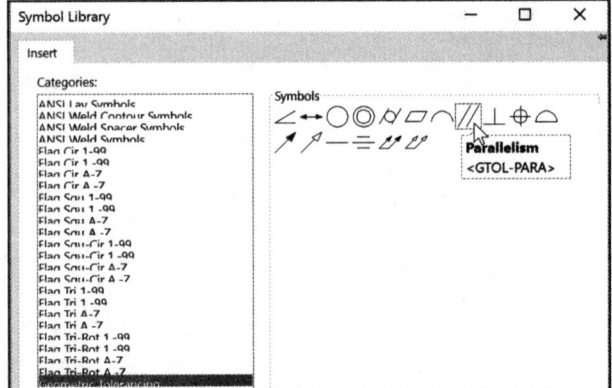

8. Build this model in SOLIDWORKS. Set document properties and identify the correct Sketch planes. Apply the correct Sketch and Feature tools, and apply material.

Calculate the overall mass of the part, volume, and locate the Center of mass with the provided information.

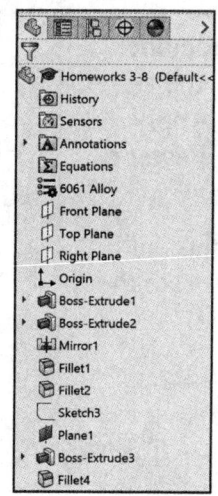

- Material: 6061

- Units: IPS

- View the provided drawing views for details.

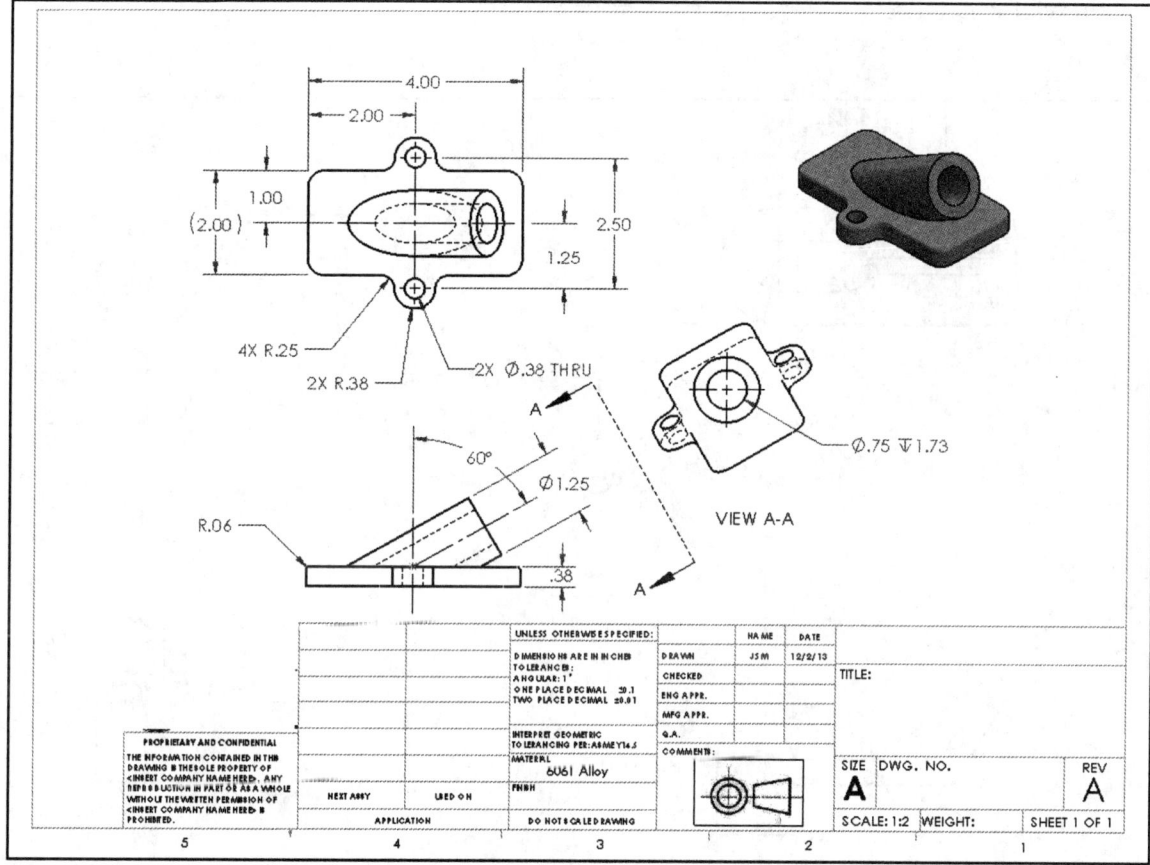

9. Build this model in SOLIDWORKS. Set document properties and identify the correct Sketch planes. Apply the correct Sketch and Feature tools, and apply material.

Calculate the overall mass of the part, volume, and locate the Center of mass with the provided information.

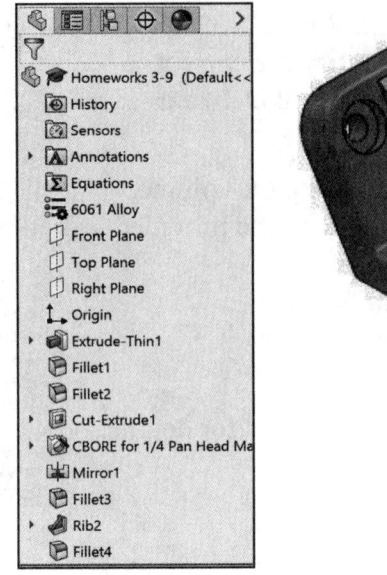

- Material: 6061

- Units: IPS

- View the provided drawing views for details.

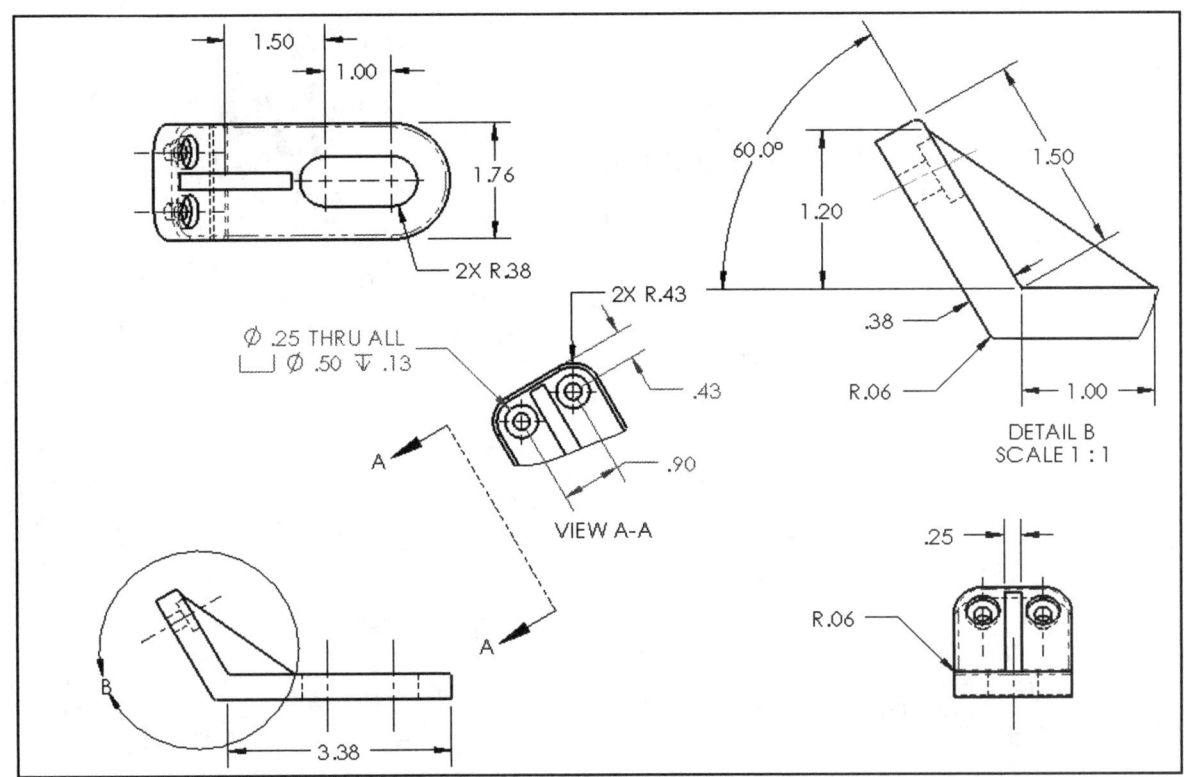

10. Build the illustrated model using SOLIDWORKS.

Calculate the overall mass and volume of the part with the provided information.

- Precision for linear dimensions = **2**.
- Material: **AISI 304**.
- Units: **MMGS**.
- All Holes ↧ **25**mm.
- All Rounds **5**mm.
- All Holes **Ø4**mm.

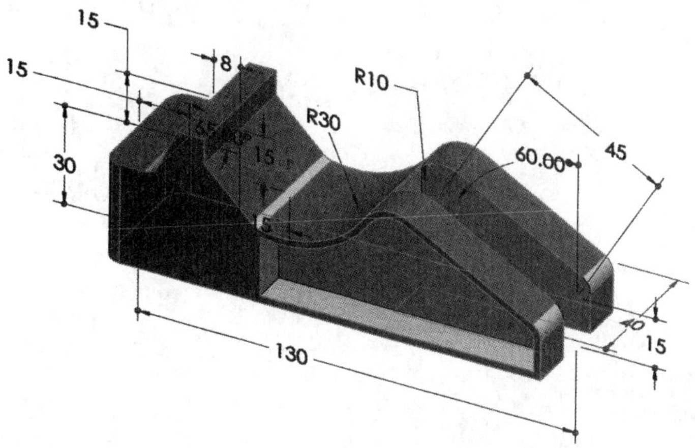

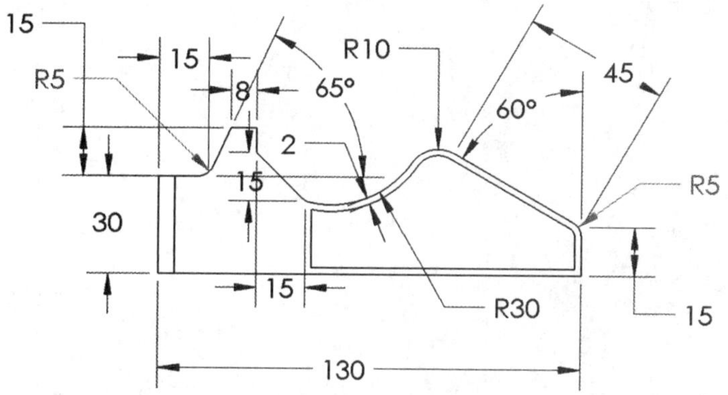

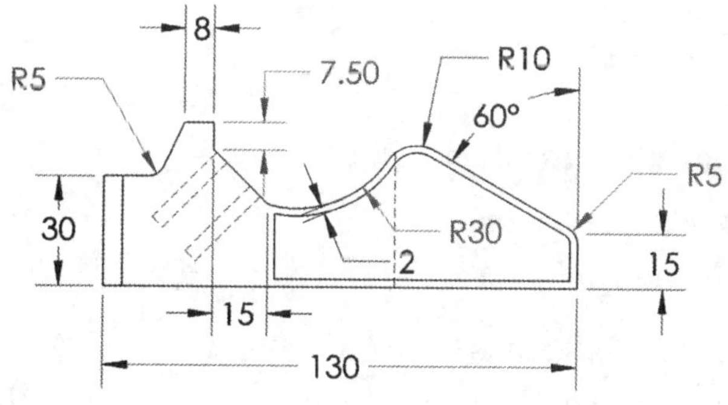

Front views

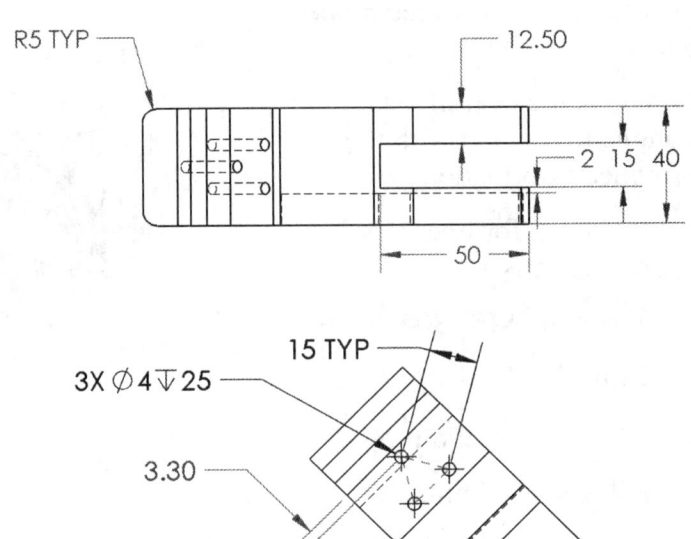

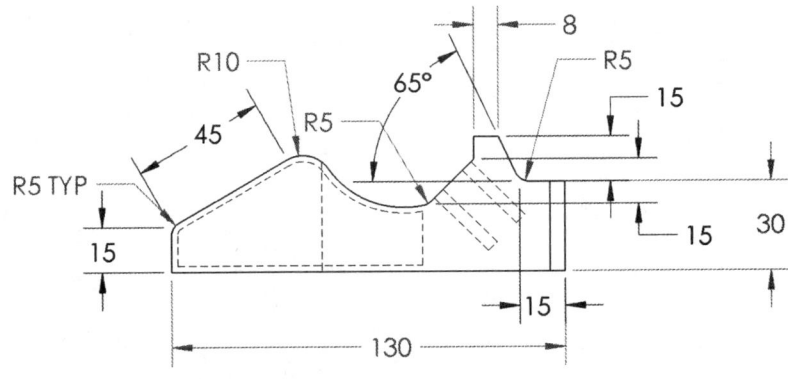

Top and Auxiliary view

Calculate the mass:

A = 888.48grams

B = 990.50grams

C = 788.48grams

D = 820.57grams

Back view

If you don't find your answer (within 1%) in the multiple choice single answer format section, recheck your solid model for precision and accuracy. It could be as simple as missing a few fillets.

Calculate the volume:

A = 102259.43 cubic millimeters
B = 133359.47 cubic millimeters
C = 111059.43 cubic millimeters
D = 125059.49 cubic millimeters

Create a new coordinate system.

Center a new coordinate system with the provided illustration. The new coordinate system location is at the front right bottom point (vertex) of the model.

Enter the Center of Mass:

X = -15.59 millimeters

Y = 15.93 millimeters

Z = -2.65 millimeters

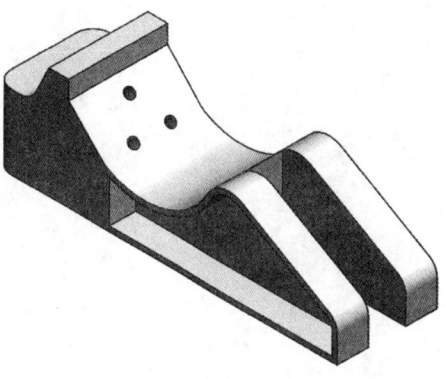

Modify the model:

- Modify all fillets (rounds) to 7mm.
- Modify the overall length to 140mm.
- Modify material to 1060 alloy.

Enter the mass:

309.75

Enter the volume:

114721.22

 If you don't find your answer (within 1%) in the multiple choice single answer format section, recheck your solid model for precision and accuracy. It could be as simple as missing a few fillets.

11. Build the illustrated model using SOLIDWORKS.

Calculate the overall mass and volume of the part with the provided information.

- Precision for linear dimensions = **2**.

- Material: **1060 Alloy**.

- Units: **MMGS**.

- TYP $\varnothing 12$.

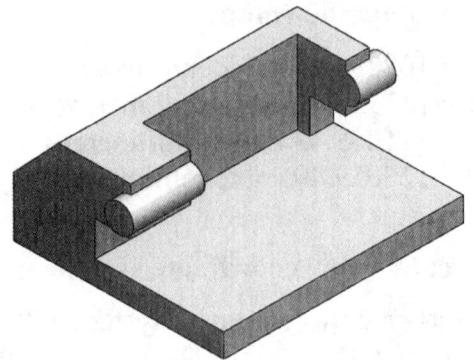

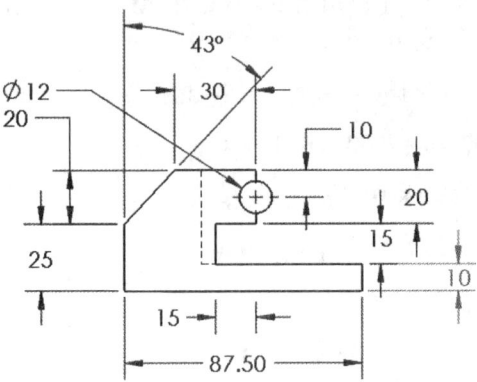

Front view

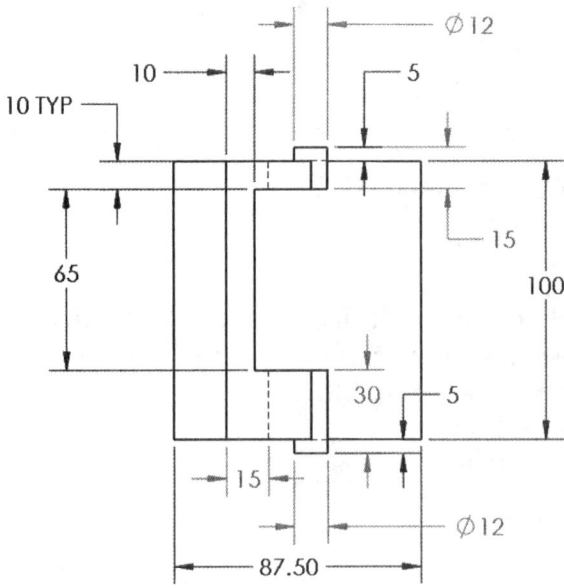

Top view

Calculate the mass:

A = 600.92 grams

B = 509.92 grams

C = 701.93 grams

D = 599.34 grams

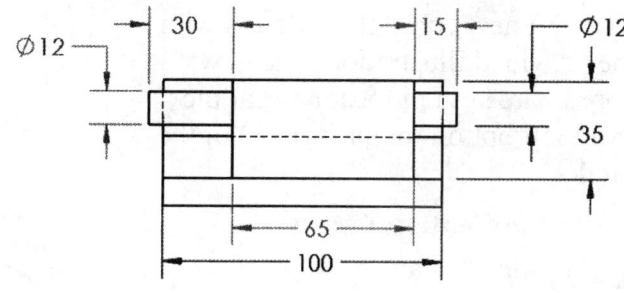

Calculate the volume:

A = 188860.93 cubic millimeters
B = 196660.93 cubic millimeters
C = 198880.65 cubic millimeters
D = 230021.67 cubic millimeters

Right view

Modify the model:

- Modify material to Plain Carbon Steel.

- Modify TYP Hole diameter from TYP ϕ 12 to TPY ϕ 10.

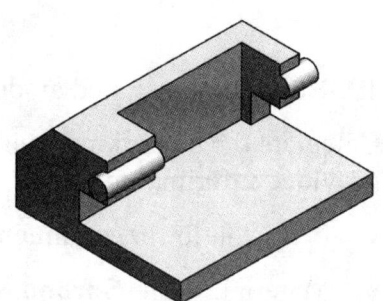

Enter the mass:

1465.70

Enter the volume:

187910.60

Create a new coordinate system.

Center a new coordinate system with the provided illustration. The new coordinate system location is at the front left bottom point (vertex) of the model.

Enter the Center of Mass:

X = 31.39

Y = 16.55

Z = -48.63

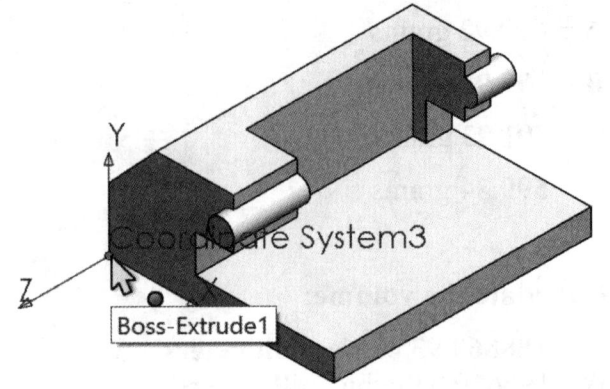

12. Build the illustrated model using SOLIDWORKS.

Calculate the overall mass and volume of the part with the provided information.

- Precision for linear dimensions = **2**.

- Material: **Plain Carbon Steel**.

- Units: **MMGS**.

- The part is **symmetrical** about the Front Plane.

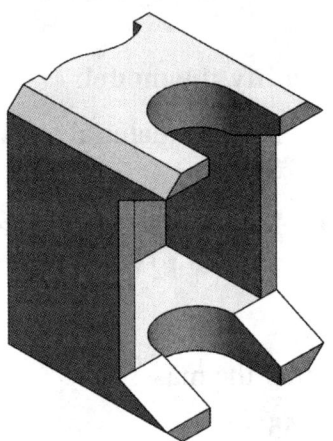

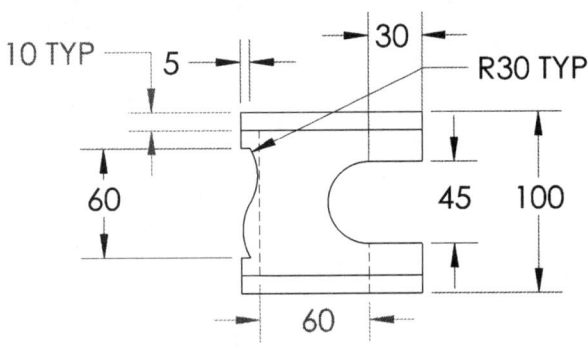

Top view

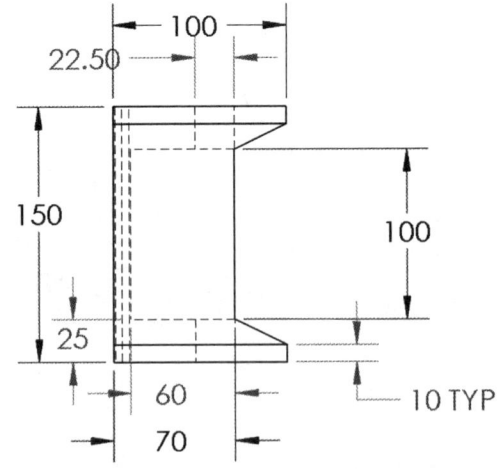

Front view

Calculate the mass:

A = 4411.5 grams

B = 4079.32 grams

C = 4234.30 grams

D = 5322.00 grams

Calculate the volume:

A = 522989.22 cubic millimeters
B = 555655.11 cubic millimeters
C = 511233.34 cubic millimeters
D = 655444.00 cubic millimeters

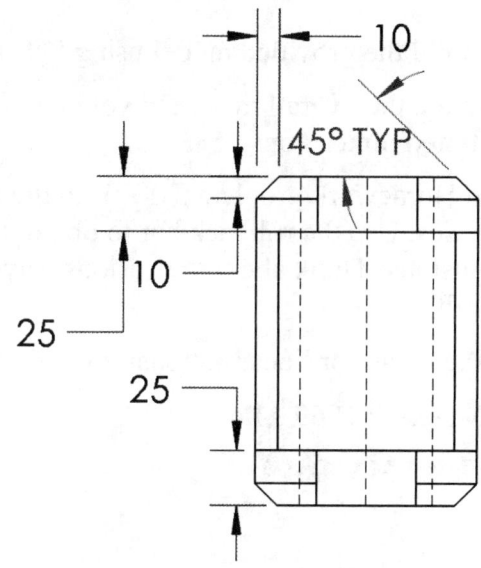

Right view

Create a new coordinate system.

Center a new coordinate system with the provided illustration. The new coordinate system location is at the back right bottom point (vertex) of the model.

Enter the Center of Mass:

X = -64.9

Y = 75.00

Z = 40.70

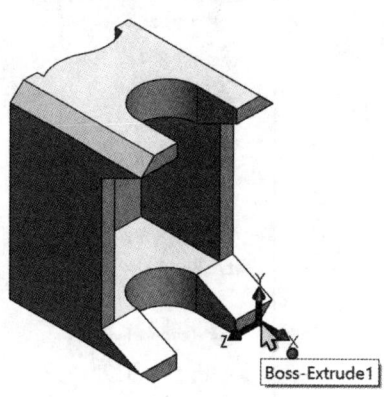

13. Build the provided model using SOLIDWORKS.

Calculate the overall mass and volume of the part. There are no illustrated dimensions.

Open Homework problem 3-13 from the Homework chapter exercises. Use the rollback bar to obtain features and dimensions. Think about the various ways that this model can be built.

- Precision for linear dimensions = **2**.

- Material: **1060 Alloy**.

- Units: **MMGS**.

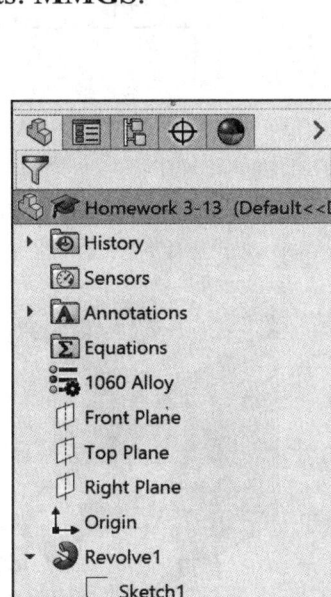

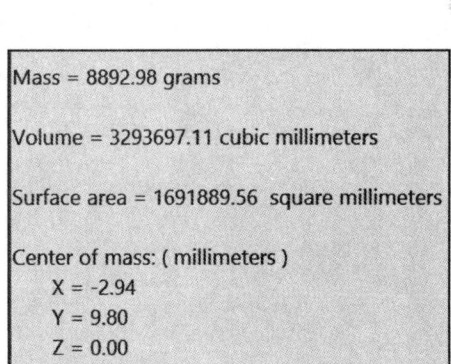

Mass = 8892.98 grams

Volume = 3293697.11 cubic millimeters

Surface area = 1691889.56 square millimeters

Center of mass: (millimeters)
   X = -2.94
   Y = 9.80
   Z = 0.00

Screen shots from an older CSWA exam for a Basic/Intermediate part.

Click on the additional views to understand the part and to provide information. Read each question carefully.

Understand the dimensions, center of mass and units. Apply needed materials.

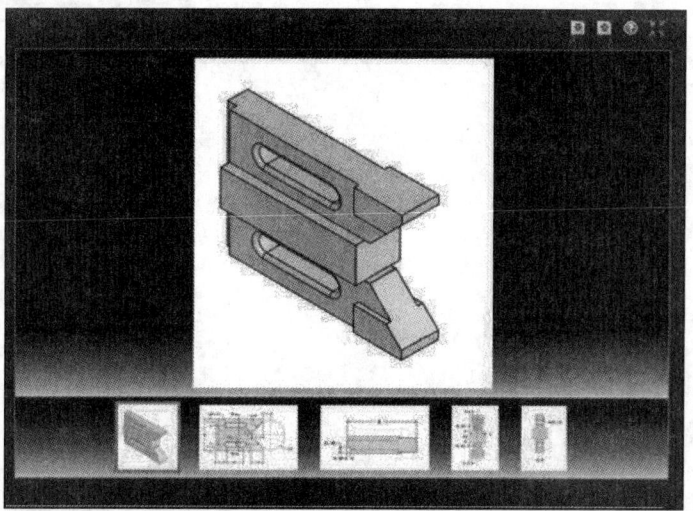

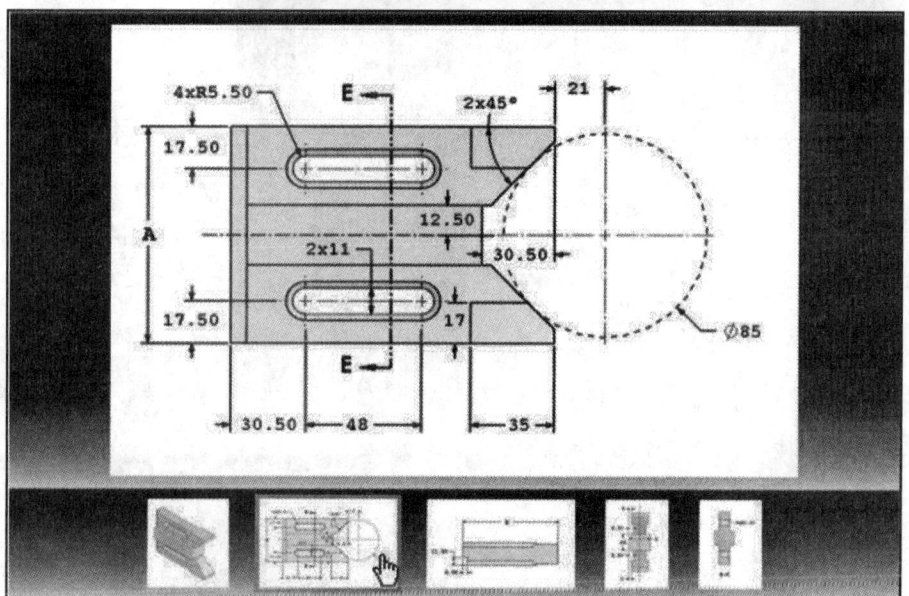

Screen shots from the exam

💡 Zoom in on the part or view if needed.

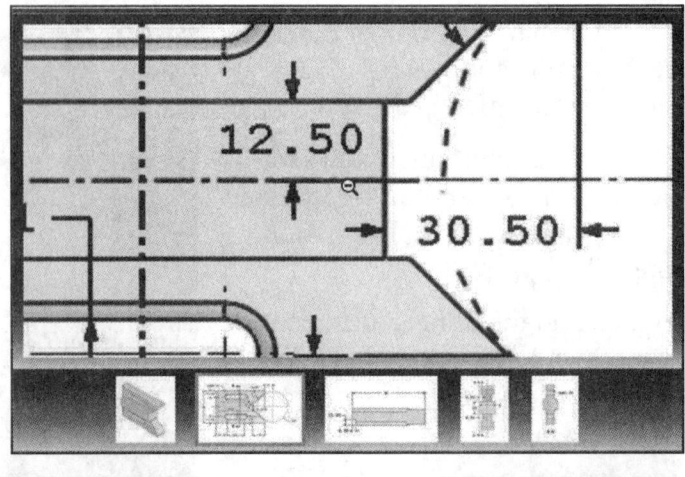

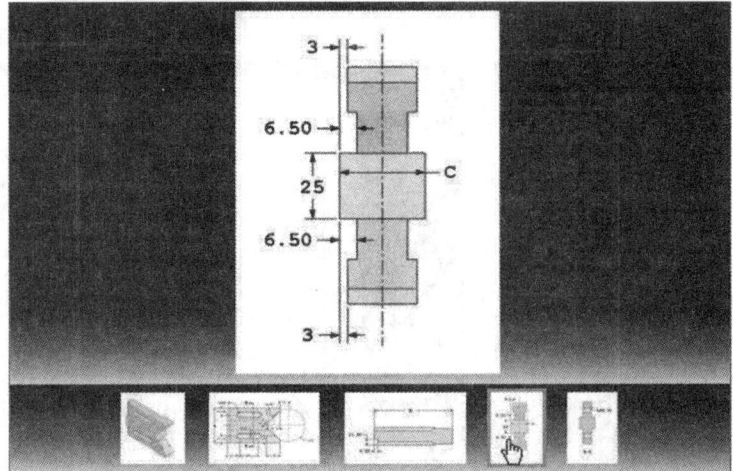

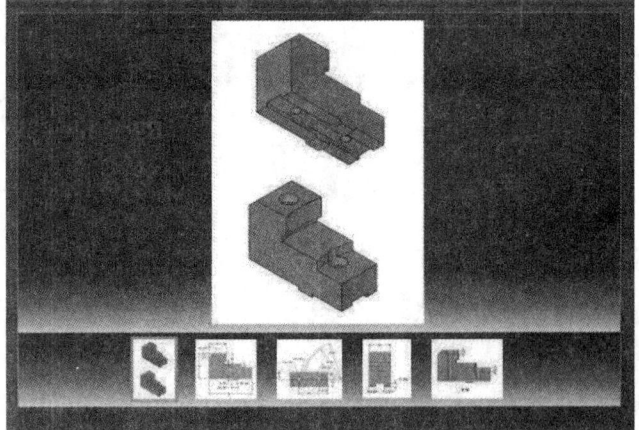

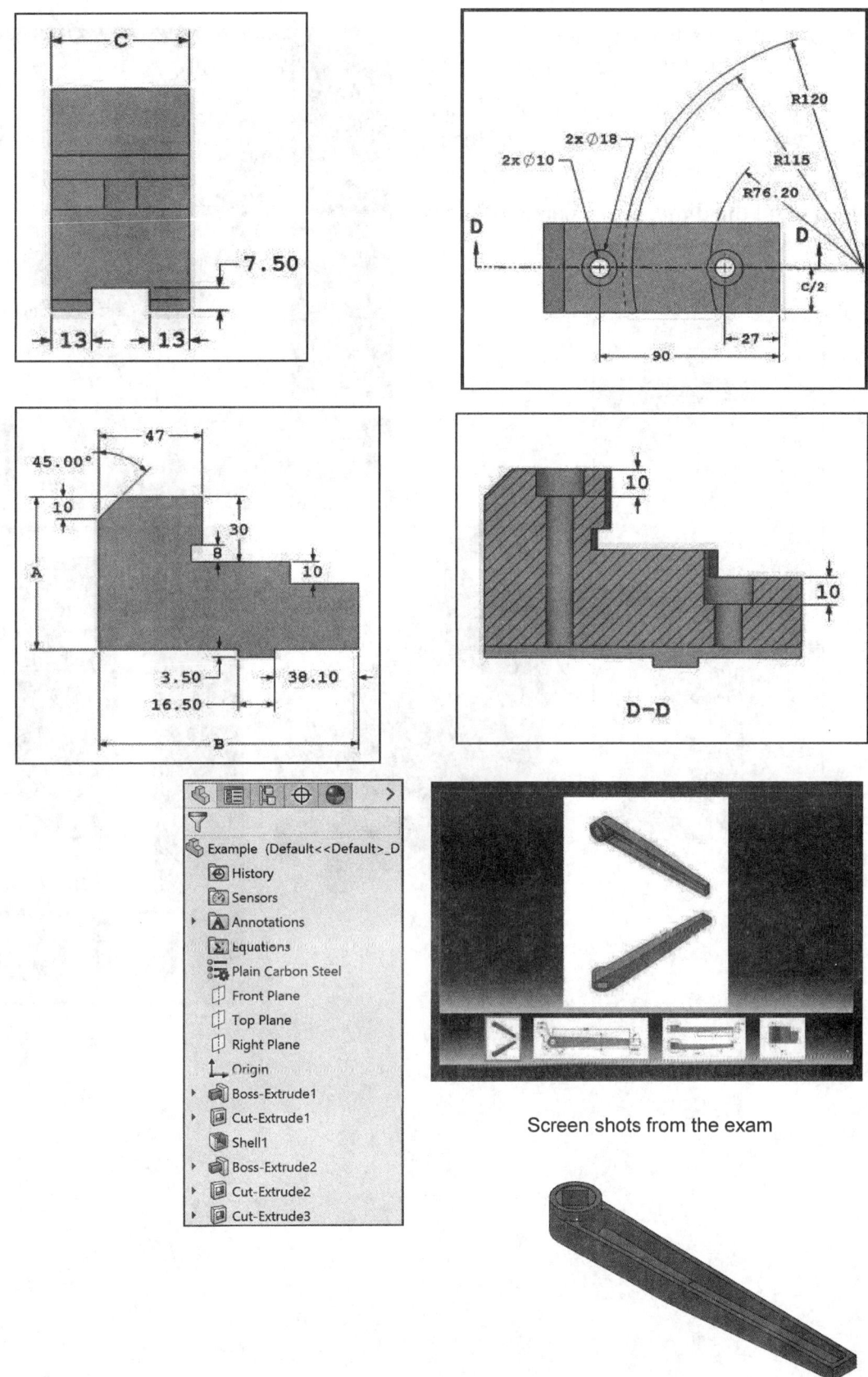

Screen shots from the exam

Screen shots from an older CSWA exam for a Basic/Intermediate part.

Click on the additional views to understand the part and to provide information. Read each question carefully.

Understand the dimensions, center of mass and units. Apply needed materials.

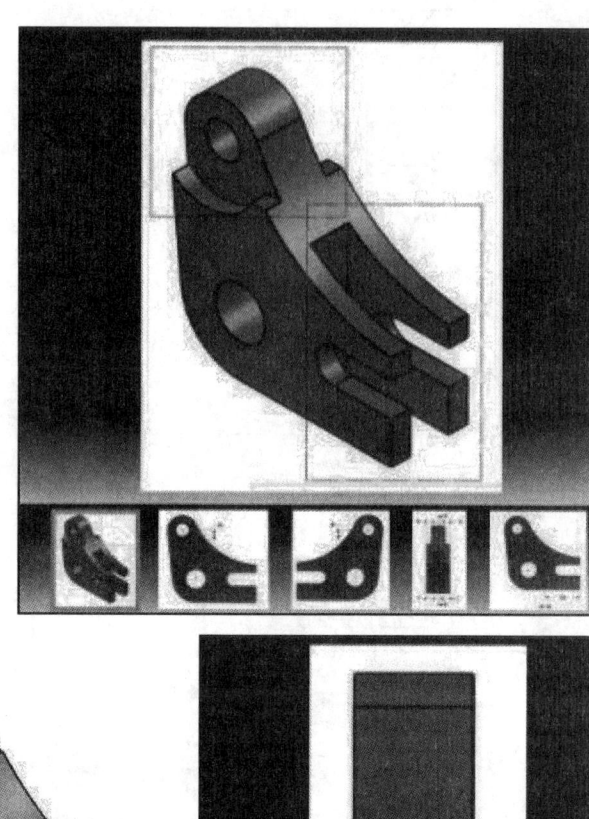

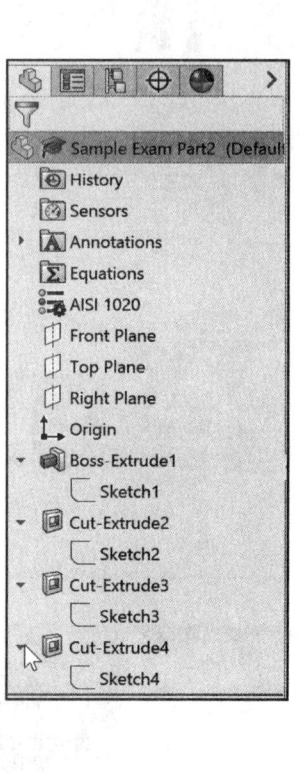

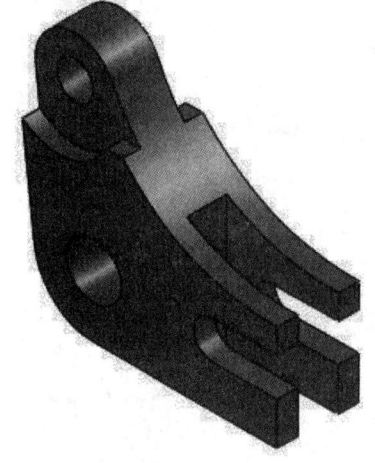

Screen shot from the new sample CSWA exam for a Basic/Intermediate part.

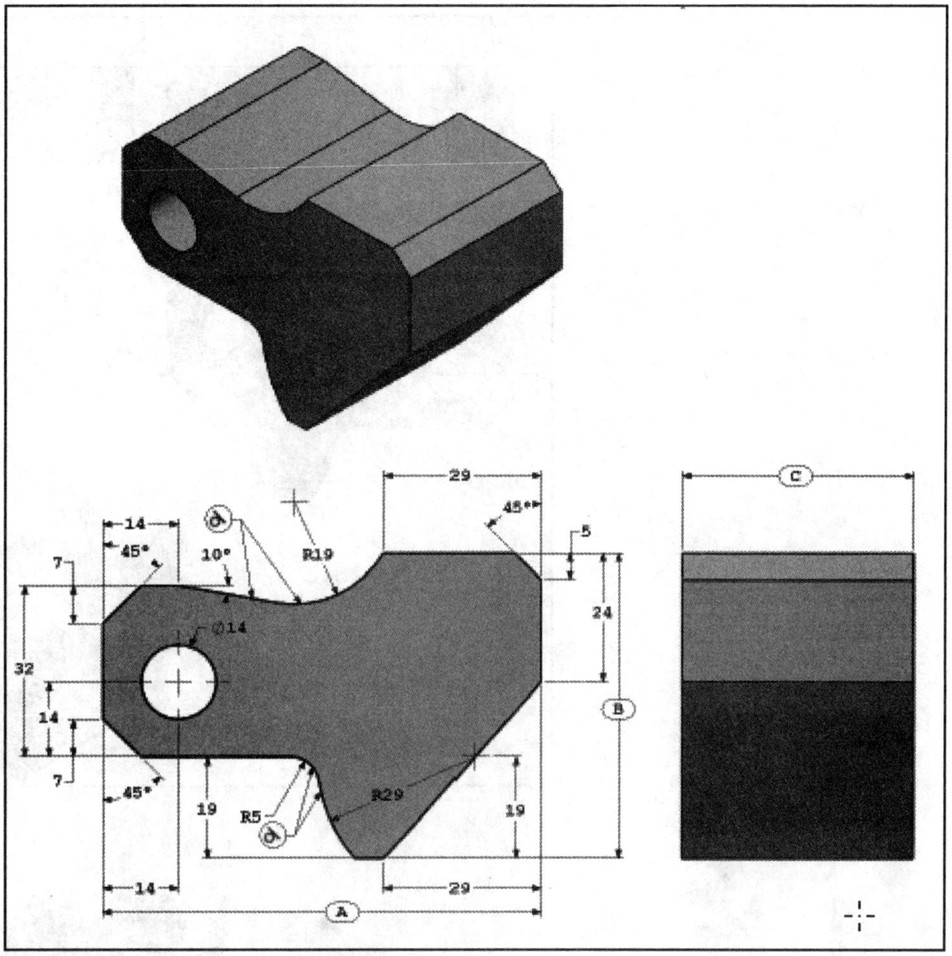

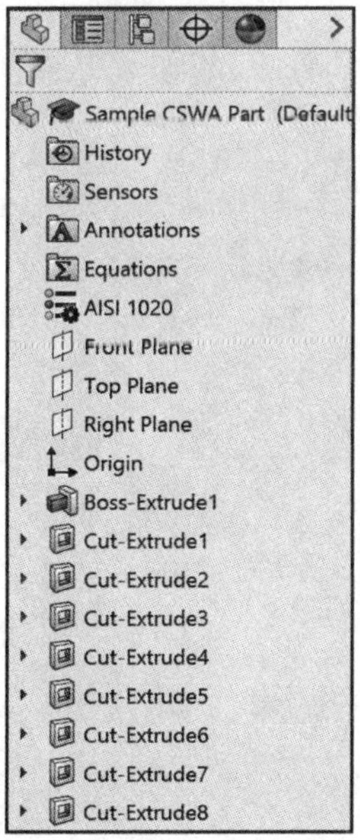

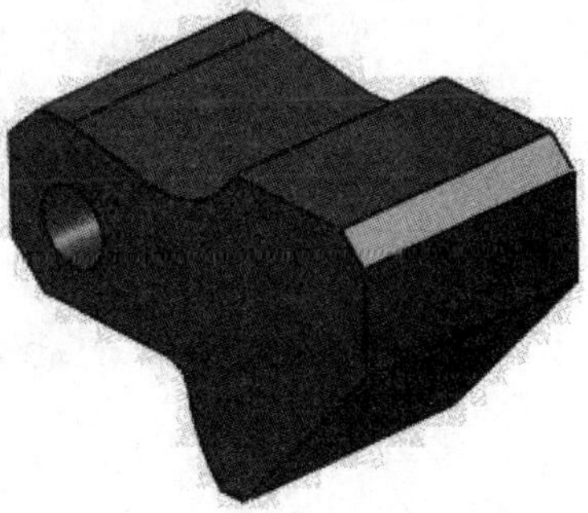

Screen shot from the new sample CSWA exam for a Basic/Intermediate part.

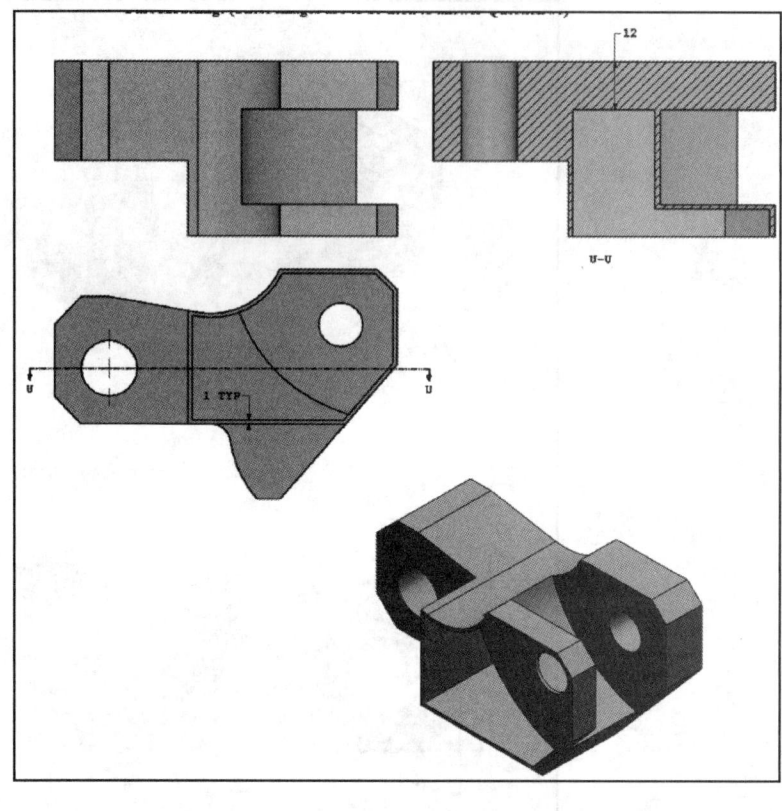

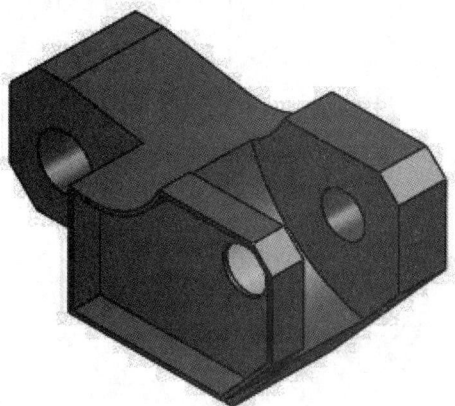

CHAPTER 4 - ADVANCED PART CREATION AND MODIFICATION

Objectives

Advanced Part Creation and Modification is one of the five categories on the CSWA exam.

The main difference between the *Advanced Part Creation and Modification* and the *Basic Part Creation and Modification* or the *Intermediate Part Creation and Modification* category is the complexity of the sketches and the number of dimensions and geometric relations along with an increased number of features.

There are three questions on the CSWA exam (part 2) in this category. The first question is in a multiple choice single answer format and the other two questions (Modification of the model) are in the fill in the blank format.

Each question is worth fifteen (15) points for a total of forty five (45) points.

You are required to build a model with six or more features and to answer a question either on the overall mass, volume, or the location of the Center of mass for the created model relative to the default part Origin location. You are then requested to modify the model and answer fill in the blank format questions.

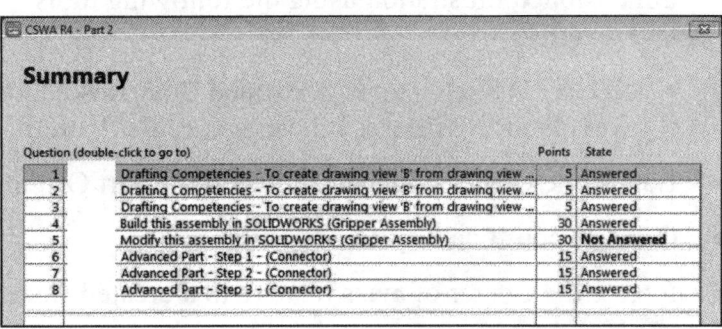

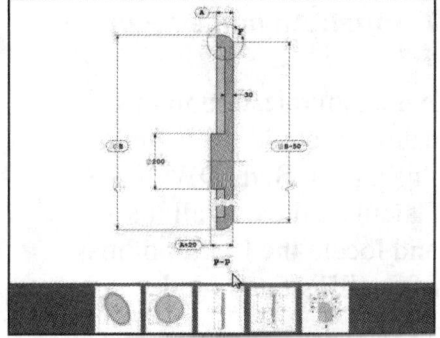

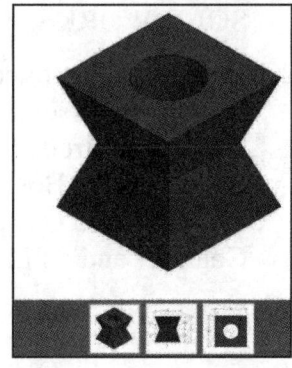

Screen shots from an exam

On the completion of the chapter, you will be able to:

- Specify Document Properties.

- Interpret Engineering terminology.

- Build an advanced part from a detailed dimensioned illustration using the following tools and features:

  - 2D & 3D Sketch tools, Extruded Boss/Base, Extruded Cut, Fillet, Mirror, Revolved Boss/Base, Linear & Circular Pattern, Chamfer and Revolved Cut.

- Locate the Center of mass relative to the part Origin.

- Create a coordinate system location.

- Locate the Center of mass relative to a created Coordinate system.

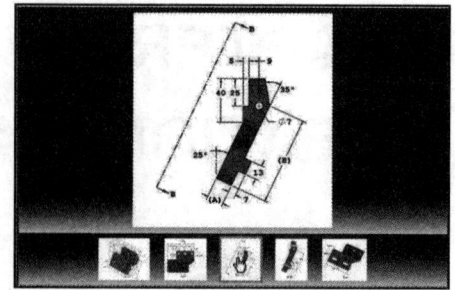

In the *Advanced Part Creation and Modification* category; there are two dimension modification questions based on the first (multiple choice) question. You should be within 1% of the multiple choice answer before you go on to the modification single answer section.

Build an Advanced Part from a detailed dimensioned illustration

Tutorial: Advanced Part 4-1

An exam question in this category could read: Build this part in SOLIDWORKS. Calculate the overall mass and locate the Center of mass of the illustrated model.

1. **Create** a new part in SOLIDWORKS.

2. **Build** the illustrated model. Insert seven features: Extruded Base, two Extruded Bosses, two Extruded Cuts, a Chamfer and a Fillet.

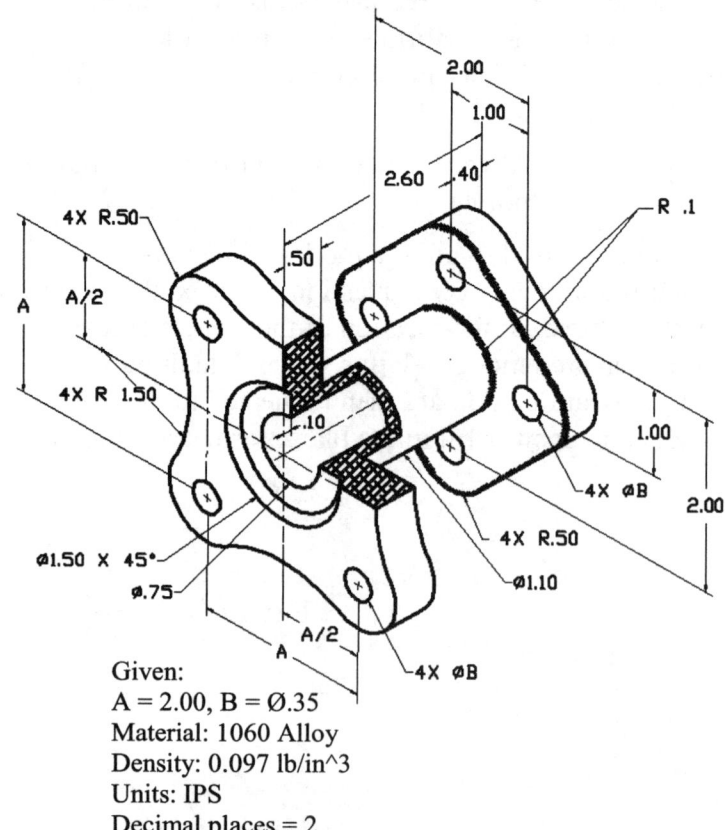

Given:
A = 2.00, B = Ø.35
Material: 1060 Alloy
Density: 0.097 lb/in^3
Units: IPS
Decimal places = 2

Think about the steps that you would take to build the illustrated part. Identify the location of the part Origin. Start with the back base flange. Review the provided dimensions and annotations in the part illustration.

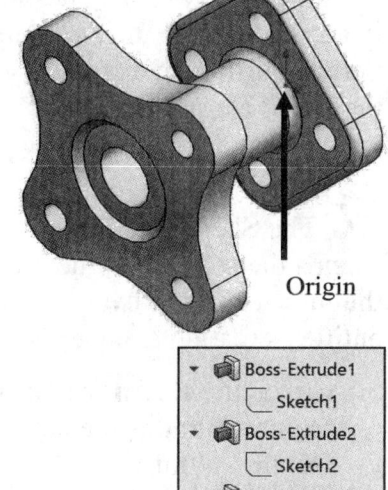

Origin

💡 The main difference between the *Advanced Part Creation and Modification* and the *Basic Part Creation and Modification* or the *Intermediate Part Creation and Modification* category is the complexity of the sketches and the number of dimensions and geometric relations along with an increased number of features.

💡 All SW models (initial and final) are provided. Copy the folders and model files to your local hard drive.

3. **Set** the document properties for the model.

4. Create **Sketch1**. Sketch1 is the Base sketch. Select the Front Plane as the Sketch plane. Apply construction geometry. Sketch a horizontal and vertical centerline. Sketch four circles. Insert an Equal relation. Insert a Symmetric relation about the vertical and horizontal centerlines. Sketch two top angled lines and a tangent arc. Apply the Mirror Sketch tool. Complete the sketch. Insert the required geometric relations and dimensions.

💡 In a Symmetric relation, the selected items remain equidistant from the centerline, on a line perpendicular to the centerline. Sketch entities to select: a centerline and two points, lines, arcs or ellipses.

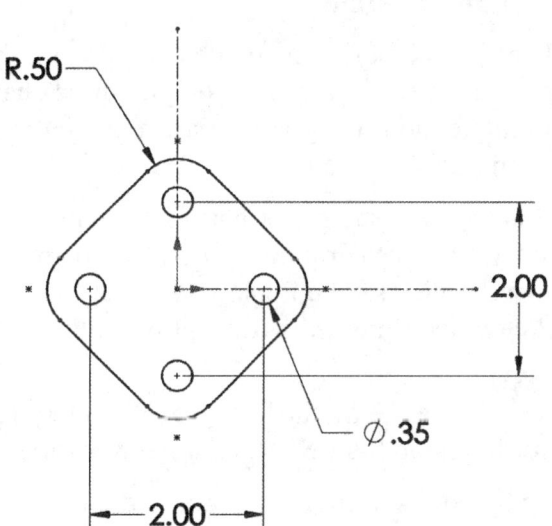

R.50

2.00

∅.35

2.00

In the exam, you are allowed to answer the questions in any order. Use the Summary Screen during the exam to view the list of all questions you have or have not answered.

The Sketch Fillet tool rounds the selected corner at the intersection of two sketch entities, creating a tangent arc.

Summary

Question (double-click to go to)		Points	State
1	Drafting Competencies - To create drawing view 'B' from drawing view ...	5	Answered
2	Drafting Competencies - To create drawing view 'B' from drawing view ...	5	Answered
3	Drafting Competencies - To create drawing view 'B' from drawing view ...	5	Answered
4	Build this assembly in SOLIDWORKS (Gripper Assembly)	30	Answered
5	Modify this assembly in SOLIDWORKS (Gripper Assembly)	30	**Not Answered**
6	Advanced Part - Step 1 - (Connector)	15	Answered
7	Advanced Part - Step 2 - (Connector)	15	Answered
8	Advanced Part - Step 3 - (Connector)	15	Answered

5. Create the **Extruded Base** feature. Boss-Extrude1 is the Base feature. Blind is the default End Condition in Direction 1. Depth = .40in.

6. Create **Sketch2**. Select the front face of Boss-Extrude1 as the Sketch plane. Sketch a circle. Insert the required geometric relation and dimension.

7. Create the first **Extruded Boss** feature. Blind is the default End Condition in Direction 1. The Extrude feature is the tube between the two flanges. Depth = 1.70in. Note: 1.70in = 2.60in - (.50in + .40in).

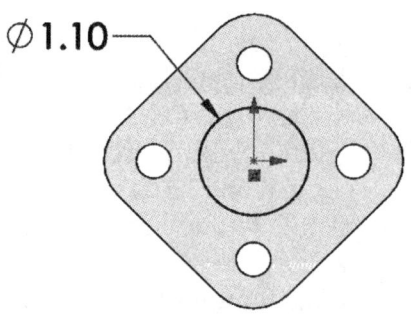

Ø 1.10

The complexity of the models along with the features progressively increases throughout this chapter to simulate the final types of parts that could be provided on the CSWA exam.

When you create a new part or assembly, the three default Planes (Front, Right and Top) are aligned with specific views. The Plane you select for the Base sketch determines the orientation of the part.

There are no Surfacing or Boundary feature questions on the CSWA exam at this time.

This book is designed to expose the new user to many tools, techniques and procedures. It may not always use the most direct tool or process.

Screen shots in the book were made using SOLIDWORKS 2016 SP2 and SOLIDWORKS 2017 SP0 running Windows® 10.

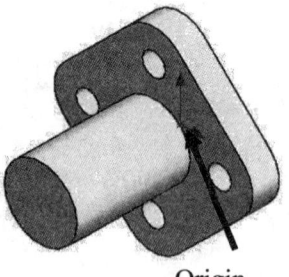

Origin

8. Create **Sketch3**. Select the front circular face of Boss-Extrude2 as the Sketch plane. Sketch a horizontal and vertical centerline. Sketch the top two circles. Insert an Equal and Symmetric relation between the two circles. Mirror the top two circles about the horizontal centerline. Insert dimensions to locate the circles from the Origin. Apply either the 3 Point Arc or the Centerpoint Arc Sketch tool. The center point of the Tangent Arc is aligned with a Vertical relation to the Origin. Complete the sketch.

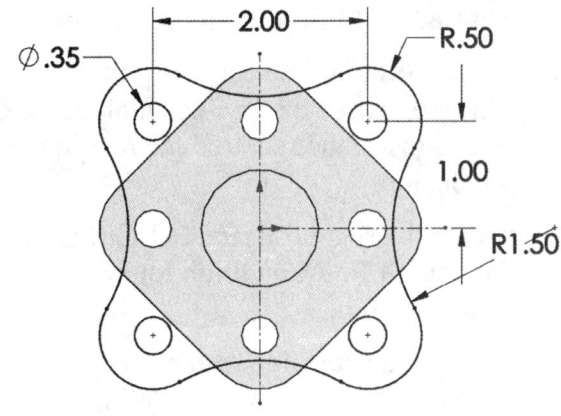

🔅 Use the Centerpoint Arc Sketch tool to create an arc from a: centerpoint, a start point, and an end point.

🔅 Apply the Tangent Arc Sketch tool to create an arc, tangent to a sketch entity.

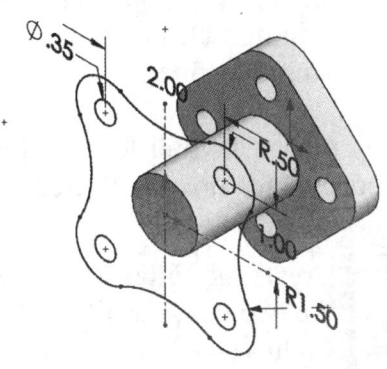

The Arc PropertyManager controls the properties of a sketched Centerpoint Arc, Tangent Arc, and 3 Point Arc.

9. Create the second **Extruded Boss** feature. Blind is the default End Condition in Direction 1. Depth = .50in.

10. Create **Sketch4**. Select the front face of the Extrude feature as the Sketch plane. Sketch a circle. Insert the required geometric relation and dimension.

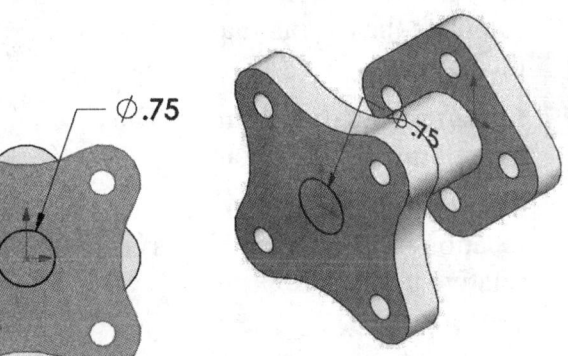

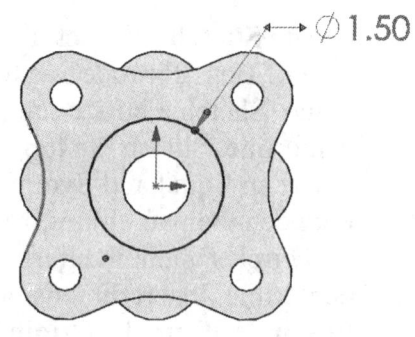

11. Create the first **Extruded Cut** feature. Select the Through All End Condition for Direction 1.

12. Create **Sketch5**. Select the front face of the Extrude feature as the Sketch plane. Sketch a circle. Insert the required geometric relation and dimension.

13. Create the second **Extruded Cut** feature. Blind is the default End Condition for Direction1. Depth = .10in.

14. Create the **Chamfer** feature. In order to have the outside circle 1.50in, select the inside edge of the sketched circle. Create an Angle Distance chamfer. Distance = .10in. Angle = 45deg.

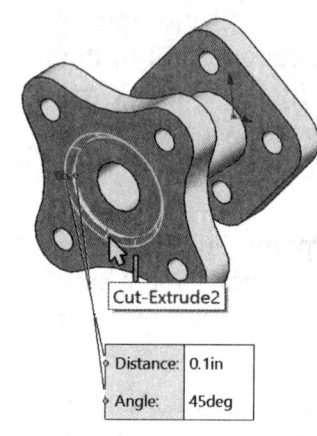

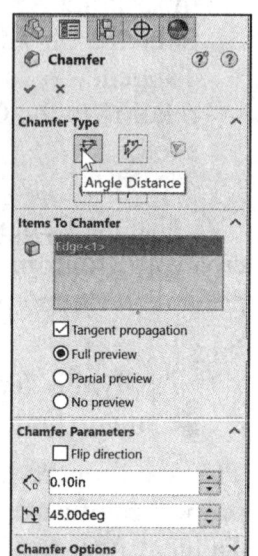

The Chamfer feature creates a beveled feature on selected edges, faces or a vertex.

15. Create the **Fillet** feature. Fillet the two edges as illustrated. Radius = .10in.

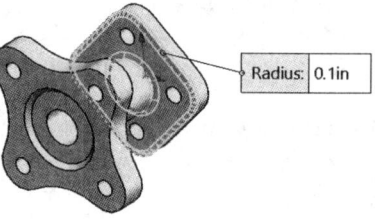

16. **Assign** 1060 Alloy material to the part. Material is required to calculate the overall mass of the part.

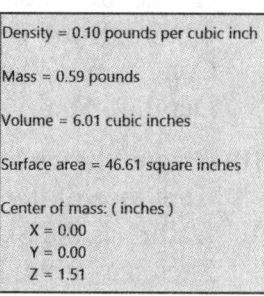

17. **Calculate** the overall mass. The overall mass = 0.59 pounds.

Density = 0.10 pounds per cubic inch

Mass = 0.59 pounds

Volume = 6.01 cubic inches

Surface area = 46.61 square inches

Center of mass: (inches)
  X = 0.00
  Y = 0.00
  Z = 1.51

18. **Locate** the Center of mass. The location of the Center of mass is relative to the part Origin.

- X: 0.00

- Y: 0.00

- Z: 1.51

19. **Save** the part and name it Advanced Part 4-1.

20. **Close** the model.

Tutorial: Advanced Part 4-2

An exam question in this category could read: Build this part in SOLIDWORKS. Calculate the overall mass and locate the Center of mass of the illustrated model.

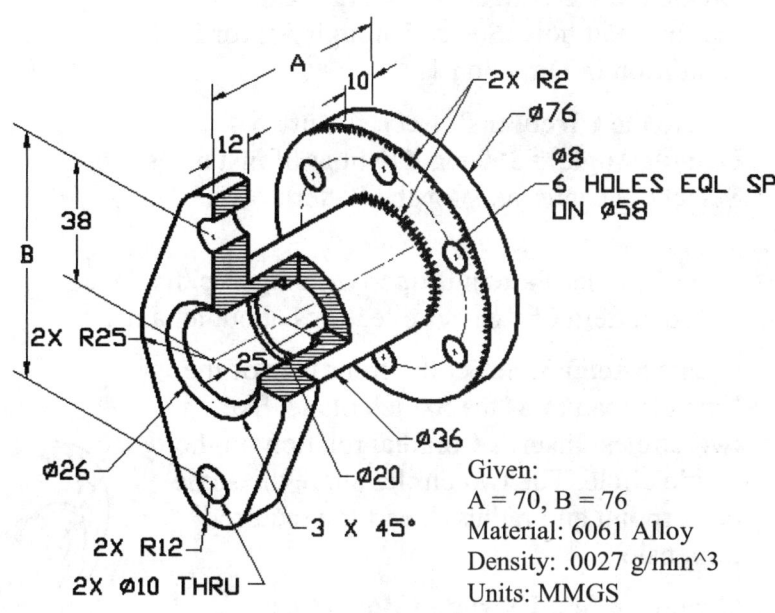

Given:
A = 70, B = 76
Material: 6061 Alloy
Density: .0027 g/mm^3
Units: MMGS

1. **Create** a new part in SOLIDWORKS.

2. **Build** the illustrated dimensioned model. Insert eight features: Extruded Base, Extruded Cut, Circular Pattern, two Extruded Bosses, Extruded Cut, Chamfer and Fillet.

Think about the steps that you would take to build the illustrated part. Review the provided information. Start with the six hole flange.

🔅 Tangent edges are displayed for educational purposes.

3. **Set** the document properties for the model.

4. Create **Sketch1**. Sketch1 is the Base sketch. Select the Front Plane as the Sketch plane. Sketch two circles. Insert the required geometric relations and dimensions.

5. Create the **Extruded Base** feature. Blind is the default End Condition in Direction 1. Depth = 10mm. Note the direction of the extrude feature to maintain the Origin location.

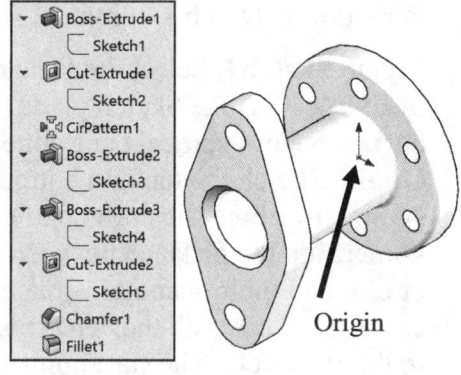

6. Create **Sketch2**. Select the front face of Boss-Extrude1 as the Sketch plane. Sketch2 is the profile for first Extruded Cut feature. The Extruded Cut feature is the seed feature for the Circular Pattern. Apply construction reference geometry. Insert the required geometric relations and dimensions.

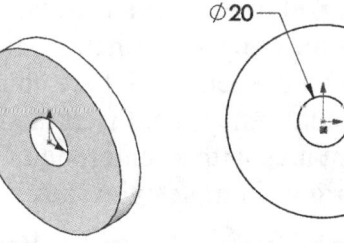

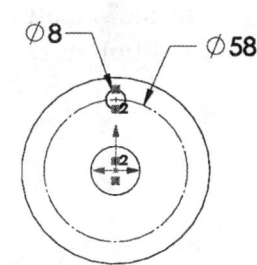

7. Create the **Extruded Cut** feature. Cut-Extrude1 is the first bolt hole. Select Through All for End Condition in Direction 1.

8. Create the **Circular Pattern** feature. Default Angle = 360deg. Number of instances = 6. Select the center axis for the Pattern Axis box.

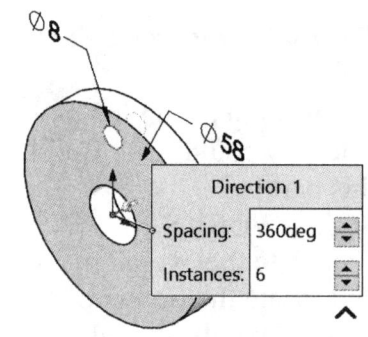

🔅 The Circular Pattern PropertyManager is displayed when you pattern one or more features about an axis.

9. Create **Sketch3**. Select the front face of the Extrude feature as the Sketch plane. Sketch two circles. Insert a Coradial relation on the inside circle. The two circles share the same centerpoint and radius. Insert the required dimension.

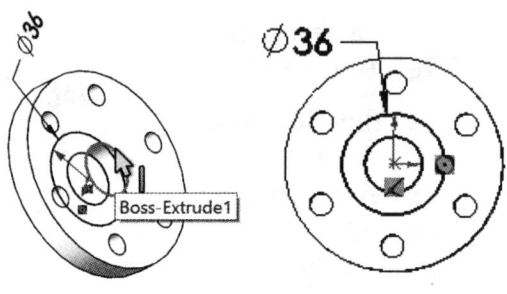

10. Create the first **Extruded Boss (Boss-Extrude2)** feature. The Boss-Extrude2 feature is the connecting tube between the two flanges. Blind is the default End Condition in Direction 1. Depth = 48mm.

11. Create **Sketch4**. Select the front circular face of Extrude3 as the Sketch plane. Sketch a horizontal and vertical centerline from the Origin. Sketch the top and bottom circles symmetric about the horizontal centerline. Dimension the distance between the two circles and their diameter. Create the top centerpoint arc with the centerpoint Coincident to the top circle. The start point and the end point of the arc are horizontal. Sketch the two top angled lines symmetric about the vertical centerline. Apply symmetry. Mirror the two lines and the centerpoint arc about the horizontal centerline. Insert the left and right tangent arcs with a centerpoint Coincident with the Origin. Complete the sketch.

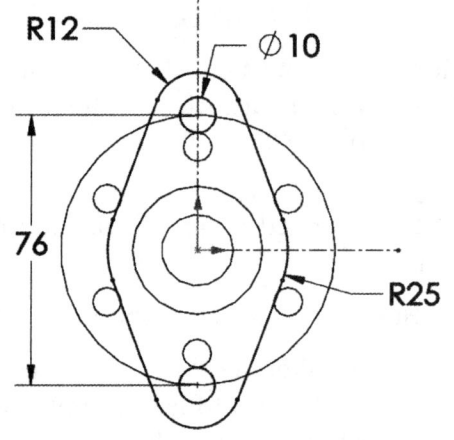

12. Create the second **Extruded Boss** (Boss-Extrude3) feature. Blind is the default End Condition in Direction 1. Depth = 12mm.

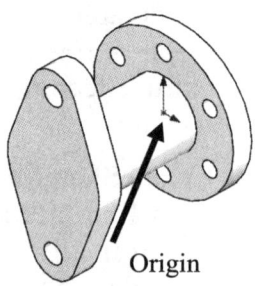

Origin

13. Create **Sketch5**. Select the front face of the Extrude feature as the Sketch plane. Sketch a circle. The part Origin is located in the center of the model. Insert the required dimension.

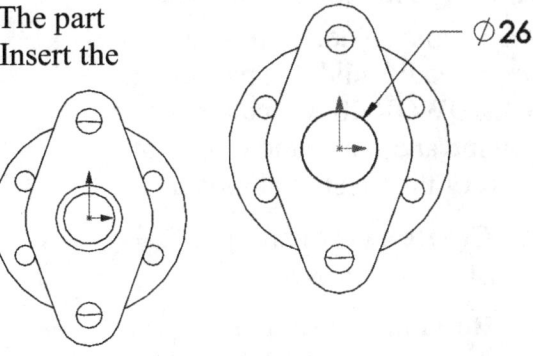

14. Create the second **Extruded Cut** feature. Blind is the default End Condition in Direction 1. Depth = 25mm.

15. Create the **Chamfer** feature. Chamfer1 is an Angle distance chamfer. Chamfer the inside edge of the Extrude feature as illustrated. Distance = 3mm. Angle = 45deg.

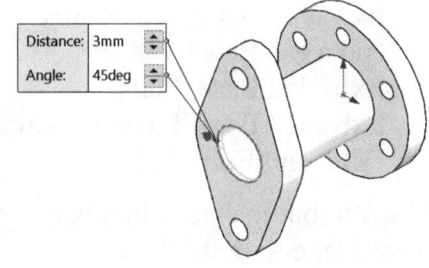

16. Create the **Fillet** feature. Fillet the two edges of Extrude1. Radius = 2mm.

17. **Assign** 6061 Alloy material to the part.

18. **Calculate** the overall mass of the part. The overall mass = 276.97 grams.

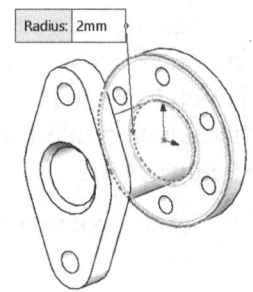

19. **Locate** the Center of mass. The location of the Center of mass is relative to the part Origin.

- X: 0.00 millimeters
- Y: 0.00 millimeters
- Z: 21.95 millimeters

20. **Save** the part and name it Advanced Part 4-2.

21. **Close** the model.

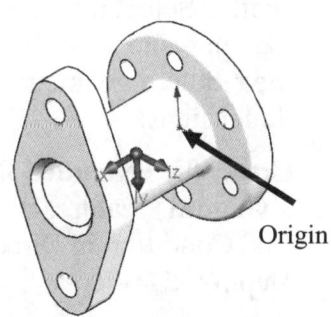

In the Advanced Part Modeling category, an exam question could read: Build this part in SOLIDWORKS. Locate the Center of mass with respect to the part Origin.

- A: X = 0.00 millimeters, Y = 0.00 millimeters, Z = 21.95 millimeters
- B: X = 21.95 millimeters, Y = 10.00 millimeters, Z = 0.00 millimeters
- C: X = 0.00 millimeters, Y = 0.00 millimeters, Z = -27.02 millimeters
- D: X= 1.00 millimeters, Y = -1.01 millimeters, Z = -0.04 millimeters

The correct answer is A.

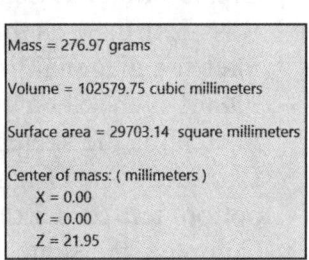

Mass = 276.97 grams

Volume = 102579.75 cubic millimeters

Surface area = 29703.14 square millimeters

Center of mass: (millimeters)
X = 0.00
Y = 0.00
Z = 21.95

Tutorial: Advanced Part 4-3

An exam question in this category could read: Build this part in SOLIDWORKS. Calculate the volume and locate the Center of mass of the illustrated model.

1. **Create** a new part in SOLIDWORKS.

2. **Build** the illustrated dimensioned model. Insert five sketches, five features and a Reference plane: Extruded Base, Plane1, Extruded Boss, Extruded Cut, Fillet and Extruded Cut.

Think about the steps that you would take to build the illustrated part. Insert a Reference plane to create the Extruded Boss feature. Create Sketch2 for Plane1. Plane1 is the Sketch plane for Sketch3. Sketch3 is the profile for Boss-Extrude2.

3. **Set** the document properties for the model.

4. Create **Sketch1**. Sketch1 is the Base sketch. Select the Top Plane as the Sketch plane. Sketch a rectangle. Insert the required geometric relations and dimensions.

5. Create the **Extruded Base (Boss-Extrude1)** feature. Blind is the default End Condition in Direction 1. Depth = .700in.

6. Create **Sketch2**. Select the top face of Boss-Extrude1 as the Sketch plane. Sketch a diagonal line as illustrated. Plane1 is the Sketch plane for Sketch3. Sketch3 is the sketch profile for Boss-Extrude2. The Origin is located in the bottom left corner of the sketch. Complete the sketch.

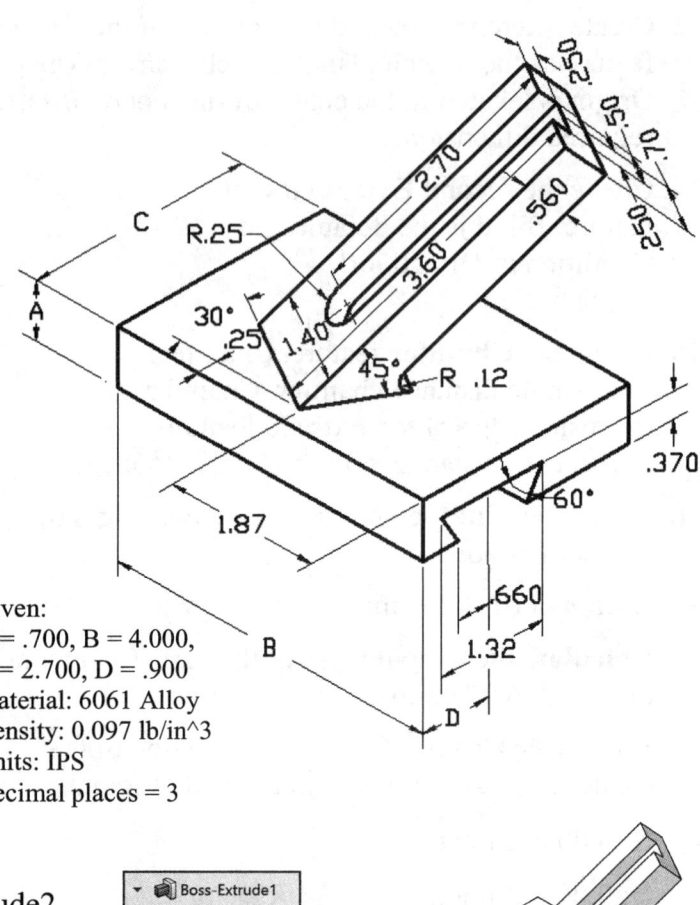

Given:
A = .700, B = 4.000,
C = 2.700, D = .900
Material: 6061 Alloy
Density: 0.097 lb/in^3
Units: IPS
Decimal places = 3

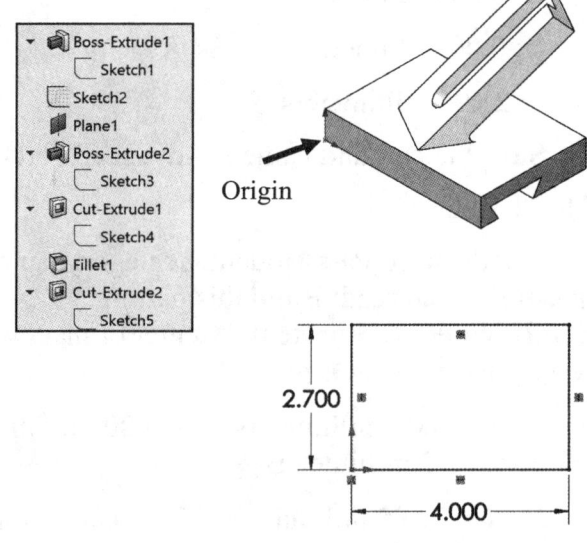

Origin

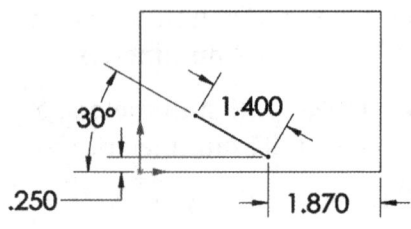

7. Create **Plane1**. Show Sketch2. Select the top face of Boss-Extrude1 and Sketch2. Sketch2 and face<1> are the Reference Entities. Angle = 45 deg.

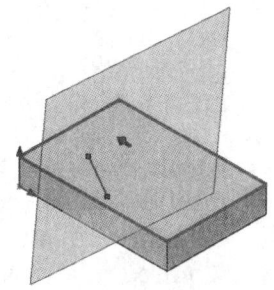

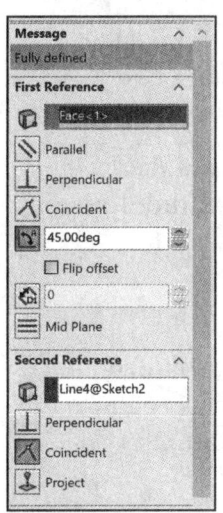

💡 Activate the Plane PropertyManager. Click **Plane** from the Reference Geometry Consolidated toolbar, or click **Insert**, **Reference Geometry**, **Plane** from the Menu bar.

💡 View Sketch2. Click **View**, **Hide/Show**, **Sketches** from the Menu bar.

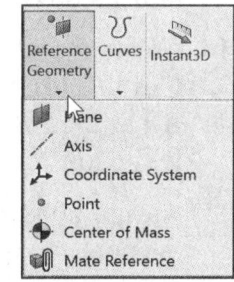

💡 View Plane1. Click **View**, **Hide/Show**, **Planes** from the Menu bar.

8. Create **Sketch3**. Select Plane1 as the Sketch plane. Select the Line Sketch tool. Use Sketch2 as a reference for the width dimension of the rectangle. Insert the required geometric relations and dimension. Sketch3 is the sketch profile for Boss-Extrude2.

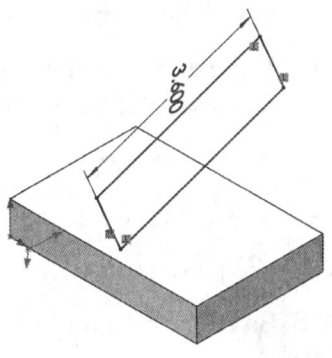

9. Create the **Extruded Boss** feature. Boss-Extrude2 is located on Plane1. Blind is the default End Condition in Direction 1. Depth = .560in.

10. Create **Sketch4**. Select the top angle face of Boss-Extrude2 as the Sketch plane. Sketch4 is the profile for the first Extruded Cut feature. Apply a Mid point relation with the Centerline Sketch tool. Insert a Parallel, Symmetric, Perpendicular, and Tangent relation. Insert the required dimensions.

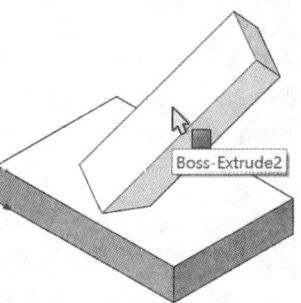

11. Create the first **Extruded Cut** feature. Blind is the default End Condition. Depth = .250in.

💡 There are numerous ways to build the models in this chapter. A goal is to display different design intents and techniques.

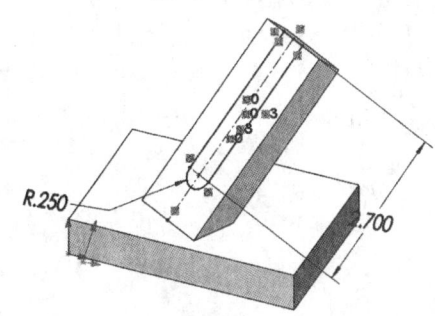

12. Create the **Fillet** feature. Fillet the illustrated edge. Edge<1> is displayed in the Items To Fillet box. Radius = .12in.

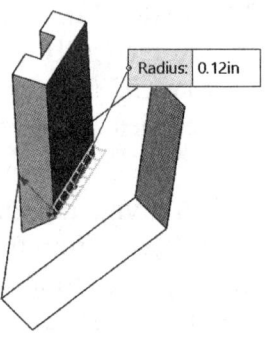

13. Create **Sketch5**. Select the right face of Boss-Extrude1 as the Sketch plane. Insert the required relations and dimensions.

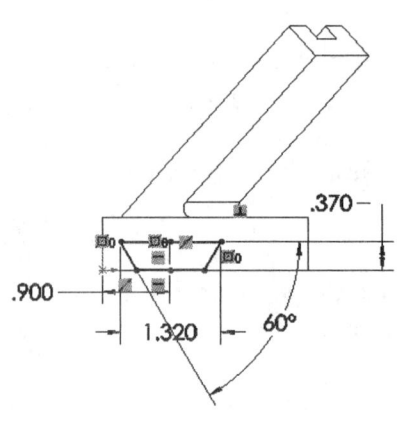

14. Create the second **Extruded Cut** feature. Select Through All as the End Condition in Direction 1.

15. **Assign** 6061 Alloy material to the part.

Mass = 0.80 pounds

Volume = 8.19 cubic inches

Surface area = 49.02 square inches

Center of mass: (inches)
X = 2.08
Y = 0.79
Z = -1.60

16. **Calculate** the volume of the part. The volume = 8.19 cubic inches.

17. **Locate** the Center of mass. The location of the Center of mass is relative to the part Origin.

- X: 2.08 inches

- Y: 0.79 inches

- Z: -1.60 inches

18. **Save** the part and name it Advanced Part 4-3.

19. **Close** the model.

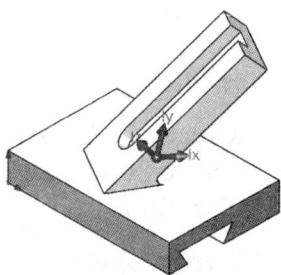

As an exercise, apply the MMGS unit system to the part. Modify the material from 6061 Alloy to ABS. Modify the Plane1 angle from 45deg to 30deg.

Mass = 134.58 grams

Volume = 131941.14 cubic millimeters

Surface area = 30575.45 square millimeters

Center of mass: (millimeters)
X = 53.89
Y = 16.98
Z = -42.47

Calculate the total mass of the part and the location of the Center of mass relative to the part Origin. Save the part and name it Advanced Part 4-3 MMGS System.

Tutorial: Advanced Part 4-4

An exam question in this category could read: Build this part in SOLIDWORKS. Calculate the volume and locate the Center of mass of the illustrated model.

1. **Create** a new part in SOLIDWORKS.

2. **Build** the illustrated dimensioned model. Create the part with eleven sketches, eleven features and a Reference plane: Extruded Base, Plane1, two Extruded Bosses, two Extruded Cuts, Extruded Boss, Extruded Cut, Extruded-Thin, Mirror, Extruded Cut and Extruded Boss.

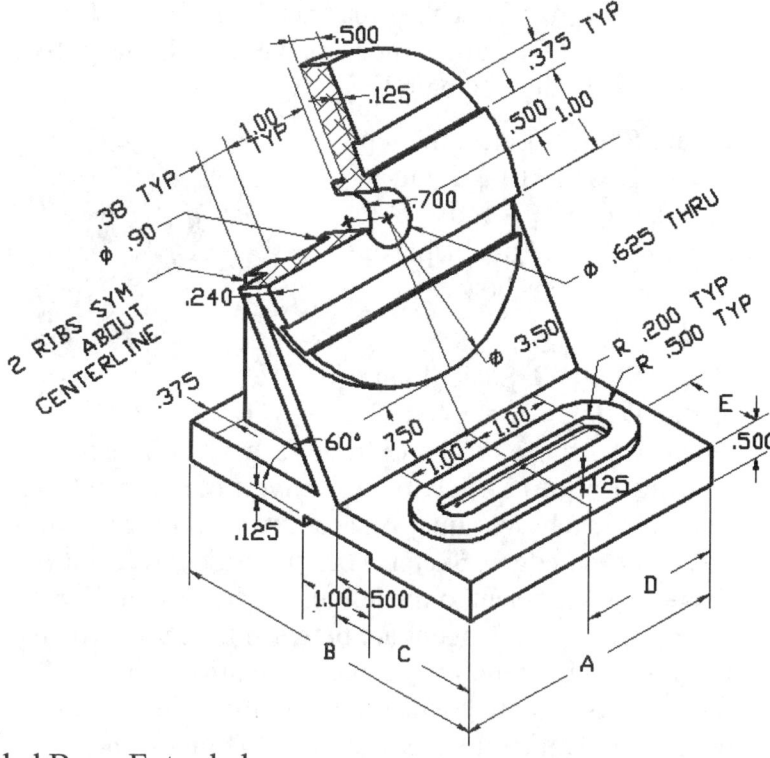

Think about the steps that you would take to build the illustrated part. Create the rectangular Base feature. Create Sketch2 for Plane1. Insert Plane1 to create the Extruded Boss feature: Boss-Extrude2. Plane1 is the Sketch plane for Sketch3. Sketch3 is the sketch profile for Boss-Extrude2.

3. **Set** the document properties for the model.

4. Create **Sketch1**. Sketch1 is the Base sketch. Select the Top Plane as the Sketch plane. Sketch a rectangle. Insert the required geometric relations and dimensions. Note the location of the Origin.

5. Create the **Extruded Base (Boss-Extrude1)** feature. Blind is the default End Condition in Direction 1. Depth = .500in.

Given:
A = 3.500, B = 4.200, C = 2.000, D = 1.750, E = 1.000
Material: 6061 Alloy
Density: 0.097 lb/in^3
Units: IPS
Decimal places = 3

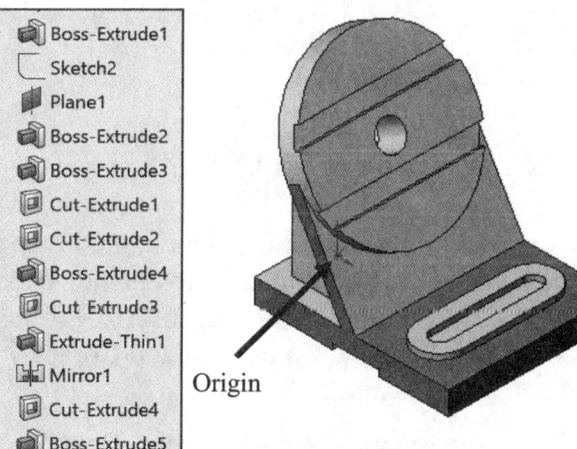

Origin

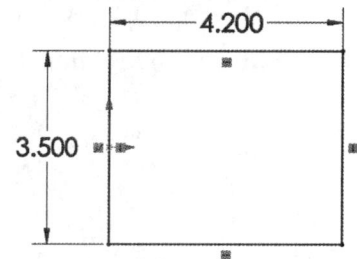

6. Create **Sketch2**. Sketch2 is the sketch profile for Plane1. Select the top face of Extrude1 as the Sketch plane. Sketch a centerline. Show Sketch2.

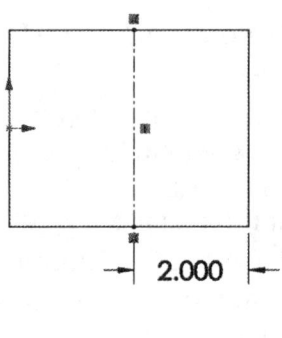

2.000

7. Create **Plane1**. Select the top face of Boss-Extrude1 and Sketch2. Face<1> and Line1@Sketch2 are displayed in the Selections box. Angle = 60deg.

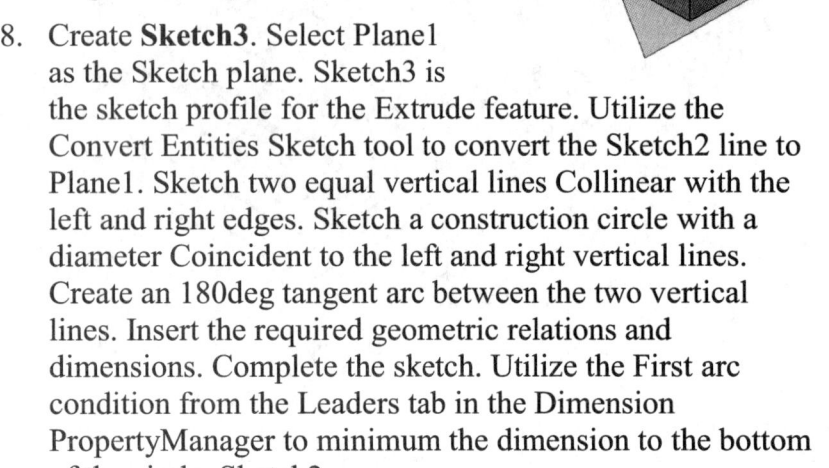

8. Create **Sketch3**. Select Plane1 as the Sketch plane. Sketch3 is the sketch profile for the Extrude feature. Utilize the Convert Entities Sketch tool to convert the Sketch2 line to Plane1. Sketch two equal vertical lines Collinear with the left and right edges. Sketch a construction circle with a diameter Coincident to the left and right vertical lines. Create an 180deg tangent arc between the two vertical lines. Insert the required geometric relations and dimensions. Complete the sketch. Utilize the First arc condition from the Leaders tab in the Dimension PropertyManager to minimum the dimension to the bottom of the circle, Sketch2.

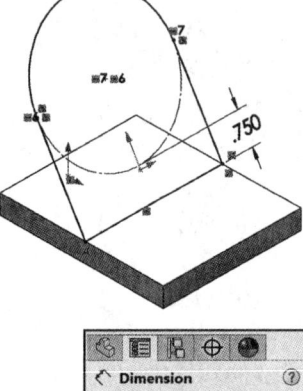

.750

Insert a Construction circle when dimensions are reference to a minimum or maximum arc condition.

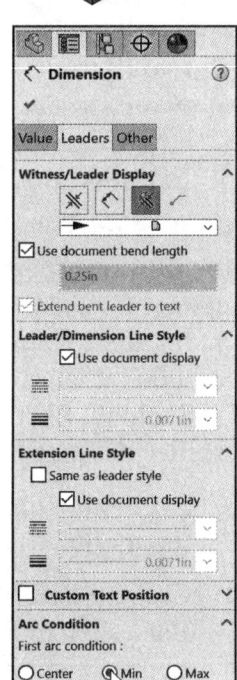

9. Create the **Extruded Boss** (Boss-Extrude2) feature. Blind is the default End Condition. Depth = .260in. Note: .260in = (.500in - .240in). The extrude direction is towards the back.

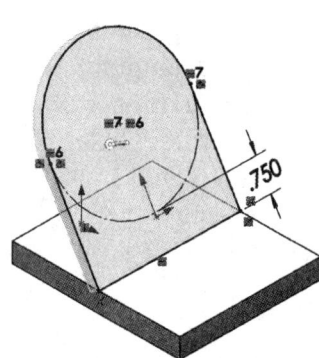

.750

10. Create **Sketch4**. Select the right angled face of the Extrude feature as the Sketch plane. Wake-up the center point of the tangent Arc. Sketch a circle. The circle is Coincident and Coradial to the Extrude feature.

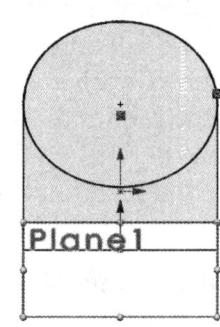

Plane1

11. Create the second **Extruded Boss** (Boss-Extrude3) feature. Blind is the default End Condition in Direction 1. Depth = .240in.

12. Create **Sketch5**. Sketch5 is the profile for the Extruded Cut feature. Select the right angle face of the Extrude feature as the Sketch plane. Apply the Convert Entities and Trim Sketch tools. Insert the required geometric relations and dimensions.

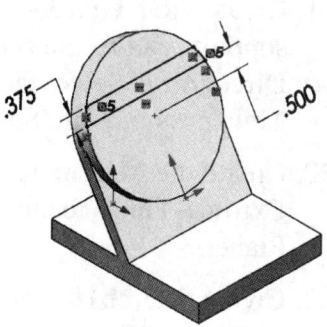

13. Create the first **Extruded Cut** feature. Blind is the default End Condition. Depth = .125in.

14. Create **Sketch6**. Select the right angle face of Boss-Extrude3 as the Sketch plane. Apply the Convert Entities and Trim Sketch tools. Insert the required geometric relations and dimensions.

15. Create the second **Extruded Cut** feature. Blind is the default End Condition. Depth = .125in.

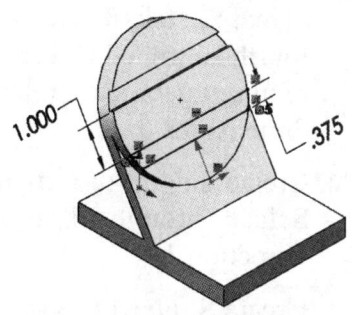

16. Create **Sketch7**. Select the left angled face of Boss-Extrude2 as the Sketch plane. Sketch a circle. Insert the required geometric relation and dimension.

17. Create the third **Extruded Boss (Boss-Extrude4)** feature. Blind is the default End Condition. Depth = .200in. Note: .200in = (.700in - .500in).

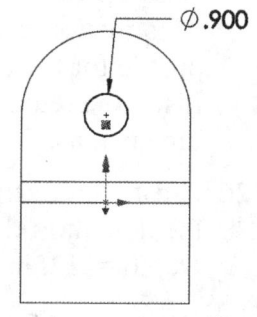

18. Create **Sketch8**. Select the flat circular face of the Extrude feature as illustrated as the Sketch plane. Sketch a circle. Insert the required dimension.

19. Create the third **Extruded Cut** feature. Select Through All for End Condition in Direction 1.

20. Create **Sketch9**. Select the left flat top face of Extrude1 as the Sketch Plane. Sketch a line parallel to the front edge as illustrated. Insert the required geometric relations and dimensions.

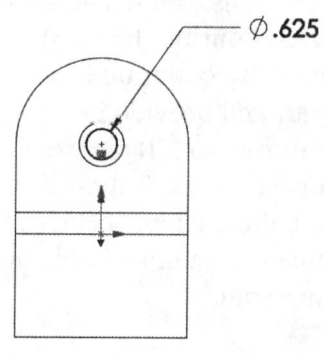

This book is designed to expose the new user to many tools, techniques and procedures. It may not always use the most direct tool or process.

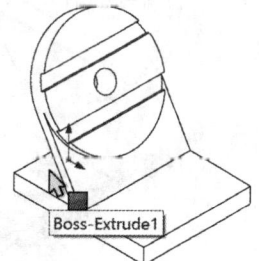

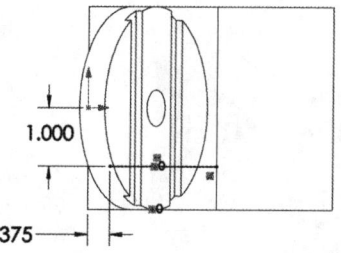

21. Create the **Extrude-Thin1** feature. Extrude-Thin1 is the left support feature. Select Up To Surface for End Condition in Direction 1. Select face<1> for direction as illustrated. Thickness = .38in. Select One-Direction.

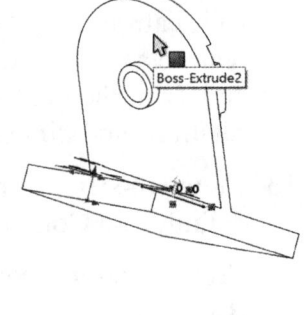

22. Create the **Mirror** feature. Mirror the Extrude-Thin1 feature about the Front Plane.

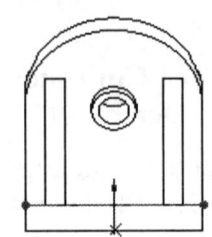

23. Create **Sketch10**. Select the bottom front flat face of Boss-Extrude1 as the Sketch plane. Sketch10 is the profile for the fourth Extruded Cut feature. Insert the required geometric relations and dimensions.

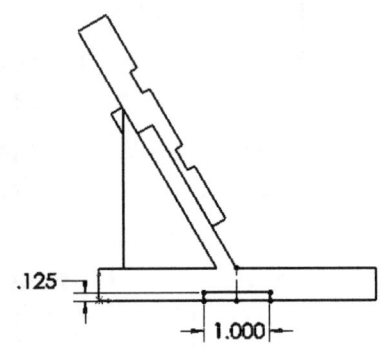

24. Create the fourth **Extruded Cut** feature. Select Through All for End Condition in Direction 1.

25. Create **Sketch11**. Select the top face of Boss-Extrude1 as the Sketch plane. Apply construction geometry. Sketch11 is the profile for the Boss-Extrude5 feature. Insert the required geometric relations and dimensions.

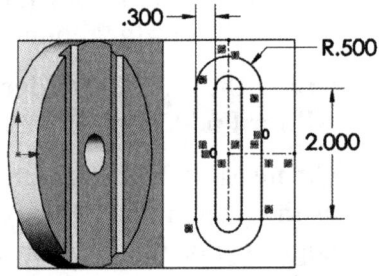

26. Create the **Extruded Boss** feature. Blind is the default End Condition in Direction 1. Depth = .125in.

Click on the additional views during the CSWA exam to better understand the part and provided information. Read each question carefully. Identify the dimensions, center of mass and units. Apply needed material.

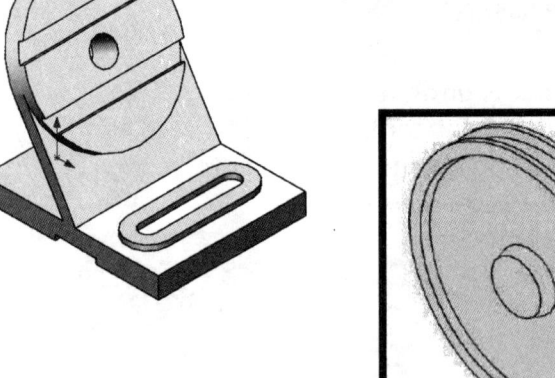

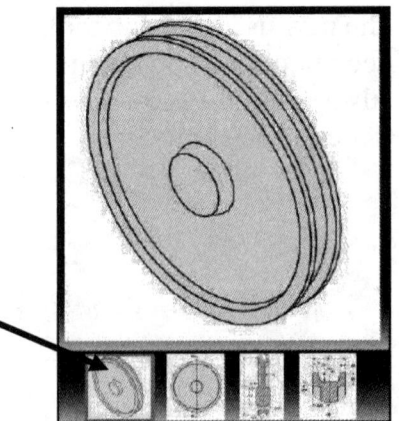

27. **Assign** 6061 Alloy material to the part.

28. **Calculate** the volume of the part. The volume = 14.05 cubic inches.

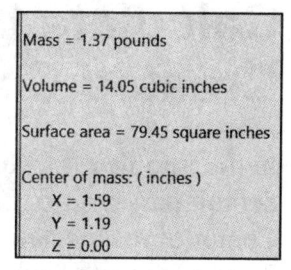

29. **Locate** the Center of mass. The location of the Center of mass is relative to the part Origin.

- X: 1.59 inches

- Y: 1.19 inches

- Z: 0.00 inches

30. **Save** the part and name it Advanced Part 4-4.

31. **Close** the model.

In the Advanced Part Modeling category, an exam question could read: Build this model. Calculate the volume of the part.

- A: 14.05 cubic inches

- B: 15.66 cubic inches

- C: 13.44 cubic inches

- D: 12.71 cubic inches

The correct answer is A.

As an exercise, modify A from 3.500in to 3.600in. Modify B from 4.200in to 4.100in. Modify the Plane1 angle from 60deg to 45deg. Modify the system units from IPS to MMGS.

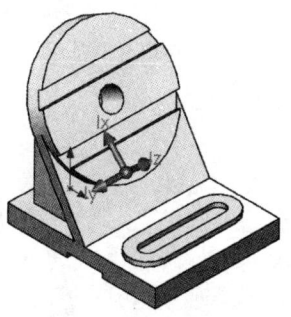

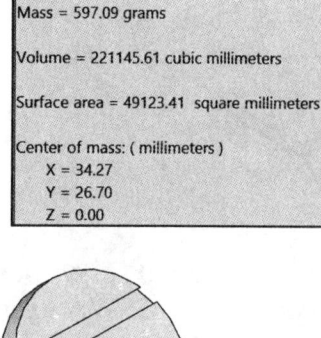

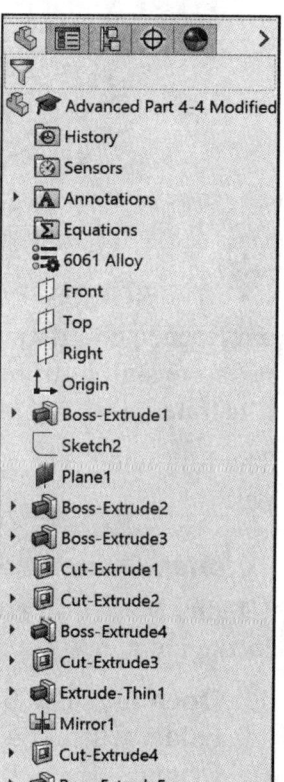

Calculate the mass and locate the Center of mass. The mass = 597.09 grams.

- X: 34.27 millimeters

- Y: 26.70 millimeters

- Z: 0.00 millimeters

32. **Save** the part and name it Advanced Part 4-4 Modified.

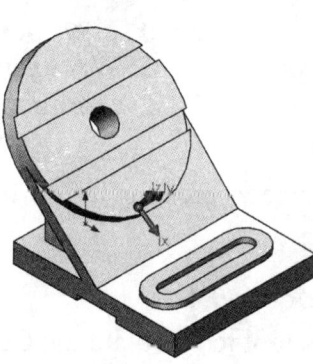

Calculate the Center of Mass Relative to a Created Coordinate System Location

In the Simple Part Modeling chapter, you located the Center of mass relative to the default part Origin. In the Advanced Part Modeling category, you may need to locate the Center of mass relative to a created coordinate system location. The exam model may display a created coordinate system location. Example:

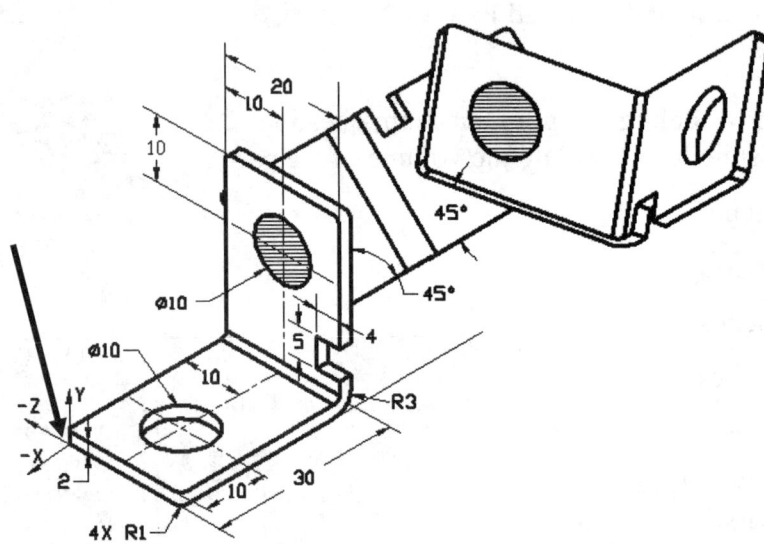

The SOLIDWORKS software displays positive values for (X, Y, Z) coordinates for a reference coordinate system. The CSWA exam displays either a positive or negative sign in front of the (X, Y, Z) coordinates to indicate direction as illustrated, (-X, +Y, -Z).

The following section reviews creating a Coordinate System location for a part.

Tutorial: Coordinate location 4-1

Use the Mass Properties tool to calculate the Center of mass for a part located at a new coordinate location through a point.

1. **Open** the Plate-3-Point part from the SOLIDWORKS CSWA Folder\Chapter 4 location. View the location of the part Origin.

2. **Locate** the Center of mass. The location of the Center of mass is relative to the part Origin.

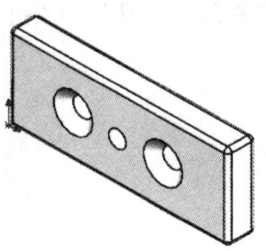

- X = 28 millimeters
- Y = 11 millimeters
- Z = -3 millimeters

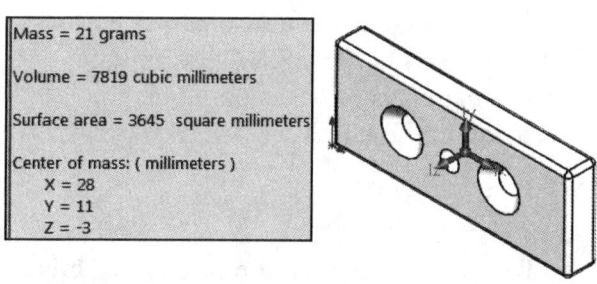

Create a new coordinate system location. Locate the new coordinate system location at the center of the center hole as illustrated.

3. **Right-click** the **front face** of Base-Extrude.

4. Click **Sketch** from the Context toolbar.

5. Click the **edge** of the center hole as illustrated.

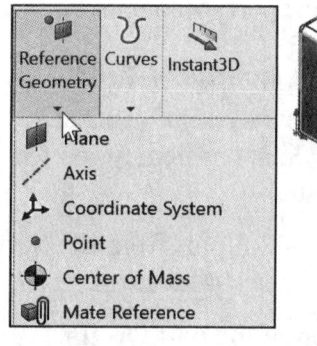

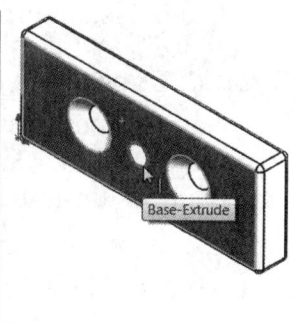

6. Click **Convert Entities** from the Sketch toolbar. The center point for the new coordinate location is displayed.

7. **Exit** the sketch. Sketch4 is displayed.

8. Click the **Coordinate System** tool from the Consolidated Reference Geometry toolbar. The Coordinate System PropertyManager is displayed.

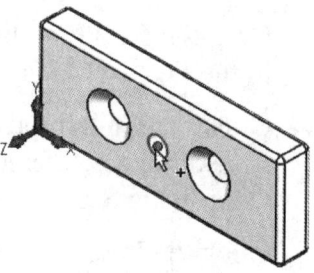

9. Click the **center point** of the center hole in the Graphics window. Point2@Sketch4 is displayed in the Selections box as the Origin.

10. Click **OK** from the Coordinate System PropertyManager. Coordinate System1 is displayed.

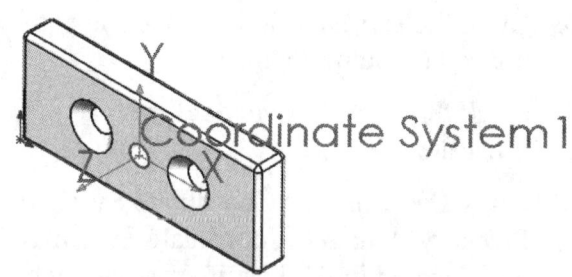

11. **View** the new coordinate location at the center of the center hole.

View the Mass Properties of the part with the new coordinate location.

12. Click the **Mass Properties** tool from the Evaluate tab.

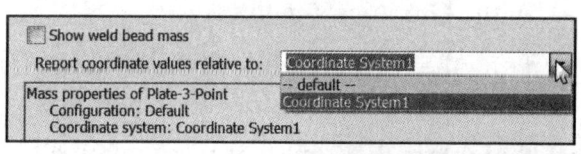

13. Select **Coordinate System1** from the Output box. The Center of mass relative to the new location is located at the following coordinates: X = 0 millimeters, Y = 0 millimeters, Z = -3 millimeters.

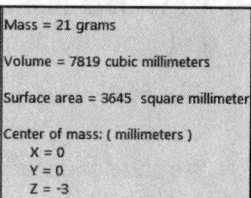

14. **Reverse** the direction of the axes as illustrated. On the CSWA exam, the coordinate system axes could be represented by: (+X, -Y, -Z).

15. **Close** the model.

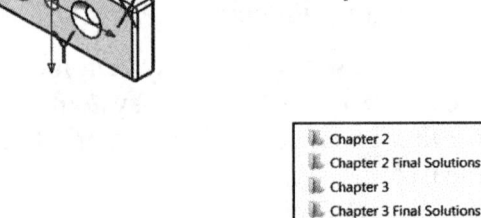

To reverse the direction of an axis, click its **Reverse Axis Direction** button in the Coordinate System PropertyManager.

Tutorial: Coordinate location 4-2

Create a new coordinate system location. Locate the new coordinate system at the top back point as illustrated.

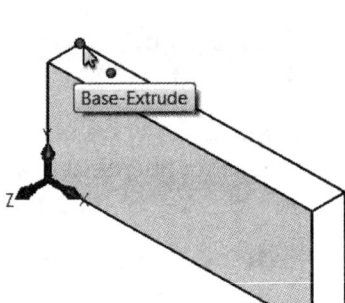

1. **Open** the Plate-X-Y-Z part from the SOLIDWORKS CSWA Folder\Chapter 4 location.

2. **View** the location of the part Origin.

3. Drag the **Rollback bar** under the Base-Extrude feature in the FeatureManager.

4. Click the **Coordinate System** tool from the Consolidated Reference Geometry toolbar. The Coordinate System PropertyManager is displayed.

5. Click the **back left vertex** as illustrated.

6. Click the **top back horizontal** edge as illustrated. Do not select the midpoint.

7. Click the **back left vertical** edge as illustrated.

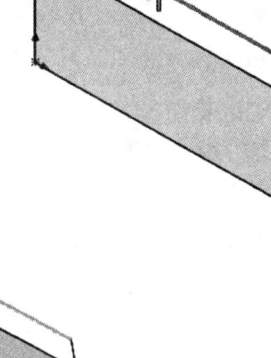

8. Click **OK** from the Coordinate System PropertyManager. Coordinate System1 is displayed in the FeatureManager and in the Graphics window.

9. Drag the **Rollback bar** to the bottom of the FeatureManager.

10. **Calculate** the Center of mass relative to the new coordinate system.

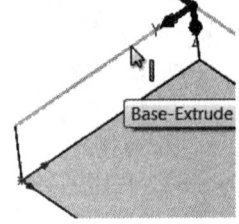

11. Select **Coordinate System1**. The Center of mass relative to the new location is located at the following coordinates:

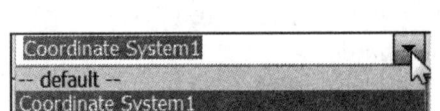

- X = -28 millimeters

- Y = 11 millimeters

- Z = 4 millimeters

Center of mass: (millimeters)
X = -28
Y = 11
Z = 4

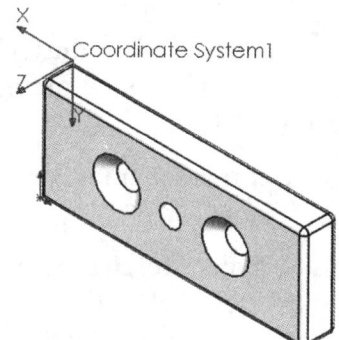

Coordinate System1

12. **Reverse** the direction of the axes as illustrated.

13. **View** the new coordinates for the center of mass.

14. **Close** the model.

Define a Coordinate system for a part or assembly. Apply a Coordinate system with the Measure and Mass Properties tool.

Tutorial: Advanced Part 4-5

An exam question in this category could read: Build this part in SOLIDWORKS. Calculate the overall mass and locate the Center of mass of the illustrated model.

1. **Create** a new part in SOLIDWORKS.

2. **Build** the illustrated dimensioned model. Insert thirteen features: Extrude-Thin1, Fillet, two Extruded Cuts, Circular Pattern, two Extruded Cuts, Mirror, Chamfer, Extruded Cut, Mirror, Extruded Cut and Mirror.

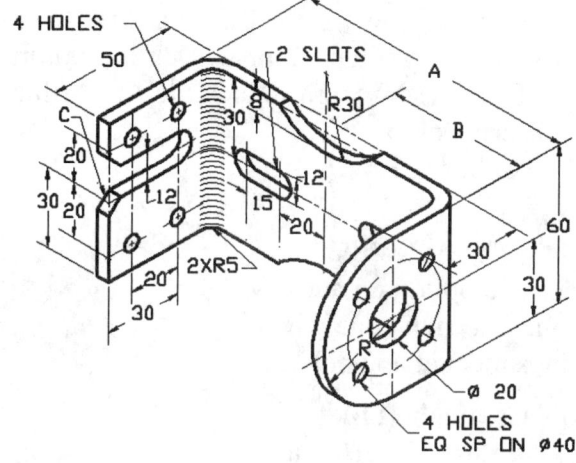

Think about the steps that you would take to build the illustrated part. Review the provided information. The depth of the left side is 50mm. The depth of the right side is 60mm.

Given:
A = 110, B = 55,
C = 5 X 45Ø CHAMFER
Material: 5MM, 6061 Alloy
Density: .0027 g/mm^3
Units: MMGS
ALL HOLES 6MM

There are numerous ways to build the models in this chapter. A goal is to display different design intents and techniques.

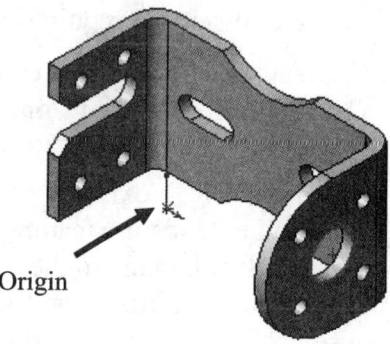

Origin

💡 If the inside radius = 5mm and the material thickness = 5mm, then the outside radius = 10mm.

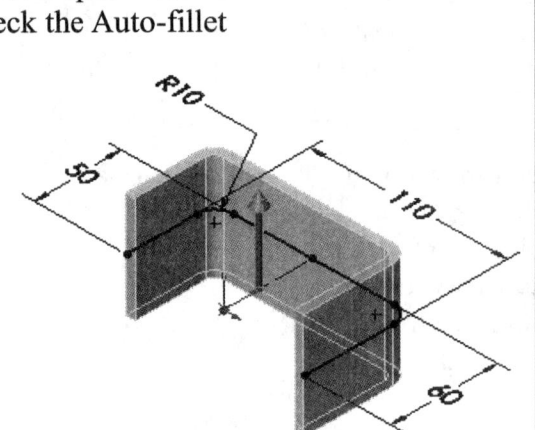

3. **Set** the document properties for the model.

4. Create **Sketch1**. Sketch1 is the Base sketch. Select the Top Plane as the Sketch plane. Apply the Line and Sketch Fillet Sketch tools. Apply construction geometry. Insert the required geometric relations and dimensions.

5. Create the **Extrude-Thin1** feature. Extrude-Thin1 is the Base feature. Apply symmetry in Direction 1. Depth = 60mm. Thickness = 5mm. Check the Auto-fillet corners box. Radius = 5mm.

💡 The Auto-fillet corners option creates a round at each edge where lines meet at an angle.

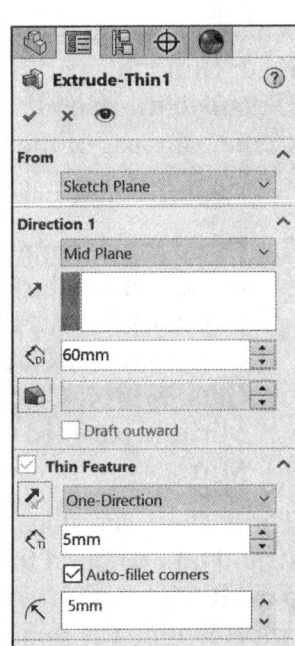

6. Create the **Fillet** feature. Fillet1 is a full round fillet. Fillet the three illustrated faces: top, front and bottom.

7. Create **Sketch2**. Select the right face as the Sketch plane. Wake-up the centerpoint. Sketch a circle. Insert the required relation and dimension.

8. Create the first **Extruded Cut** feature. Select Up To Next for the End Condition in Direction 1.

💡 The Up To Next End Condition extends the feature from the sketch plane to the next surface that intercepts the entire profile. The intercepting surface must be on the same part.

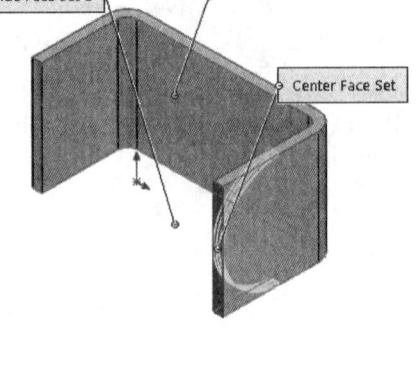

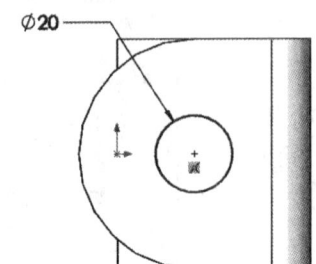

9. Create **Sketch3**. Select the right face as the Sketch plane. Create the profile for the second Extruded Cut feature. This is the seed feature for CirPattern1. Apply construction geometry to locate the center point of Sketch3. Insert the required relations and dimensions.

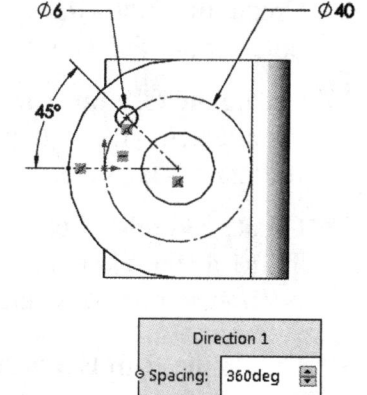

10. Create the second **Extruded Cut** feature. Select Up To Next for the End Condition in Direction 1.

11. Create the **Circular Pattern** feature. Number of Instances = 4. Default angle = 360deg.

12. Create **Sketch4**. Select the left outside face of Extrude-Thin1 as the Sketch plane. Apply the Line and Tangent Arc Sketch tool to create Sketch4. Insert the required geometric relations and dimensions.

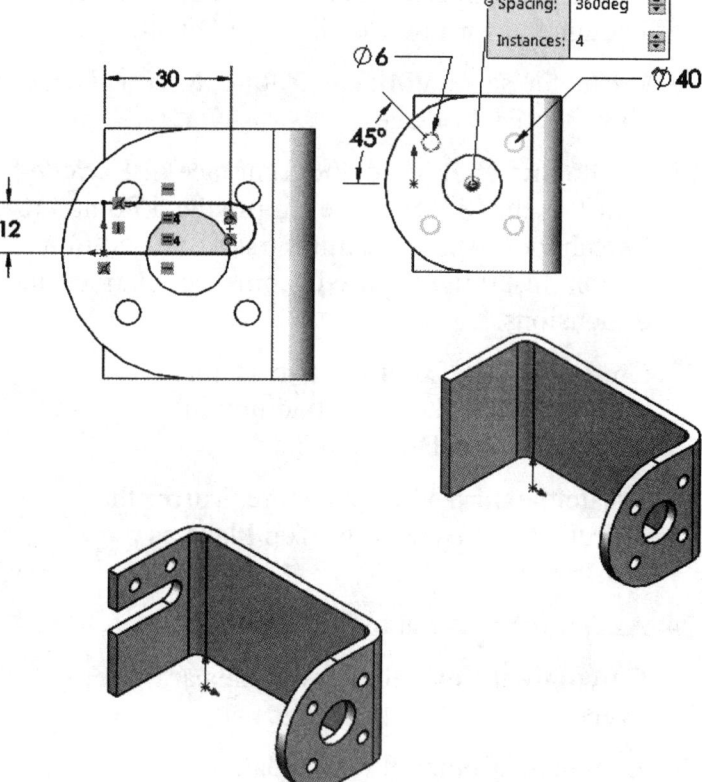

13. Create the third **Extruded Cut** feature. Select Up To Next for End Condition in Direction 1. The Slot on the left side of Extrude-Thin1 is created.

14. Create **Sketch5**. Select the left outside face of Extrude-Thin1 as the Sketch plane. Sketch two circles. Insert the required geometric relations and dimensions.

15. Create the fourth **Extruded Cut** feature. Select Up To Next for End Condition in Direction 1.

🔅 There are numerous ways to create the models in this chapter. A goal is to display different design intents and techniques

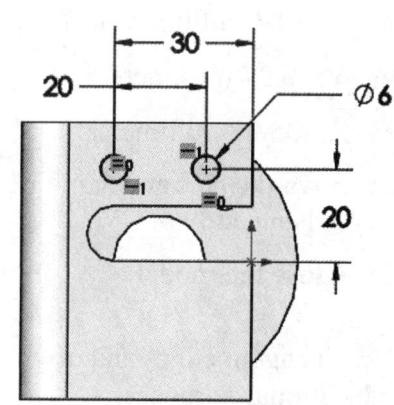

16. Create the first **Mirror** feature. Mirror the top two holes about the Top Plane.

17. Create the **Chamfer** feature. Create an Angle distance chamfer. Chamfer the selected edges as illustrated. Distance = 5mm. Angle = 45deg.

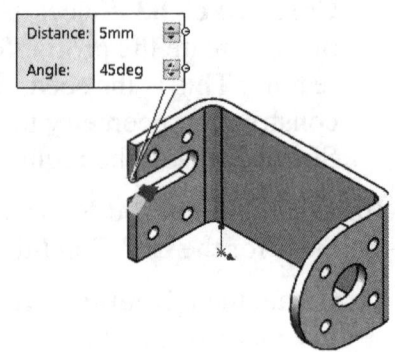

18. Create **Sketch6**. Select the front face of Extrude-Thin1 as the Sketch plane. Insert the required geometric relations and dimensions.

19. Create the fifth **Extruded Cut** feature. Select Though All for End Condition in Direction 1.

20. Create the second **Mirror** feature. Mirror Extrude5 about the Right Plane.

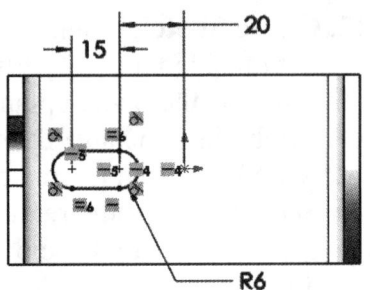

21. Create **Sketch7**. Select the front face of Extrude-Thin1 as the Sketch plane. Apply the 3 Point Arc Sketch tool. Apply the min First Arc Condition option. Insert the required geometric relations and dimensions.

22. Create the last **Extruded Cut** feature. Through All is the End Condition in Direction 1 and Direction 2.

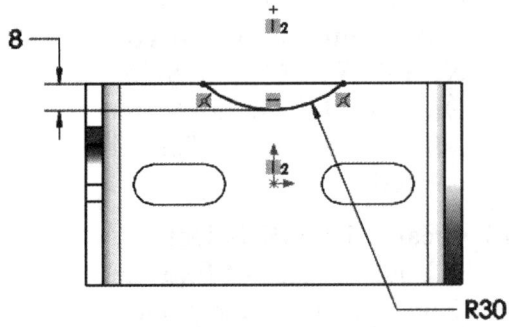

23. Create the third **Mirror** feature. Mirror the Extrude feature about the Top Plane as illustrated.

24. **Assign** the material to the part.

25. **Calculate** the overall mass of the part. The overall mass = 132.45 grams.

26. **Locate** the Center of mass relative to the part Origin:

- X: 1.83 millimeters

- Y: -0.27 millimeters

- Z: -35.38 millimeters

Mass = 132.45 grams
Volume = 49055.56 cubic millimeters
Surface area = 24219.80 square millimeters
Center of mass: (millimeters)
X = 1.83
Y = -0.27
Z = -35.38

27. **Save** the part and name it Advanced Part 4-5.

28. **Close** the model.

Tangent edges and origin are displayed for educational purposes.

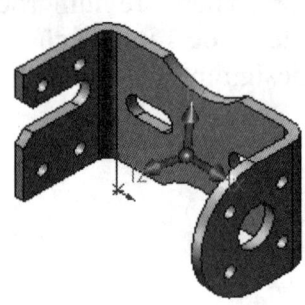

All questions on the exam are in a multiple choice single answer or fill in the blank format. In the Advanced Part Modeling category, an exam question could read: Build this model. Calculate the overall mass of the part with the provided information.

- A: 139.34 grams

- B: 155.19 grams

- C: 132.45 grams

- D: 143.91 grams

The correct answer is C.

☀ Use the Options button in the Mass Properties dialog box to apply custom settings to units.

Tutorial: Advanced Part 4-5A

An exam question in this category could read: Build this part in SOLIDWORKS. Locate the Center of mass. Note the coordinate system location of the model as illustrated.

Where do you start? Build the model as you did in the Tutorial: Advanced Part 4-5. Create Coordinate System1 to locate the Center of mass.

1. **Open** Advanced Part 4-5 from your SOLIDWORKS folder.

Create the illustrated coordinate system location.

2. Show **Sketch2** from the FeatureManager design tree.

3. Click the **center point** of Sketch2 in the Graphics window as illustrated.

☀ Click on the additional views during the CSWA exam to better understand the part and provided information.

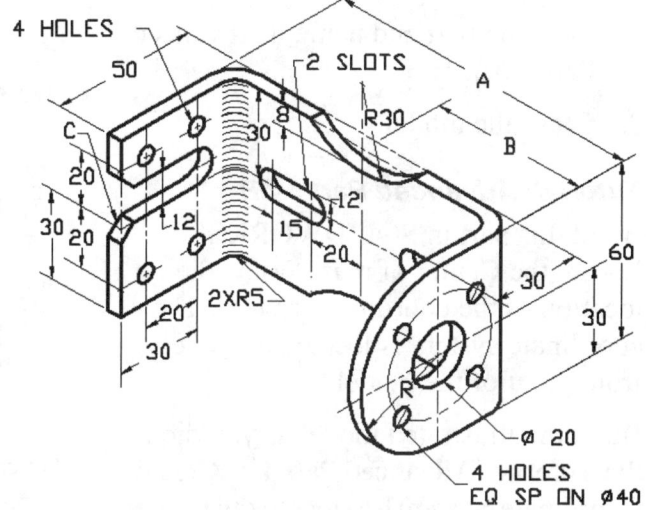

A = 110, B = 55, C = 5 X 45Ø CHAMFER
Material: 5MM, 6061 Alloy
Density: .0027 g/mm^3
Units: MMGS
ALL HOLES 6MM

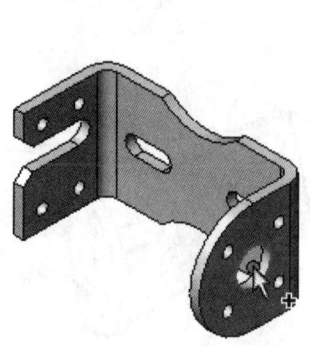
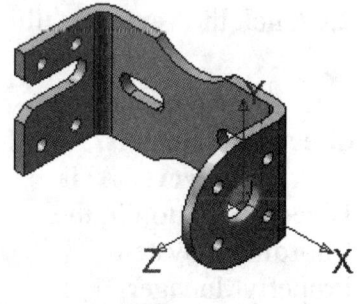

Coordinate system: +X, +Y, +Z

4. Click the **Coordinate System** tool from the Consolidated Reference Geometry toolbar. The Coordinate System PropertyManager is displayed. Point2@Sketch2 is displayed in the Origin box.

5. Click **OK** from the Coordinate System PropertyManager. Coordinate System1 is displayed.

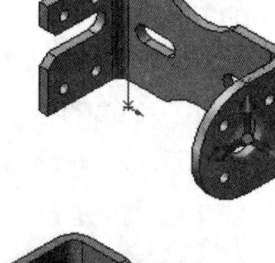

6. **Locate** the Center of mass based on the location of the illustrated coordinate system. Select Coordinate System1.

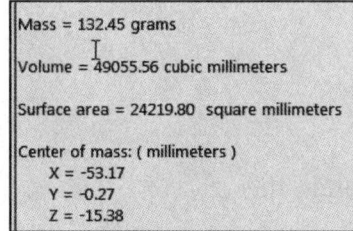

Mass = 132.45 grams

Volume = 49055.56 cubic millimeters

Surface area = 24219.80 square millimeters

Center of mass: (millimeters)
    X = -53.17
    Y = -0.27
    Z = -15.38

- X: -53.17 millimeters

- Y: -0.27 millimeters

- Z: -15.38 millimeters

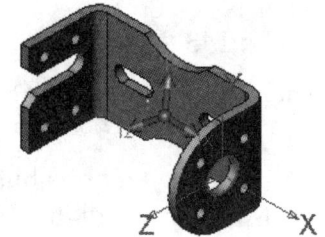

7. **Save** the part and name it Advanced Part 4-5A.

8. **Close** the model.

Tutorial: Advanced Part 4-5B

Build this part in SOLIDWORKS. Locate the Center of mass. View the location of the coordinate system. The coordinate system is located at the left front point of the model.

Build the illustrated model as you did in the Tutorial: Advanced Part 4-5. Create Coordinate System1 to locate the Center of mass for the model.

1. **Open** Advanced Part 4-5 from your SOLIDWORKS folder.

Create the illustrated coordinate system.

2. Click the **vertex** as illustrated for the Origin location.

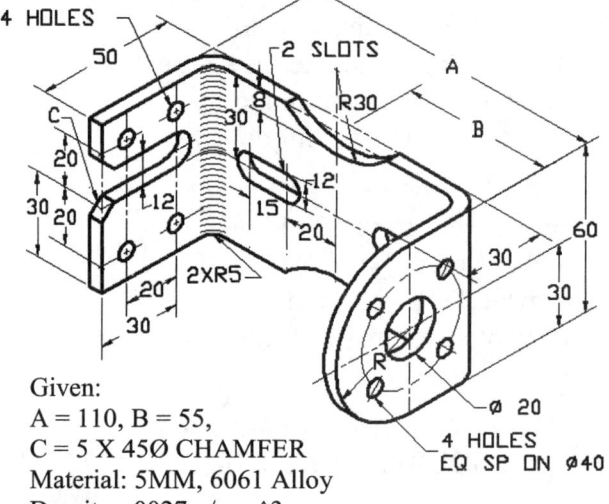

Given:
A = 110, B = 55,
C = 5 X 45Ø CHAMFER
Material: 5MM, 6061 Alloy
Density: .0027 g/mm^3
Units: MMGS
ALL HOLES 6MM

To reverse the direction of an axis, click the **Reverse Axis Direction** button in the Coordinate System PropertyManager.

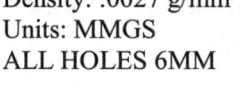

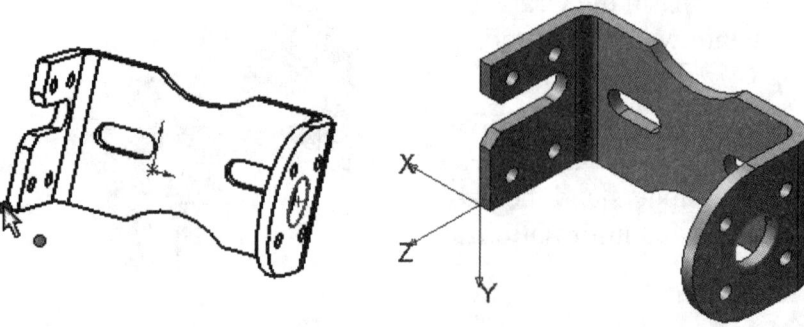

3. Click the **Coordinate System** tool from the Consolidated Reference Geometry toolbar. The Coordinate System PropertyManager is displayed. Vertex<1> is displayed in the Origin box.

4. Click the **bottom horizontal edge** as illustrated. Edge<1> is displayed in the X Axis Direction box.

5. Click the **left back vertical edge** as illustrated. Edge<2> is displayed in the Y Axis Direction box.

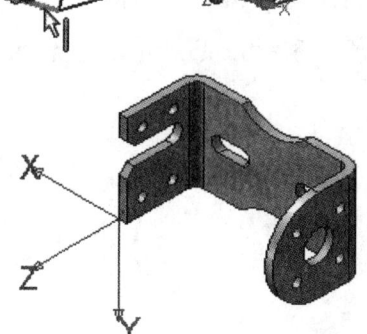

6. Click **OK** from the Coordinate System PropertyManager. Coordinate System1 is displayed.

7. **Locate** the Center of mass based on the location of the illustrated coordinate system. Select Coordinate System1.

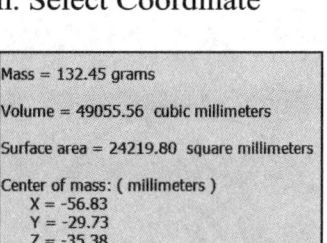

- X: -56.83 millimeters

- Y: -29.73 millimeters

- Z: -35.38 millimeters

Mass = 132.45 grams

Volume = 49055.56 cubic millimeters

Surface area = 24219.80 square millimeters

Center of mass: (millimeters)
  X = -56.83
  Y = -29.73
  Z = -35.38

8. **Save** the part and name it Advanced Part 4-5B.

9. **Close** the model.

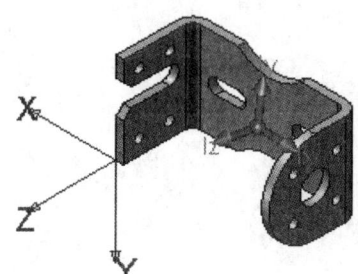

In the Advanced Part Modeling category, an exam question could read: Build this model. Locate the Center of mass.

- A: X = -56.83 millimeters, Y = -29.73 millimeters, Z = -35.38 millimeters

- B: X = 1.80 millimeters, Y = -0.27 millimeters, Z = -35.54 millimeters

- C: X = -59.20 millimeters, Y = -0.27 millimeters, Z = -15.54 millimeters

- D: X= -1.80 millimeters, Y = 1.05 millimeters, Z = -0.14 millimeters

The correct answer is A.

Tutorial: Advanced Part 4-6

An exam question in this category could read: Build this part in SOLIDWORKS. Calculate the overall mass and locate the Center of mass of the illustrated model.

1. **Create** a new part in SOLIDWORKS.

2. **Build** the illustrated dimensioned model. Insert twelve features and a Reference plane: Extrude-Thin1, two Extruded Bosses, Extruded Cut, Extruded Boss, Extruded Cut, Plane1, Mirror and five Extruded Cuts.

Think about the steps that you would take to build the illustrated part. Create an Extrude-Thin1 feature as the Base feature.

3. **Set** the document properties for the model. Review the given information.

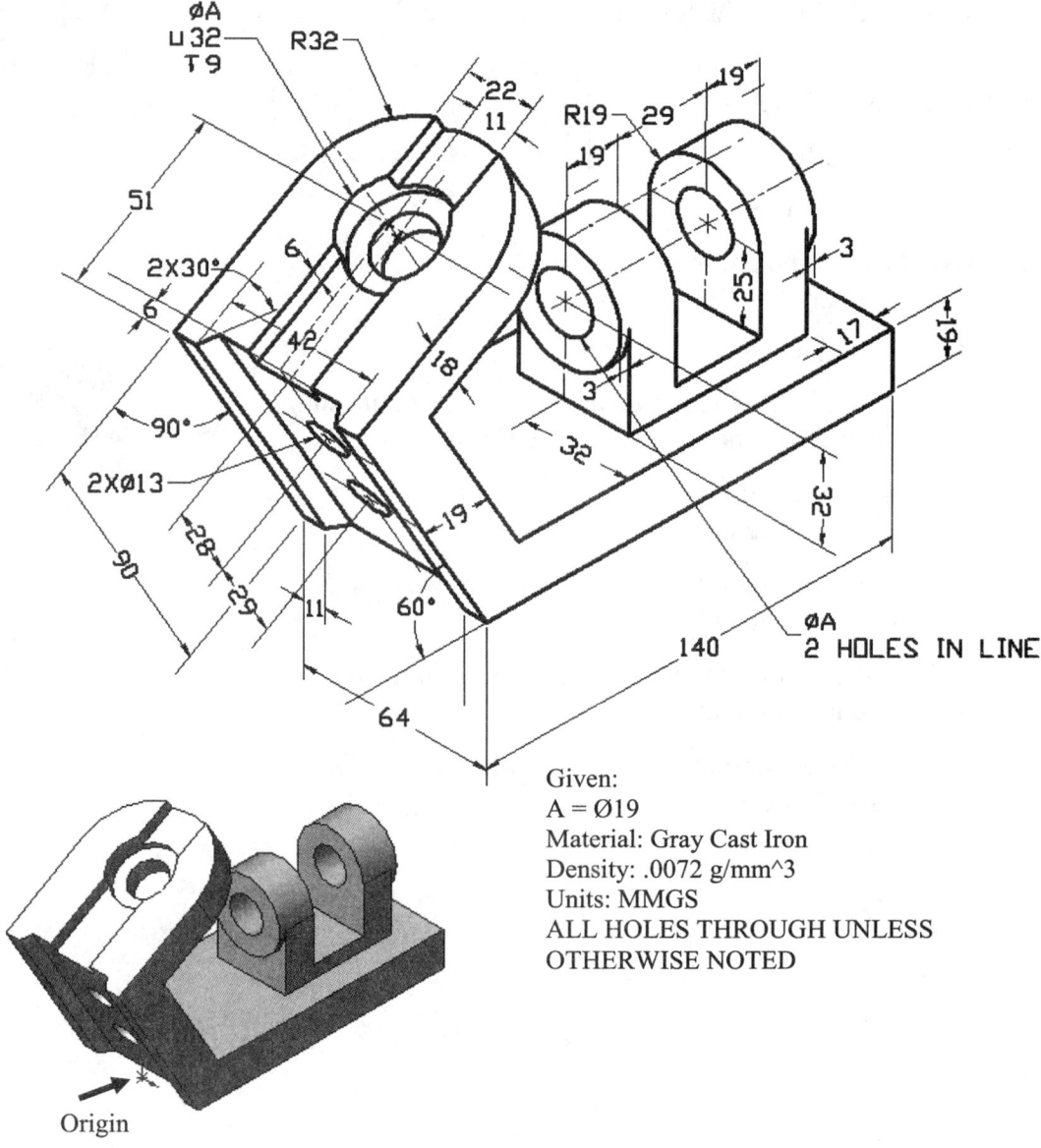

Given:
A = Ø19
Material: Gray Cast Iron
Density: .0072 g/mm^3
Units: MMGS
ALL HOLES THROUGH UNLESS
OTHERWISE NOTED

Origin

4. Create **Sketch1**. Sketch1 is the Base sketch. Select the Right Plane as the Sketch plane. Apply construction geometry. Insert the required geometric relations and dimensions. Sketch1 is the profile for Extrude-Thin1. Note the location of the Origin.

5. Create the **Extrude-Thin1** feature. Apply symmetry. Select Mid Plane as the End Condition in Direction 1. Depth = 64mm. Thickness = 19mm.

6. Create **Sketch2**. Select the top narrow face of Extrude-Thin1 as the Sketch plane. Sketch three lines: two vertical and one horizontal and a tangent arc. Insert the required geometric relations and dimensions.

7. Create the **Boss-Extrude1** feature. Blind is the default End Condition in Direction 1. Depth = 18mm.

8. Create **Sketch3**. Select the Right Plane as the Sketch plane. Sketch a rectangle. Insert the required geometric relations and dimensions. Note: 61mm = (19mm - 3mm) x 2 + 29mm.

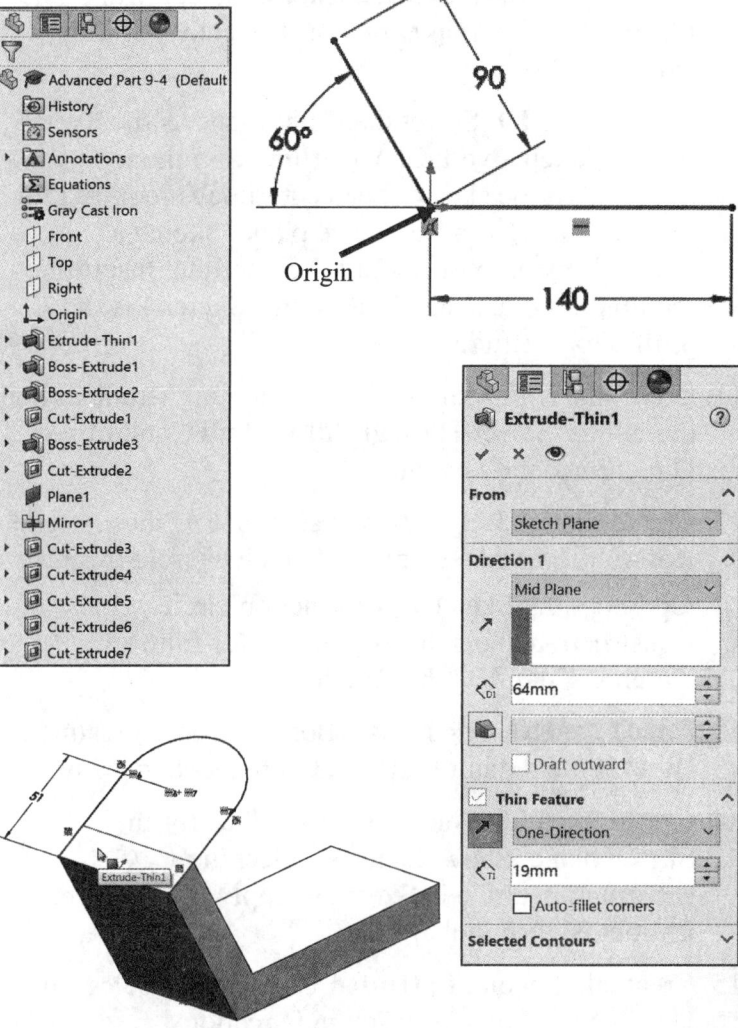

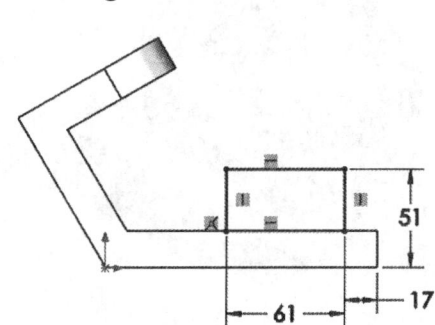

9. Create the **Boss-Extrude2** feature. Select Mid Plane for End Condition in Direction 1. Depth = 38mm. Note: 2 x R19.

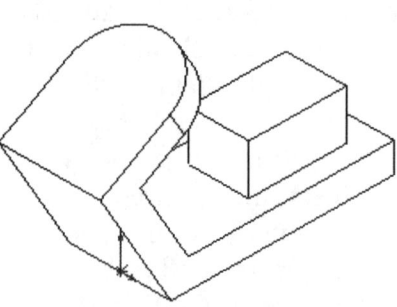

10. Create **Sketch4**. Select the Right Plane as the Sketch plane. Sketch a vertical centerline from the top midpoint of the sketch. The centerline is required for Plane1. Plane1 is a Reference plane. Sketch a rectangle symmetric about the centerline. Insert the required relations and dimensions. Sketch4 is the profile for Extrude3.

11. Create the first **Extruded Cut** feature. Extrude in both directions. Select Through All for End Condition in Direction 1 and Direction 2.

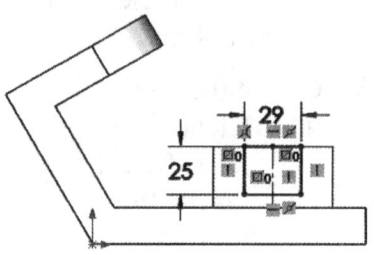

12. Create **Sketch5**. Select the inside face of the Extrude feature for the Sketch plane. Sketch a circle from the top midpoint. Sketch a construction circle. Construction geometry is required for future features. Complete the sketch.

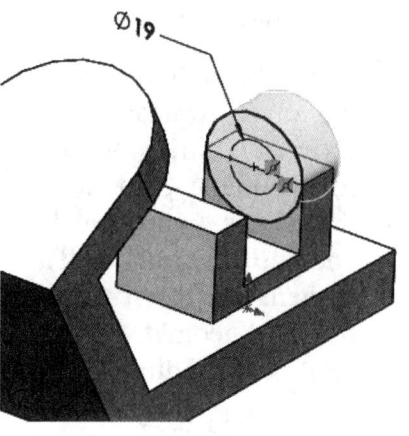

13. Create the **Extruded Boss** (Boss-Extrude3) feature. Blind is the default End Condition. Depth = 19mm.

14. Create **Sketch6**. Select the inside face for the Sketch plane. Show Sketch5. Select the construction circle in Sketch5. Apply the Convert Entities Sketch tool.

15. Create the second **Extruded Cut** feature. Select the Up To Next End Condition in Direction 1.

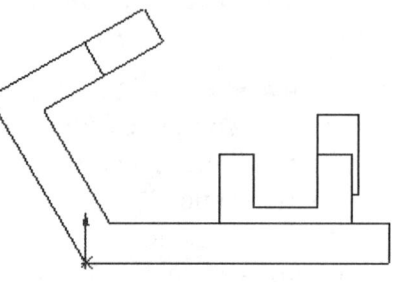

There are numerous ways to create the models in this chapter. A goal is to display different design intents and techniques

Tangent edges and origin are displayed for educational purposes.

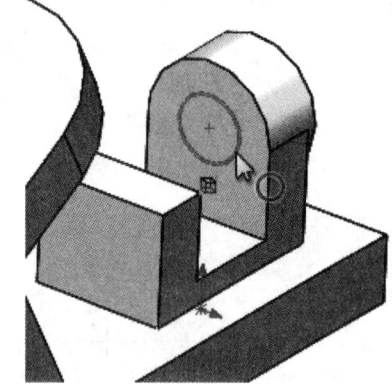

16. Create **Plane1**. Apply symmetry. Create Plane1 to mirror Cut-Extrude2 and Boss-Extrude3. Create a Parallel Plane at Point. Select the midpoint of Sketch4, and Face<1> as illustrated. Point1@Sketch4 and Face<1> is displayed in the Selections box.

17. Create the **Mirror** feature. Mirror Cut-Extrude2 and Boss-Extrude3 about Plane1.

The Mirror feature creates a copy of a feature (or multiple features) mirrored about a face or a plane. You can select the feature or you can select the faces that comprise the feature.

18. Create **Sketch7**. Select the top front angled face of Extrude-Thin1 as the Sketch plane. Apply the Centerline Sketch tool. Insert the required geometric relations and dimensions.

19. Create the third **Extruded Cut** feature. Select Through All for End Condition in Direction 1. Select the angle edge for the vector to extrude as illustrated.

Click on the additional views during the CSWA exam to better understand the part and provided information. Read each question carefully. Identify the dimensions, center of mass and units. Apply needed material.

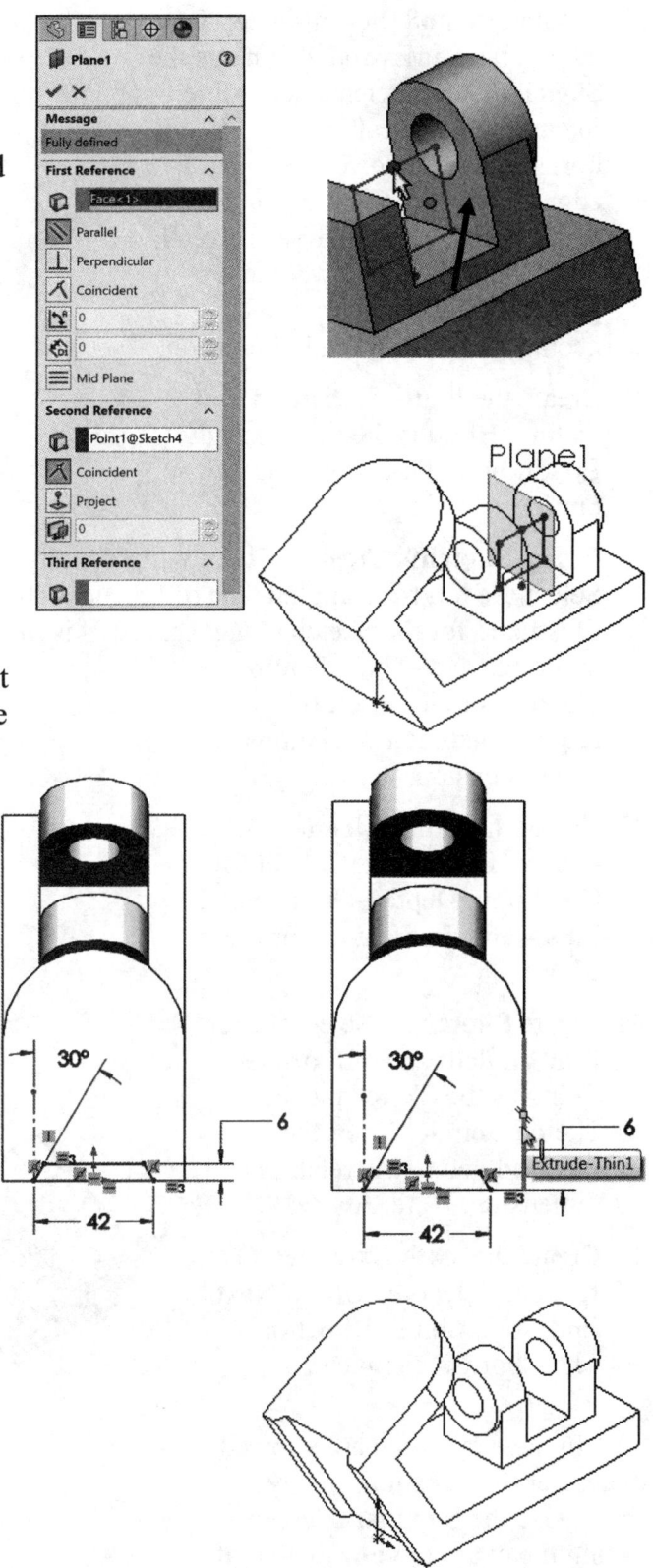

20. Create **Sketch8**. Select the top front angled face of Extrude-Thin1 as the Sketch plane. Sketch a centerline. Sketch two vertical lines and a horizontal line. Select the top arc edge. Apply the Convert Entities Sketch tool. Apply the Trim Sketch tool to remove the unwanted arc geometry. Insert the required geometric relations and dimension.

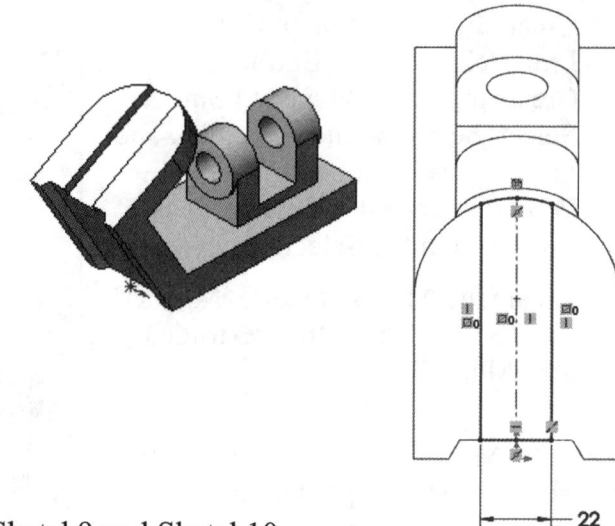

21. Create the fourth **Extruded Cut** feature. Blind is the default End Condition in Direction 1. Depth = 6mm.

22. Create **Sketch9**. Create a Cbore with Sketch9 and Sketch10. Select the top front angled face of Extrude-Thin1 as illustrated for the Sketch plane. Extrude8 is the center hole in the Extrude-Thin1 feature. Sketch a circle. Insert the required geometric relations and dimension.

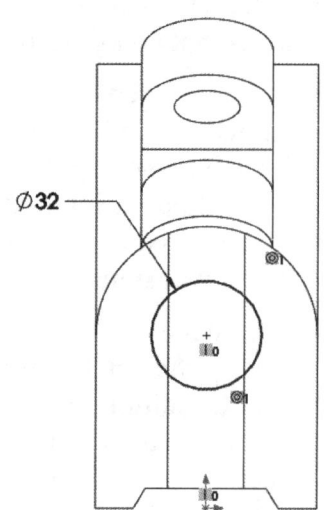

23. Create the fifth **Extrude Cut** feature. Blind is the default End Condition. Depth = 9mm. Note: This is the first feature for the Cbore.

24. Create **Sketch10**. Select the top front angled face of Extrude-Thin1 as the Sketch plane. Sketch a circle. Insert the required geometric relation and dimension. Note: A = Ø19.

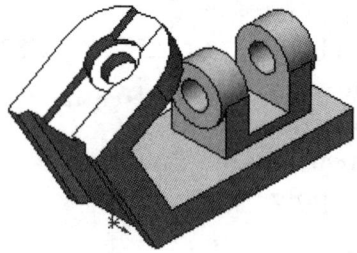

25. Create the sixth **Extruded Cut** feature. Select the Up To Next End Condition in Direction 1. The Cbore is complete.

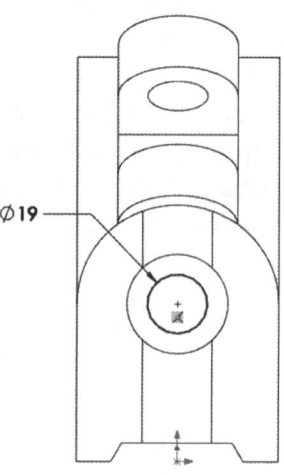

☀ In the exam, you are allowed to answer the questions in any order. Use the Summary Screen during the exam to view the list of all questions you have or have not answered.

26. Create **Sketch11**. Select the front angle face of the Extrude feature for the Sketch plane. Sketch two circles. Insert the required geometric relations and dimensions.

27. Create the last **Extruded Cut** feature. Select the Up To Next End Condition in Direction 1.

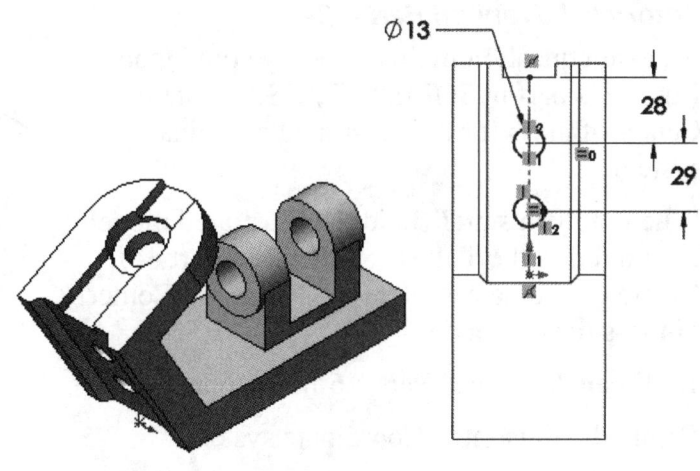

💡 The FilletXpert manages, organizes and reorders constant radius fillets.

💡 The FilletXpert automatically calls the FeatureXpert tool when it has trouble placing a fillet on the specified geometry.

28. **Assign** the material to the part.

29. **Calculate** the overall mass of the part. The overall mass = 2536.59 grams.

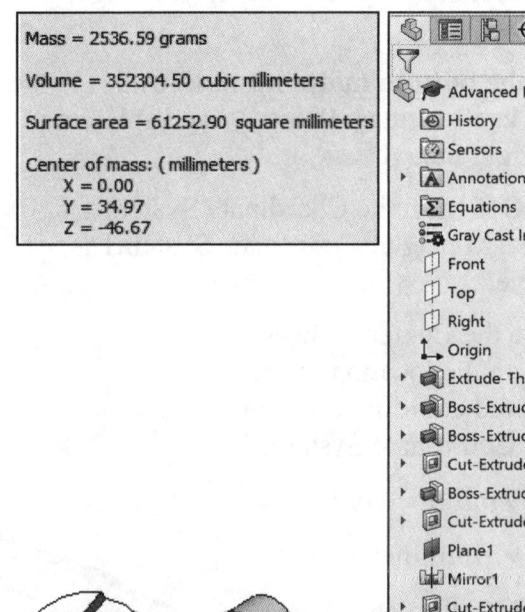

30. **Locate** the Center of mass relative to the part Origin:

- X: 0.00 millimeters

- Y: 34.97 millimeters

- Z: -46.67 millimeters

31. **Save** the part and name it Advanced Part 4-6.

💡 This book is designed to expose the new user to many tools, techniques and procedures. It may not always use the most direct tool or process.

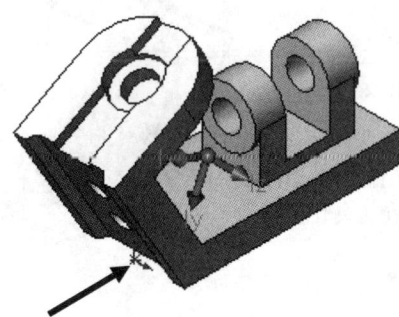

Origin

Tutorial: Advanced Part 4-6A

An exam question in this category could read: Build this part in SOLIDWORKS. Locate the Center of mass for the illustrated coordinate system.

Where do you start? Build the illustrated model as you did in the Tutorial: Advanced Part 4-6. Create Coordinate System1 to locate the Center of mass for the model.

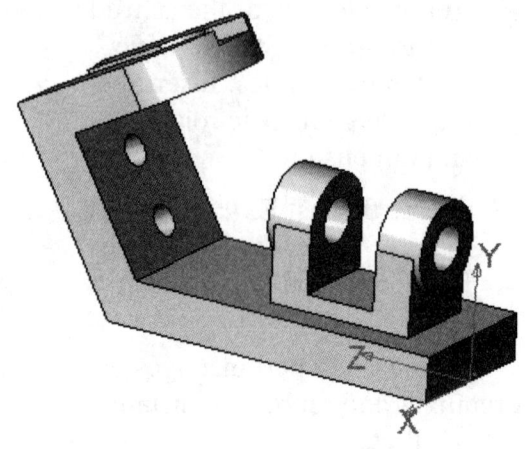

1. **Open** Advanced Part 4-6 from your folder.

Create the illustrated Coordinate system.

2. Click the **Coordinate System** tool from the Consolidated Reference Geometry toolbar. The Coordinate System PropertyManager is displayed.

3. Click the **bottom midpoint** of Extrude-Thin1 as illustrated. Point<1> is displayed in the Origin box.

4. Click **OK** from the Coordinate System PropertyManager. Coordinate System1 is displayed.

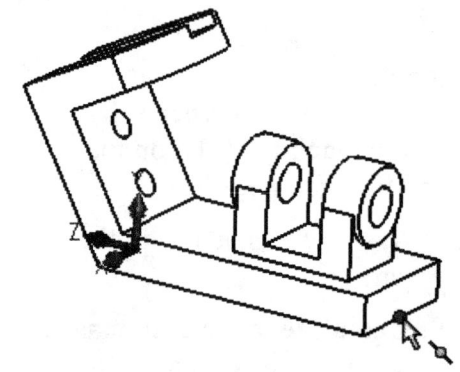

5. **Locate** the Center of mass based on the location of the illustrated coordinate system. Select Coordinate System1.

- X: 0.00 millimeters

- Y: 34.97 millimeters

- Z: 93.33 millimeters

Mass = 2536.59 grams

Volume = 352304.50 cubic millimeters

Surface area = 61252.90 square millimeters

Center of mass: (millimeters)
   X = 0.00
   Y = 34.97
   Z = 93.33

6. **Save** the part and name it Advanced Part 4-6A.

7. **View** the Center of mass with the default coordinate system.

8. **Close** the model.

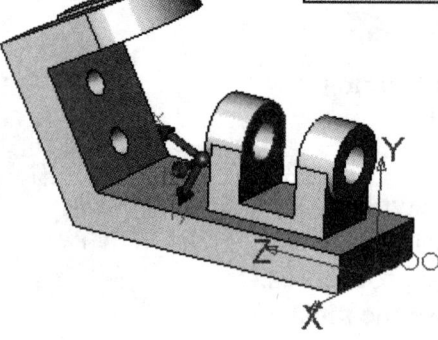

Tutorial: Advanced Part 4-7

An exam question in this category could read: Build this part in SOLIDWORKS. Calculate the overall mass and locate the Center of mass of the illustrated model.

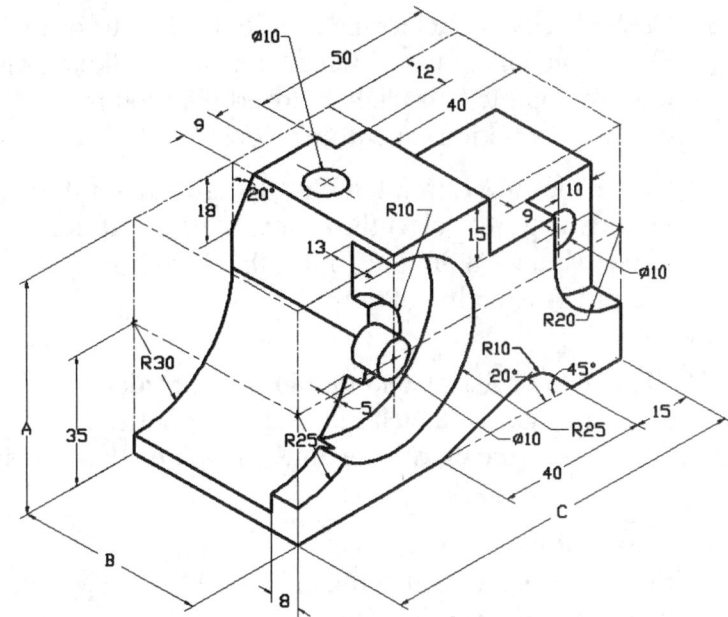

💡 If needed, see additional model views and dimensions at the end of this tutorial.

1. **Create** a new part in SOLIDWORKS.

2. **Build** the illustrated dimensioned model. Insert thirteen features: Extruded Base, nine Extruded Cuts, two Extruded Bosses and a Chamfer. Note: The center point of the top hole is located 30mm from the top right edge.

Think about the steps that you would take to build the illustrated part. Review the centerlines that outline the overall size of the part.

3. **Set** the document properties for the model.

4. Create **Sketch1**. Sketch1 is the Base sketch. Select the Right Plane as the Sketch plane. Sketch a rectangle. Insert the required geometric relations and dimensions. The part Origin is located in the bottom left corner of the sketch.

5. Create the **Extruded Base** feature. Blind is the default End Condition in Direction 1. Depth = 50mm. Boss-Extrude1 is the Base feature.

Given:
A = 63, B = 50, C = 100
Material: Copper
Units: MMGS
Density: .0089 g/mm^3
Top hole is 20mm from the top front edge.
All HOLES THROUGH ALL

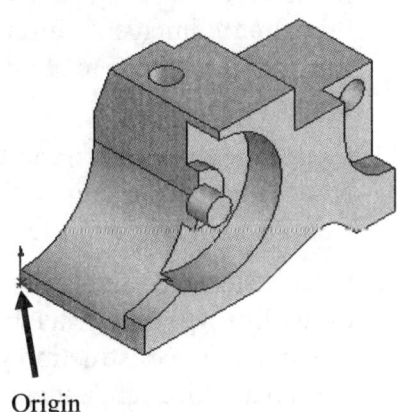

Origin

6. Create **Sketch2**. Select the right face of Extrude1 as the Sketch plane. Sketch a 90deg tangent arc. Sketch three lines to complete the sketch. Insert the required geometric relations and dimensions.

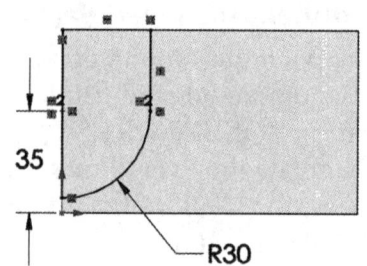

7. Create the first **Extruded Cut** feature. Offset the extrude feature. Select the Offset Start Condition. Offset value = 8.0mm. Blind is the default End Condition. Depth = 50mm.

The default Start Condition in the Extrude PropertyManager is Sketch Plane. The Offset start condition starts the extrude feature on a plane that is offset from the current Sketch plane.

8. Create **Sketch3**. Select the right face as the Sketch plane. Create the Extrude profile. Insert the required geometric relations and dimensions.

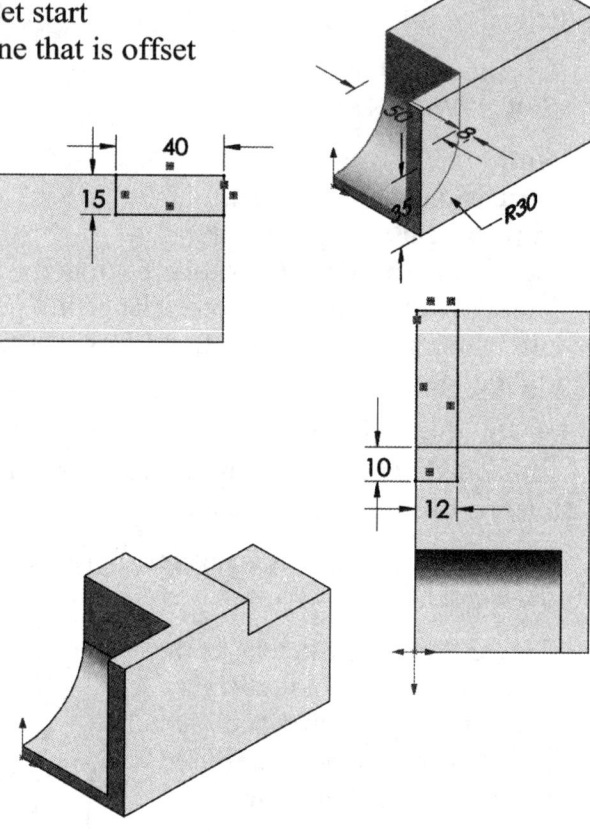

9. Create the second **Extruded Cut** feature. Select Through All for End Condition in Direction 1.

10. Create **Sketch4**. Select the top face of the Extrude feature as the Sketch Plane. Select the top edge to reference the 10mm dimension. Insert the required geometric relations and dimensions.

11. Create the third **Extruded Cut** feature. Select Through All for End Condition in Direction 1.

12. Create **Sketch5**. Select the right face of the Extrude feature as the Sketch Plane. Apply construction geometry. Sketch a 90deg tangent arc. Sketch three lines to complete the sketch. Insert the required geometric relations and dimensions.

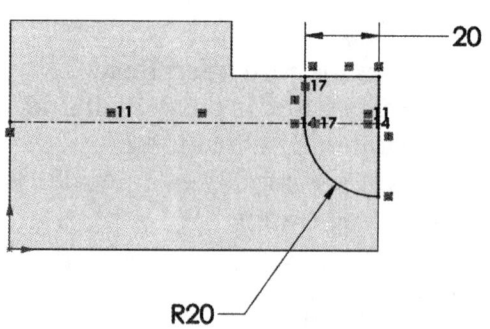

13. Create the fourth **Extruded Cut** feature. Blind is the default End Condition. Depth = 9mm.

14. Create **Sketch6**. Select the right face of the Extrude feature as the Sketch plane. Sketch a circle. Insert the required dimensions.

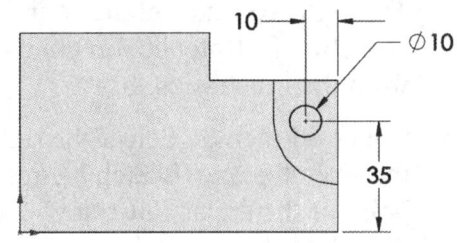

15. Create the fifth **Extruded Cut** feature. Select Through All for End Condition in Direction 1.

16. Create **Sketch7**. The top hole is 20mm from the top front edge. Select the top face of Extrude1 as the Sketch Plane. Sketch a circle. Insert the required dimensions and relations.

17. Create the sixth **Extruded Cut** feature. Select Through All for End Condition in Direction 1.

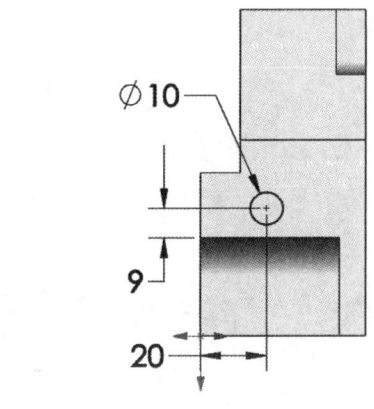

There are numerous ways to create the models in this chapter. A goal of this text is to display different design intents and techniques.

18. Create **Sketch8**. Select the right face of Extrude1 as the Sketch plane. Insert a tangent arc as illustrated. Complete the sketch. Insert the required relations and dimensions.

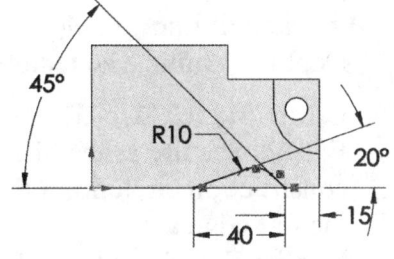

19. Create the seventh **Extruded Cut** feature. Apply symmetry. Select the Through All End Condition in Direction 1 and Direction 2.

20. Create **Sketch9**. Select the right face of Extrude1 as the Sketch plane. Select Hidden Lines Visible. Sketch two construction circles centered about the end point of the arc. Apply the 3 Point Arc Sketch tool. Complete the sketch. Insert the required relations and dimensions.

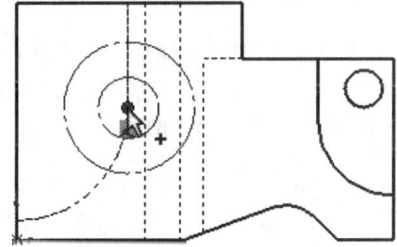

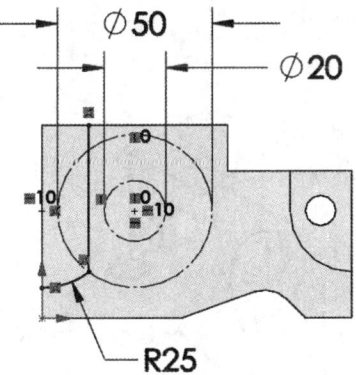

21. Create the eighth **Extruded Cut** feature. Select the Through All End Condition in Direction 1 and Direction 2. Note the direction of the extrude feature from the illustration.

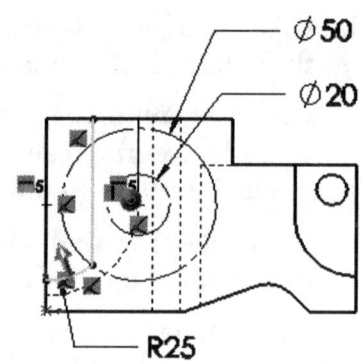

22. Create **Sketch10**. Select the right face of Extrude1 as the Sketch plane. Sketch a circle centered at the end point of the arc as illustrated. Apply the Trim Entities Sketch tool. Display Sketch9. Complete the sketch. Insert the required geometric relations.

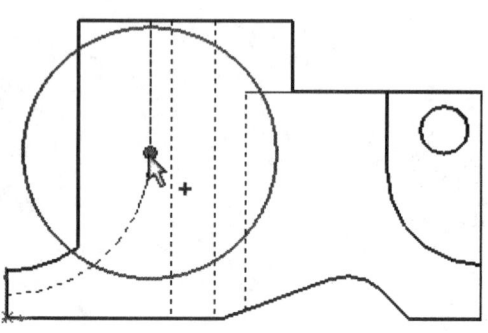
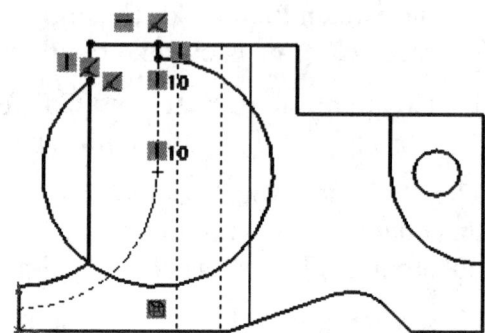

23. Create the ninth **Extruded Cut** feature. Blind is the default End Condition in Direction 1. Depth = 13mm. The feature is displayed.

24. Create **Sketch11**. Select the right face of the Extrude feature as the Sketch plane. Select the construction circle from Sketch9, the left arc, and the left edge as illustrated. Apply the Convert Entities Sketch tool. Apply the Trim Sketch tool. Insert the required relations.

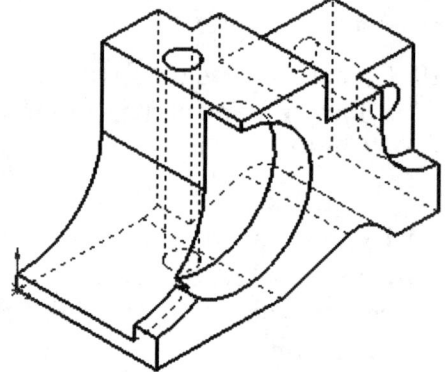

25. Create the **Extruded Boss** feature. Blind is the default End Condition in Direction 1. Depth = 5.00mm.

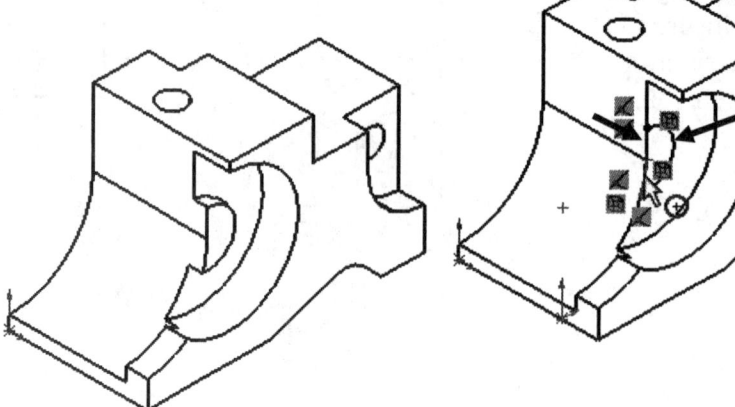

26. Create **Sketch12**. Select the right face of the Extrude feature as the Sketch plane. Sketch a circle. Insert the required relation and dimension.

27. Create the **Extruded Boss** feature. Select the Up To Surface End Condition in Direction 1. Select the right face of Extrude1 for Direction 1.

28. Create the **Chamfer** feature. Chamfer the left edge as illustrated. Distance = 18mm. Angle = 20deg.

29. **Assign** the material to the part.

30. **Calculate** the overall mass of the part. The overall mass = 1280.33 grams.

31. **Locate** the Center of mass relative to the part Origin:

- X: 26.81 millimeters

- Y: 25.80 millimeters

- Z: -56.06 millimeters

32. **Save** the part and name it Advanced Part 4-7.

33. **Close** the model.

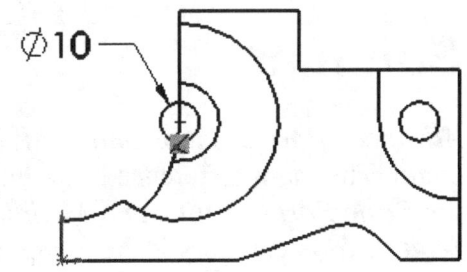

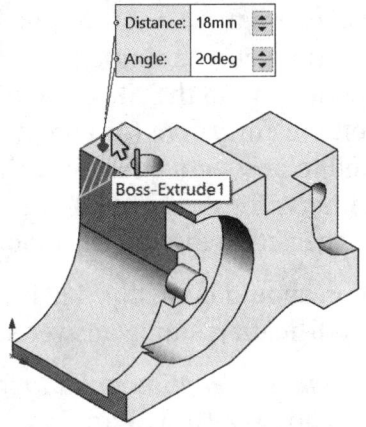

This example was taken from the SOLIDWORKS website as an example of an Advanced Part on the CSWA exam. This model has thirteen features and twelve sketches. As stated throughout the text, there are numerous ways to create the models in these chapters.

A goal in this text is to display different design intents and techniques, and to provide you with the ability to successfully address the models in the given time frame of the CSWA exam.

Click on the different provided views to obtain additional model information.

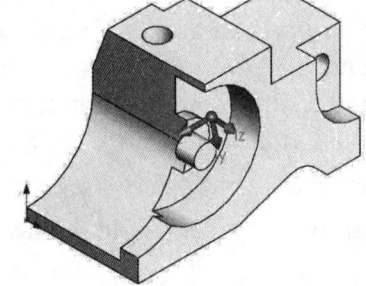

Mass = 1280.33 grams

Volume = 143857.58 cubic millimeters

Surface area = 26112.48 square millimeters

Center of mass: (millimeters)
X = 26.81
Y = 25.80
Z = -56.06

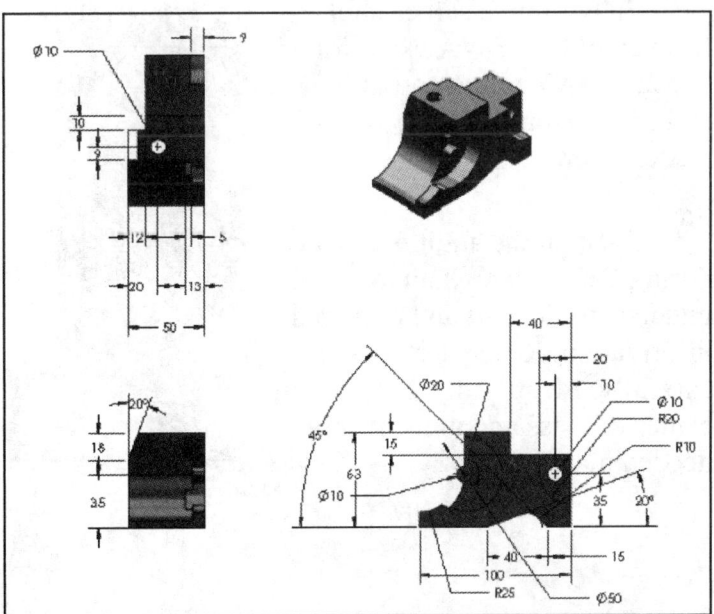

Summary

Advanced Part Creation and Modification is one of the five categories on the CSWA exam. The main difference between the *Advanced Part Creation and Modification* and the *Basic Part Creation and Modification* or the *Intermediate Part Creation and Modification* category is the complexity of the sketches and the number of dimensions and geometric relations along with an increased number of features.

There are three questions on the CSWA exam in this category. One question is in a multiple choice single answer format and the other two questions (Modification of the model) are in the fill in the blank format. Each question is worth fifteen (15) points for a total of forty-five (45) points. You are required to build a model with six or more features and to answer a question either on the overall mass, volume, or the location of the Center of mass for the created model relative to the default part Origin location. You are then requested to modify the model and answer a fill in the blank format question.

You should be within 1% of the multiple choice answer before you go on to the modification single answer section.

Assembly Creation and Modification (Bottom-up) is the next chapter in this book. Up to this point, a Basic Part, Intermediate Part or an Advanced part was the focus. The *Assembly Creation and Modification* category addresses an assembly with numerous sub-components. All subcomponents are provided to you in the exam. The next chapter covers the general concepts and terminology used in the *Assembly Creation and Modification* category and then addresses the core elements. Knowledge of Standard mates is required in this category.

There are four questions - Multiple Choice/Single Answer in the category. Each question is worth 30 points.

View sample screen shots from an older CSWA exam for an Advanced Modeling part at the end of the Homework section in this chapter.

Click on the additional views during the CSWA exam to better understand the part and provided information. Read each question carefully. Identify the dimensions, center of mass and units. Apply needed material.

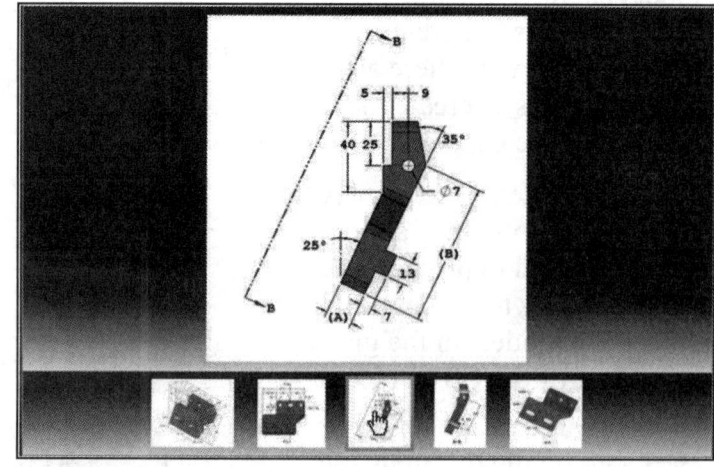

Questions

1. In Tutorial, Advanced Part 4-1 you created the illustrated part. Modify the Base flange thickness from .40in to .50in. Modify the Chamfer feature angle from 45deg to 33deg. Modify the Fillet feature radius from .10in to .125in. Modify the material from 1060 Alloy to Nickel.

Calculate the overall mass of the part, volume, and locate the Center of mass with the provided information.

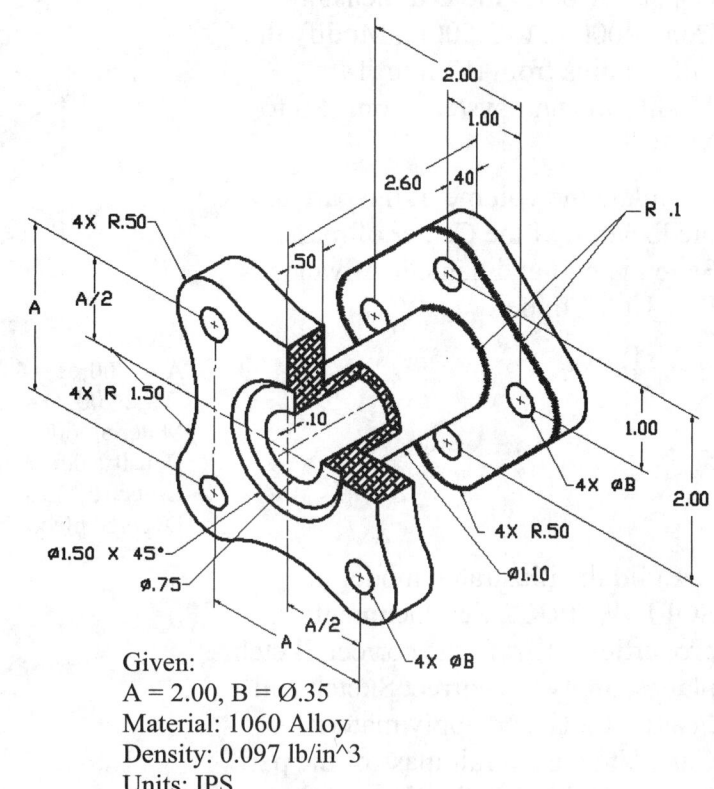

Given:
A = 2.00, B = Ø.35
Material: 1060 Alloy
Density: 0.097 lb/in^3
Units: IPS
Decimal places = 2

2. In Tutorial, Advanced Part 4-2 you created the illustrated part. Modify the CirPattern1 feature. Modify the number of instances from 6 to 8. Modify the seed feature from an 8mm diameter to a 6mm diameter.

Calculate the overall mass, volume, and the location of the Center of mass relative to the part Origin.

Given:
A = 70, B = 76
Material: 6061 Alloy
Density: .0027 g/mm^3
Units: MMGS

3. In Tutorial, Advanced Part 4-3 you created the illustrated part. Modify the material from 6061 Alloy to Copper. Modify the B dimension from 4.000in. to 3.500in. Modify the Fillet radius from .12in to .14in. Modify the unit system from IPS to MMGS.

Calculate the volume of the part and the location of the Center of mass. Save the part and name it Advance Part 10-3 Copper.

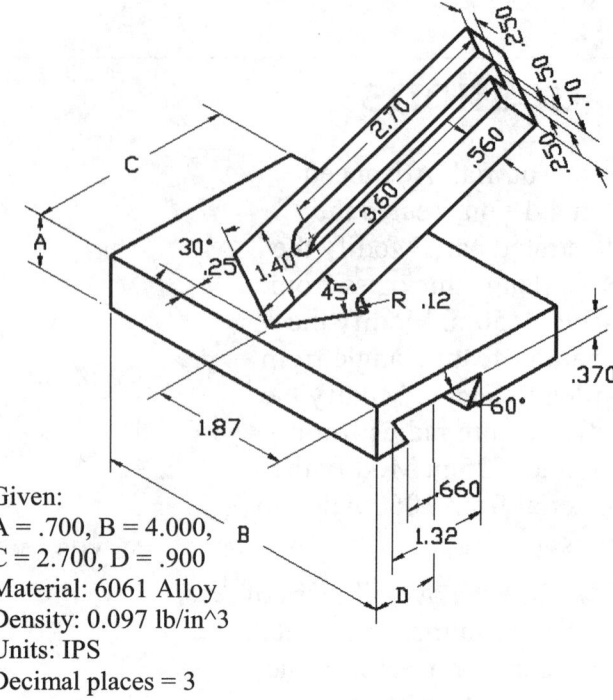

Given:
A = .700, B = 4.000,
C = 2.700, D = .900
Material: 6061 Alloy
Density: 0.097 lb/in^3
Units: IPS
Decimal places = 3

4. Build the illustrated model in SOLIDWORKS. Set document properties, identify the correct Sketch planes, apply the correct Sketch and Feature tools, and apply material. Calculate the overall mass of the part, volume and locate the Center of mass with the provided information.

- Material: 6061 Alloy

- Units: MMGS

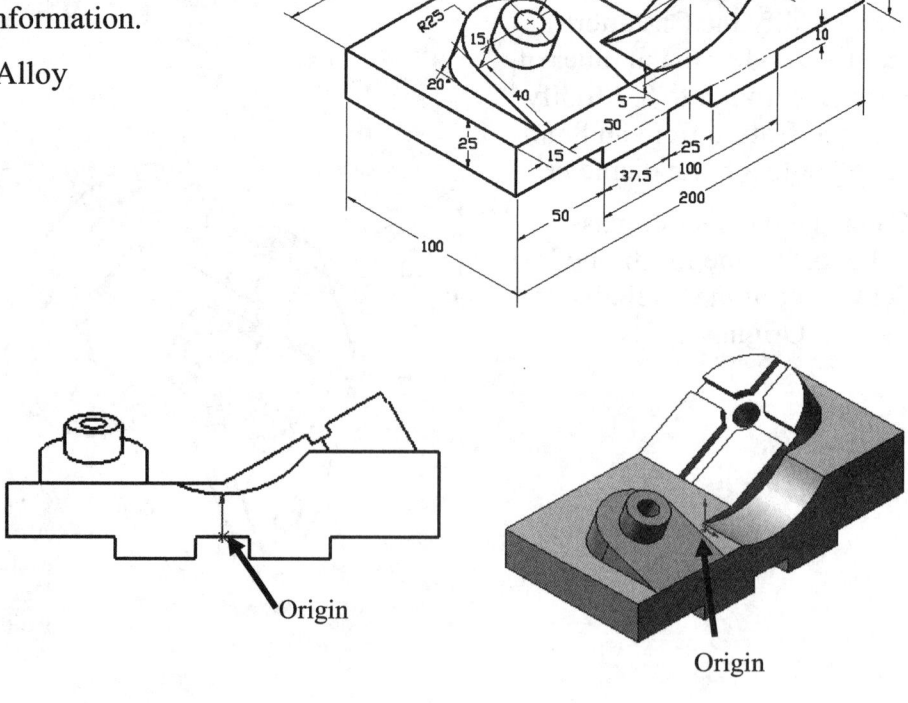

5. Build the illustrated model in SOLIDWORKS. Calculate the overall mass of the part, volume and locate the Center of mass with the provided information. Where do you start? Build the model as you did in the above exercise. Create Coordinate System1 to locate the Center of mass for the model.

- Material: 6061 Alloy

- Units: MMGS

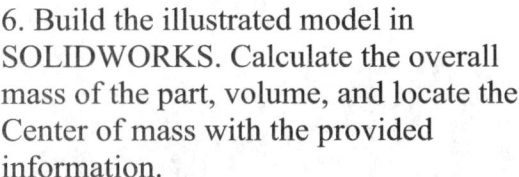

6. Build the illustrated model in SOLIDWORKS. Calculate the overall mass of the part, volume, and locate the Center of mass with the provided information.

- Material: 6061 Alloy

- Units: MMGS

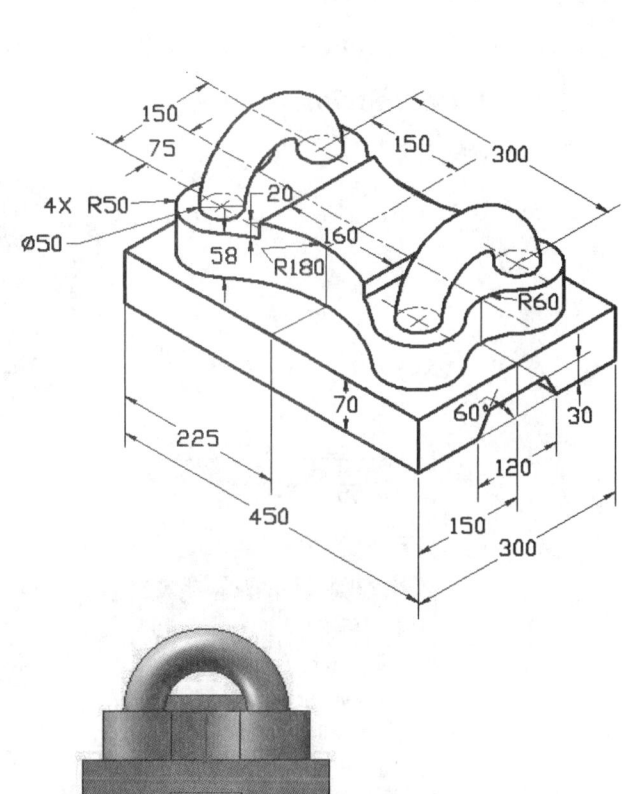

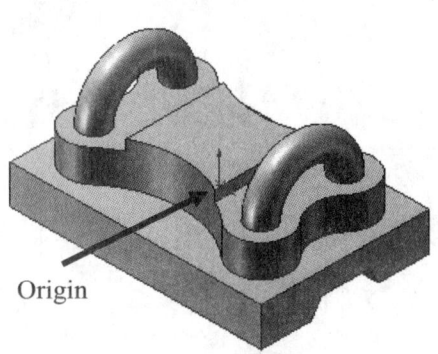

Origin

7. Build the model in SOLIDWORKS. Calculate the overall mass of the part, volume and locate the Center of mass with the provided information. Where do you start? Build the model as you did in the above exercise. Create Coordinate System1 to locate the Center of mass for the model

- Material: 6061 Alloy

- Units: MMGS

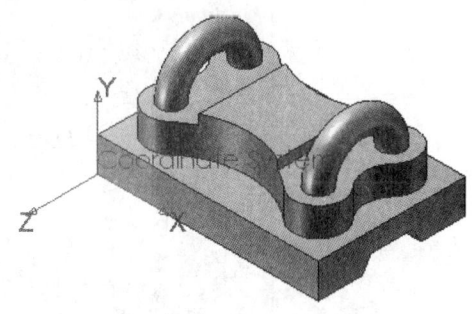

8. Build the model using SOLIDWORKS.

The model is provided in the SOILDWORKS CSWA Folder\Chapter 4 folder.

Open Homework 4.8.

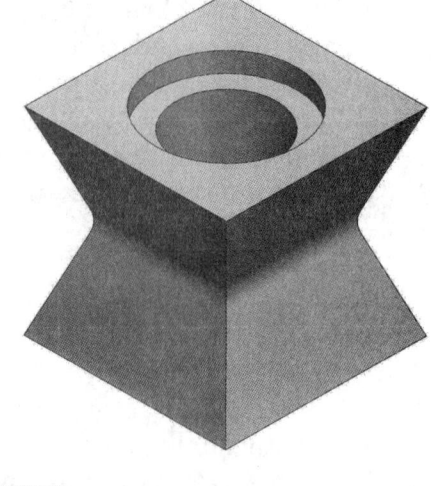

Utilize the rollback bar to view the sketches and features. Note: There are many ways to create this model.

Calculate the overall mass and volume of part with the provided information.

- Precision for linear dimensions = **2**

- Material: **Case Stainless Steel**

- Units: **MMGS**

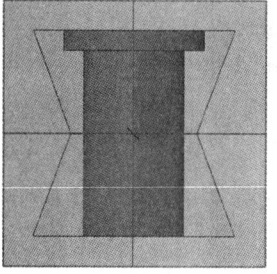

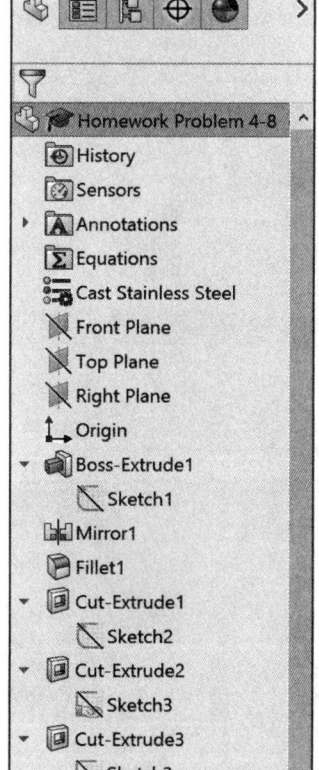
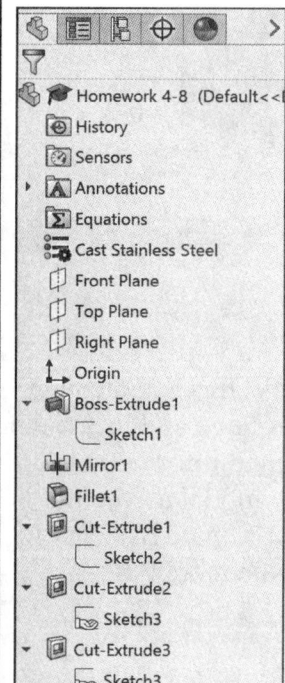
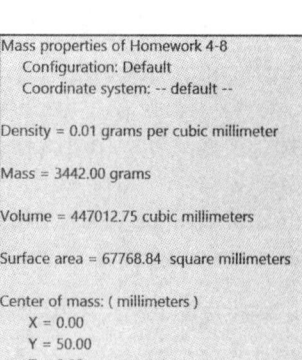

💡 Screen shots from an older CSWA exam for an Advanced Part Creation and Modification question.

Click on the additional views to understand the part and provided information.
Read each question carefully.

Understand the dimensions, center of mass and units.
Apply needed materials.

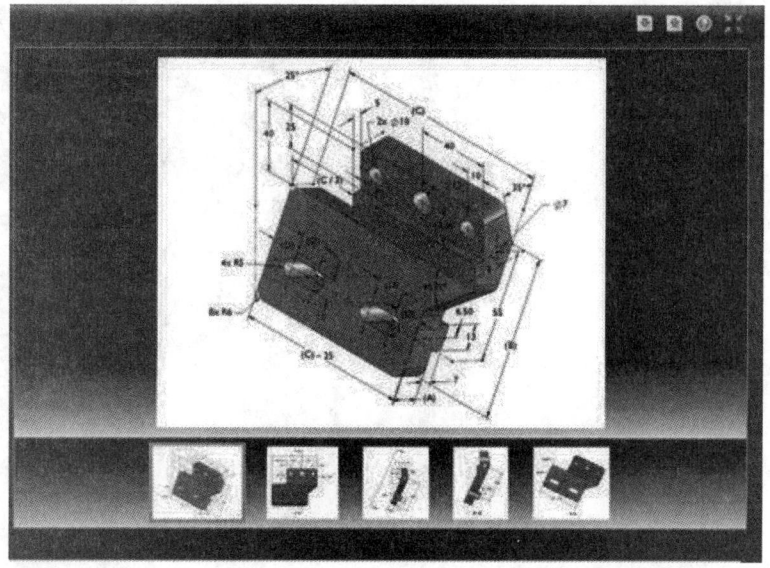

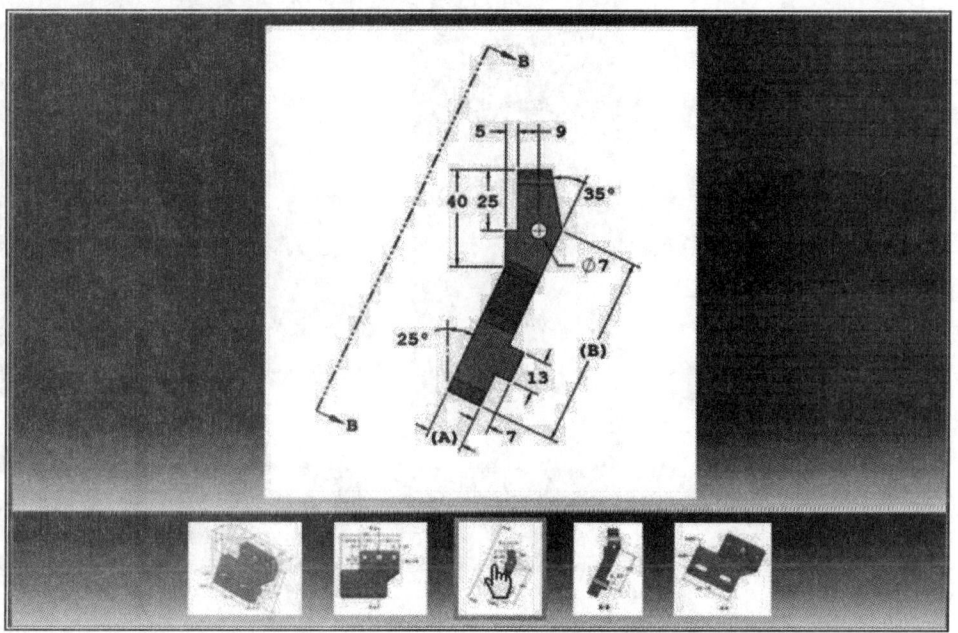

💡 Zoom in on the part if needed.

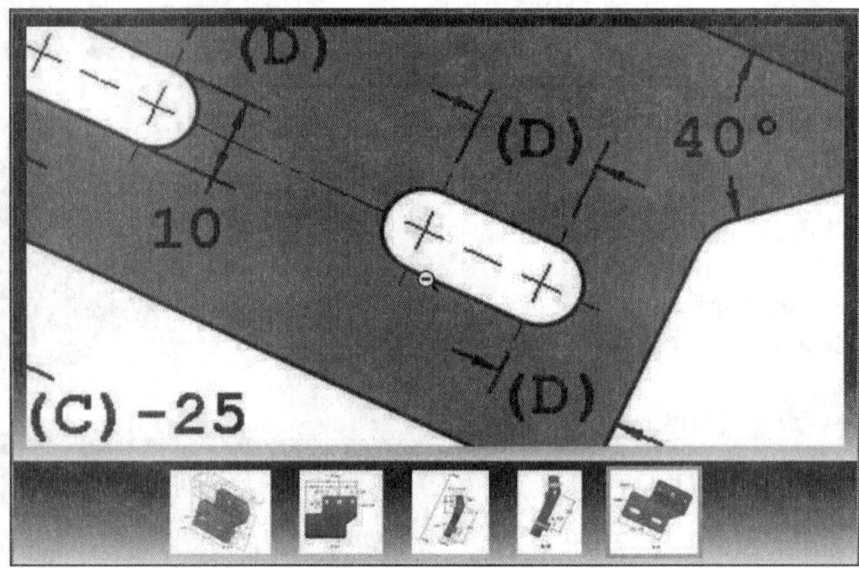

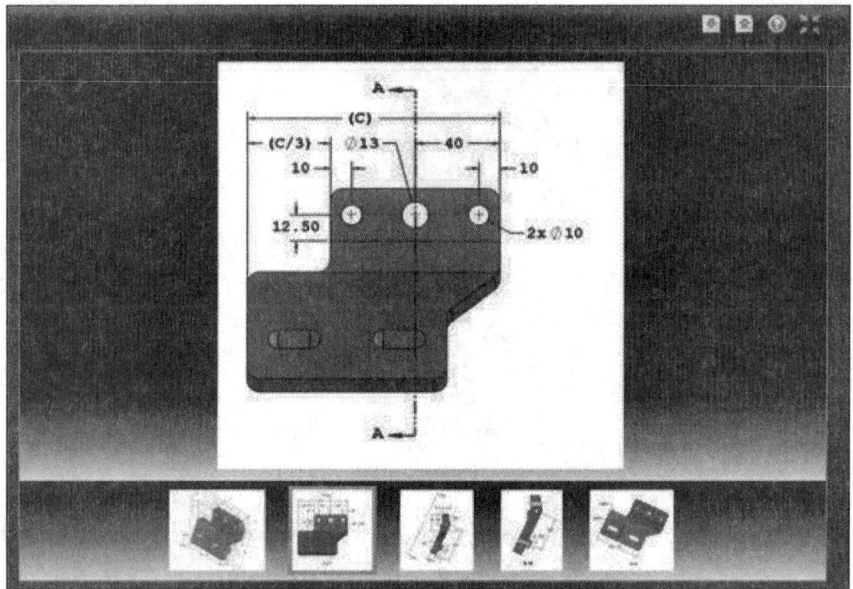

Click on the additional views to understand the part and provided information.

Read each question carefully. Understand the dimensions, center of mass and units.

Apply needed materials.

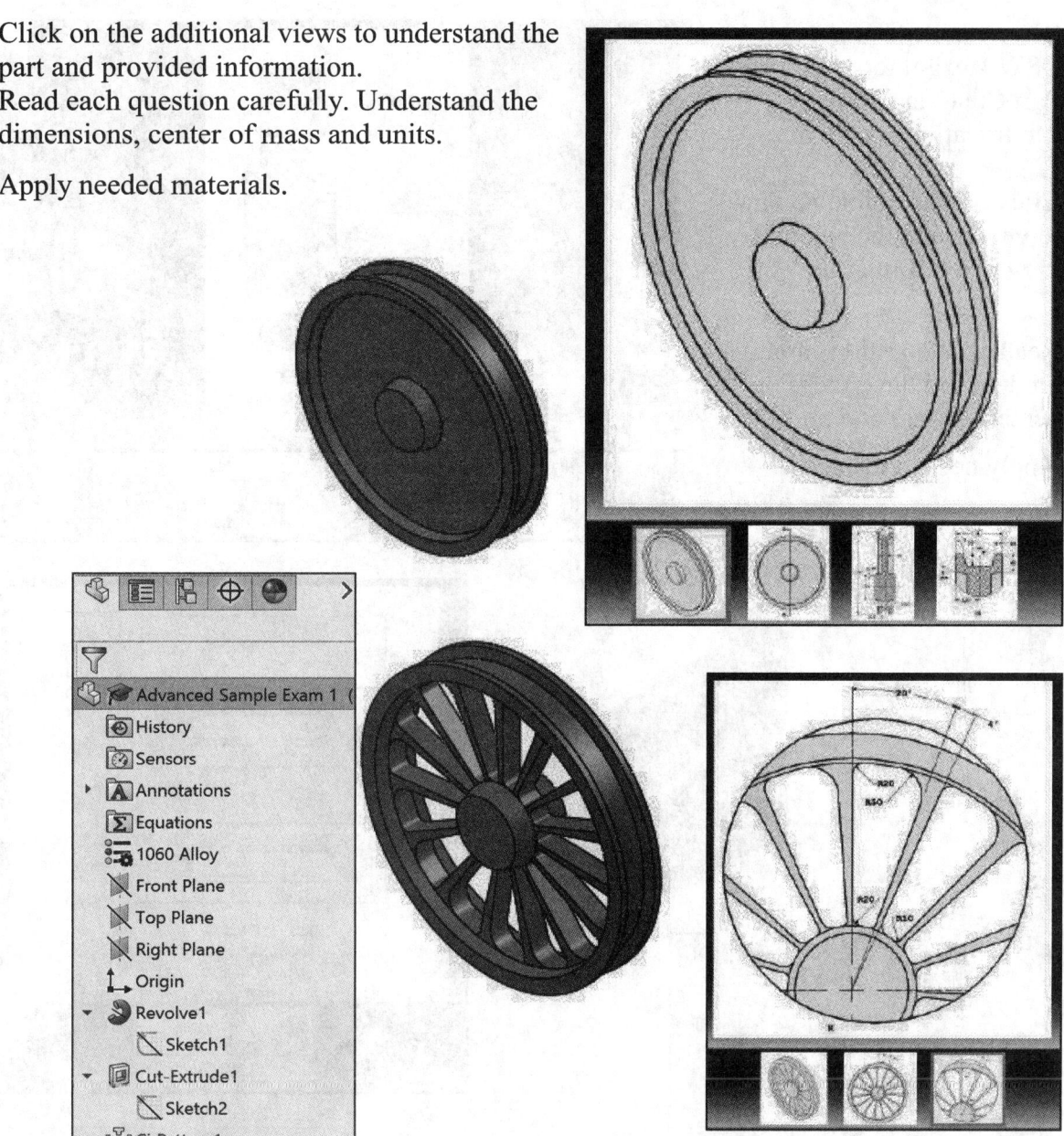

Screen shots from an older
CSWA exam for an Advanced
Part Creation and
Modification question.

Click on the additional views
to understand the part and
provided information.

Read each question carefully.
Understand the dimensions,
center of mass and units.

Apply needed materials.

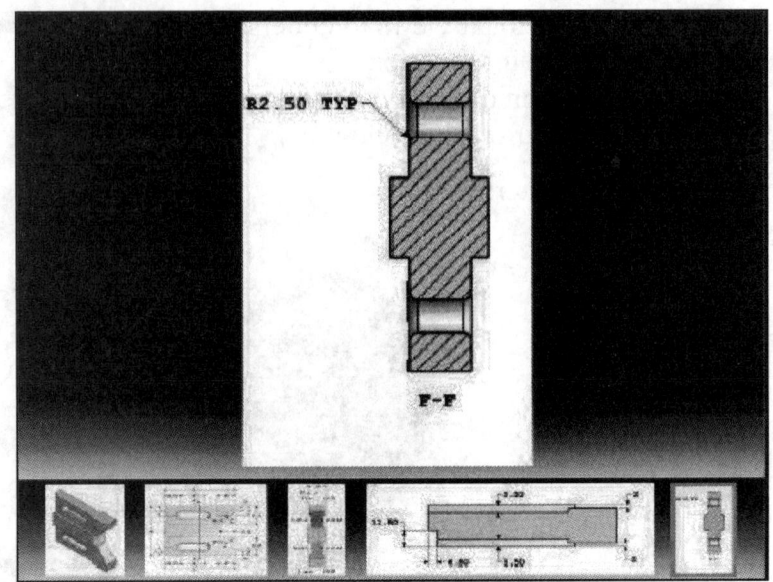

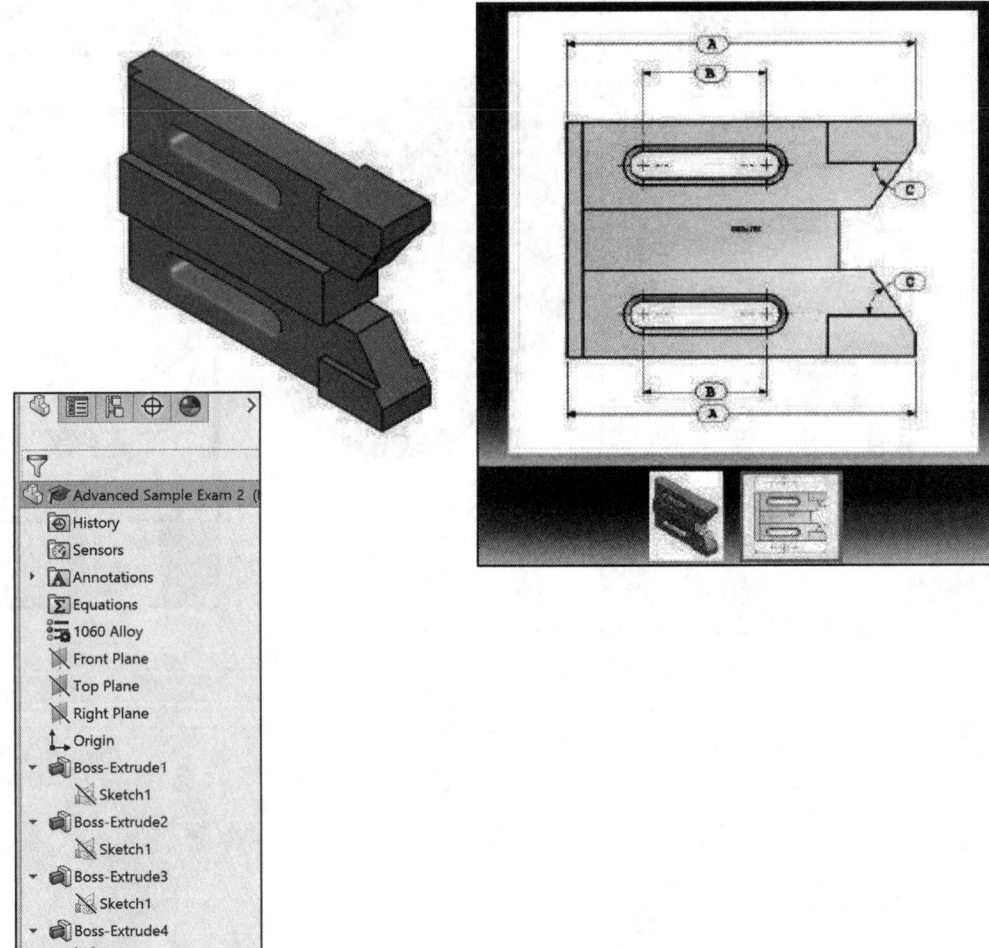

CHAPTER 5 - ASSEMBLY CREATION AND MODIFICATION

Objectives

Assembly Creation and Modification is one of the five categories on the CSWA exam. In the last two chapters, a Basic, Intermediate or Advanced model was the focus. The Assembly Creation and Modification (Bottom-up) category addresses an assembly with numerous components.

This chapter covers the general concepts and terminology used in Assembly modeling and then addresses the core elements that are aligned to the CSWA exam. Knowledge to insert Standard mates and to create a new Coordinate system location is required in this category.

There are four questions on the CSWA exam (2 questions in part 1, 2 questions in part 2) in the Assembly Creation and Modification category: (2) different assemblies - (4) questions - (2) multiple choice/(2) single answer - 30 points each.

The first question is in a multiple choice single answer format. You should be within 1% of the multiple choice answer before you move on to the modification single answer section, (fill in the blank format).

You are required to download the needed components from a provided zip file and insert them correctly to create the assembly.

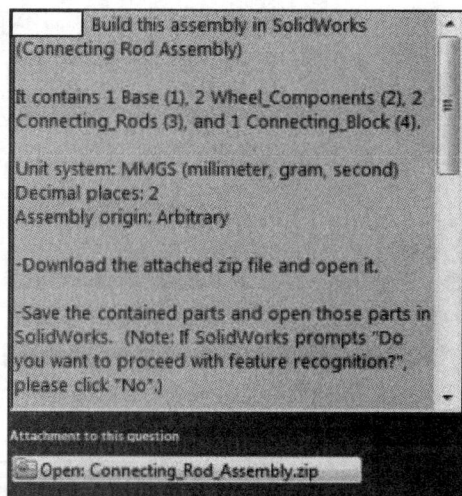

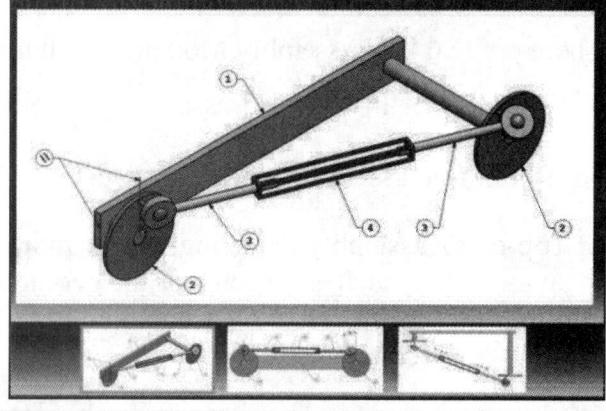

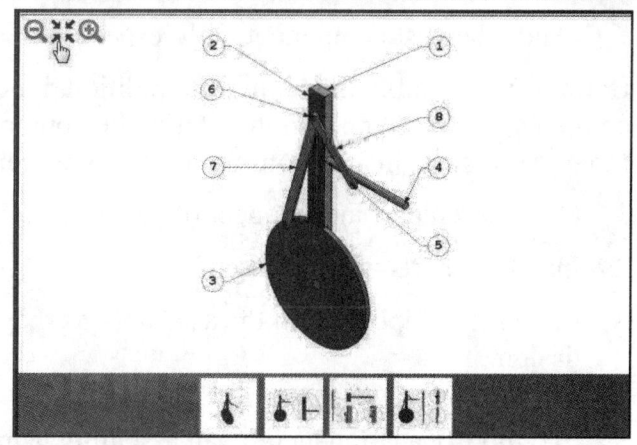

Screen shots from a CSWA exam

On the completion of the chapter, you will be able to:

- Specify Document Properties.

- Identify the first fixed component in an assembly.

- Create a Bottom-up assembly with the following Standard mates:

  - Coincident, Concentric, Perpendicular, Parallel, Tangent, Distance, Angle, and Aligned, Anti-Aligned options.

- Apply the Mirror Component tool.

- Locate the Center of mass relative to the assembly Origin.

- Create a Coordinate system location.

- Locate the Center of mass relative to a created Coordinate system.

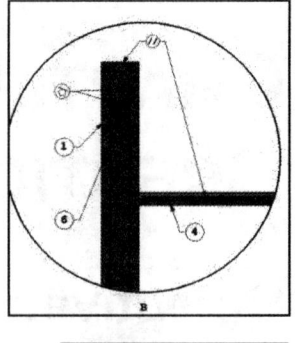

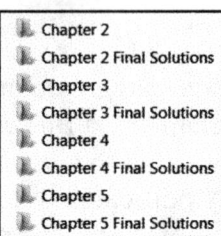

 All SOLIDWORKS models (initial and final) are provided in the SOLIDWORKS CSWA Model Folder. Copy the needed folders to your local hard drive.

Assembly Modeling

There are two key Assembly Modeling techniques:

- Top-down, "In-Context" assembly modeling.

- Bottom-up assembly modeling.

In Top-down assembly modeling, one or more features of a part are defined by something in an assembly, such as a sketch or the geometry of another component. The design intent comes from the top, and moves down into the individual components, hence the name Top-down assembly modeling.

Mate the first component with respect to the assembly reference planes.

Bottom-up assembly modeling is a traditional method that combines individual components. Based on design criteria, the components are developed independently. The three major steps in a Bottom-up design approach are:

1. Create each part independent of any other component in the assembly.

2. Insert the parts into the assembly.

3. Mate the components in the assembly as they relate to the physical constraints of your design.

To modify a component in an assembly using the bottom-up assembly approach, you must edit the individual part.

Build an Assembly from a Detailed Dimensioned illustration

An exam question in this category could read; Build this assembly in SOLIDWORKS. Locate the Center of mass of the model with respect to the illustrated coordinate system. Set decimal place to 2."

The assembly contains the following: (1) Clevis component, (3) Axle components, (2) 5 Hole Link components, (2) 3 Hole Link components, and (6) Collar components. All holes Ø.190 THRU unless otherwise noted. Angle A = 150deg. Angle B = 120deg. Unit system: IPS.

Note: The location of the illustrated coordinate system (+X, +Y, +Z).

In the exam, download the zip file of the components. Unzip the components. Do not use feature recognition when you open the downloaded components. This is a timed exam. You do not need the additional feature information.

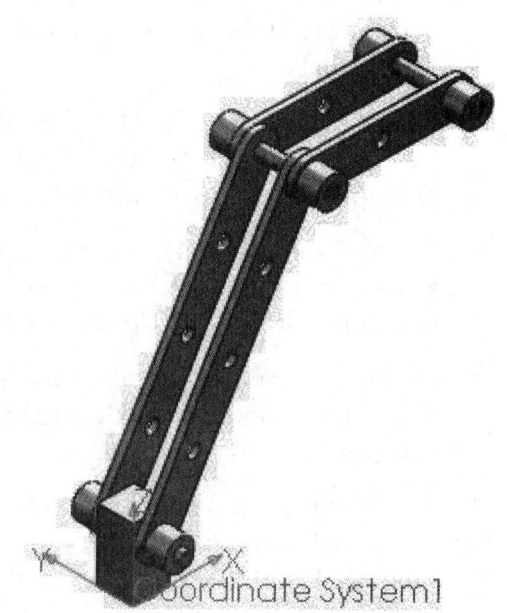

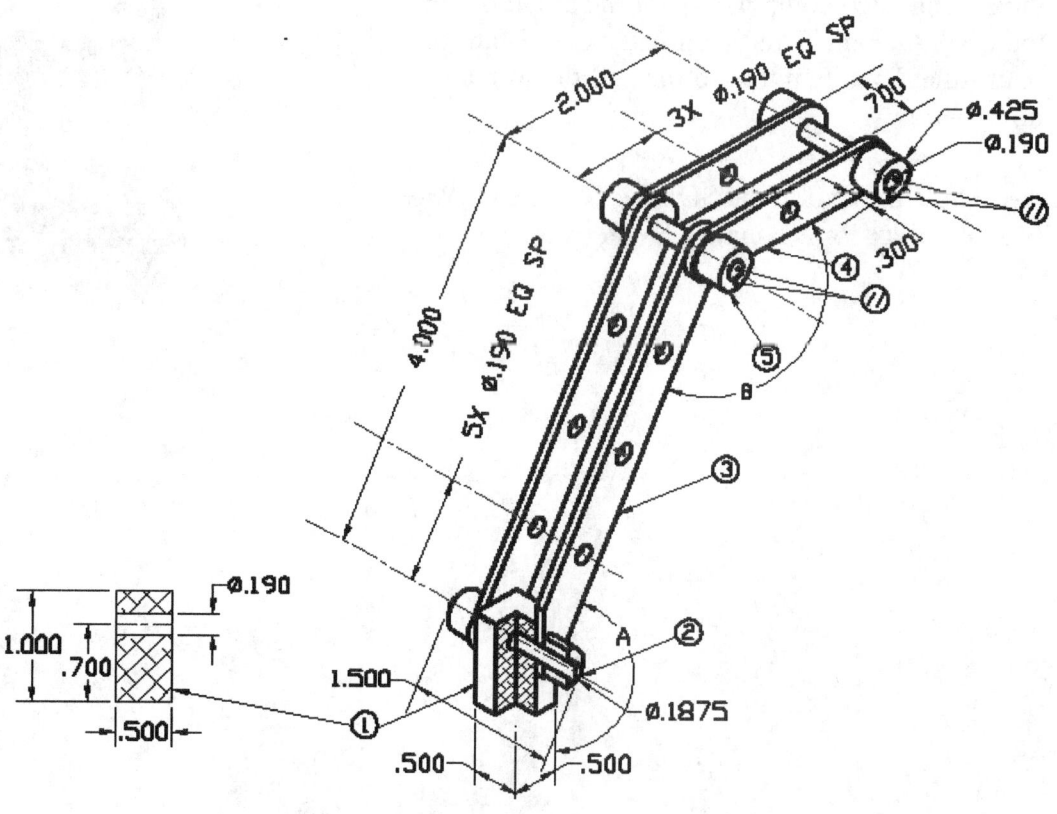

- Clevis, (Item 1): Material: 6061 Alloy. The two (5) Hole Link components are positioned with equal Angle mates, (150deg) to the Clevis component.

- Axle, (Item 2): Material: AISI 304. The first Axle component is mated Concentric and Coincident to the Clevis. The second and third Axle components are mated Concentric and Coincident to the 5 Hole Link and the 3 Hole Link components respectively.

- 5 Hole Link, (Item 3): Material: 6061 Alloy. Material thickness = .100in. Radius = .250in. Five holes located 1in. on center. The 5 Hole Link components are positioned with equal Angle mates, (120deg) to the 3 Hole Link components.

- 3 Hole Link, (Item 4): Material: 6061 Alloy. Material thickness = .100in. Radius = .250in. Three holes located 1in. on center. The 3 Hole Link components are positioned with equal Angle mates, (120deg) to the 5 Hole Link components.

- Collar, (Item 5): Material: 6061 Alloy. The Collar components are mated Concentric and Coincident to the Axle and the 5 Hole Link and 3 Hole Link components respectively.

Think about the steps that you would take to build the illustrated assembly. Identify the first fixed component. Insert the required Standard mates.

Locate the Center of mass of the model with respect to the illustrated coordinate system. In this example, start with the Clevis component.

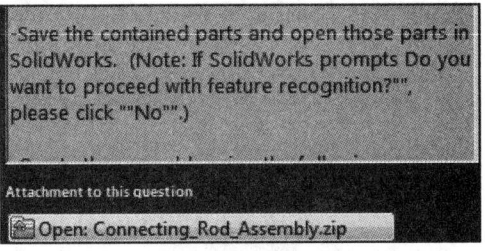

☀ Do not use feature recognition when you open the downloaded components for the assembly in the CSWA exam. This is a timed exam. Manage your time. You do not need the additional feature information.

☀ View the .pdf in the SOLIDWORKS CSWA Model Folder for a sample CSWA exam.

Screen shot from an exam

Tutorial: Assembly Model 5-1

Build the assembly in SOLIDWORKS.

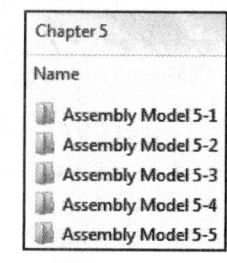

1. **Download** the needed components from the SOLIDWORKS CSWA Model Folder\Chapter 5\Assembly Model 5-1 folder.

2. **Create** a new IPS assembly in SOLIDWORKS.

3. Click **Cancel** ✖ from the Begin Assembly PropertyManager. Assem1 is the default document name. Assembly documents end with the extension .sldasm.

4. **Set** the document properties for the model.

5. **Insert** the Clevis part.

6. **Fix** the component to the assembly Origin. Click OK from the Insert Component PropertyManager. The Clevis is displayed in the Assembly FeatureManager and in the Graphics window.

💡 The first component or sub-assembly should be fixed **(f)** to the origin, fully defined to the assembly document or mated to an axis about the assembly origin.

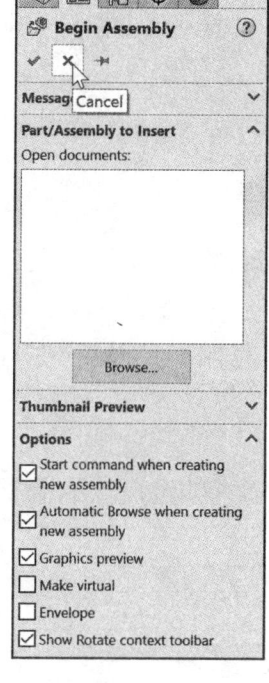

💡 Only insert the required mates (timed exam) to obtain the needed Mass properties information.

7. **Insert** the Axle part above the Clevis component as illustrated.

8. **Insert** a Concentric mate between the inside cylindrical face of the Clevis and the outside cylindrical face of the Axle.

9. **Insert** a Coincident mate between the Right Plane of the Clevis and the Right Plane of the Axle.

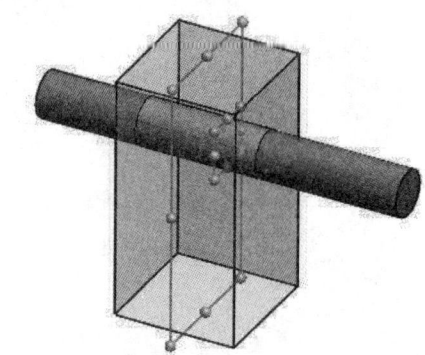

10. **Insert** the 5 Hole Link part.
    Locate and rotate the component
    as illustrated.

11. **Insert** a Concentric mate
    between the outside cylindrical
    face of the Axle and the inside
    cylindrical face of the 5 Hole
    Link. Concentric2 is created.

12. **Insert** a Coincident mate
    between the right face of the
    Clevis and the left face of the 5
    Hole Link. Coincident2 is
    created.

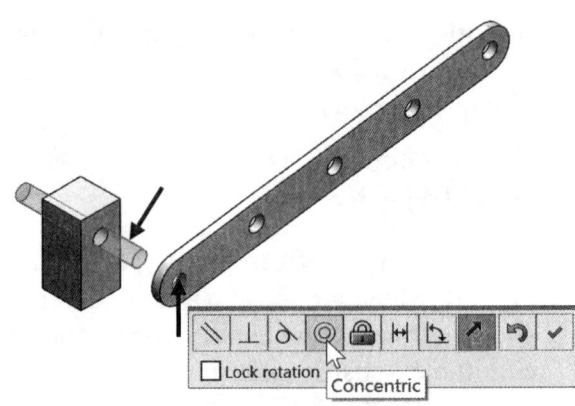

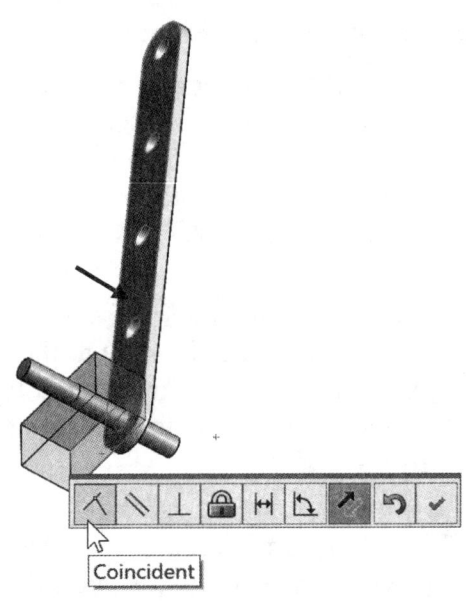

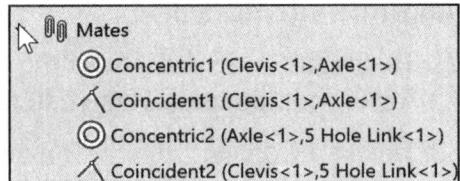

13. **Insert** an Angle mate between the bottom face of the 5 Hole Link and the back face of the Clevis. Angle = 30deg. The selected faces are displayed in the Mate Selections box. Angle1 is created. Flip direction if needed.

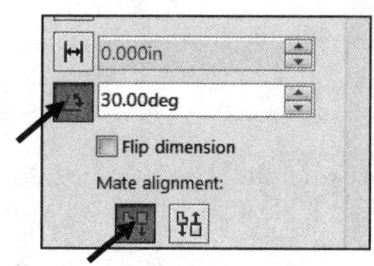

💡 Depending on the component orientation, select the Flip direction option and/or enter the supplement of the angle.

14. **Insert** the second Axle part. Locate the second Axle component near the end of the 5 Hole Link as illustrated.

15. **Insert** a Concentric mate between the inside cylindrical face of the 5 Hole Link and the outside cylindrical face of the Axle. Concentric3 is created.

16. **Insert** a Coincident mate between the Right Plane of the assembly and the Right Plane of the Axle. Coincident3 is created.

17. **Insert** the 3 Hole Link part. Locate and rotate the component as illustrated.

18. **Insert** a Concentric mate between the outside cylindrical face of the Axle and the inside cylindrical face of the 3 Hole Link. Concentric4 is created.

19. **Insert** a Coincident mate between the right face of the 5 Hole Link and the left face of the 3 Hole Link.

20. **Insert** an Angle mate between the bottom face of the 5 Hole Link and the bottom face of the 3 Hole Link. Angle − 60deg. Angle2 is created.

💡 Depending on the component orientation, select the Flip direction option and/or enter the supplement of the angle when needed.

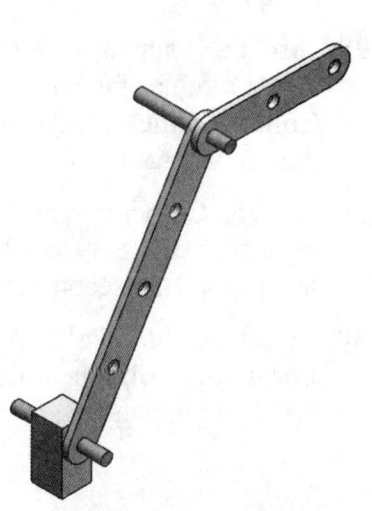

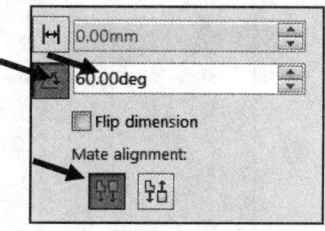

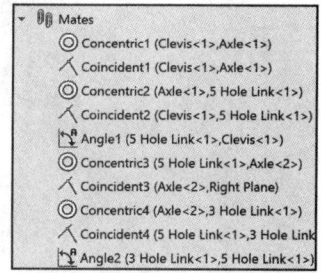

Mates
- ⊚ Concentric1 (Clevis<1>,Axle<1>)
- ⟨ Coincident1 (Clevis<1>,Axle<1>)
- ⊚ Concentric2 (Axle<1>,5 Hole Link<1>)
- ⟨ Coincident2 (Clevis<1>,5 Hole Link<1>)
- ⟨ Angle1 (5 Hole Link<1>,Clevis<1>)
- ⊚ Concentric3 (5 Hole Link<1>,Axle<2>)
- ⟨ Coincident3 (Axle<2>,Right Plane)
- ⊚ Concentric4 (Axle<2>,3 Hole Link<1>)
- ⟨ Coincident4 (5 Hole Link<1>,3 Hole Link
- ⟨ Angle2 (3 Hole Link<1>,5 Hole Link<1>)

💡 Apply the Measure tool to check the angle.

21. **Insert** the third Axle part.

22. **Insert** a Concentric mate between the inside cylindrical face of the 3 Hole Link and the outside cylindrical face of the Axle.

23. **Insert** a Coincident mate between the Right Plane of the assembly and the Right Plane of the Axle.

24. **Insert** the Collar part. Locate the Collar near the first Axle component.

25. **Insert** a Concentric mate between the inside cylindrical face of the Collar and the outside cylindrical face of the first Axle.

26. **Insert** a Coincident mate between the right face of the 5 Hole Link and the left face of the Collar.

27. **Insert** the second Collar part. Locate the Collar near the second Axle component.

28. **Insert** a Concentric mate between the inside circular face of the second Collar and the outside circular face of the second Axle.

29. **Insert** a Coincident mate between the right face of the 3 Hole Link and the left face of the second Collar.

30. **Insert** the third Collar part. Locate the Collar near the third Axle component.

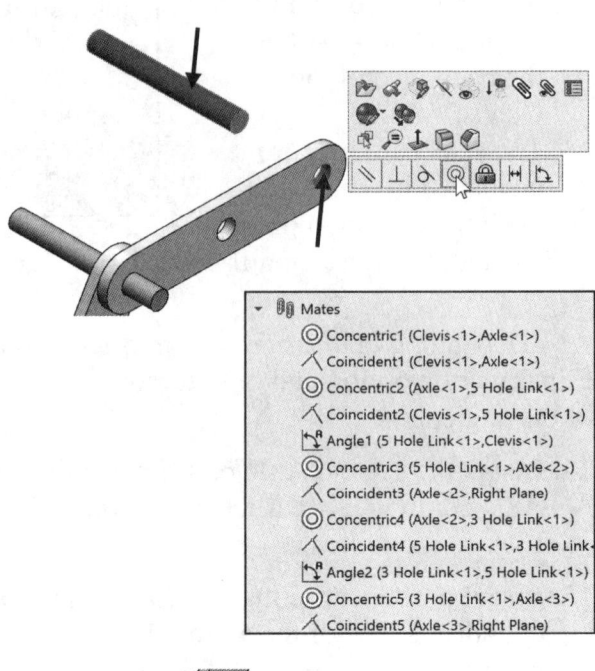

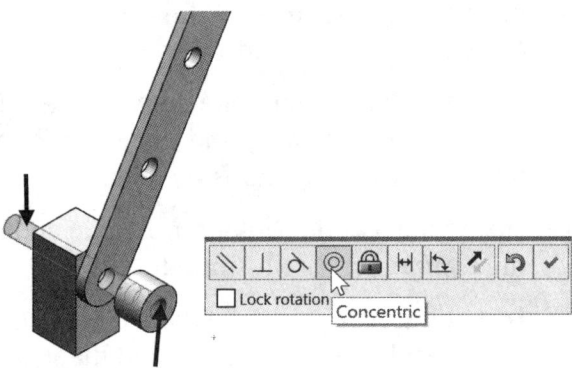

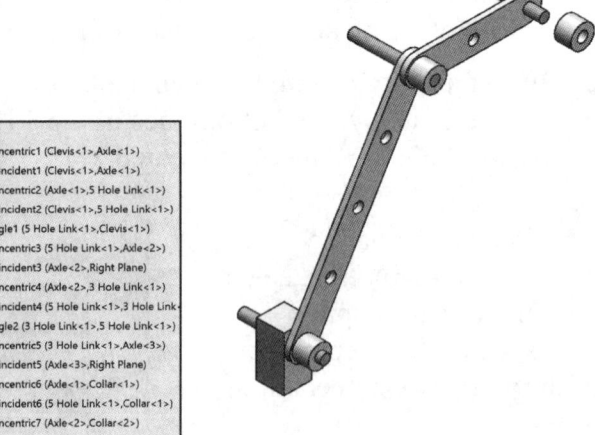

31. **Insert** a Concentric mate between the inside cylindrical face of the Collar and the outside cylindrical face of the third Axle.

32. **Insert** a Coincident mate between the right face of the 3 Hole Link and the left face of the third Collar.

33. **Mirror** the components. Mirror the three Collars, 5 Hole Link and 3 Hole Link about the Right Plane. If using an older version of SOLIDWORKS, check the Recreate mates to new components box. Click Next in the Mirror Components PropertyManager. Check the Preview instanced components box.

Click **Insert**, **Mirror Components** from the Menu bar menu or click the **Mirror Components** tool from the Linear Component Pattern Consolidated toolbar.

If using an older release of SOLIDWORKS, no check mark in the Components to Mirror box indicates that the components are copied. The geometry of a copied component is unchanged from the original, only the orientation of the component is different.

If using an older release of SOLIDWORKS, a check mark in the Components to Mirror box indicates that the selected is mirrored. The geometry of the mirrored component changes to create a truly mirrored component.

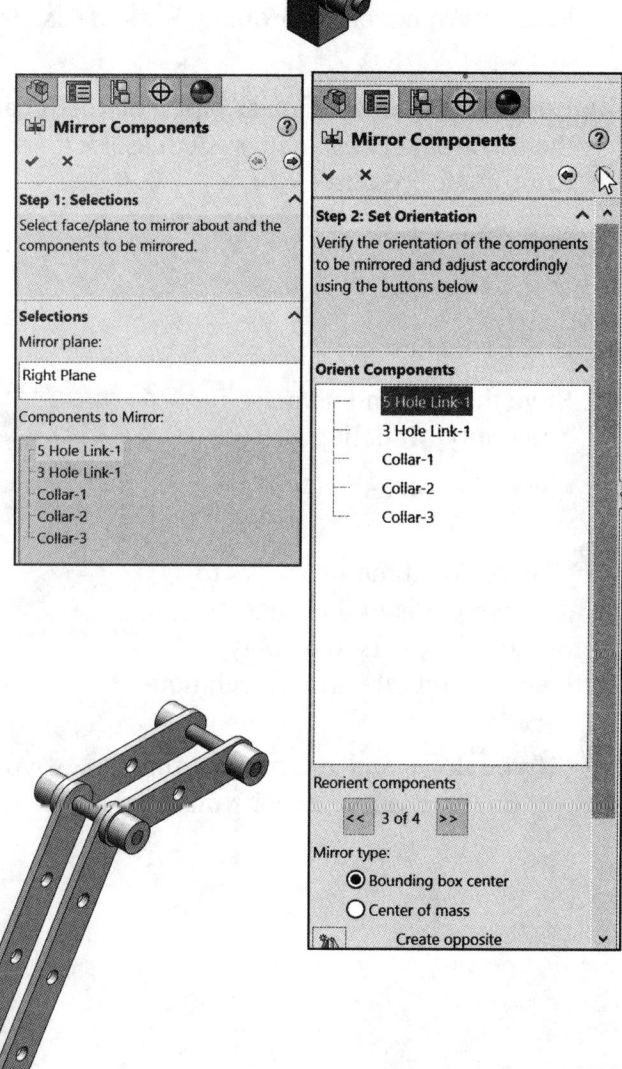

Create the coordinate system location for the assembly.

34. Select the front right **vertex** of the Clevis component as illustrated.

35. Click the **Coordinate System** tool from the Reference Geometry Consolidated toolbar. The Coordinate System PropertyManager is displayed.

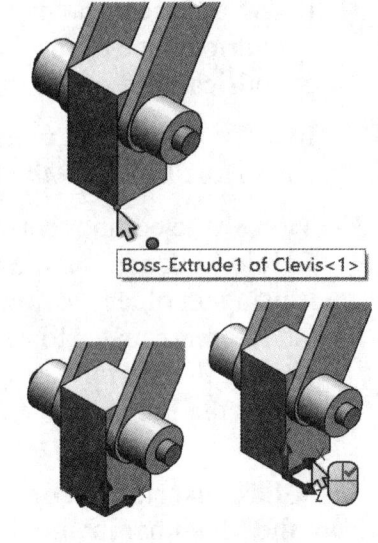

36. Click the **right bottom edge** of the Clevis component.

37. Click the **front bottom edge** of the Clevis component as illustrated.

38. Address the **direction** for X, Y, Z as illustrated.

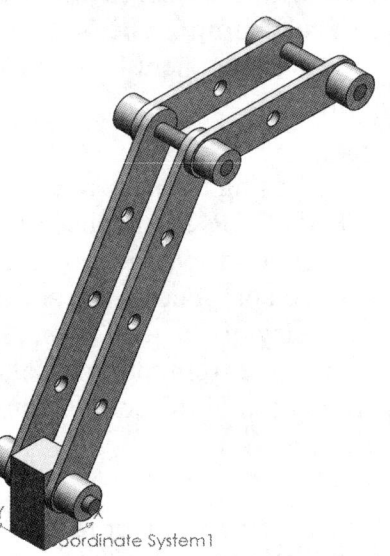

39. Click **OK** from the Coordinate System PropertyManager. Coordinate System1 is displayed.

40. **Locate** the Center of mass based on the location of the illustrated coordinate system. Select Coordinate System1.

- X: 1.79 inches

- Y: 0.25 inches

- Z: 2.61 inches

41. **Save** the part and name it Assembly Modeling 5-1.

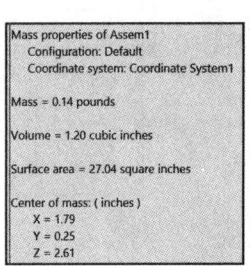

Mass properties of Assem1
  Configuration: Default
  Coordinate system: Coordinate System1

Mass = 0.14 pounds

Volume = 1.20 cubic inches

Surface area = 27.04 square inches

Center of mass: (inches)
  X = 1.79
  Y = 0.25
  Z = 2.61

42. **Close** the model.

☀ There are numerous ways to create the models in this chapter. A goal in this text is to display different design intents and techniques.

☀ If you don't find an option within 1% of your answer on the exam re-check your assembly.

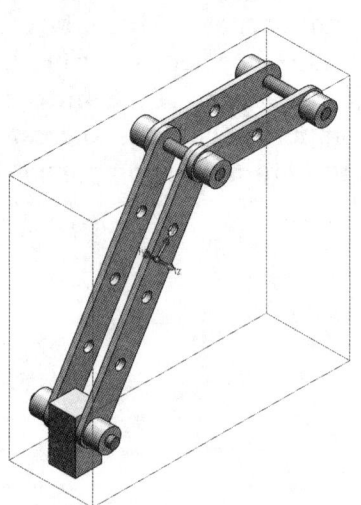

Tutorial: Assembly Model 5-2

An exam question in this category could read; Build this assembly in SOLIDWORKS. Locate the Center of mass of the model with the illustrated coordinate system. Set decimal place to 2. Unit system: MMGS."

The assembly contains the following: (2) U-Bracket components, (4) Pin components and (1) Square block component.

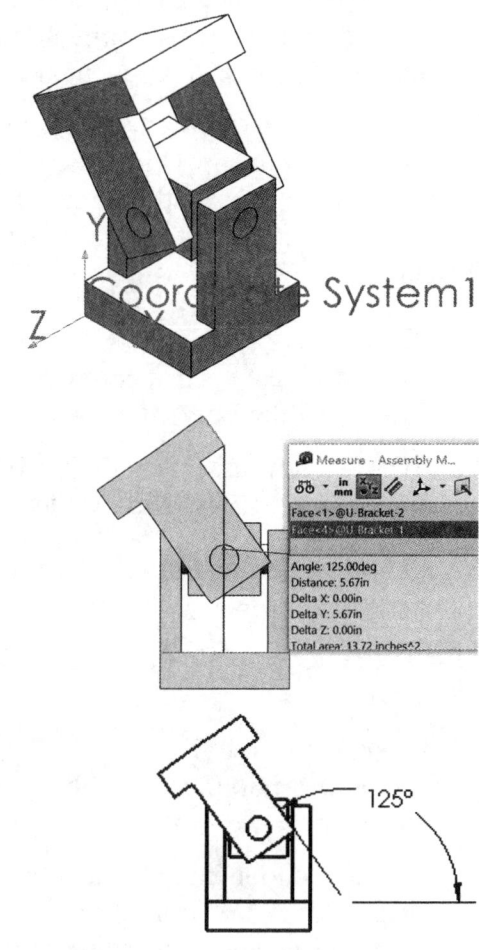

- U-Bracket, (Item 1): Material: AISI 304. Two U-Bracket components are combined together Concentric to opposite holes of the Square block component. The second U-Bracket component is positioned with an Angle mate to the right face of the first U-Bracket and a Parallel mate between the top face of the first U-Bracket and the top face of the Square block component. Angle A = 125deg.

- Square block, (Item 2): Material: AISI 304. The Pin components are mated Concentric and Coincident to the 4 holes in the Square block (no clearance). The depth of each hole = 10mm.

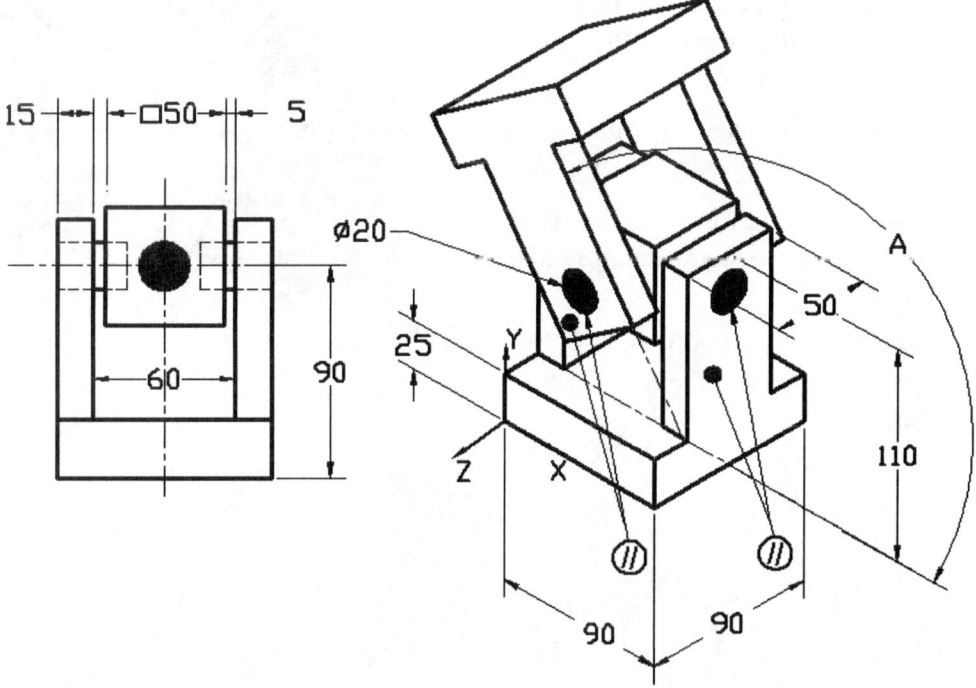

- Pin, (Item 3): Material: AISI 304. The Pin components are mated Concentric to the hole (no clearance). The end face of the Pin components are Coincident to the outer face of the U-Bracket components. The Pin component has a 5mm spacing between the Square block component and the two U-Bracket components.

Think about the steps that you would take to build the illustrated assembly. Identify the first fixed component. This is the Base component of the assembly. Insert the required Standard mates. Locate the Center of mass of the model with respect to the illustrated coordinate system. In this example, start with the U-Bracket part.

Create the assembly.

1. **Download** the needed components from the SOLIDWORKS CSWA Model Folder\Chapter 5\Assembly Model 5-2 folder.

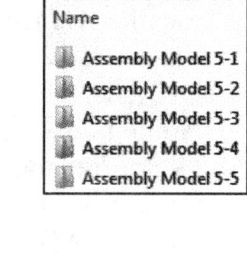

2. **Create** a new assembly in SOLIDWORKS. The created models are displayed in the Open documents box.

3. Click **Cancel** ✖ from the Begin Assembly PropertyManager.

4. **Set** the document properties for the model.

5. **Insert** the first U-Bracket component into the assembly document.

6. **Fix** the component to the assembly Origin. Click OK from the PropertyManager. The U-Bracket is displayed in the Assembly FeatureManager and in the Graphics window.

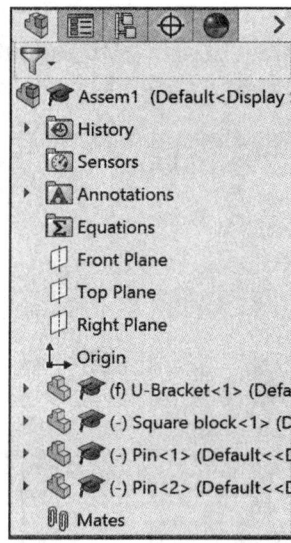

7. **Insert** the Square block above the U-Bracket component as illustrated.

8. **Insert** the first Pin part. Locate the first Pin to the front of the Square block.

9. **Insert** the second Pin part. Locate the second Pin to the back of the Square block.

10. **Insert** the third Pin part. Locate the third Pin to the left side of the Square block. Rotate the Pin as illustrated.

11. **Insert** the fourth Pin part. Locate the fourth Pin to the right side of the Square block. Rotate the Pin as illustrated.

12. **Insert** a Concentric mate between the inside cylindrical face of the Square block and the outside cylindrical face of the first Pin. Concentric1 is created.

13. **Insert** a Coincident mate between the inside back circular face of the Square block and the flat back face of the first Pin. Coincident1 mate is created.

14. **Insert** a Concentric mate between the inside cylindrical face of the Square block and the outside cylindrical face of the second Pin. Concentric2 is created.

15. **Insert** a Coincident mate between the inside back circular face of the Square block and the front flat face of the second Pin. Coincident2 mate is created.

16. **Insert** a Concentric mate between the inside cylindrical face of the Square block and the outside cylindrical face of the third Pin. Concentric3 is created.

17. **Insert** a Coincident mate between the inside back circular face of the Square block and the right flat face of the third Pin. Coincident3 mate is created.

18. **Insert** a Concentric mate between the inside circular face of the Square block and the outside cylindrical face of the fourth Pin. Concentric4 is created.

19. **Insert** a Coincident mate between the inside back circular face of the Square block and the left flat face of the fourth Pin. Coincident4 mate is created.

> ▾ 🔗 Mates
> ◎ Concentric1 (Square block<1>,Pin<1>)
> ⋀ Coincident1 (Square block<1>,Pin<1>)
> ◎ Concentric2 (Square block<1>,Pin<2>)
> ⋀ Coincident2 (Square block<1>,Pin<2>)
> ◎ Concentric3 (Square block<1>,Pin<3>)
> ⋀ Coincident3 (Square block<1>,Pin<3>)
> ◎ Concentric4 (Square block<1>,Pin<4>)
> ⋀ Coincident4 (Square block<1>,Pin<4>)

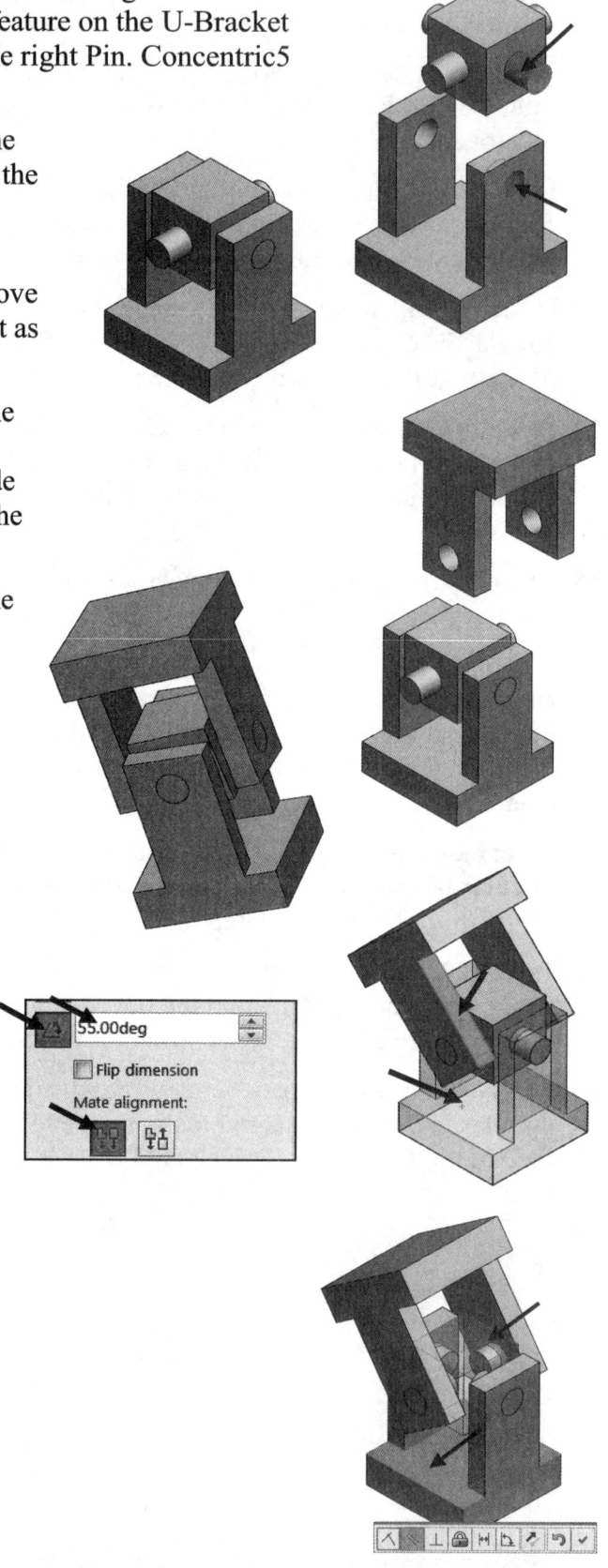

20. **Insert** a Concentric mate between the inside right cylindrical face of the Cut-Extrude feature on the U-Bracket and the outside cylindrical face of the right Pin. Concentric5 is created.

21. **Insert** a Coincident mate between the Right Plane of the Square block and the Right Plane of the assembly. Coincident5 is created.

22. **Insert** the second U-Bracket part above the assembly. Position the U-Bracket as illustrated.

23. **Insert** a Concentric mate between the inside cylindrical face of the second U-Bracket component and the outside cylindrical face of the second Pin. The mate is created.

24. **Insert** a Coincident mate between the outside circular edge of the second U-Bracket and the back flat face of the second Pin. The mate is created.

🔆 There are numerous ways to mate the models in this chapter. A goal is to display different design intents and techniques.

25. **Insert** an Angle mate between the top flat face of the first U-Bracket component and the front narrow face of the second U-Bracket component as illustrated. Angle1 is created. An Angle mate is required to obtain the correct Center of mass.

26. **Insert** a Parallel mate between the top flat face of the first U-Bracket and the top flat face of the Square block component.

27. **Expand** the Mates folder and the components from the FeatureManager. View the created mates.

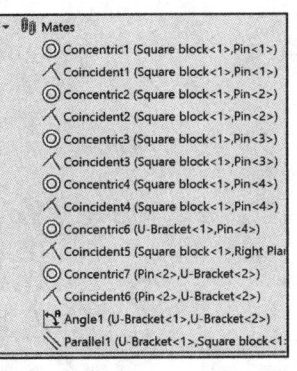

Create the coordinate location for the assembly.

28. Select the front **bottom left vertex** of the first U-Bracket component as illustrated.

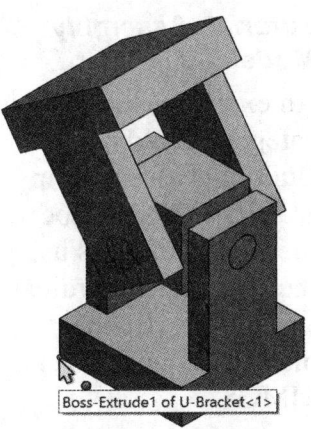

29. Click the **Coordinate System** tool from the Reference Geometry Consolidated toolbar. The Coordinate System PropertyManager is displayed.

30. Click **OK** from the Coordinate System PropertyManager. Coordinate System1 is displayed.

31. **Locate** the Center of mass based on the location of the illustrated coordinate system. Select Coordinate System1.

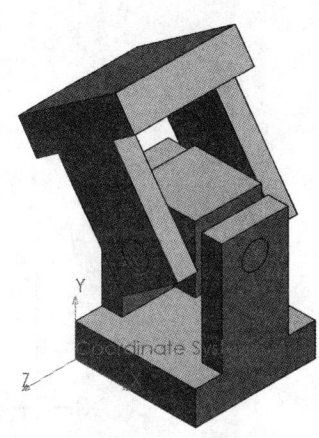

- X: 31.54 millimeters

- Y: 85.76 millimeters

- Z: -45.00 millimeters

32. **Save** the part and name it Assembly Modeling 5-2.

33. **Close** the model.

💡 If you don't find an option within 1% of your answer on the exam re-check your assembly.

💡 Click on the additional views during the CSWA exam to better understand the assembly\component. Read each question carefully. Identify the dimensions, center of mass and units. Apply needed material.

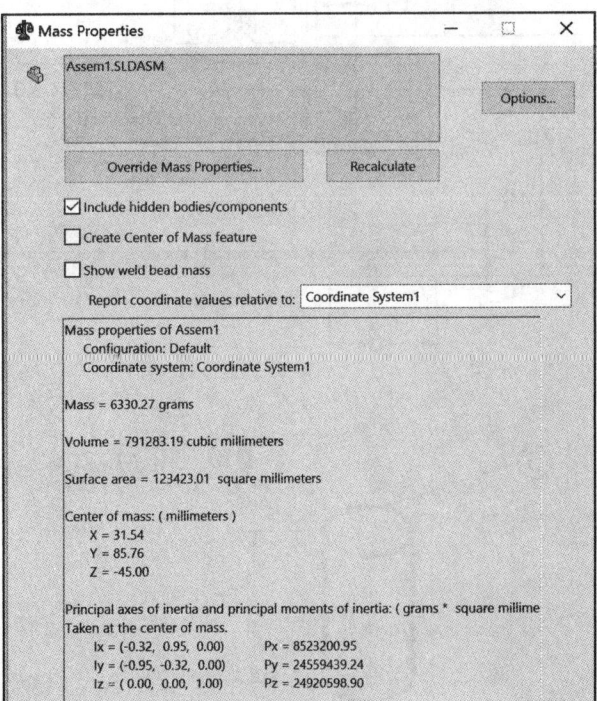

Tutorial: Assembly Model 5-3

An exam question in this category could read; Build this assembly in SOLIDWORKS. Locate the Center of mass using the illustrated coordinate system. Set decimal place to 2. Unit system: MMGS.

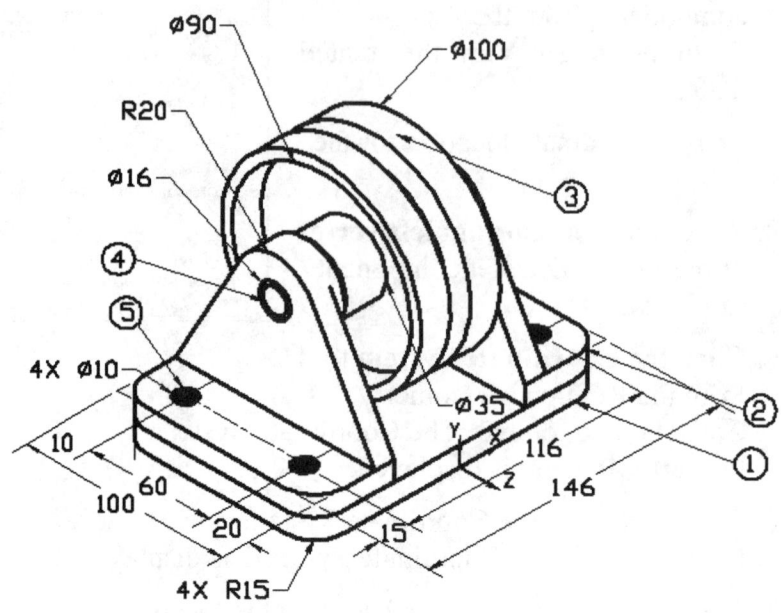

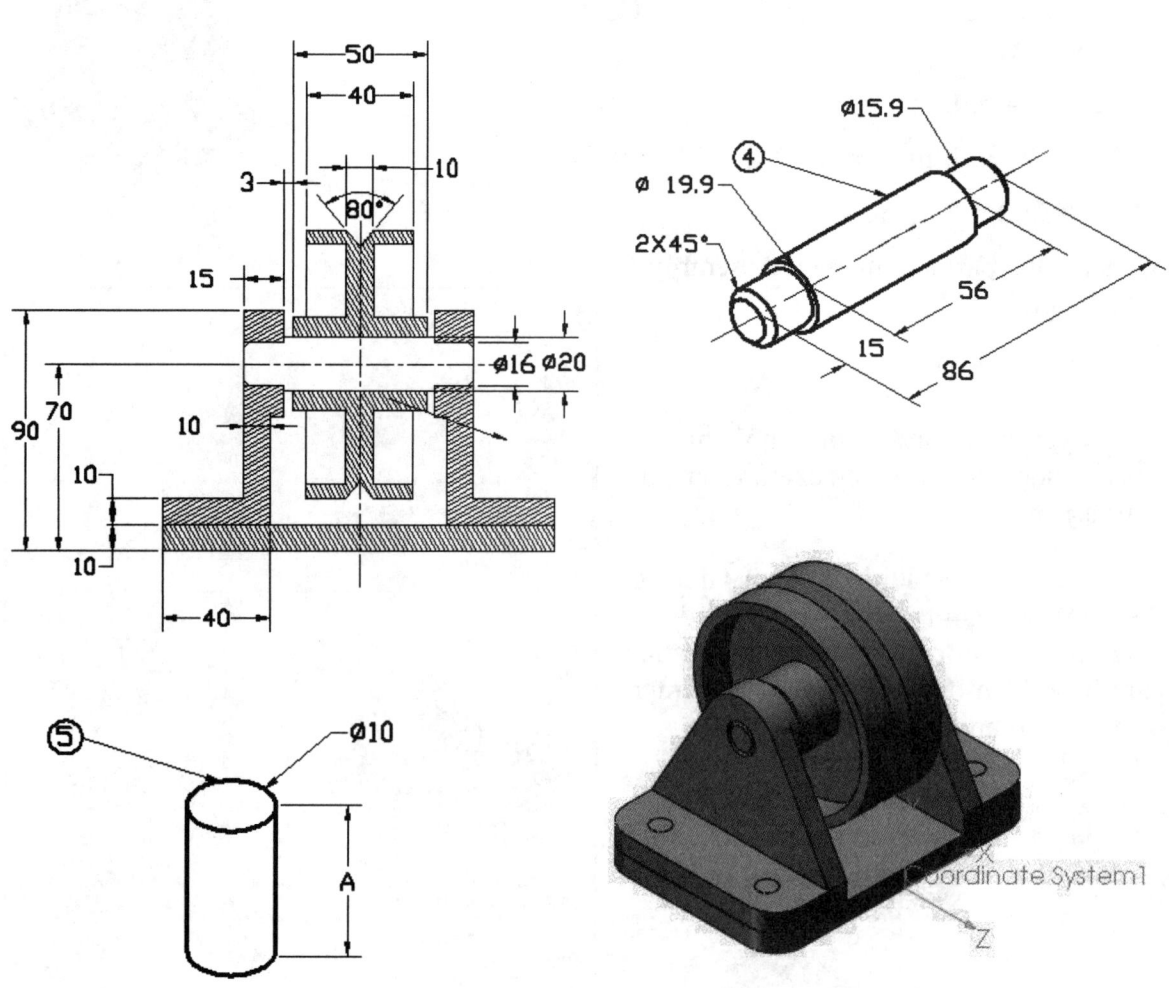

The assembly contains the following: (1) WheelPlate component, (2) Bracket100 components, (1) Axle40 component, (1) Wheel1 component and (4) Pin-4 components.

- WheelPlate, (Item 1): Material: AISI 304. The WheelPlate contains 4-Ø10 holes. The holes are aligned to the left Bracket100 and the right Bracket100 components. All holes are THRU ALL. The thickness of the WheelPlate = 10 mm.

- Bracket100, (Item 2): Material: AISI 304. The Bracket100 component contains 2-Ø10 holes and 1- Ø16 hole. All holes are through-all.

- Wheel1, (Item 3): Material AISI 304: The center hole of the Wheel1 component is Concentric with the Axle40 component. There is a 3mm gap between the inside faces of the Bracket100 components and the end faces of the Wheel hub.

- Axle40, (Item 4): Material AISI 304: The end faces of the Axle40 are Coincident with the outside faces of the Bracket100 components.

- Pin-4, (Item 5): Material AISI 304: The Pin-4 components are mated Concentric to the holes of the Bracket100 components (no clearance). The end faces are Coincident to the WheelPlate bottom face and the Bracket100 top face.

Think about the steps that you would take to build the illustrated assembly. Identify the first fixed component. This is the Base component of the assembly. Insert the required Standard mates.

Locate the Center of mass of the illustrated model with respect to the referenced coordinate system.

The referenced coordinate system is located at the bottom, right, midpoint of the Wheelplate. In this example, start with the WheelPlate part.

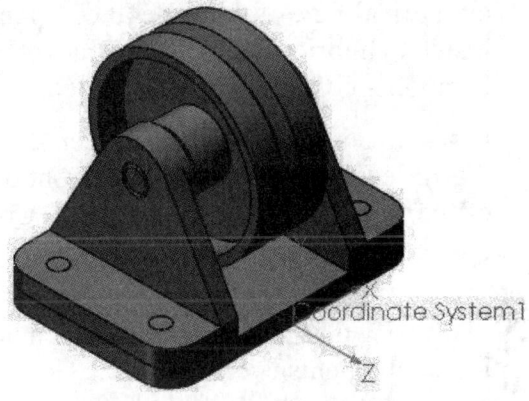

1. **Download** the needed components from the SOLIDWORKS CSWA Model Folder\Chapter 5\Assembly Model 5-3 folder.

2. **Create** a new assembly in SOLIDWORKS.

3. Click **Cancel** ✖ from the Begin Assembly PropertyManager.

4. **Set** the document properties for the assembly.

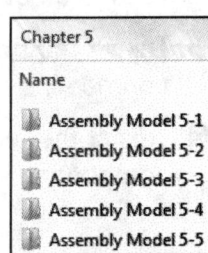

Chapter 5
Name
Assembly Model 5-1
Assembly Model 5-2
Assembly Model 5-3
Assembly Model 5-4
Assembly Model 5-5

5. **Insert** the first component. Insert the WheelPlate. Fix the component to the assembly Origin. The WheelPlate is displayed in the Assembly FeatureManager and in the Graphics window. The WheelPlate component is fixed.

6. **Insert** the first Bracket100 part above the WheelPlate component as illustrated.

7. **Insert** a Concentric mate between the inside front left cylindrical face of the Bracket100 component and the inside front left cylindrical face of the WheelPlate. Concentric1 is created.

8. **Insert** a Concentric mate between the inside front right cylindrical face of the Bracket100 component and the inside front right cylindrical face of the WheelPlate. Concentric2 is created.

9. **Insert** a Coincident mate between the bottom flat face of the Bracket100 component and the top flat face of the WheelPlate component. Coincident1 is created.

10. **Insert** the Axle40 part above the first Bracket100 component as illustrated.

11. **Insert** a Concentric mate between the outside cylindrical face of the Axle40 component and the inside cylindrical face of the Bracket100 component. Concentric3 is created.

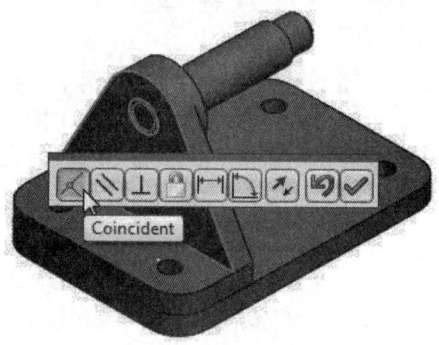

12. **Insert** a Coincident mate between the flat face of the Axle40 component and the front outside edge of the first Bracket100 component. Coincident2 is created.

To verify that the distance between holes of mating components is equal, utilize Concentric mates between pairs of cylindrical hole faces.

13. **Insert** the first Pin-4 part above the Bracket100 component.

14. **Insert** the second Pin-4 part above the Bracket100 component.

15. **Insert** a Concentric mate between the outside cylindrical face of the first Pin-4 component and the inside front left cylindrical face of the Bracket100 component. Concentric4 is created.

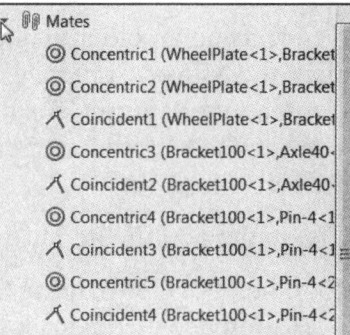

16. **Insert** a Coincident mate between the flat top face of the first Pin-4 component and the top face of the first Bracket100 component. Coincident3 is created.

17. **Insert** a Concentric mate between the outside cylindrical face of the second Pin-4 component and the inside front right cylindrical face of the Bracket100 component. Concentric5 is created.

18. **Insert** a Coincident mate between the flat top face of the second Pin-4 component and the top face of the first Bracket100 component. Coincident4 is created.

19. **Insert** the Wheel1 part as illustrated.

20. **Insert** a Concentric mate between the outside cylindrical face of Axle40 and the inside front cylindrical face of the Wheel1 component. Concentric6 is created.

21. **Insert** a Coincident mate between the Front Plane of Axle40 and the Front Plane of Wheel1. Coincident5 is created.

22. **Mirror** the components. Mirror the Bracket100 and the two Pin-4 components about the Front Plane.

☀ Click **Insert**, **Mirror Components** from the Menu bar menu or click the **Mirror Components** tool from the Linear Component Pattern Consolidated toolbar.

💡 If using an older version of SOLIDWORKS, click the Mirror Component tool from the Linear Component Pattern Consolidated toolbar to activate the Mirror Components PropertyManager.

Create the coordinate location for the assembly.

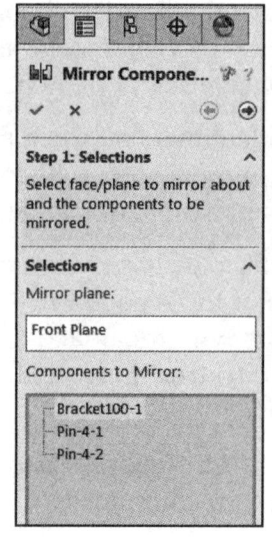

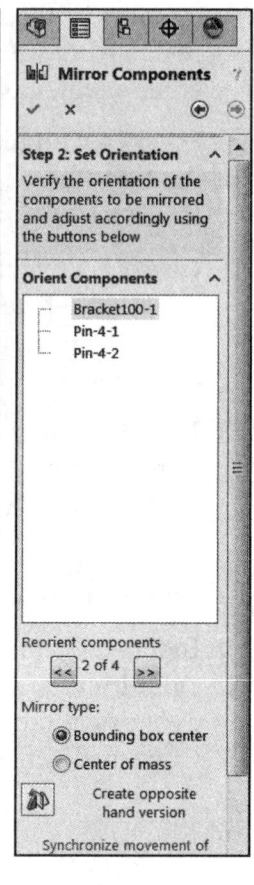

23. Click the **Coordinate System** tool from the Reference Geometry Consolidated toolbar. The Coordinate System PropertyManager is displayed.

24. **Select** the right bottom midpoint as the Origin location as illustrated.

25. **Select** the bottom right edge as the X axis direction reference as illustrated.

26. Click **OK** from the Coordinate System PropertyManager. Coordinate System1 is displayed.

27. **Locate** the Center of mass based on the location of the illustrated coordinate system. Select Coordinate System1.

- X: = 0.00 millimeters

- Y: = 37.14 millimeters

- Z: = -50.00 millimeters

💡 If you don't find an option within 1% of your answer on the exam re-check your assembly.

28. **Save** the part and name it Assembly Modeling 5-3.

29. **Close** the model.

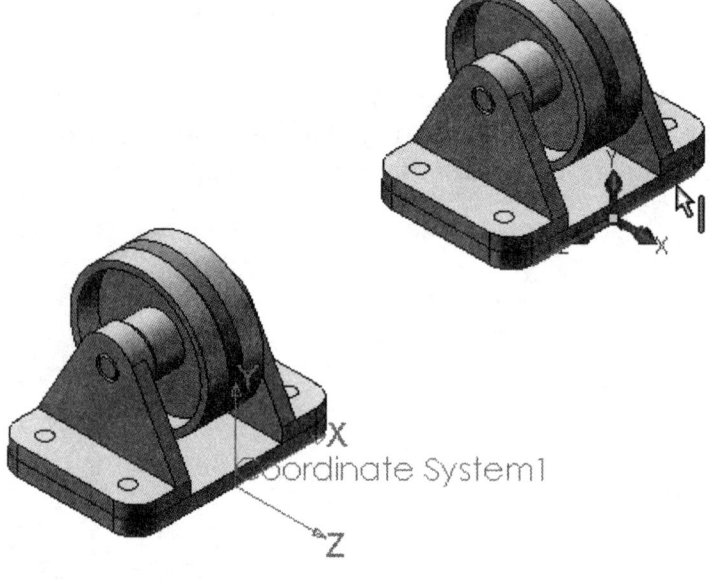

Mate the First Component with Respect to the Assembly Reference Planes

You can fix the position of a component so that it cannot move with respect to the assembly Origin. By default, the first part in an assembly is fixed; however, you can float it at any time.

It is recommended that at least one assembly component is either fixed, or mated to the assembly planes or Origin. This provides a frame of reference for all other mates, and prevents unexpected movement of components when mates are added.

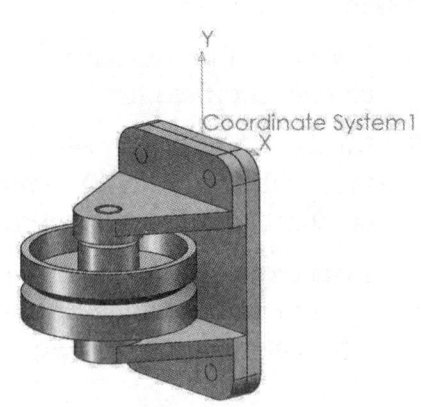

Up to this point, you identified the first fixed component, and built the required Base component of the assembly. The component features were orientated correctly to the illustrated assembly. In the exam, what if you created the Base component where the component features were not orientated correctly to the illustrated assembly?

In the next tutorial, build the illustrated assembly. Insert the Base component, float the component, then mate the first component with respect to the assembly reference planes.

Complete the assembly with the components from the Tutorial: Assembly model 5-3. Set decimal place to 2.

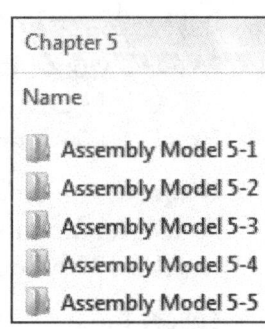

Tutorial: Assembly Model 5-4

1. **Create** a new assembly in SOLIDWORKS.

2. **Set** document settings. Set decimal place to 2. Unit system: MMGS.

3. **Insert** the illustrated WheelPlate part from the book.

4. **Float** the WheelPlate component from the FeatureManager.

5. **Insert** a Coincident mate between the Front Plane of the assembly and the bottom flat face of the WheelPlate. Coincident1 is created.

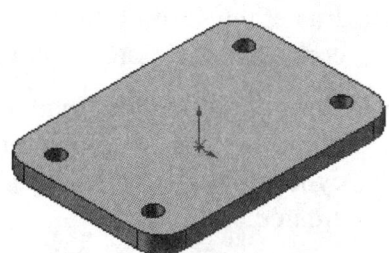

6. **Insert** a Coincident mate between the Right Plane of the assembly and the Right Plane of the WheelPlate. Coincident2 is created.

7. **Insert** a Coincident mate between the Top Plane of the assembly and the Front Plane of the WheelPlate. Coincident3 is created.

🔆 When the Base component is mated to three assembly reference planes, no component status symbol is displayed in the Assembly FeatureManager.

8. **Insert** the first Bracket100 part as illustrated. Rotate the component if required.

9. **Insert** a Concentric mate between the inside back left circular face of the Bracket100 component and the inside top left circular face of the WheelPlate. Concentric1 is created.

10. **Insert** a Concentric mate between the inside back right cylindrical face of the Bracket100 component and the inside top right cylindrical face of the WheelPlate. Concentric2 is created.

11. **Insert** a Coincident mate between the flat back face of the Bracket100 component and the front flat face of the WheelPlate component. Coincident4 is created.

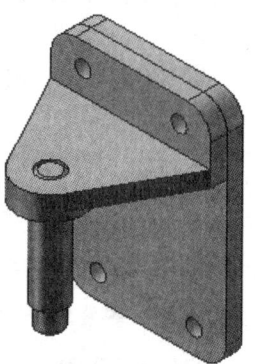

12. **Insert** the Axle40 part as illustrated. Rotate the component if required.

13. **Insert** a Concentric mate between the outside cylindrical face of the Axle40 component and the inside cylindrical face of the Bracket100 component. Concentric3 is created.

14. **Insert** a Coincident mate between the top flat face of the Axle40 component and the top outside circular edge of the Bracket100 component. Coincident5 is created.

15. **Insert** the first Pin-4 part above the Bracket100 component. Rotate the component.

16. **Insert** the second Pin-4 part above the Bracket100 component. Rotate the component.

17. **Insert** a Concentric mate between the outside cylindrical face of the first Pin-4 component and the inside front left cylindrical face of the Bracket100 component. Concentric4 is created.

18. **Insert** a Coincident mate between the flat front face of the first Pin-4 component and the top flat front face of the Bracket100 component. Coincident6 is created.

19. **Insert** a Concentric mate between the outside cylindrical face of the second Pin-4 component and the inside front right cylindrical face of the Bracket100 component. Concentric5 is created.

20. **Insert** a Coincident mate between the flat front face of the second Pin-4 component and the top flat front face of the Bracket100 component. Coincident7 is created.

21. **Insert** the Wheel1 part as illustrated.

22. **Insert** a Concentric mate between the outside cylindrical face of Axle40 and the inside top cylindrical face of the Wheel1 component. Concentric6 is created.

23. **Insert** a Coincident mate between the Right Plane of Axle40 and the Right Plane of the Wheel1 component. Coincident8 is created.

24. **Insert** a Coincident mate between the Front Plane of Axle40 and the Front Plane of the Wheel1 component. Coincident9 is created.

25. **Mirror** the components. Mirror the Bracket100, and the two Pin-4 components about the Top Plane. Do not check any components in the Components to Mirror box. Check the Recreate mates to new components box. Click Next in the PropertyManager. Check the Preview instanced components box.

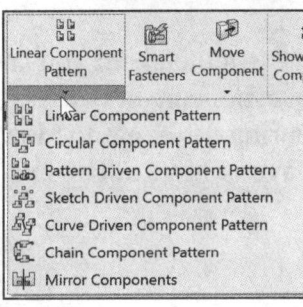

Create the coordinate location for the assembly.

26. Click the **Coordinate System** tool from the Reference Geometry Consolidated toolbar. The Coordinate System PropertyManager is displayed.

27. **Select** the top back midpoint for the Origin location as illustrated.

28. Click **OK** from the Coordinate System PropertyManager. Coordinate System1 is displayed.

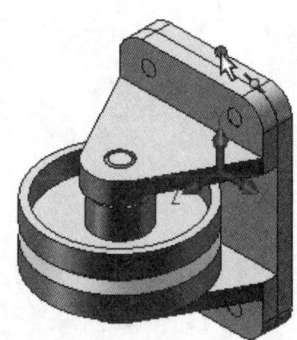

29. **Locate** the Center of mass based on the location of the illustrated coordinate system. Select Coordinate System1.

- X: = 0.00 millimeters

- Y: = -73.00 millimeters

- Z: = 37.14 millimeters

30. **Save** the part and name it Assembly Modeling 5-4.

31. **Close** the model.

In a multi choice format - the question is displayed as:

What is the center of mass of the assembly (millimeters)?

A) X = 0.00, Y = -73.00, Z = 37.14

B) X = 308.53, Y = -109.89, Z = -61.40

C) X = 298.66, Y = -17.48, Z = -89.22

D) X = 448.66, Y = -208.48, Z = -34.64

If you don't find an option within 1% of your answer on the exam re-check your assembly.

In the exam you are allowed to answer the questions in any order. Use the Summary Screen during the exam to view the list of all questions you have or have not answered.

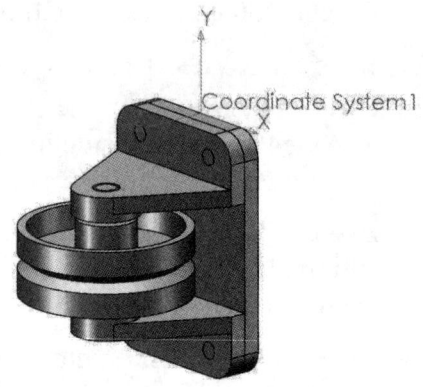

Mass = 3797.32 grams

Volume = 474665.19 cubic millimeters

Surface area = 130119.83 square millimeters

Center of mass: (millimeters)
  X = 0.00
  Y = -73.00
  Z = 37.14

Coordinate System1

Tutorial: Assembly Model 5-5

An exam question in this category could read:

Build this assembly in SOLIDWORKS (Chain Link Assembly). It contains 2 long_pins (1), 3 short_pins (2), and 4 chain_links (3).

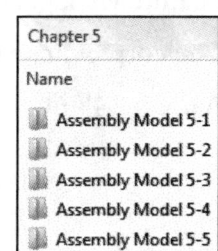

- Unit system: MMGS (millimeter, gram, second).

- Decimal places: 2.

- Assembly origin: Arbitrary.

Download the needed components from the SOLIDWORKS CSWA Model Folder\Chapter 5\Assembly Model 5-5 folder to create the Assembly document.

IMPORTANT: Create the assembly with respect to the Origin as shown in the Isometric view. (This is important for calculating the proper Center of Mass.) Create the assembly using the following conditions:

1. Pins are mated concentric to chain link holes (no clearance).

2. Pin end faces are coincident to chain link side faces.

A = 25 degrees, B = 125 degrees, C = 130 degrees

What is the center of mass of the assembly (millimeters)?

Hint: If you don't find an option within 1% of your answer please re-check your assembly.

A) X = 348.66, Y = -88.48, Z = -91.40

B) X = 308.53, Y = -109.89, Z = -61.40

C) X = 298.66, Y = -17.48, Z = -89.22

D) X = 448.66, Y = -208.48, Z = -34.64

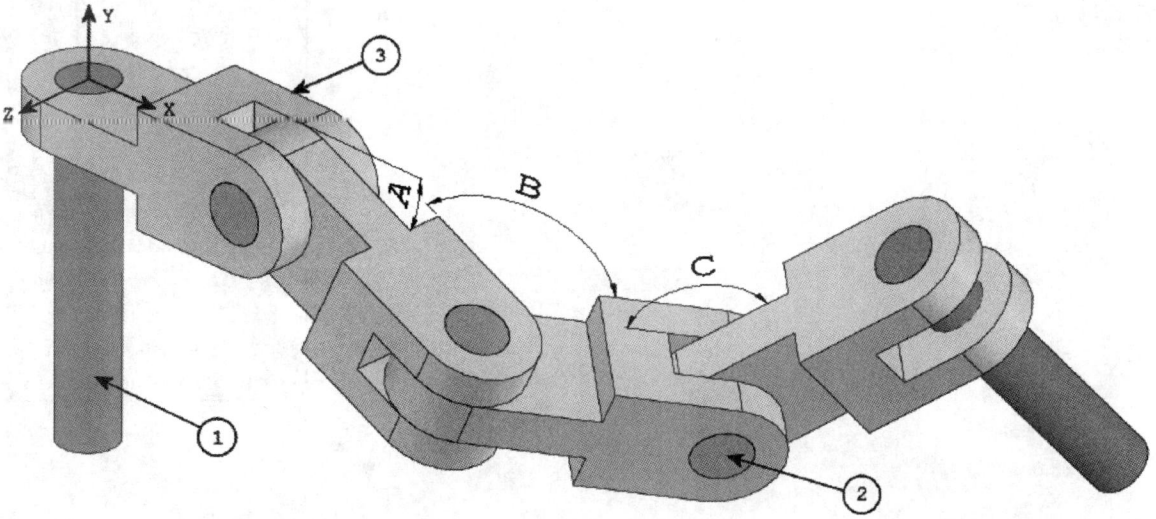

There are no step by step procedures in this section. Below are various Assembly FeatureManagers that created the above assembly and obtained the correct answer.

The correct answer is:

A) X = 348.66, Y = -88.48, Z = -91.40

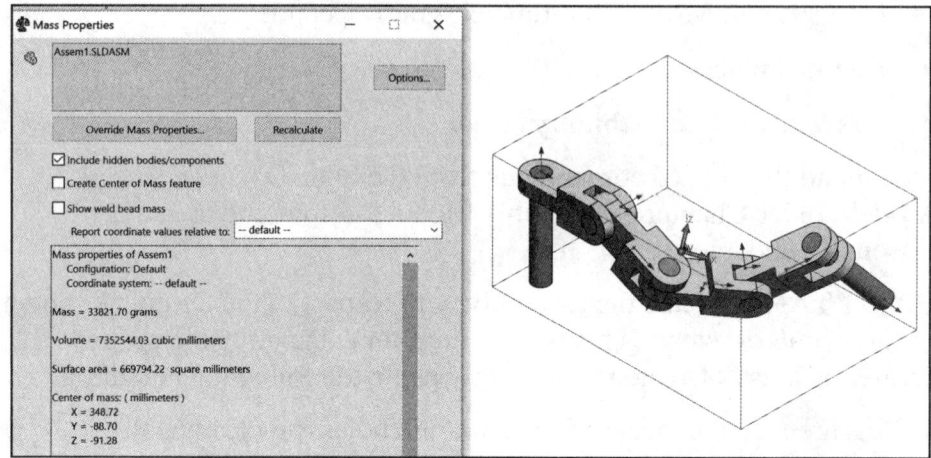

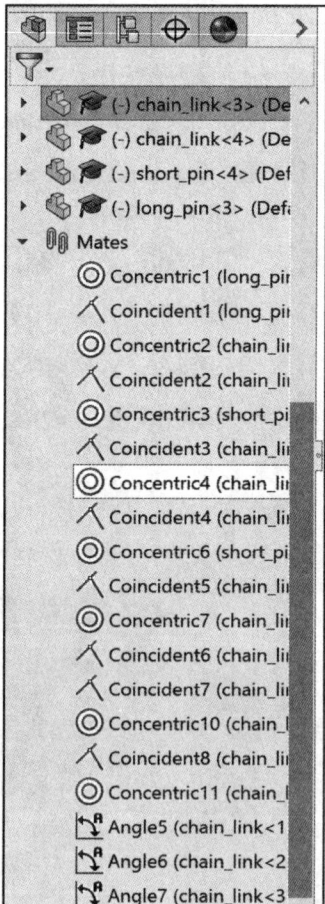

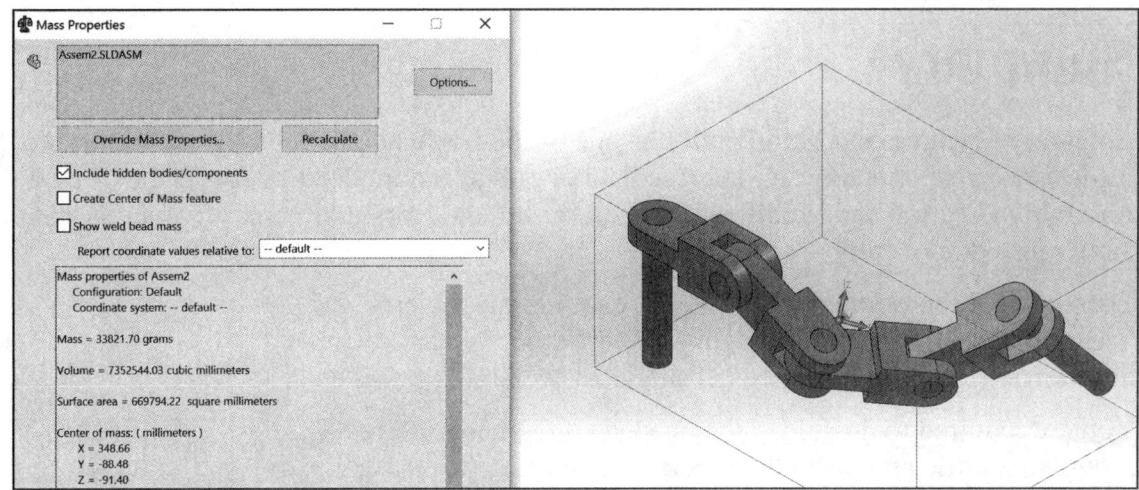

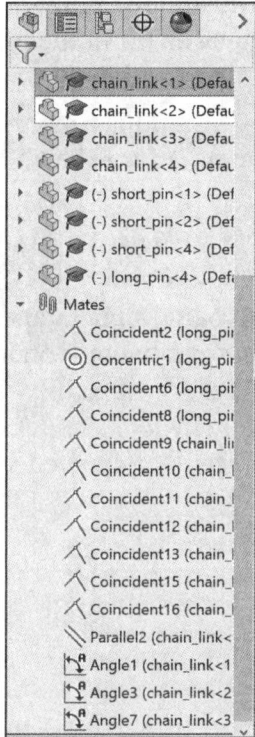

Summary

Assembly Creation and Modification is one of the five categories on the CSWA exam. In the last two chapters, a Basic, Intermediate or Advanced model was the focus. The Assembly Creation and Modification (Bottom-up) category addresses an assembly with numerous components.

There are four questions on the CSWA exam in the Assembly Creation and Modification category: (2) different assemblies - (4) questions - (2) multiple choice\(2) single answers - 30 points each.

You are required to download the needed components from a provided zip file and insert them correctly to create the assembly as illustrated. You are then requested to modify the assembly and answer fill in the blank format questions.

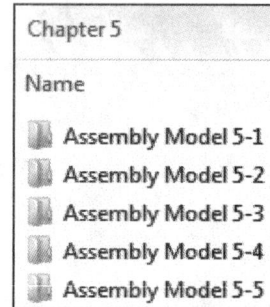

At this time, Advanced Mates and Mechanical Mates are not required for the CSWA exam.

Click on the additional views during the CSWA exam to better understand the assembly/component. Read each question carefully. Identify the dimensions, center of mass and units. Apply needed material.

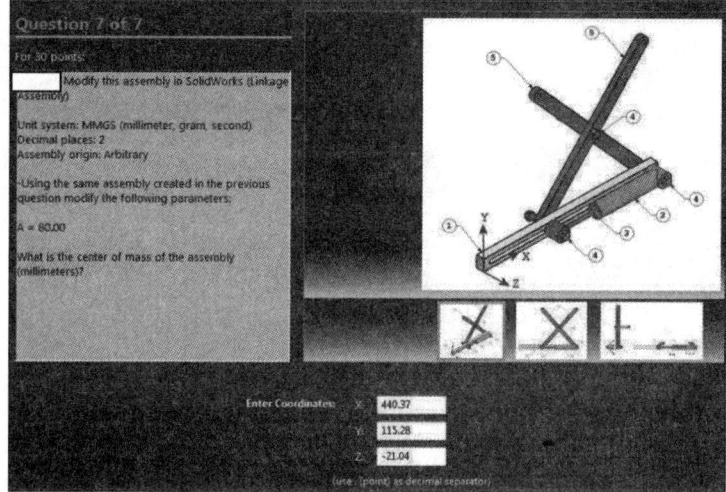

Questions

1. Build this ANSI MMGS assembly from the provided information in SOLIDWORKS.

Calculate the overall mass and volume of the assembly.

Locate the Center of mass using the illustrated coordinate system.

The assembly contains the following: one Base100 component, one Yoke component, and one AdjustingPin component.

- Base100, (Item 1): Material 1060 Alloy. The distance between the front face of the Base100 component and the front face of the Yoke = 60mm.
- Yoke, (Item 2): Material 1060 Alloy. The Yoke fits inside the left and right square channels of the Base100 component (no clearance). The top face of the Yoke contains a Ø12mm through all hole.
- AdjustingPin, (Item 3): Material 1060 alloy. The bottom face of the AdjustingPin head is located 40mm from the top face of the Yoke component. The AdjustingPin component contains an Ø5mm Though All hole.

The Coordinate system is located in the lower left corner of the Base100 component. The X axis points to the right.

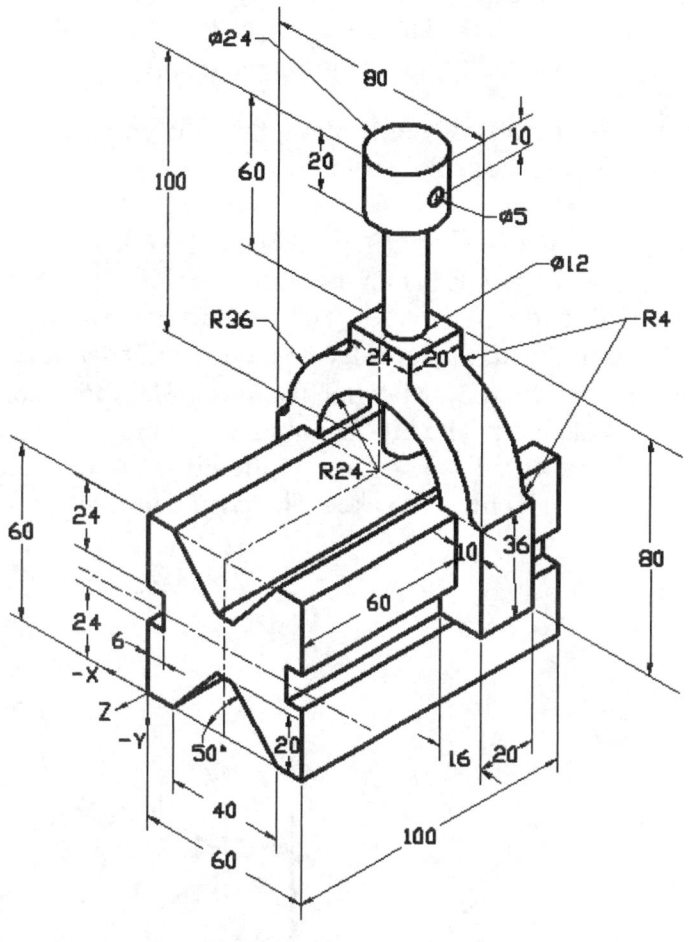

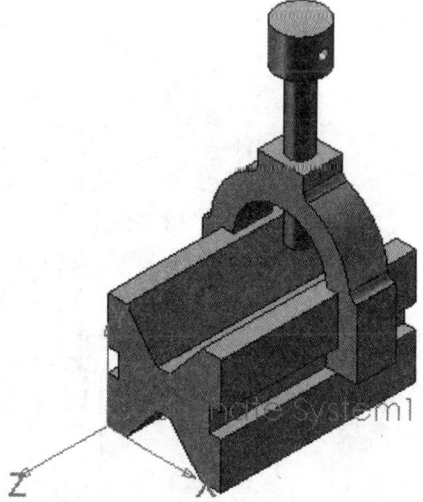

2. Build the assembly from the provided information in SOLIDWORKS. Calculate the overall mass and volume of the assembly. Locate the Center of mass using the illustrated coordinate system. The assembly contains the following: three MachinedBracket components and two Pin-5 components. Apply the MMGS unit system.

Insert the Base component, float the component, then mate the first component with respect to the assembly reference planes.

- MachinedBracket, (Item 1): Material 6061 Alloy. The MachinedBracket component contains two Ø10mm through all holes. Each MachinedBracket component is mated with two Angle mates. The Angle mate = 45deg. The top edge of the notch is located 20mm from the top edge of the MachinedBracket.
- Pin-5, (Item 2): Material Titanium. The Pin-5 component is 5mms in length and equal in diameter. The Pin-5 component is mated Concentric to the MachinedBracket (no clearance). The end faces of the Pin-5 component is Coincident with the outer faces of the MachinedBracket. There is a 1mm gap between the MachinedBracket components.

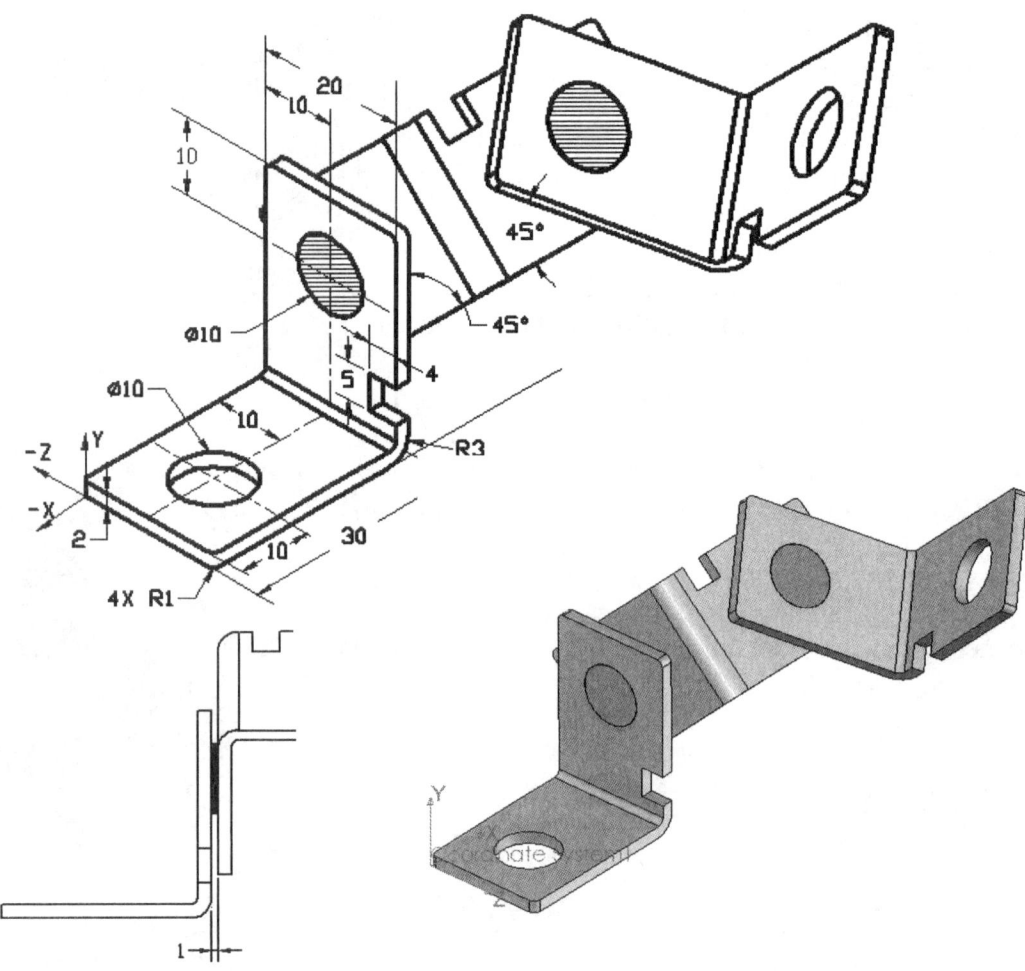

3. Build the assembly from the provided information in SOLIDWORKS. Calculate the overall mass and volume of the assembly. Locate the Center of mass using the illustrated coordinate system. The illustrated assembly contains the following components: three MachinedBracket components and two Pin-6 components. Apply the MMGS unit system.

Insert the Base component, float the component, then mate the first component with respect to the assembly reference planes.

- MachinedBracket, (Item 1): Material 6061 Alloy. The MachineBracket component contains two Ø10mm through all holes. Each MachinedBracket component is mated with two Angle mates. The Angle mate = 45deg. The top edge of the notch is located 20mm from the top edge of the MachinedBracket.
- Pin-6, (Item 2): Material Titanium. The Pin-6 component is 5mms in length and equal in diameter. The Pin-5 component is mated Concentric to the MachinedBracket (no clearance). The end faces of the Pin-6 component is Coincident with the outer faces of the MachinedBracket. There is a 1mm gap between the MachinedBracket components.

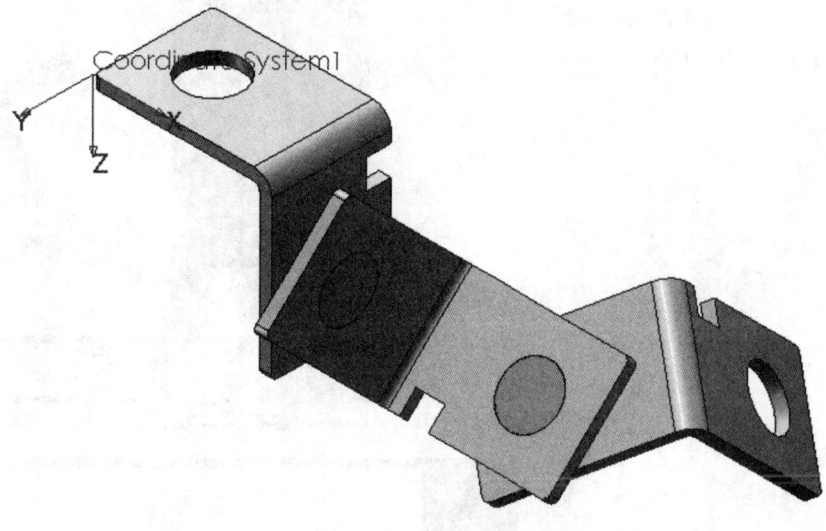

💡 Sample screen shots from an older CSWA exam for an assembly. Click on the additional views to understand the assembly and provided information. Read each question carefully. Understand the dimensions, center of mass and units. Apply needed materials.

💡 Zoom in on the part if needed.

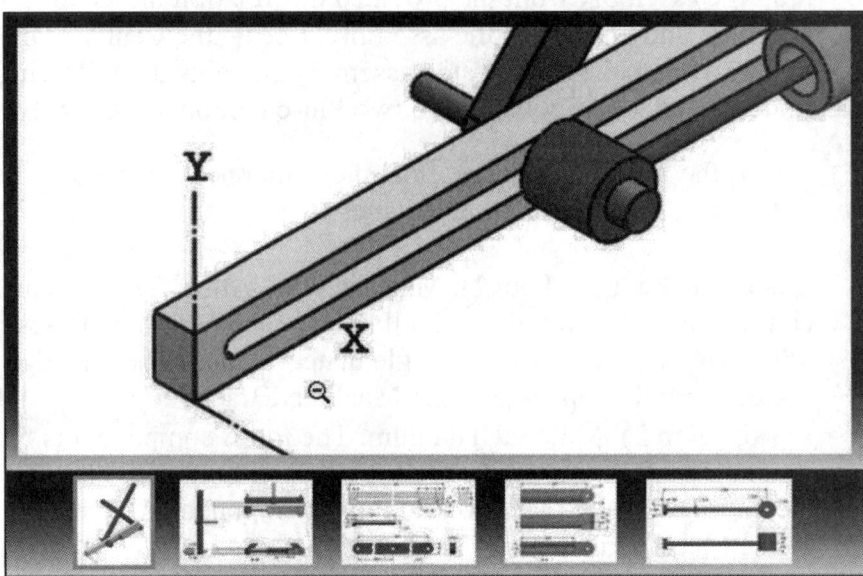

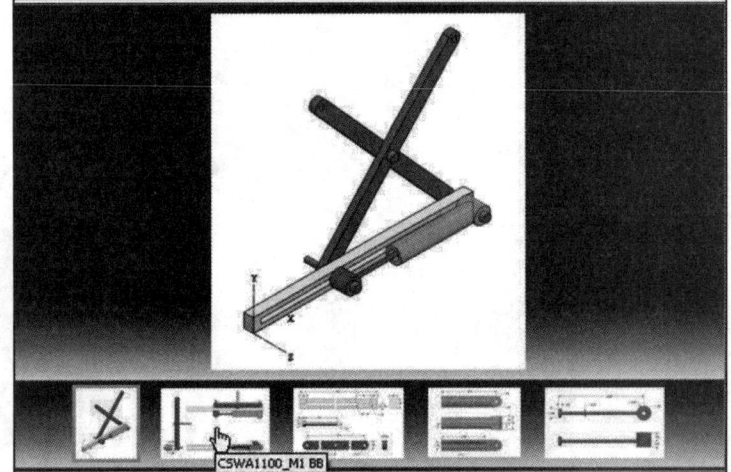

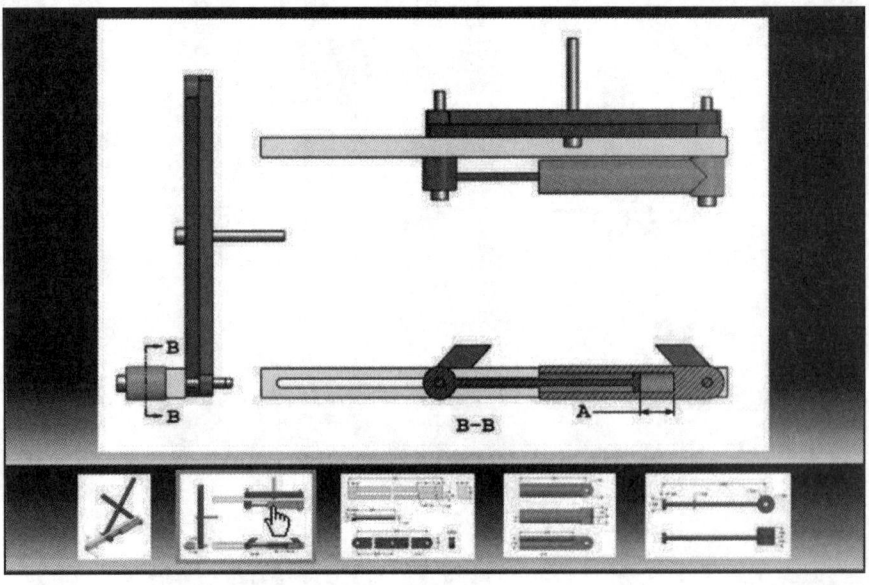

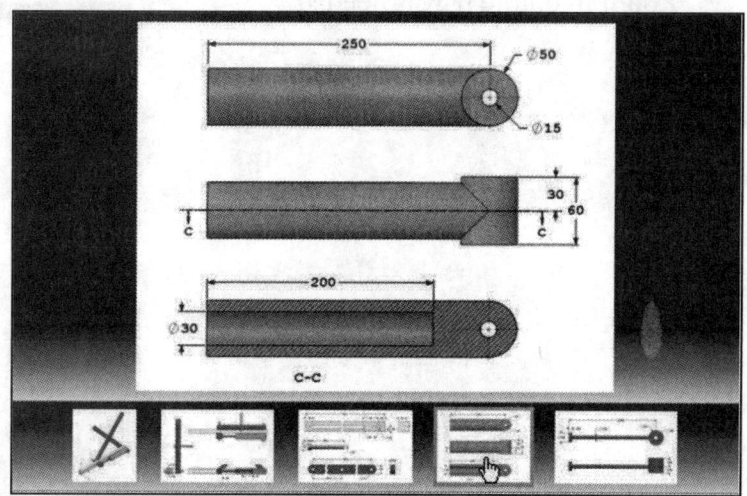

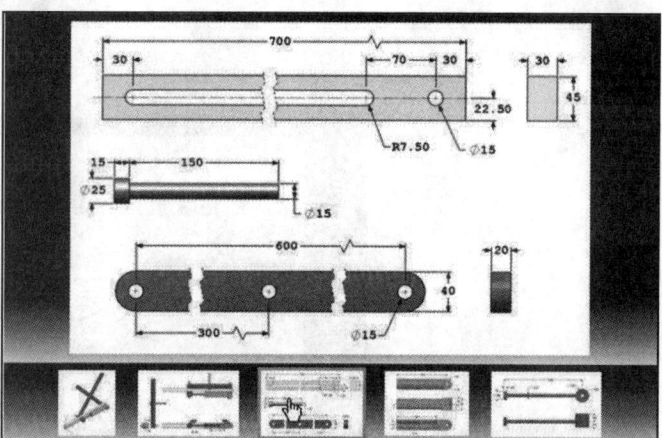

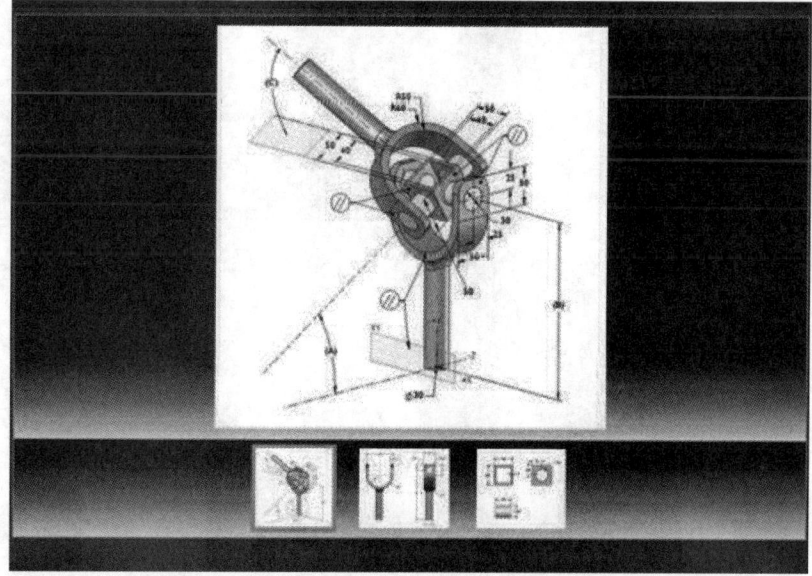

Screen shots from an exam

Zoom in on the part if needed.

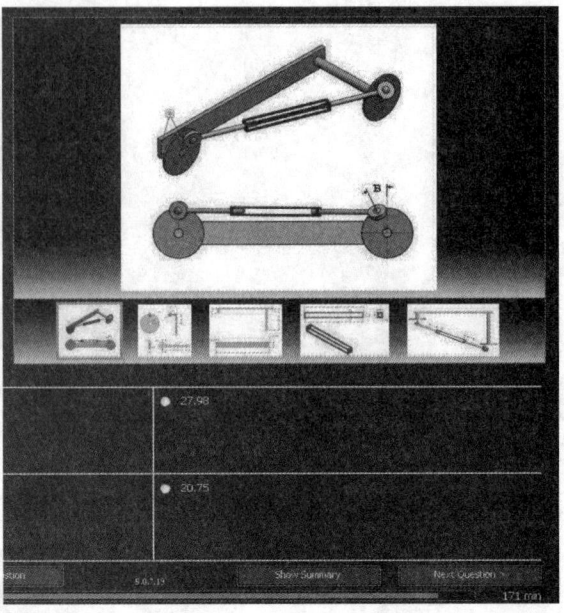

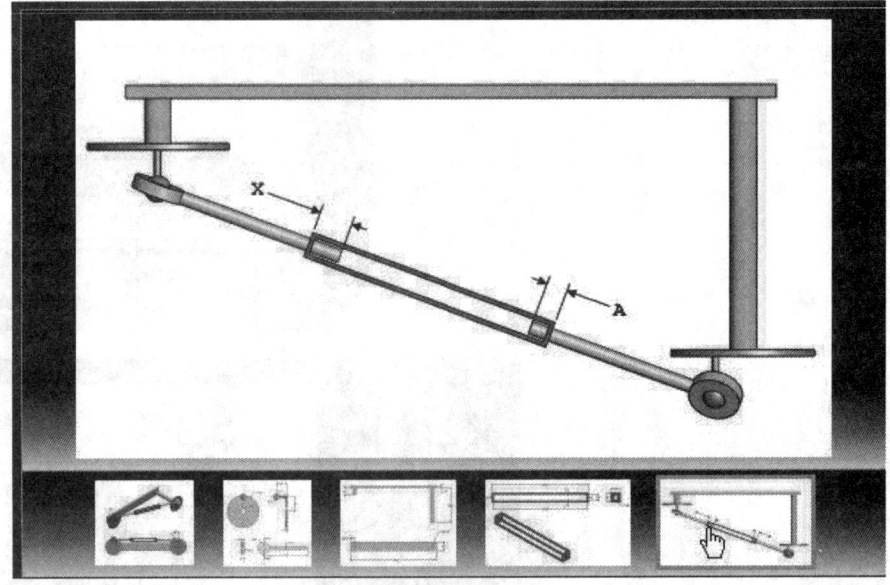

Screen shots from an exam

CHAPTER 6 - CERTIFIED SOLIDWORKS SUSTAINABLE DESIGN ASSOCIATE (CSDA)

Introduction

DS SOLIDWORKS Corp. offers various types of certification. Each stage represents increasing levels of expertise in 3D CAD: Certified SOLIDWORKS Associate (CSWA), Certified SOLIDWORKS Professional (CSWP) and Certified SOLIDWORKS Expert (CSWE) along with specialty fields.

The Certified SOLIDWORKS Sustainable Design Associate (CSDA) certification indicates a foundation in and apprentice knowledge of demonstrating an understanding in the principles of environmental assessment and sustainable design.

The main requirement for obtaining the CSDA certification is to take and pass the online 30 minute exam (minimum of 24 out of 30 points).

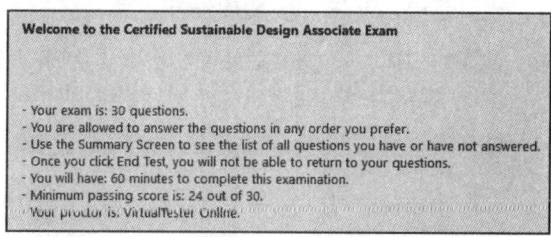

The CSDA exam consists of a total of 30 questions in various key categories: *Environmental Assessment, Introduction to sustainability* and *Sustainable design.*

All questions are in a multiple choice/multi answer format. SOLIDWORKS does not require that you have a copy of SOLIDWORKS Sustainability, or even SOLIDWORKS. No SOLIDWORKS models need to be created for this exam.

You are allowed to answer the questions in any order you prefer. Use the Summary Screen during the CSDA exam to view the list of all questions you have or have not answered.

As a Certified SOLIDWORKS Sustainable Design Associate (CSDA), you will prepare for today's competitive job market by demonstrating an understanding in the principles of environmental assessment and sustainable design.

Visit the following link http://www.SOLIDWORKS.com/sustainability/sustainable-design-guide.htm to read, learn and answer the questions for the CSDA certification exam and to better understand the principles and industry standards of sustainability.

The chapter covers the general concepts and terminology used in the CSDA certification along with the link to the Certified SOLIDWORKS Sustainable Design Associate (CSDA) certification guide.

Review the information presented in this chapter and the guide (from the following link: http://www.SOLIDWORKS.com/sustainability/sustainable-design-guide.htm) in detail and then address the categories that are aligned to the CSDA exam.

On the completion of the chapter and reading the guide, you will learn:

- Introductory concepts of sustainability and sustainable business.

- Broad sustainable design concepts, such as Design for Disassembly (DfD), Extended Producer Responsibility (EPR) and Biomimicry.

- The stages of a product life cycle.

- Considerations for properly setting up an Environmental Assessment study, such as environmental indicators, scope of the assessment, and metrics to use.

- Goal and Scope variables for an Environmental Assessment study, such as system boundary and functional unit.

- Common tools for performing Environmental Assessments, such as Product Scorecards and Life Cycle Assessment.

- Basic steps for performing a Life Cycle Assessment (LCA) study.

- Interpreting the results of a product Environmental Assessment.

- Universal strategies for sustainable design.

- Proper communication of environmental assessment results and use of environmental marketing claims (green marketing).

Recommended, although ***no hands on usage of SOLIDWORKS*** is required for the CSDA certification exam, it is a good idea to review the SOLIDWORKS SustainablityXpress and SOLIDWORKS Sustainability tutorials inside of SOLIDWORKS to better understand the actual workflow.

Even if you do not have SOLIDWORKS Sustainability, you can read through the SOLIDWORKS Sustainability tutorials.

Illustrations may vary slightly depending on your SOLIDWORKS version.

SOLIDWORKS
SustainabilityXpress, for parts,
is supplied in all
SOLIDWORKS product
configurations.

SOLIDWORKS Sustainability
for assemblies, is an Add-in on
the commercial versions of
SOLIDWORKS and is
contained in the
SOLIDWORKS Education
Edition and SOLIDWORKS
Student Edition.

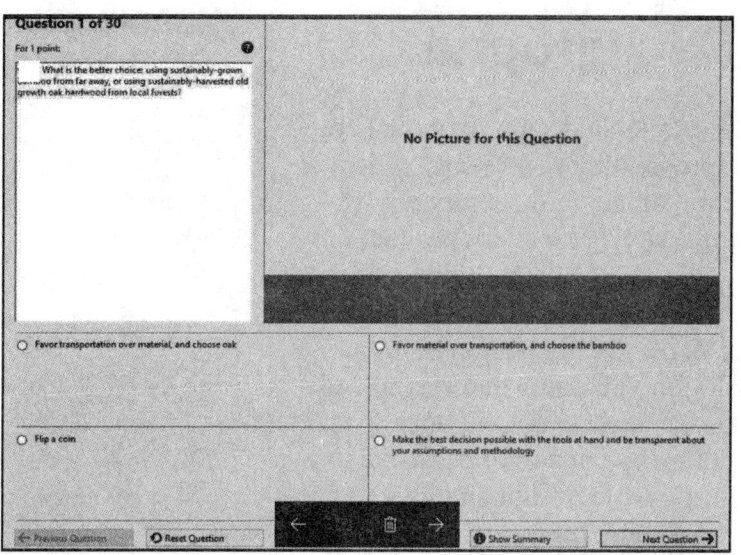

You are allowed to
answer the questions in any
order you prefer. Use the Summary Screen during the
CSDA exam to view the list of all questions you have
or have not answered.

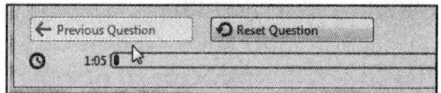

During the exam, use the control keys at the bottom of
the screen to:

- *Show the Previous the Question.*

- *Reset the Question.*

- *Show the Summary Screen.*

- *Move to the Next Question.*

Goals

The primary goal is not only to help you pass the CSDA exam, but also to ensure that you
understand and comprehend the concepts and implementation details of the CSDA
process.

The second goal is to provide the most comprehensive coverage of CSDA exam related
topics available, without too much coverage of topics not on the exam.

The third and ultimate goal is to get you from where you are today to the point that you
can confidently pass the CSDA exam.

Screen shots in this chapter were made using SOLIDWORKS 2016 SP2 and
SOLIDWORKS 2017 SP0.

Background

Sustainable design, like quality, time to market, and cost, will soon dictate how engineers approach most every product they develop. Choosing products based on their carbon footprint will be equally as important as design validation. To stay ahead of the curve, you and your company need to understand sustainable design and how to implement it now.

Sustainable engineering is the integration of social, environmental, and economic conditions into a product or process. Soon all design will be Sustainable Design.

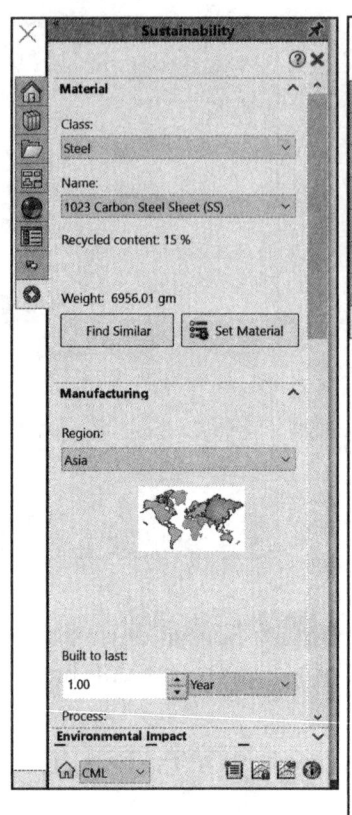
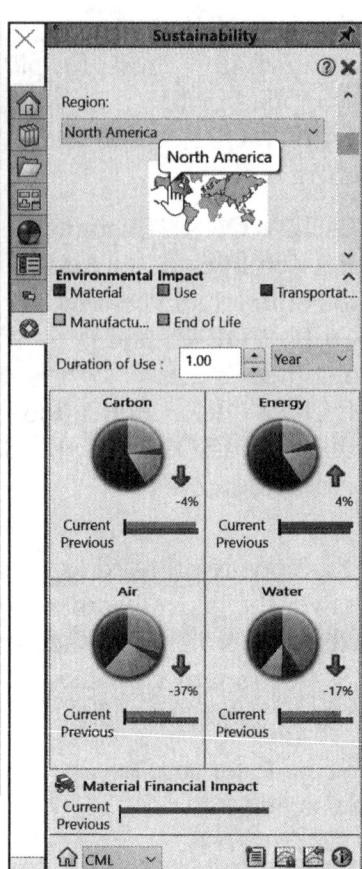

SOLIDWORKS Sustainability allows students and designers to be environmentally conscious about their designs.

Every license of SOLIDWORKS obtains a copy of SustainabilityXpress. SustainabilityXpress calculates environmental impact on a part in four key areas:

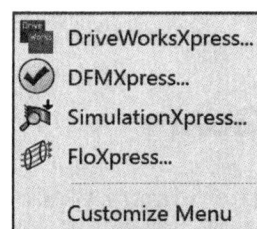

- *Carbon Footprint.*

- *Energy Consumption.*

- *Air Acidification.*

- *Water Eutrophication.*

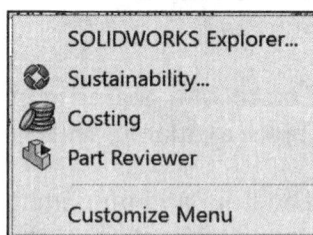

Material and Manufacturing process region and Transportation Usage region are used as input variables. Two SOLIDWORKS Sustainability products are available: *SOLIDWORKS SustainabilityXpress* and *SOLIDWORKS Sustainability.*

SOLIDWORKS SustainabilityXpress: Handles part documents and is included in the core software.

SOLIDWORKS Sustainability: Provides the following functions:

- Same functions as SustainabilityXpress.

- Life Cycle Assessment (LCA) of assemblies.

- Configuration support:

  o Save inputs and results per configuration.

- Expanded reporting capabilities for assemblies.

- Specify amount & type of energy consumed during use.

- Specify method of transportation.

- Support for Assembly Visualization.

SOLIDWORKS Sustainability provides real-time feedback on key impact factors in the Environmental Impact Dashboard, which updates dynamically with any changes by the user. You can generate customized reports to share the results.

SOLIDWORKS Sustainability for assemblies, is an Add-in on the commercial versions of SOLIDWORKS and is contained in the SOLIDWORKS Education Edition and SOLIDWORKS Student Edition.

Life Cycle Assessment

Life Cycle Assessment is a method to quantitatively assess the environmental impact of a product throughout its entire lifecycle, from the procurement of the raw materials, through the production, distribution, use, disposal and recycling of that product.

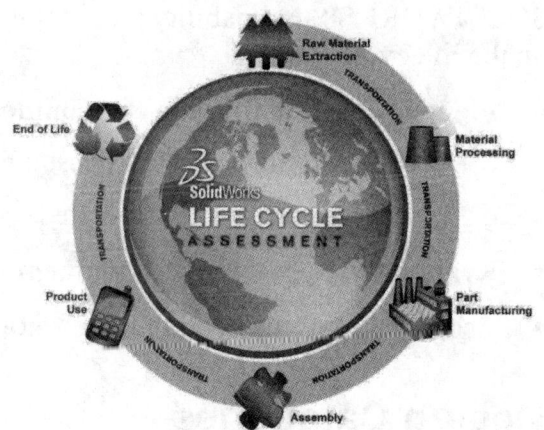

- **Raw Material Extraction:**

  o Planting, growing, and harvesting of trees.

  o Mining of raw ore (example: bauxite).

  o Drilling and pumping of oil.

- **Material Processing** - The processing of raw materials into engineered materials:
  - Oil into Plastic.
  - Iron into Steel.
  - Bauxite into Aluminum.
- **Part Manufacturing** - Processing of material into finished parts:
  - Injection molding.
  - Milling and Turning.
  - Casting.
  - Stamping.
- **Assembly -** Assemble all of the finished parts to create the final product.
- **Product Use -** End consumer uses product for intended lifespan of product.
- **End of Life -** Once the product reaches the end of its useful life, how is it disposed of:
  - Landfill.
  - Recycled.
  - Incinerated.

Life Cycle Assessment Key Elements

SOLIDWORKS Sustainability provides the ability to assess the following key elements on the life cycle:

- **Identify and quantify the environmental loads involved:**
  - Energy and raw materials consumed.
  - Emissions and wastes generated.
- **Evaluate the potential environmental impacts of these loads.**
- **Assess the options available for reducing these environmental impacts.**

Design Categories

Materials: Provides the ability to select various material classes and Names for the part from the drop-down menu.

Manufacturing: Provides the ability to select both the process and usage region for the part. At this time, there are four different areas to choose from: North America, Europe, Asia and Japan.

Process: Provides the ability to select between multiple production techniques to manufacture the part.

Environmental Impact: This area included four quantities: *Carbon Footprint*, *Total Energy*, *Air Acidification*, and *Water Eutrophication*. Each graph presents a graphical breakdown in: Material Impact, Transportation and Use, Manufacturing and End of Life.

- **Carbon Footprint**: A measure of carbon-dioxide and other greenhouse gas emissions such as methane (in CO_2 equivalent units, CO_{2e}) which contributes to emissions, predominantly caused by burning fossil fuels. Global warming Potential (GWP) is also commonly referred to as a carbon footprint.

- **Energy Consumption**: A measure of the non-renewable energy sources associated with the part's lifecycle in units of Mega Joules (MJ). This impact includes not only the electricity of fuels used during the product's lifecycle, but also the upstream energy required to obtain and process these fuels, and the embodied energy of materials which would be released if burned. Energy Consumed is expressed as the net calorific value of energy demand from non-renewable resources (petroleum, natural gas, etc.).

☼ Efficiencies in energy conversion (power, heat, steam, etc.) are taken into account.

- **Air Acidification**: Sulfur dioxide, nitrous oxides, and other acidic emissions into the air cause an increase in the acidity of rain water, which in turn acidifies lakes and soil. These acids can make the land and water toxic for plants and aquatic life. Acid rain can also slowly dissolve man-made building materials such as concrete. This impact is typically measured in units of either kg sulfur dioxide equivalent SO_{2e} or moles H+ equivalent.

- **Water Eutrophication**: When an overabundance of nutrients are added to a water ecosystem, Eutrophication occurs, nitrogen and phosphorous from waste water and agricultural fertilizers cause an overabundance of algae to bloom, which then depletes the water of oxygen and results in the death of both plant and animal life. This impact is typically measured in either kg phosphate equivalent (PO_{4e}) or kg nitrogen (N) equivalent.

Generate a Report: Provides the ability to generate a customer report that captures your baseline design and comparison between the various input parameters.

The CSDA exam is timed. Work efficiently. Use the information presented in the guide (from the following link: http://www.SOLIDWORKS.com/sustainability/sustainable-design-guide.htm) during the exam.

The Guide to Sustainability is translated into: French, Italian, German, Spanish, Turkish, Chinese, Korean, and Japanese.

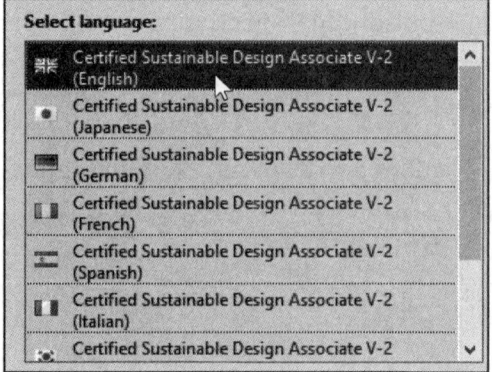

References

It is very important to understand definitions and how SOLIDWORKS information is obtained on the above areas for baseline calculations and comparative calculations. The following standards and agencies were used in the development cycles of this tool:

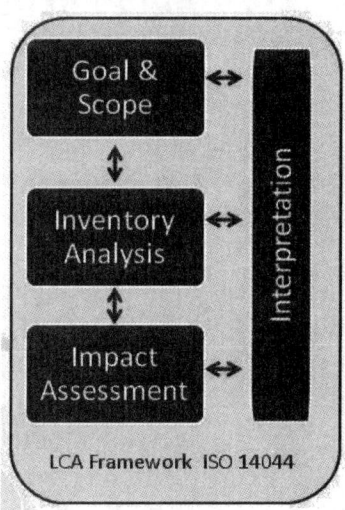

- **Underlying LCA Technology: PE International:**
  - 20 years of LCA experience.
  - LCA international database.
  - GaBi 4 - leading software application for product sustainability.
  - www.pe-international.com.

- **International LCA Standards:**
  - Environmental Management Life Cycle Assessment Principles and Framework ISO 14040/44 www.iso.org.

- **US EPA LCA Resources:**
  - https://www.epa.gov/environmental-topics

SOLIDWORKS Sustainability Methodology

The following chart was created to provide a visualization of the Methodology used in SOLIDWORKS Sustainability. Note the Input variables and the Output areas along with the ability to create and send a customer report are based on your selected decisions.

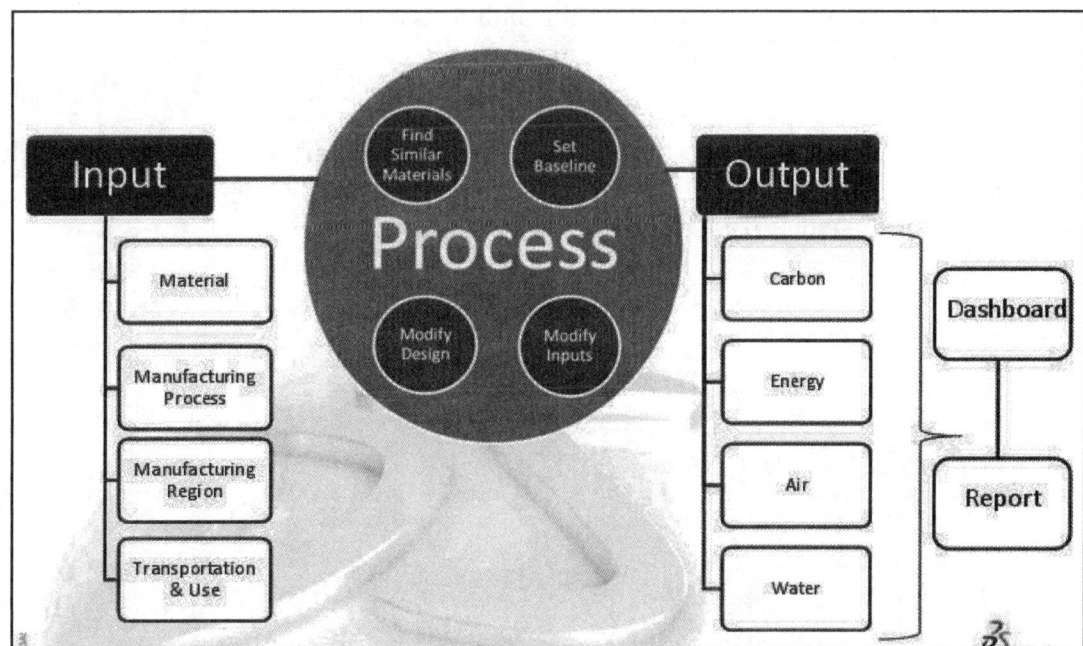

Sustainable Design Guide

The idea of "Sustainable Design" is cropping up more and more in today's product design conversations. But what is sustainable design, and how do I do it? Visit the following link http://www.SOLIDWORKS.com/sustainability/sustainable-design-guide.htm to read, learn and answer the questions for the CSDA certification exam and to better understand the principles and industry standards of sustainability.

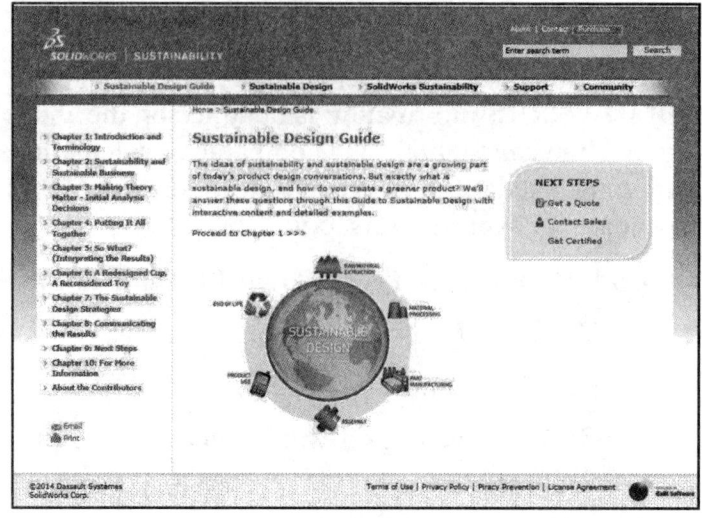

The Guide is divided into ten chapters. First, feel free to jump around. This guide was made to be consumed in sections, and in no particular order. The Guide addresses terminology early on, so if you find concepts that you're unfamiliar with, navigate to the appropriate section to learn more. Going through the entire Guide and playing with some of the examples should take approximately 5-7 hours, so it's a good idea to pace yourself.

To take the CSDA certification, SOLIDWORKS does not require that you have a copy of SOLIDWORKS Sustainability, or even SOLIDWORKS, handy. The Guide is designed to be interesting and informative without having access to the design software.

However, there are examples that you can download into your copy of SOLIDWORKS to make the theory come alive. As you go through the Guide, you'll be alerted to such examples by one of the following two boxes.

SOLIDWORKS Sustainability for assemblies is an additional application on the commercial versions of SOLIDWORKS and is contained in the SOLIDWORKS Education Edition and SOLIDWORKS Student Edition.

Activity: Run Sustainability - Analyze a simple part

Close all parts, assemblies and drawings. Run Sustainability/SustainabilityXpress. Perform a simple analysis on a part. The below procedure uses SOLIDWORKS 2017. There are a few variations between years.

1. Open the **CLAMP2** part from the CSDA\Sustainability folder.

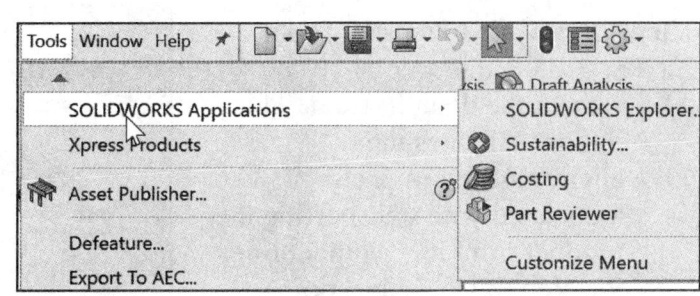

Activate Sustainability.

2. Click **Tools, SOLIDWORKS Applications, Sustainability** from the Main menu. The Sustainability Wizard is displayed in the Task Pane area.

View the SOLIDWORKS Sustainability dialog box.

3. Click **Continue**.

Select the Material Class.

4. Click the **Drop-down arrow** under Class. View your options. Select **Steel** from the drop-down menu as illustrated.

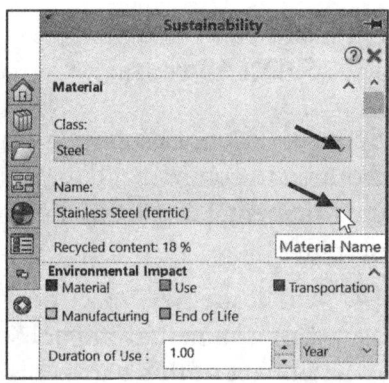

Select the Material Name. Material Name is Class dependent.

5. Click the **Drop-down arrow** under Name. View your options. Select **Stainless Steel (ferritic)** from the drop-down menu.

Select the Manufacturing Region. Each region produces energy by different method combinations. Impact of a kWh is different for each region. Example methods include: Fossil Fuels, Nuclear and Hydro-electric.

6. Position the **mouse pointer** over the map. View your available options. Click **Asia** as illustrated.

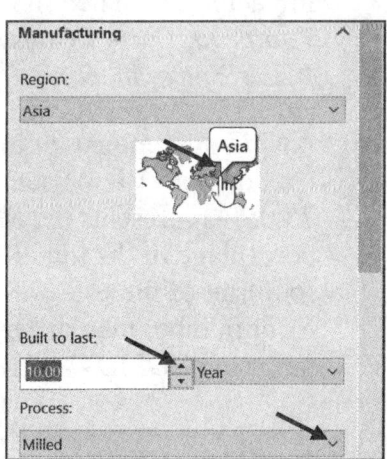

Select Build to last Period.

7. Select **10 years** as illustrated.

Select Manufacturing Process. Manufacturing Process is Material Name dependent.

8. Select **Milled** from the drop-down menu. View the provided information on energy and scrap rate. Note: No paint is selected by default.

Select the Use region.

9. Position the **mouse pointer** over the map. View your available options.

10. Click **North America**.

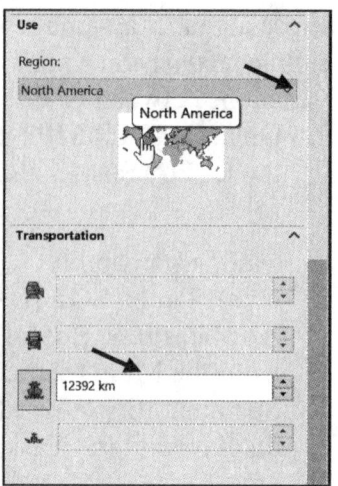

View the provided Transportation modes.

11. Accept the default: **Boat**. This option estimates the environmental impacts associated with transporting the product from its manufacturing location to its use location.

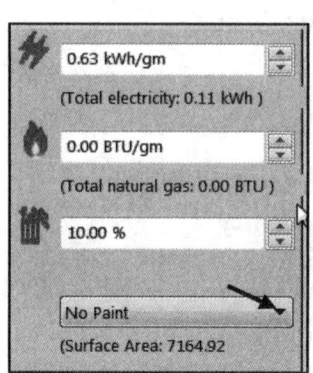

View the provided information on End of Life.

12. **Accept** the default.

Set Duration of Use period.

13. Select **10 years**.

Set your design Baseline. A Baseline is required to comprehend the environmental impact of the original design.

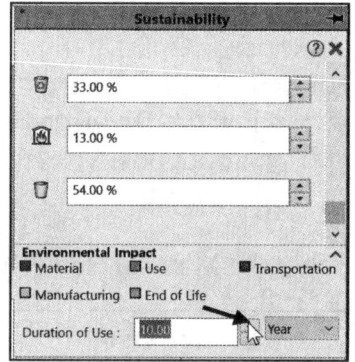

14. Click the **Set Baseline** [icon] tool from the bottom of the Environmental Impact screen. The Environmental Impact of this part is displayed. The Environmental Impact is calculated in four key areas: *Carbon Footprint, Energy Consumption, Air Acidification* and *Water Eutrophication*.

15. Position the **mouse pointer** over the Carbon box. View Factor percentage. 75.05% represents the Material percentage of the total Carbon footprint of the part (0.871kg). Note: Your number may differ if you are not using SOLIDWORKS 2017.

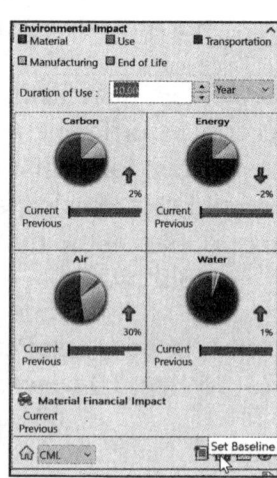

☀ 75.05% represents the Material percentage of the Energy footprint of the part.

16. Click inside the **Carbon** box to display a Baseline bar chart of the Carbon Footprint. View the results.

17. Click the **Home** 🏠 icon to return to the Environmental Impact display.

18. Click inside the **Energy** Consumption impact screen to display a Baseline bar chart of Energy Consumption. View the results.

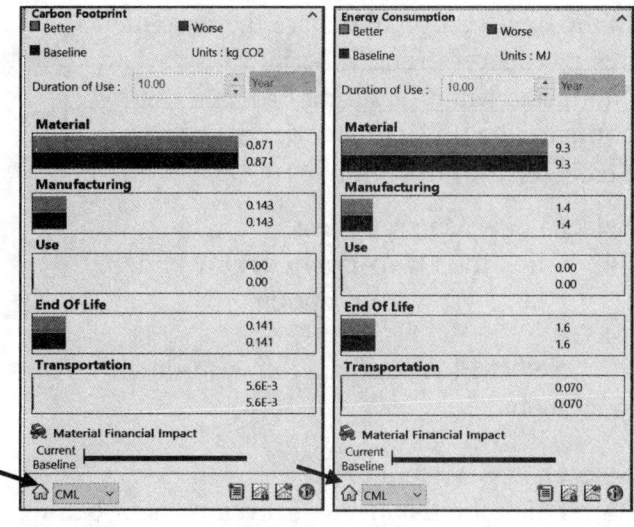

19. Click the **Home** 🏠 icon to return to the Environmental Impact display.

20. Click inside the **Air** Consumption impact screen to display a Baseline bar chart of Air Acidification. View the results.

21. Click the **Home** 🏠 icon to return to the Environmental Impact display.

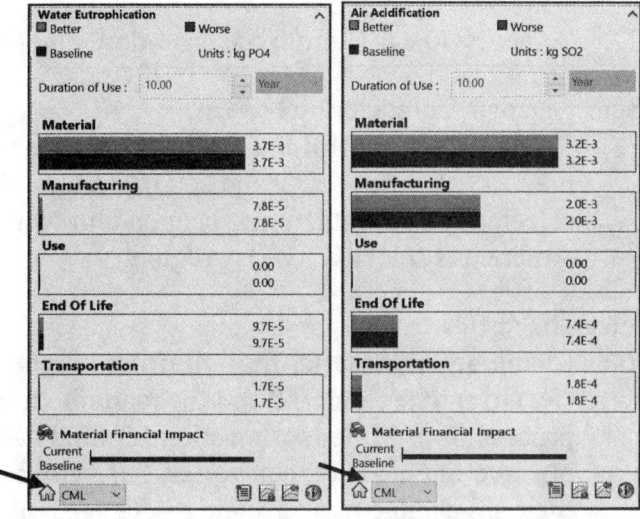

22. Click inside the **Water** Consumption impact screen to display a Baseline bar chart of Water Eutrophication. View the results.

23. Click the **Home** 🏠 icon to return to the Environmental Impact display.

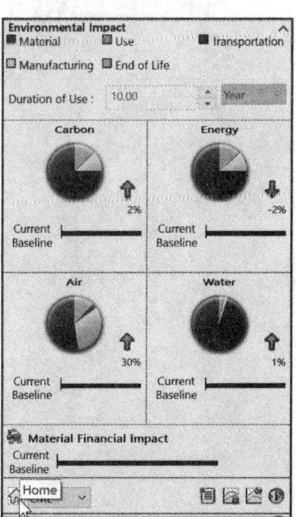

In the next section, compare the baseline design to a different Material Class, Name and Manufacturing Process. Let's compare the present material Stainless Steel (ferritic) to Nylon 6/10.

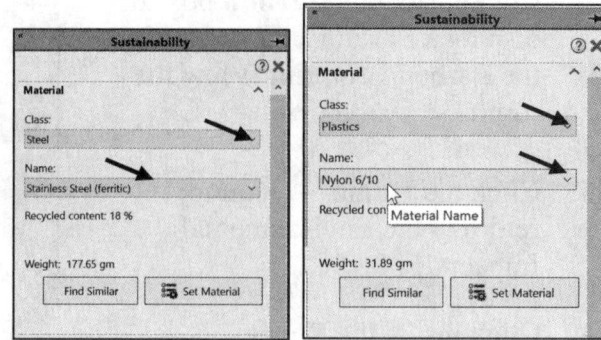

Select a new Material Class.

24. Click the **Drop-down arrow** under Class. View your options.

25. Select **Plastics** from the drop-down menu.

Select a new Material Name.

26. Click the **Drop-down arrow** under Name. View your options.

27. Select **Nylon 6/10** from the drop-down menu.

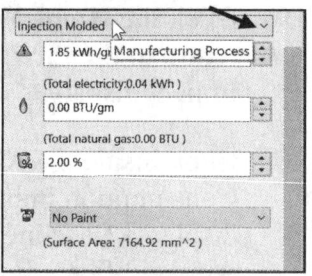

Select a new Manufacturing Process.

28. Select **Injection Molded** from the drop-down menu. Note: the energy and scrap changes. Asia is selected for Manufacturing Region and North America is selected for Use region.

View the results.

29. Changing the material from **Stainless Steel (ferritic)** to **Nylon 6/10** and the manufacturing process from Milled to Injection Molded had a positive impact in all categories, but a further material change may provide a better result. Your numbers may vary depending on your release and version year. What is important is the trend.

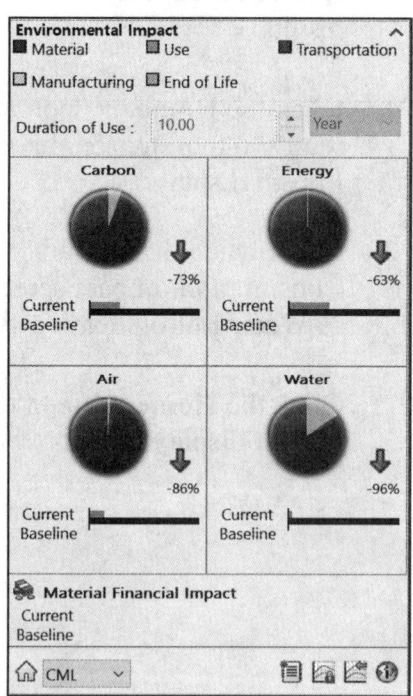

Find a similar material and compare the Environmental Impact to Nylon 6/10. This function is a real time saver.

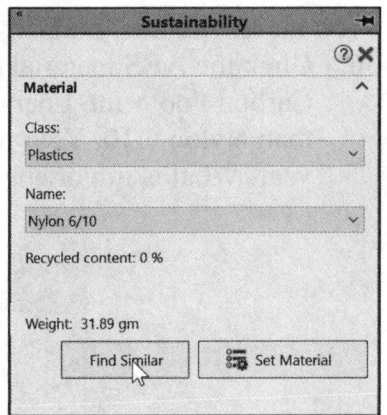

30. Click the **Find Similar** button as illustrated. The Find Similar Material dialog box is displayed.

31. Click the **Value (-any-)** drop-down arrow. View your options.

32. Select **Plastics**. You can perform a general search or customize your search on physical properties of the material.

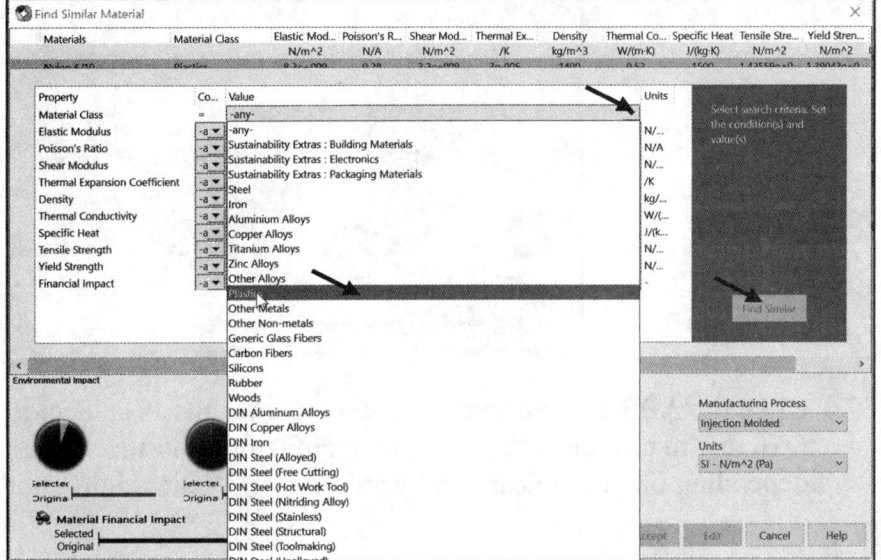

Select a Similar Material from the provided list. You can find similar materials based on the following Properties: *Material Class, Thermal Expansion Coefficient, Specific Heat, Density, Elastic Modulus, Shear Modulus, Thermal Conductivity, Poisson's Ratio, Tensile Strength and Yield Strength.* The definitions are listed at the end of the chapter.

☀ SOLIDWORKS Simulation provides the ability to search on various materials properties. Select either Greater than, Less than or approximately from the drop-down menu.

33. Click the **Find Similar** button as illustrated. SOLIDWORKS provides a full list of comparable materials that you can further refine.

34. Check the **ABS** material box. Check the **ABS PC** material box.

35. Click **inside the top left box (Show Selected Only)** as illustrated. The selected materials are displayed with their properties.

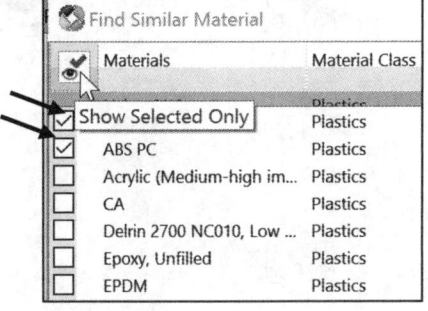

View the Environment Impact for the alternative materials.

36.   Click the **ABS** material row as illustrated. View the results. The material is lower in Carbon Footprint, Energy Consumption, Air Acidification and Water Eutrophication than Nylon 6/10. Your numbers may vary depending on your release and version year. What is important is the trend.

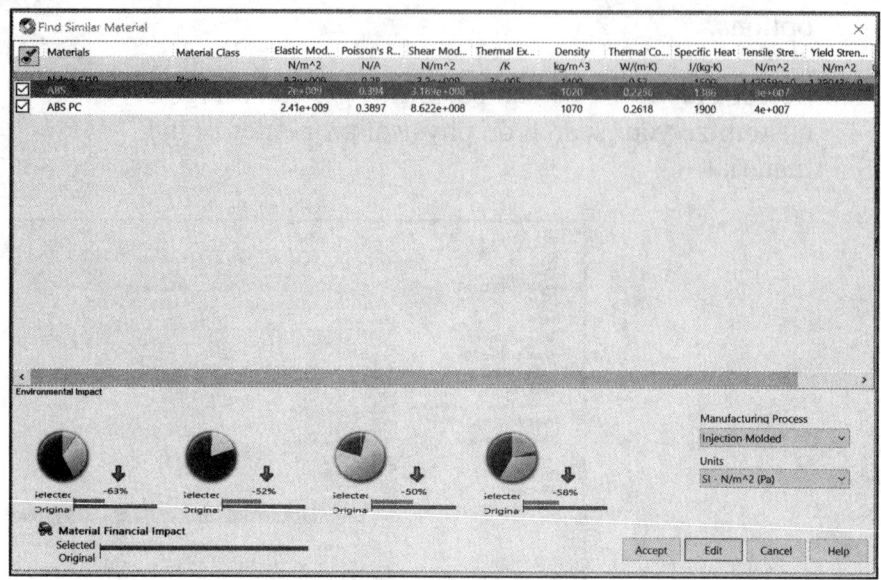

37.   Click the **ABS PC** material row. View the results. You decide to stay with Nylon 6/10 due to cost and other design manufacturing issues. Your numbers may vary depending on your release and version year. What is important is the trend.

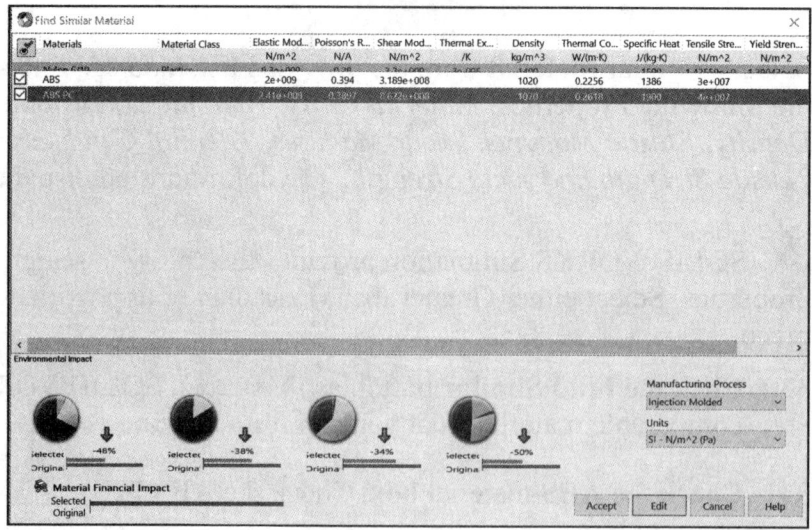

38. Click the **Cancel** button from the Find Similar Material dialog box.

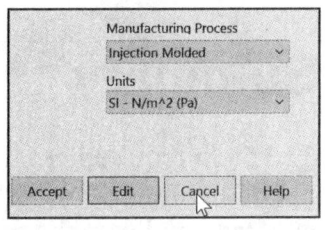

Run a Report.

39. Click the **Save As** or the **Generate Report** button as illustrated depending on your SOLIDWORKS version. SOLIDWORKS provides the ability to communicate this report information throughout your organization. Sustainability generates a report that will compare designs (material, regions) and explain each category of Environmental Impact and show how each design compares to the Base line.

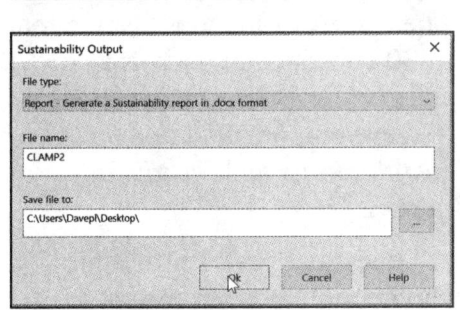

40. Click **OK**.

 You can't generate a report if Microsoft Word is running.

41. Review the Generated report. **Ctrl - Click here for alternative units such as Miles Driven In a Car.** View the results. Note: Internet access is required

42. **View the Glossary** in the report section and the other hyperlinks for additional information.

Close the Report and part. You are finished with this section.

43. **Close** the report.

44. **Close** the part.

 The CSDA exam consists of a total of 30 questions in various categories: *Environmental Assessment*, *Introduction to sustainability* and *Sustainable design* in a multiple choice/multi answer format. No SOLIDWORKS models need to be created for this exam. The above was a simple exercise to perform Sustainability.

Summary

The main requirement for obtaining the CSDA certification is to take and pass the online 30 minute exam (minimum of 24 out of 30 points).

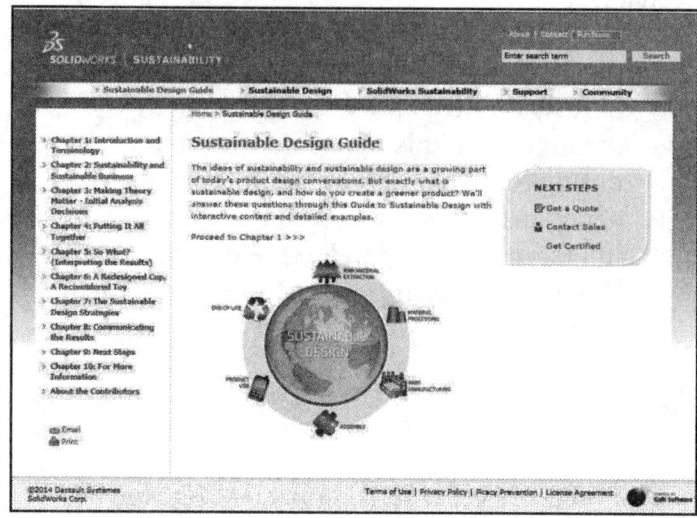

The CSDA exam consists of a total of 30 questions in various key categories: *Environmental Assessment, Introduction to sustainability* and *Sustainable design.*

All questions are in a multiple choice/multi answer format. SOLIDWORKS does not require that you have a copy of SOLIDWORKS Sustainability, or even SOLIDWORKS. No SOLIDWORKS models need to be created for this exam.

You are allowed to answer the questions in any order you prefer. Use the Summary Screen during the CSDA exam to view the list of all questions you have or have not answered.

Download the Sustainable Design Guide http://www.SOLIDWORKS.com/sustainability/sustainable-design-guide.htm to learn and answer these questions and to apply your knowledge for the CSDA certification exam. SOLIDWORKS does not require that you have a copy of SOLIDWORKS Sustainability, or even SOLIDWORKS.

Review the information presented in this chapter and guide in detail and then address the key categories that are aligned to the CSDA exam.

Sample Exam Questions

These questions are examples of what to expect on the certification exam. The multiple choice questions should serve as a check for your knowledge of the exam materials.

1. Environmental Product Declarations, or EPDs, are an increasingly used method for communicating sustainability results with:

A. Suppliers and Customers.

B. Engineers.

C. Managers.

D. None of the Above.

2. The commonly referenced definition of sustainable development put forth by the Brundtland Commission reads as follows:

A. "Sustainability requires closed material loops and energy independence."

B. "Sustainable development is development that meets the needs of the present without compromising the ability of future generations to meet their own needs."

C. "Sustainable development is the use of environmental claims in marketing."

D. None of the above.

3. The study of sustainable development broadly covers these three elements:

A. Land, air, and water.

B. Natural, man-made, hybrid.

C. Environment, social equity, economics.

D. Animal, vegetable, mineral.

4. This answer choice is NOT part of a long-term, working definition of a "sustainable company" ideal:

A. Generates wastes that are useful as inputs by industry or nature.

B. Sources recycled waste material and minimal virgin resources.

C. Follows all current environmental regulations.

D. Uses minimal energy that is ultimately from renewable sources.

5. "The intelligent application of the principles of sustainability to the realm of engineering and design" is a working definition for the following concept:

A. Sustainable design.

B. Sustainable business.

C. Life cycle assessment.

D. SOLIDWORKS Sustainability.

6. A focus on product design that ensures the ultimate recyclability of a product you're developing is a sustainable design technique most specifically called:

A. Design for Environment (DfE).

B. Design for Disassembly (DfD).

C. Life Cycle Assessment (LCA).

D. Design for Total Life Assessment (TLA).

7. The sustainable design technique that promotes systematically using natural inspiration and technologies found in nature to design products is known as:

A. Biomimicry.

B. Cradle to Cradle.

C. Environmental Management System (EMS).

D. Intelligent Design.

8. The sustainable design technique that can most simply be characterized by the concept that the waste from one entity equals the food of another is:

A. Cradle to Cradle.

B. Design for Disassembly (DfD).

C. Life Cycle Assessment (LCA).

D. Intelligent Design.

9. The sustainable design technique that focuses on re-formulating the raw materials we use to design out their toxicity and environmental impacts is known as:

A. Green chemistry.

B. Design for Environment (DfE).

C. Life cycle assessment (LCA).

D. Cradle to cradle.

10. The following is an example of green marketing:

A. A brochure of a product painted green, printed on 100% post-consumer recycled paper.

B. An ad touting the cost savings you can get from driving an efficient vehicle.

C. A label that indicates how many trees will be saved by purchasing this product.

D. None of the above.

11. A green product is defined as one that:

A. Is made of 100% recycled content, and is itself recyclable.

B. Uses no energy or only renewable energy.

C. Has been designed using SOLIDWORKS Sustainability.

D. There is no such thing as a green product - the only "green" product is the one that's never made.

12. LCA stands for:

A. Life Cycle Analysis, because LCA is an exact science, similar to Finite Element Analysis (FEA).

B. Life Cycle Assessment, because LCA is an approximate and pragmatic method, like medicine.

C. Left Cymbal Assassination, because LCA practitioners rove the world destroying half of all percussion equipment.

D. None of the above.

13. Photochemical oxidation (smog) and ozone layer depletion are examples of environmental impacts that fall into the following domain:

A. Air impacts.

B. Terrestrial & aquatic impacts.

C. Natural resource depletion.

D. Climate effects.

14. The "global warming potential" (GWP) from greenhouse gases emitted throughout a product's lifecycle, such as carbon dioxide and methane, is a measure of the product's tendency to affect:

A. Human toxicity.

B. Climate change.

C. Ionizing radiation.

D. Air acidification.

15. The following: "(1) raw material extraction, (2) material processing, (3) part manufacturing, (4) assembly, (5) transportation, (6) product use, and (7) end of life" describes a product's:

A. Environmental indicators.

B. Metrics.

C. Lifecycle stages.

D. Good times.

CHAPTER 7 - CERTIFIED SOLIDWORKS SIMULATION ASSOCIATE - FINITE ELEMENT ANALYSIS (CSWSA-FEA) EXAM

Introduction

DS SOLIDWORKS Corp. offers various types of certification. Each stage represents increasing levels of expertise in 3D CAD: *Certified SOLIDWORKS Associate (CSWA), Certified SOLIDWORKS Professional (CSWP) and Certified SOLIDWORKS Expert (CSWE)* along with specialty fields in Drawings, Simulation, Sheet Metal, Weldments, Molds, Surfacing, Sustainable Design and more.

The Certified SOLIDWORKS Simulation Associate - Finite Element Analysis (CSWSA-FEA) certification indicates a foundation in and apprentice knowledge of demonstrating an understanding in the principles of stress analysis and the Finite Element Method (FEM).

The main requirement for obtaining the CSWSA-FEA certification is to take and pass the online 120 minute exam which consists of 20 questions. The questions consist of 3 hands-on problems, single answer, multiple choice, yes/no and multiple selection for a total of 100 points.

Point allocation ranges from 3 points to 20 points, depending on the difficulty. A passing grade is 70% (70 out of 100) or higher.

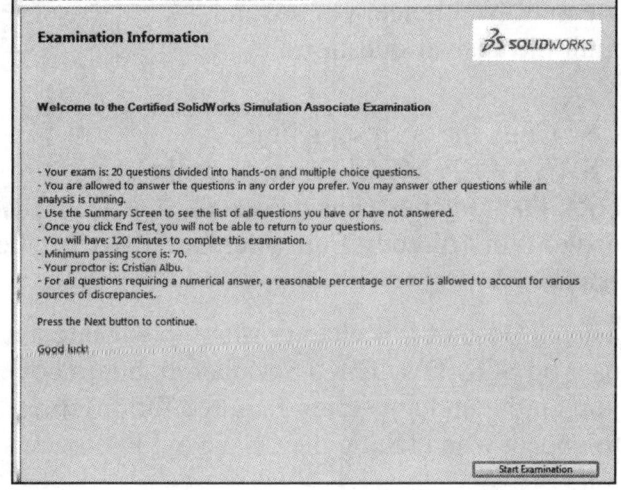

You are allowed to answer the questions in any order. Use the Summary Screen during the CSWSA-FEA exam to view the list of all questions you have or have not answered.

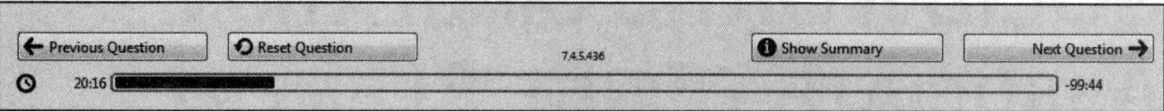

The SOLIDWORKS Simulation hands-on problems require you to modify material, fixtures, loads, or results and then answer a single value to a specified number of decimal places. SOLIDWORKS 2012 or higher is required to take the exam.

Timing yourself is crucial. One exam strategy is to answer all the hands-on questions first within 90 minutes. Here you will gain the most points. Leave 30 minutes to answer the multiple choice, yes/no, and multiple answer questions.

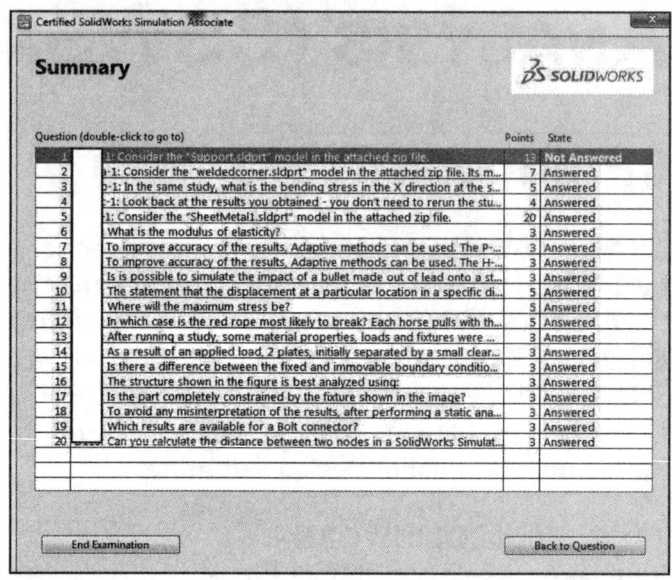

Screen shots from the exam

Copy the corresponding CSWSA-FEA Model folder from the book that matches your release of SOLIDWORKS to your hard drive. Work directly from your hard drive on the tutorials in this book.

The purpose of this chapter is not to educate a new or intermediate user on SOLIDWORKS Simulation, but to cover and to inform you on the understanding required for questions, layout and what to expect when taking the CSWSA-FEA exam.

ASSOCIATE
Simulation

Name

Model 7-1
Model 7-2
Model 7-3
Model 7-4
Model 7-5
Model 7-6

CSWSA-FEA Exam Audience

The intended audience for this book trying to take and pass the CSWSA-FEA exam is anyone with a minimum of 6 - 9 months of SOLIDWORKS and SOLIDWORKS Simulation experience and knowledge in the following areas:

- Engineering Mechanics - Statics.

- Strength of Materials.

- Finite Element Method/Finite Element Analysis Theory.

- Applied concepts in SOLIDWORKS Simulation:

  o Define a Static Analysis Study.

  o Apply material to a part.

  o Work with Solid and Sheet Metal models.

  o Define Solid, Shell and Beam elements.

  o Apply and modify Connections, Contact Set and Contact Type.

  o Define Standard and Advanced Fixtures and External loads.

  o Knowledge of setting and modifying SI/English units.

  o Define Local and Global coordinate systems.

  o Understand the axial forces, sheer forces, bending moments and factor of safety.

  o Define Connector properties such as Contact Sets, No Penetration and Bonded.

  o Set and modify plots to display in the Results folder.

  o Work with Multi-body parts as different solid bodies.

  o Create different mesh types, quality and parameters for parts and assemblies.

  o Select different solvers as directed to optimize problems.

  o Determine if the result is valid.

  o Understand the types of problems SOLIDWORKS Simulation can solve.

  o Ability to use SOLIDWORKS Simulation Help.

Basic FEA Concepts

SOLIDWORKS Simulation uses the Finite Element Method (FEM). FEM is a numerical technique for analyzing engineering designs. FEM is accepted as the standard analysis method due to its generality and suitability for computer implementation.

FEM divides the model into many small pieces of simple shapes called elements, effectively replacing a complex problem by many simple problems that need to be solved simultaneously.

Elements share common points called nodes. The process of dividing the model into small pieces is called meshing.

 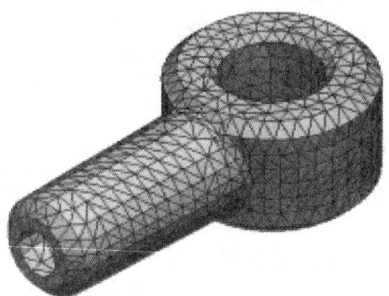

The behavior of each element is well known under all possible support and load scenarios. The finite element method uses elements with different shapes.

The response at any point in an element is interpolated from the response at the element nodes. Each node is fully described by a number of parameters depending on the analysis type and the element used.

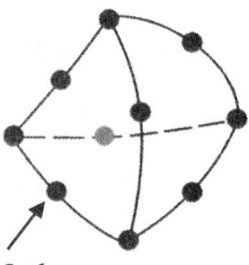

Node

Tetrahedral

For example, the temperature of a node fully describes its response in thermal analysis. For structural analyses, the response of a node is described, in general, by three translations and three rotations. These are called degrees of freedom (DOFs). Analysis using the FEM is called a Finite Element Analysis (FEA).

SOLIDWORKS Simulation formulates the equations governing the behavior of each element taking into consideration its connectivity to other elements. These equations relate the response to known material properties, restraints, and loads.

Next, SOLIDWORKS Simulation organizes the equations into a large set of simultaneous algebraic equations and solves for the unknowns.

In stress analysis, for example, the solver finds the displacements at each node and then the program calculates strains and finally stresses.

Static studies calculate displacements, reaction forces, strains, stresses, and factor of safety distribution. Material fails at locations where stresses exceed a certain level. Factor of safety calculations are based on one of the following failure criteria:

- **Maximum von Mises Stress**.

- **Maximum shear stress (Tresca)**.

- **Mohr-Coulomb stress**.

- **Maximum Normal stress**.

- **Automatic** (Automatically selects the most appropriate failure criterion across all element types).

Static studies can help avoid failure due to high stresses. A factor of safety less than unity indicates material failure. Large factors of safety in a contiguous region indicate low stresses and that you can probably remove some material from this region.

Simulation Advisor

Simulation Advisor is a set of tools that guide you through the analysis process. By answering a series of questions, these tools collect the necessary data to help you perform your analysis. Simulation Advisor includes:

- **Study Advisor**. Recommends study types and outputs to expect. Helps you define sensors and creates studies automatically.

- **Bodies and Materials Advisor**. Specifies how to treat bodies within a part or an assembly and apply materials to components.

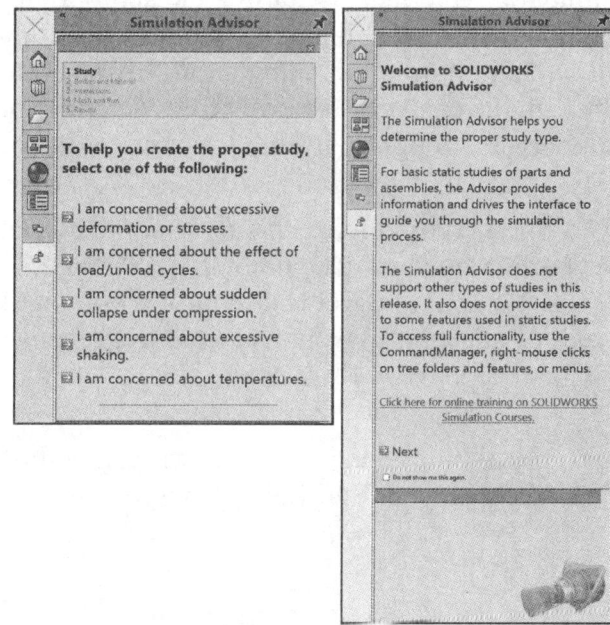

Apply material in SOLIDWORKS Simulation. Right-click on the part icon in the study. Click Apply/Edit Material.

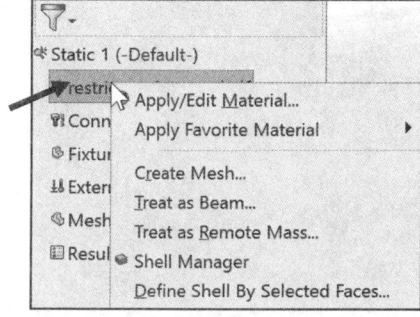

Interactions Advisor. Defines internal interactions between bodies in the model as well as external interactions between the model and the environment. Interactions can include loads, fixtures, connectors, and contacts.

- **Mesh and Run Advisor**. Helps you specify the mesh and run the study.

- **Results Advisor**. Provides tips for interpreting and viewing the output of the simulation. Also helps determine if frequency or buckling might be areas of concern.

While taking the CSWSA-FEA exam, the Simulation Advisor and/or SOLIDWORKS Simulation Help topics may provide required information to answer the exam questions.

Simulation Advisor works with the SOLIDWORKS Simulation interface by starting the appropriate PropertyManager and linking to online help topics for additional information. Simulation Advisor leads you through the analysis workflow from determining the study type through analyzing the simulation output.

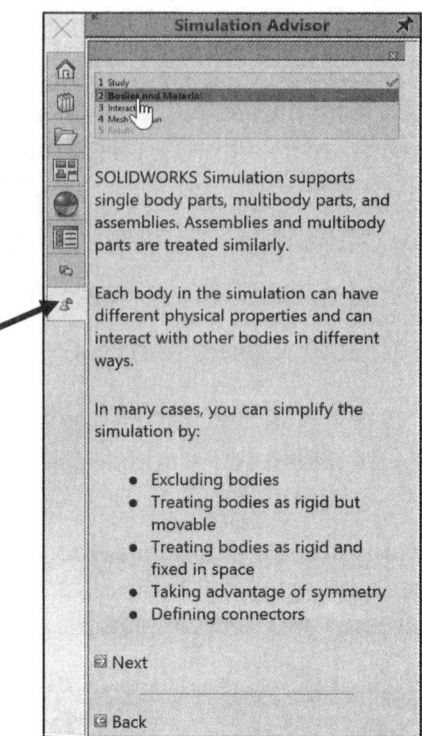

☀ The purpose of this chapter is not to educate a new or intermediate user on SOLIDWORKS Simulation but to cover and to inform you on the types of questions, layout and what to expect when taking the CSWSA-FEA exam.

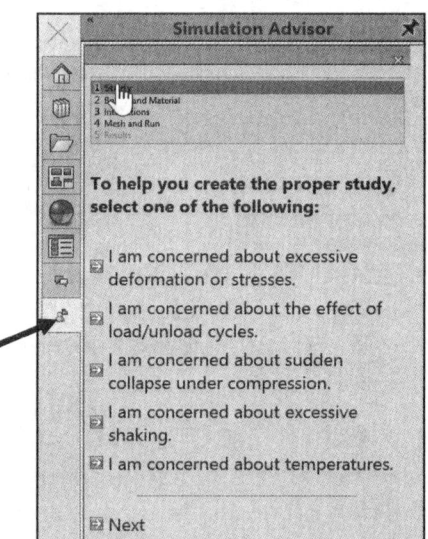

☀ Illustrations and values may vary slightly depending on your SOLIDWORKS release.

SOLIDWORKS Simulation Help & Tutorials

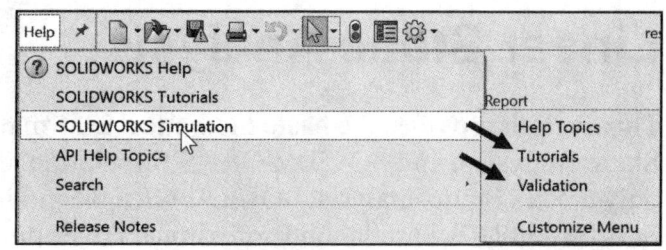

SOLIDWORKS Simulation is an Add-in. Use SOLIDWORKS Simulation during the CSWSA-FEA exam to discover information during the exam. Utilize the Contents and Search tabs to locate subject matter.

Review the SOLIDWORKS Simulation Tutorials on Static parts and assemblies. Understand your options and setup parameters. Questions in these areas will be on the exam.

Review the SOLIDWORKS Simulation Validation, Verification Problems, Static section and the SOLIDWORKS Simulation, Verification, NAFEMS Benchmarks, Linear Static section.

Access SOLIDWORKS Simulation directly from the SOLIDWORKS Add-Ins tab in the CommandManager.

A model needs to be open to access SOLIDWORKS Simulation Help or SOLIDWORKS Simulation Tutorials.

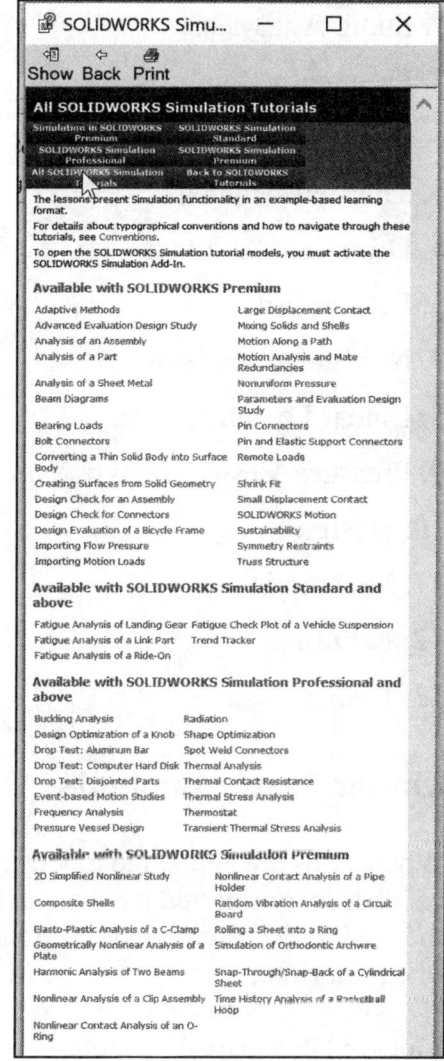

Linear Static Analysis

This section provides the basic theoretical information required for a Static analysis using SOLIDWORKS Simulation. The CSWSA-FEA only covers Static analysis. SOLIDWORKS Simulation and SOLIDWORKS Simulation Professional cover the following topics:

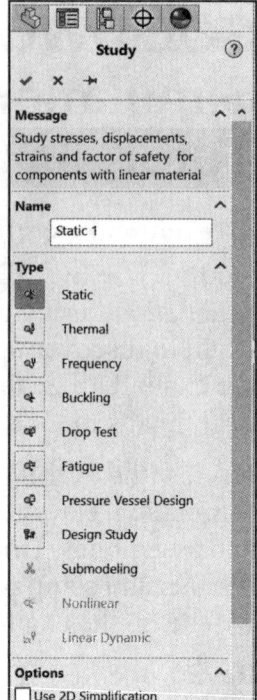

1. Static Analysis.

2. Frequency Analysis.

3. Buckling Analysis.

4. Thermal Analysis.

5. Drop Test Analysis.

6. Fatigue Analysis.

7. Nonlinear Analysis.

8. Linear Dynamic Analysis.

9. Pressure Vessel Design Analysis.

10. Design Study.

11. Sub-modeling

12. Nonlinear.

13. Linear Dynamic.

Linear Static Analysis

When loads are applied to a body, the body deforms and the effect of loads is transmitted throughout the body. The external loads induce internal forces and reactions to render the body into a state of equilibrium.

Linear Static analysis calculates displacements, strains, stresses, and reaction forces under the effect of applied loads.

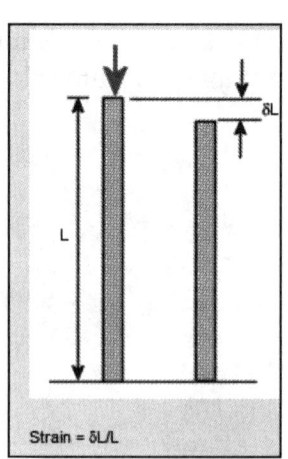

Strain ε is the ratio of change, δ L, to the original length, L. Strain, which is a dimensionless quantity. Stress σ is defined in terms of Force per unit Area.

Linear Static analysis makes the following assumptions:

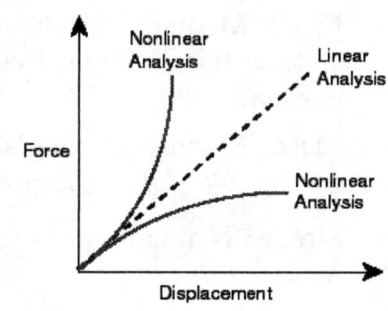

- **Static Assumption**. All loads are applied *slowly* and gradually until they reach their full magnitudes. After reaching their full magnitudes, loads *remain constant* (time-invariant). This assumption neglects inertial and damping forces.

  Time-variant loads that induce considerable inertial and/or damping forces require dynamic analysis.

  Dynamic loads change with time and in many cases induce considerable inertial and damping forces that cannot be neglected.

- **Linearity Assumption**. The relationship between loads and induced responses is linear. For example, if you double the loads, the response of the model (displacements, strains, and stresses), will also double. Apply the linearity assumption if:

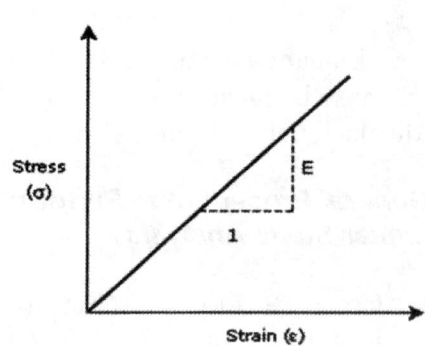

  - All materials in the model comply with Hooke's law; that is, stress is directly proportional to strain.
  - The induced displacements are small enough to ignore the change in stiffness caused by loading.
  - Boundary conditions do not vary during the application of loads. Loads must be constant in magnitude, direction, and distribution. They should not change while the model is deforming.

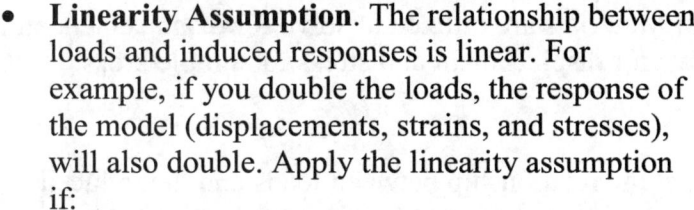 For Static analysis, all displacements are small relative to the model geometry (unless the Large Displacements option is activated).

SOLIDWORKS Simulation assumes that the normals to contact areas do not change direction during loading. Hence, it applies the full load in one step. This approach may lead to inaccurate results or convergence difficulties in cases where these assumptions are not valid.

- Elastic Modulus, E is the stress required to cause one unit of strain. The material behaves linearly in the Elastic range. The slope of the Stress-Strain curve is in a linear portion.

- Elastic Modulus (Young's Modulus) is the slope defined as stress divided by strain. *E = modulus of elasticity (Pa (N/m²), N/mm², psi).*

- Stress σ is proportional to strain in a Linear Elastic Material. Units: *(Pa (N/m²), N/mm², psi).*

You must be able to work in SI and English units for the CSWSA-FEA exam within the same problem. For example, you apply a Force in Newton and then you determine displacement in inches.

Different materials have different stress property levels. Mathematical equations derived from Elasticity theory and Strength of Materials are utilized to solve for displacement and stress. These analytical equations solve for displacement and stress for simple cross sections.

Linear static analysis assumes that the relationship between loads and the induced response is linear. For example, if you double the magnitude of loads, the response (displacements, strains, stresses, reaction forces, etc.) will also double.

General Procedure to Perform a Linear Static Analysis

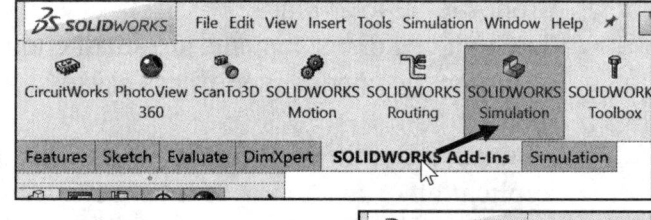

- Complete a Linear Static study by performing the following steps:

- Add-in SOLIDWORKS Simulation.

- Select the Simulation tab.

- Create a new Study. To create a new study, expand the Study Advisor and select New Study.

- Define Material. To define a material, right-click on the model icon in the Simulation study tree and select Apply/Edit Material.

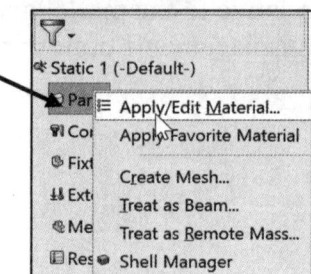

- Define Restraints/Fixtures/Connections.

- Define External Loads. Right-click the External Loads icon in the Simulation study tree and select from the list.

- For assemblies and multi-body parts, use component contact and contact sets to simulate the behavior of the model.

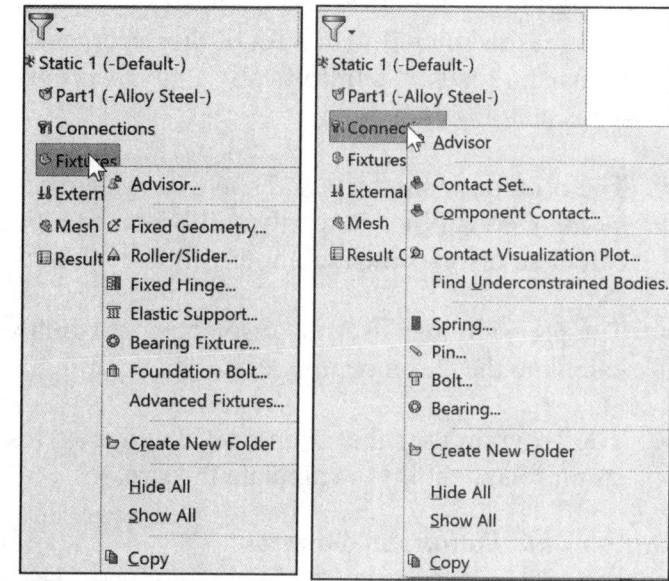

- Mesh the model and Run the study. Select Mesh type and parameters. The Mesh PropertyManager lets you mesh models for solid, shell, and mixed mesh studies.

- View the results. In viewing the results after running a study, you can generate plots, lists, graphs, and reports depending on the study and result types.

- Double-click an icon in a results folder to display the associated plot.

- To define a new plot, right-click the Results folder, and select the desired option. You can plot displacements, stresses, strains, and deformations.

- To assess failure based on a yield criterion, right-click the Results folder, and select Define Factor of Safety Plot.

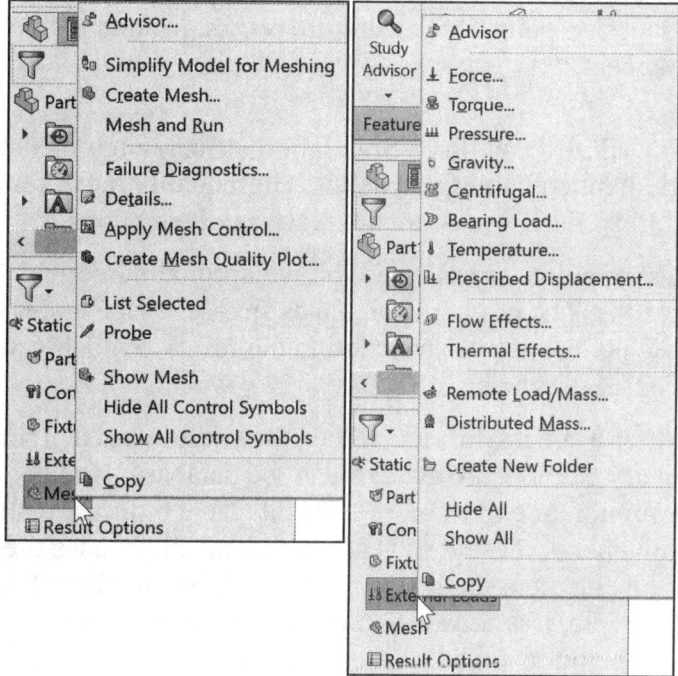

Sequence of Calculations in General

Given a meshed model with a set of displacement restraints and loads, the linear static analysis program proceeds as follows:

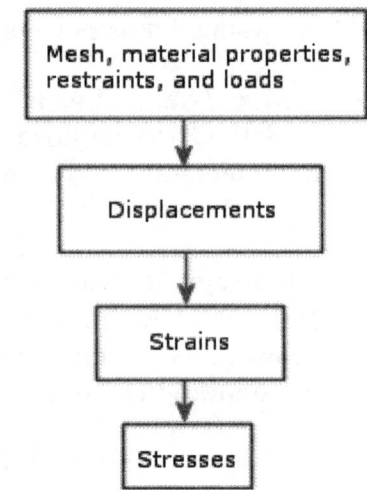

- The program constructs and solves a system of linear simultaneous finite element equilibrium equations to calculate displacement components at each node.

- The program then uses the displacement results to calculate the strain components.

- The program uses the strain results and the stress-strain relationships to calculate the stresses.

Stress Calculations in General

Stress results are first calculated at special points, called Gaussian points or Quadrature points, located inside each element.

☀ SOLIDWORKS Simulation utilizes a tetrahedral element containing 10 nodes (High quality mesh for a Solid). Each node contains a series of equations.

These points are selected to give optimal numerical results. The program calculates stresses at the nodes of each element by extrapolating the results available at the Gaussian points.

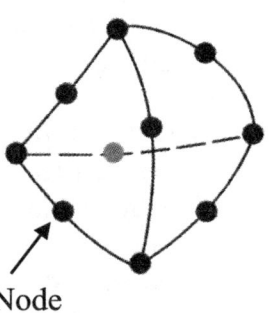

Node

Tetrahedral

After a successful run, nodal stress results at each node of every element are available in the database. Nodes common to two or more elements have multiple results. In general, these results are not identical because the finite element method is an approximate method. For example, if a node is common to three elements, there can be three slightly different values for every stress component at that node.

Overview of the Yield or Inflection Point in a Stress-Strain curve

When viewing stress results, you can ask for element stresses or nodal stresses. To calculate element stresses, the program averages the corresponding nodal stresses for each element.

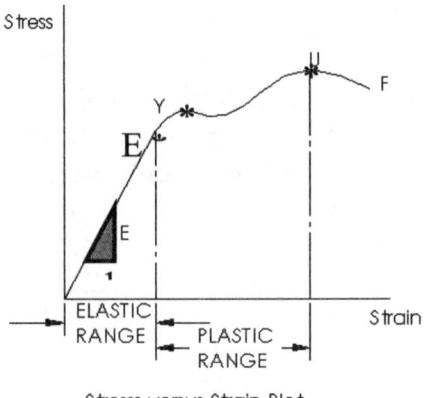

Stresss versus Strain Plot
Linearly Elastic Material

To calculate nodal stresses, the program averages the corresponding results from all elements sharing that node.

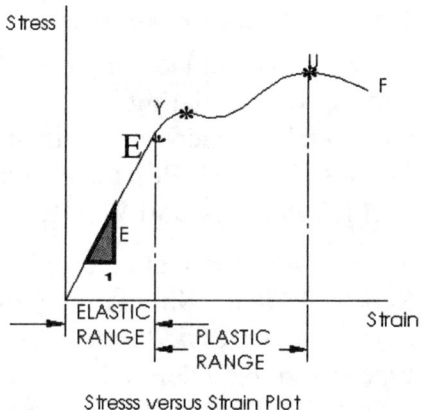

Stresss versus Strain Plot
Linearly Elastic Material

- The material remains in the Elastic Range until it reaches the elastic limit.

- The point E is the elastic limit. The material begins Plastic deformation.

- Yield Stress is the stress level at which the material ceases to behave elastically.

- The point Y is called the Yield Point. The material begins to deform at a faster rate. In the Plastic Range the material behaves non-linearly.

- The point U is called the ultimate tensile strength. Point U is the maximum value of the non-linear curve. Point U represents the maximum tensile stress a material can handle before a fracture or failure.

- Point F represents where the material will fracture.

- Designers utilize maximum and minimum stress calculations to determine if a part is safe. Simulation reports a recommended Factor of Safety during the analysis.

- The Simulation Factor of Safety is a ratio between the material strength and the calculated stress.

Brittle materials do not have a specific yield point and hence it is not recommended to use the yield strength to define the limit stress for the criterion.

Material Properties in General

Before running a study, you must define all material properties required by the associated analysis type and the specified material model. A material model describes the behavior of the material and determines the required material properties. Linear isotropic and orthotropic material models are available for all structural and thermal studies. Other material models are available for nonlinear stress studies. The von Misses plasticity model is available for drop test studies. Material properties can be specified as function of temperature.

- For solid assemblies, each component can have a different material.

- For shell models, each shell can have a different material and thickness.

- For beam models, each beam can have a different material.

- For mixed mesh models, you must define the required material properties for solid and shell separately.

Connections in General

A connection replaces a piece of hardware or fastener by simulating its effect on the rest of the model. Connections include Bolts, Springs, Flexible Support, Bearings, Bonding - Weld/Adhesives, and Welds.

The automatic detection tool in SOLIDWORKS Simulation defines Contact Sets. Sometimes additional contact sets and types need to be defined. The SOLIDWORKS Simulation Study Advisor can help.

For example, the behavior of an adhesive depends on its strength and thickness. You can select the Type manually.

Fixtures: Adequate restraints to prevent the body from rigid body motion. If your model is not adequately constrained, check the Use soft springs to stabilize the model option in the Static dialog box.

When importing loads from SOLIDWORKS Motion, make sure that Use inertial relief option is checked. These options are available for the Direct Sparse solver and FFEPlus solver.

See SOLIDWORKS Simulation Help for additional information.

Restraint Types

The Fixture PropertyManager provides the ability to prescribe zero or non-zero displacements on vertices, edges, or faces for use with static, frequency, buckling, dynamic and nonlinear studies. This section will only address standard restraint types, namely: Fixed Geometry and Immovable (No translation).

The Immovable option is displayed for Sheet Metal parts.

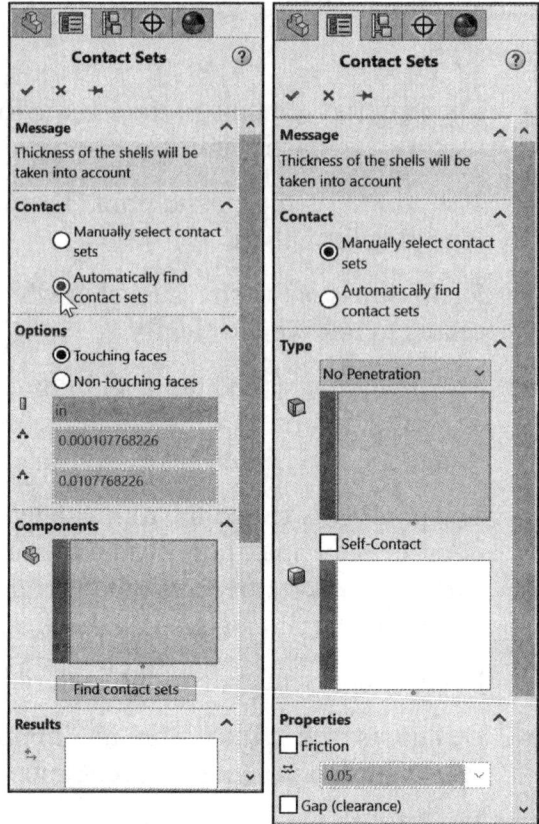

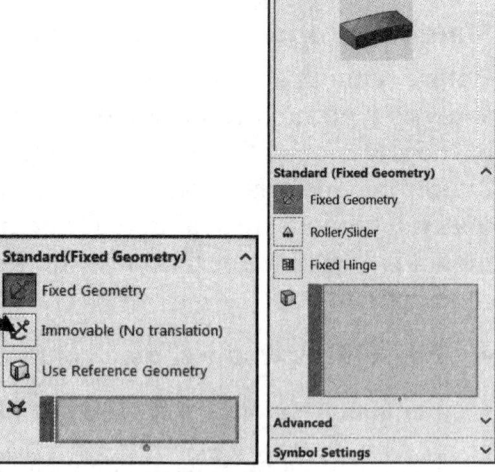

Fixed: For solids, this restraint type sets all translational degrees of freedom to zero. For shells and beams, it sets the translational and the rotational degrees of freedom to zero. For truss joints, it sets the translational degrees of freedom to zero. When using this restraint type, no reference geometry is needed.

View the illustrated table for the attributes and input needed for this restraint.

Attribute	Value
DOFs restrained for solid meshes	3 translations
DOFs restrained for shells and beams	3 translations and 3 rotations
DOFs restrained for truss joints	3 translations
3D symbol (the arrows are for translations and the discs are for rotations)	
Selectable entities	Vertices, edges, faces and beam joints
Selectable reference entity	N/A
Translations	N/A
Rotations	N/A

Immovable (No translation): This restraint type sets all translational degrees of freedom to zero. It is the same for shells, beams and trusses. No reference geometry is used.

To access the immovable restraint, right-click on Fixtures in the Simulation study tree and select Fixed Geometry. Under Standard, select Immovable (No translation). View the illustrated table for the attributes and input needed for this restraint.

Attribute	Value
DOFs restrained for shell meshes	3 translations
DOFs restrained for beam and truss meshes	3 translations
3D symbol	
Selectable entities	Vertices, edges, faces and beam joints
Selectable reference entity	N/A
Translations	N/A
Rotations	N/A

There are differences for Shells and Beams between Immovable (No translation) and Fixed restraint types.

The Immovable option is not available for Solids.

The Fixture PropertyManager allows you to prescribe zero or non-zero displacements on vertices, edges, or faces for use with static, frequency, buckling, dynamic and nonlinear studies.

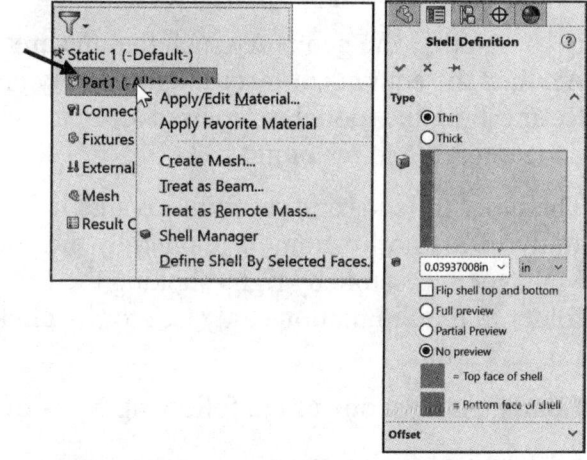

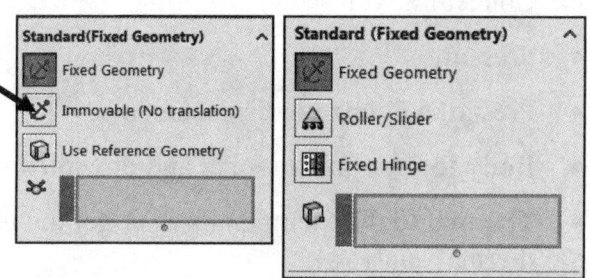

The Fixed Geometry Fixture allows for additional Advanced options: Symmetry, Circular Symmetry, User Reference Geometry, On Flat Faces, On Cylindrical Faces, and On Spherical Faces.

Attributes of each option are available in SOLIDWORKS Simulation Help.

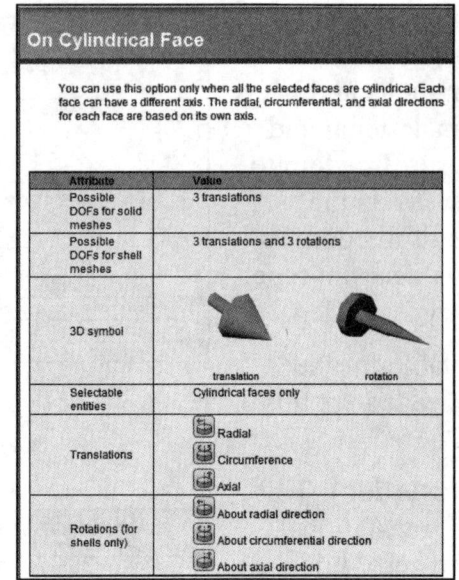

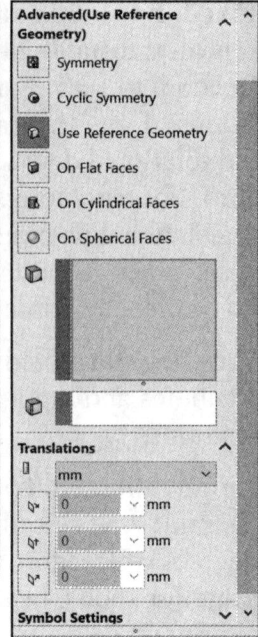

Loads and Restraints in General

Loads and restraints are necessary to define the service environment of the model. The results of analysis directly depend on the specified loads and restraints.

Loads and restraints are applied to geometric entities as features that are fully associative to geometry and automatically adjust to geometric changes.

For example, if you apply a pressure P to a face of area A_1, the equivalent force applied to the face is PA_1.

If you modify the geometry such that the area of the face changes to A_2, then the equivalent force automatically changes to PA_2. Re-meshing the model is required after any change in geometry to update loads and restraints.

The types of loads and restraints available depend on the type of the study. A load or restraint is applied by the corresponding Property Manager accessible by right-clicking the Fixtures or External Loads folder in the Simulation study tree, or by clicking Simulation, Loads/Fixture.

Loads: At least one of the following types of loading is required:

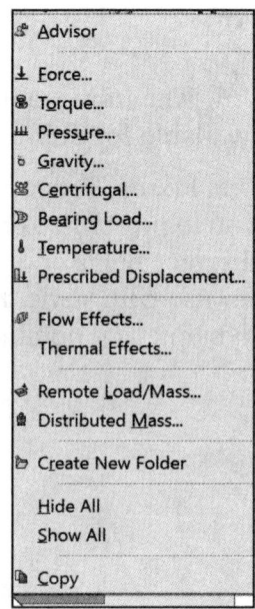

- Concentrated force.

- Pressure.

- Prescribed nonzero displacements.

- Body forces (gravitational and/or centrifugal).

- Thermal (define temperatures or get the temperature profile from thermal analysis).

- Imported loads from SOLIDWORKS Motion.

- Imported temperature and pressure from Flow Simulation.

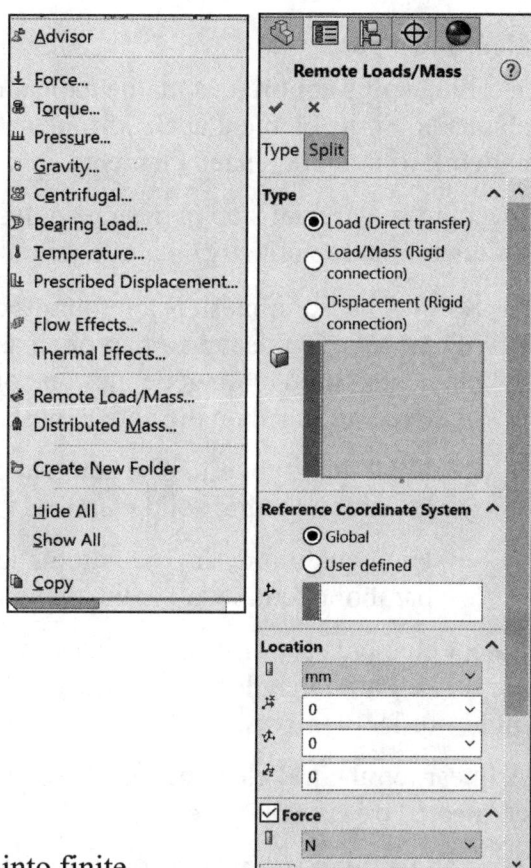

🔆 In a linear static thermal stress analysis for an assembly it is possible to input different temperature boundary conditions for different parts.

Under the External Loads folder you can define Remote Load/Mass and Distributed Mass. In the Remote Load/Mass you define Load, Load/Mass or Displacement. Input values are required for the Remote Location and the Force.

By default, the Location is set to x=0, y=0, z=0. The Force is set to $F_x=0$, $F_y=0$, $F_z=0$. The Force requires you to first select the direction and then enter the value.

Meshing in General

Meshing splits continuous mathematical models into finite elements. The types of elements created by this process depend on the type of geometry meshed. SOLIDWORKS Simulation offers three types of elements:

- Solid elements - solid geometry.

- Shell elements - surface geometry.

- Beam elements - wire frame geometry.

In CAD terminology, "Solid" denotes the type of geometry. In FEA terminology, "Solid" denotes the type of element used to mesh the solid CAD Geometry.

Meshing Types

Meshing splits continuous mathematical models into finite elements. Finite element analysis looks at the model as a network of interconnected elements.

Meshing is a crucial step in design analysis. SOLIDWORKS Simulation automatically creates a mixed mesh of:

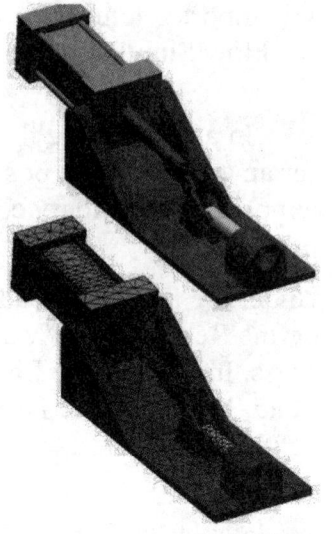

- **Solid**: The Solid mesh is appropriate for bulky or complex 3D models. In meshing a part or an assembly with solid elements, Simulation generates one of the following types of elements based on the active mesh options for the study:

  - Draft quality mesh. The automatic mesher generates linear tetrahedral solid elements **(4 nodes)**.

  - High quality mesh. The automatic mesher generates parabolic tetrahedral solid elements **(10 nodes)**.

Linear elements are also called first-order, or lower-order elements. Parabolic elements are also called second-order, or higher-order elements.

A linear tetrahedral element is defined by four corner nodes connected by six straight edges.

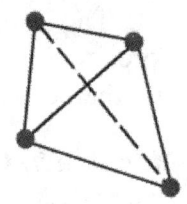

Linear solid element

A parabolic tetrahedral element assigns 10 nodes to each solid element: four corner nodes and one node at the middle of each edge (a total of six mid-side nodes).

In general, for the same mesh density (number of elements), parabolic elements yield better results than linear elements because:

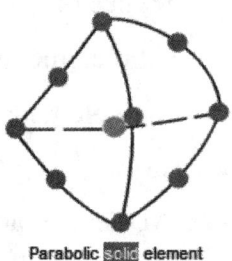

Parabolic solid element

- They represent curved boundaries more accurately.

- They produce better mathematical approximations; however, parabolic elements require greater computational resources than linear elements.

For structural problems, each node in a solid element has three degrees of freedom that represent the translations in three orthogonal directions.

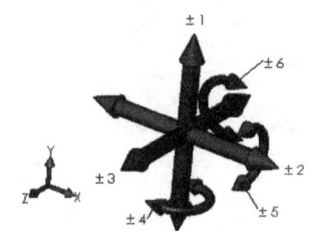

SOLIDWORKS Simulation uses the X, Y, and Z directions of the global Cartesian coordinate system in formulating the problem.

- **Shell**: Shell elements are suitable for thin parts (sheet metal models). Shell elements are 2D elements capable of resisting membrane and bending loads. When using shell elements, Simulation generates one of the following types of elements depending on the active meshing options for the study:

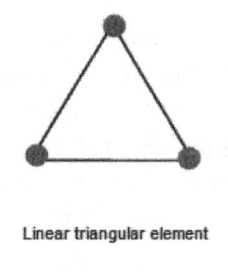

Linear triangular element

  - Draft quality mesh. The automatic mesher generates linear triangular shell elements **(3 nodes)**.

  - High quality mesh. The automatic mesher generates parabolic triangular shell elements **(6 nodes)**.

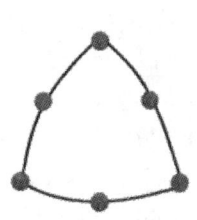

Parabolic triangular element

A linear triangular shell element is defined by three corner nodes connected by three straight edges.

A parabolic triangular element is defined by three corner nodes, three mid-side nodes, and three parabolic edges.

The Shell Definition PropertyManager is used to define the thickness of thin and thick shell elements. The program automatically extracts and assigns the thickness of the sheet metal to the shell. You cannot modify the thickness. You can select between the thin shell and thick shell formulations. You can also define a shell as a composite for static, frequency, and buckling studies. In general use thin shells when the thickness-to-span ratio is less than 0.05.

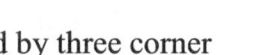

 Surface models can only be meshed with shell elements.

- **Beam or Truss**: Beam or Truss elements are suitable for extruded or revolved objects and structural members with constant cross-sections. Beam elements can resist bending, shear, and torsional loads. The typical frame shown is modeled with beam elements to transfer the load to the supports. Modeling such frames with truss elements fails since there is no mechanism to transfer the applied horizontal load to the supports.

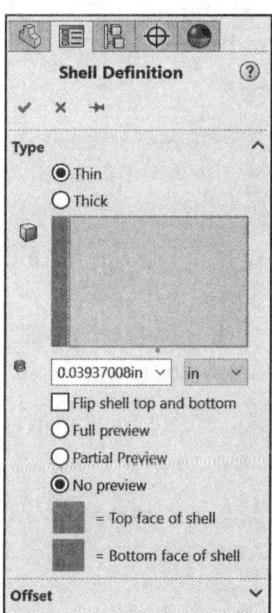

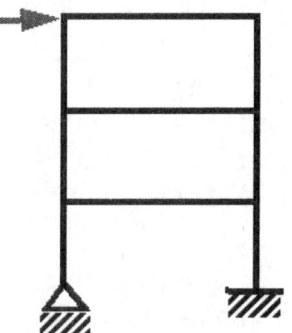

A truss is a special beam element that can resist axial deformation only.

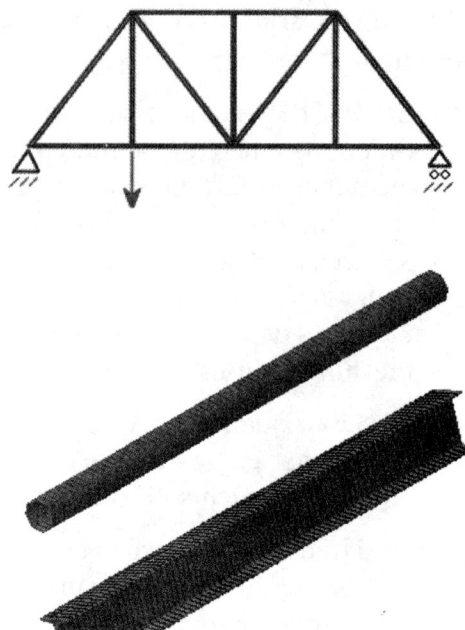

Beam elements require defining the exact cross section so that the program can calculate the moments of inertia, neutral axes and the distances from the extreme fibers to the neutral axes. The stresses vary within the plane of the cross-section and along the beam. A beam element is a line element defined by two end points and a cross-section.

Consider a 3D beam with cross-sectional area (A) and the associated mesh. Beam elements can be displayed on actual beam geometry or as hollow cylinders regardless of their actual cross-section.

Beam elements are capable of resisting axial, bending, shear, and torsional loads. Trusses resist axial loads only. When used with weldments, the software defines cross-sectional properties and detects joints.

Mesh on cyclinders and beam geometry

Beam and truss members can be displayed on actual beam geometry or as hollow cylinders regardless of their actual cross-sectional shape.

A Beam element has 3 nodes (one at each end) with 6 degrees of freedom (3 translational and 3 rotational) per node plus one node to define the orientation of the beam cross section.

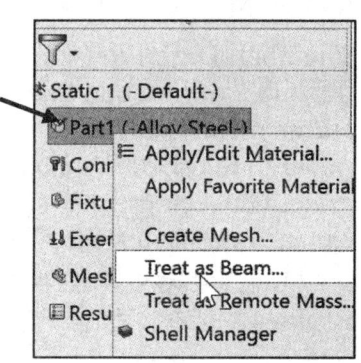

A Truss element has 2 nodes with 3 translational degrees of freedom per node.

The accuracy of the solution depends on the quality of the mesh. In general, the finer the mesh the better the accuracy.

A compatible mesh is a mesh where elements on touching bodies have overlaying nodes.

The curvature-based mesher supports multi-threaded surface and volume meshing for assembly and multi-body part documents. The standard mesher supports only multi-threaded volume meshing.

It is possible to mesh a part or assembly with a combination of solids, shells and beam elements (mixed mesh) in SOLIDWORKS Simulation.

SOLIDWORKS Simulation Meshing Tips

SOLIDWORKS Simulation Help lists the following Meshing tips that you should know for the CSWSA-FEA exam.

When you mesh a study, the SOLIDWORKS Simulation meshes all unsuppressed solids, shells, and beams:

- Use Solid mesh for bulky objects.

- Use Shell elements for thin objects like sheet metals.

- Use Beam or Truss elements for extruded or revolved objects with constant cross-sections.

- Simplify structural beams to optimize performance in Simulation to be modeled with beam elements. The size of the problem and the resources required are dramatically reduced in this case. For the beam formulation to produce acceptable results, the length of the beam should be 10 times larger than the largest dimension of its cross section.

- Compatible meshing (a mesh where elements on touching bodies have overlaying nodes) is more accurate than incompatible meshing in the interface region. Requesting compatible meshing can cause mesh failure in some cases. Requesting incompatible meshing can result in successful results. You can request compatible meshing and select Re-mesh failed parts with incompatible mesh so that the software uses incompatible meshing only for bodies that fail to mesh.

- Check for interferences between bodies when using a compatible mesh with the curvature-based mesher. If you specify a bonded contact condition between bodies, they should be touching. If interferences are detected, meshing stops, and you can access the Interference Detection PropertyManager to view the interfering parts. Make sure to resolve all interferences before you mesh again.

- If meshing fails, use the Failure Diagnostics tool to locate the cause of mesh failure. Try the proposed options to solve the problem. You can also try different element size, define mesh control, or activate Enable automatic looping for solids.

- The SOLIDWORKS Simplify utility lets you suppress features that meet a specified simplification factor. In the Simulation study tree, right-click Mesh and select Simplify Model for Meshing. This displays the Simplify utility.

- It is good practice to check mesh options before meshing. For example, the Automatic transition can result in generating an unnecessarily large number of elements for models with many small features. The high quality mesh is recommended for most cases. The Automatic looping can help solve meshing problems automatically, but you can adjust its settings for a particular model. The Curvature-based mesher automatically uses smaller element sizes in regions with high curvature.

- To improve results in important areas, use mesh control to set a smaller element size. When meshing an assembly with a wide range of component sizes, default meshing results in a relatively coarse mesh for small components. Component mesh control offers an easy way to give more importance to the selected small components. Use this option to identify important small components.

- For assemblies, check component interference. To detect interference in an assembly, click Tools, Interference Detection. Interference is allowed only when using shrink fit. The Treat coincidence as interference and Include multi-body part interference options allow you to detect touching areas. These are the only areas affected by the global and component contact settings.

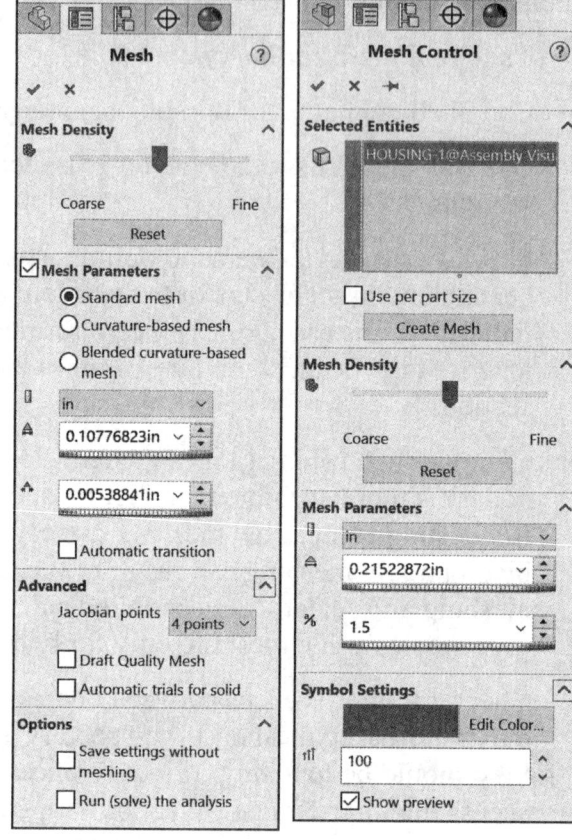

Use the mesh and displacement plots to calculate the distance between two nodes using SOLIDWORKS Simulation.

The Global element size parameter provides the ability to set the global average element size. SOLIDWORKS suggests a default value based on the model volume and surface area. This option is only available for a standard mesh.

The Ratio value in Mesh Control provides the geometric growth ratio from one layer of elements to the next. To access Mesh Control, right-click the Mesh folder in the Simulation study tree and click Apply Mesh Control.

Running the Study

When you run a study, Simulation calculates the results based on the specified input for materials, restraints, loads and mesh.

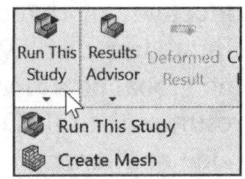

Set the default plots that you want to see in your Simulation Study tree under Simulation, Options from the Main menu.

When you run one or multiple studies, they run as background processes.

In viewing the results after running a study, you can generate plots, lists, graphs, and reports depending on the study and result types.

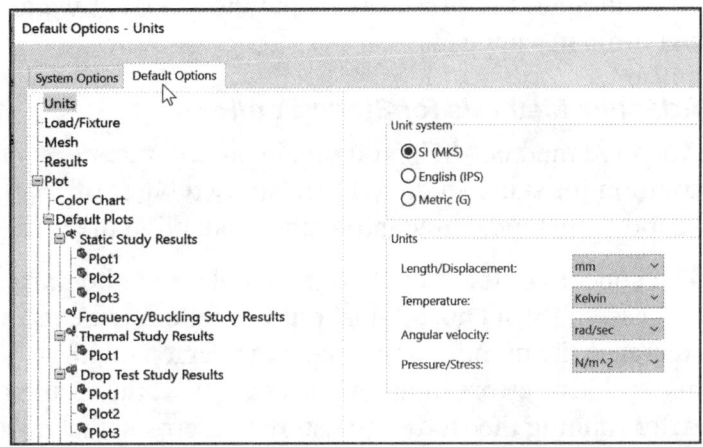

Run multiple studies (batches) either by using the SOLIDWORKS Task Scheduler or the Run all Studies command.

If you modify the study (force, material, etc.) you only need to re-run the study to update the results. You do not need to re-mesh unless you modified contact conditions.

Displacement Plot - Output of Linear Static Analysis

The Displacement Plot PropertyManager allows you to plot displacement and reaction force results for static, nonlinear, dynamic, drop test studies, or mode shapes for bucking and frequency studies. By default, directions X, Y, and Z refer to the global coordinate system.

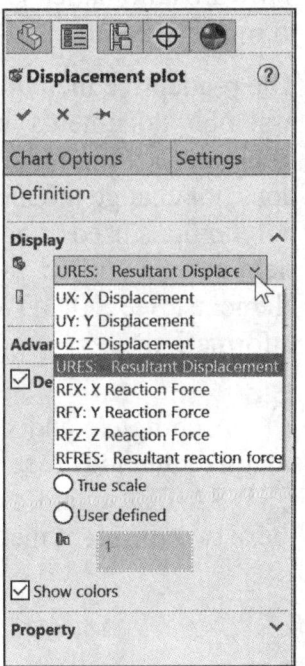

If you choose a reference geometry, these directions refer to the selected reference entity. Displacement components are:

UX = Displacement in the X-direction.

UY = Displacement in the Y-direction.

UZ = Displacement in the Z-direction.

URES = Resultant displacement.

RFX = Reaction force in the X-direction.

RFY = Reaction force in the Y-direction.

RFZ = Reaction force in the Z-axis.

RFRES = Resultant reaction force.

The Probe function allows you to query a plot and view the values of plotted quantities at defined nodes or centers of elements. When you probe a mesh plot, Simulation displays the node or element number and the global coordinates of the node. When you probe a result plot, SOLIDWORKS Simulation displays the node or element number, the value of the plotted result, and the global coordinates of the node or center of the element. For example, in a nodal stress plot, the node number, the stress value, and the global x, y and z coordinates appear.

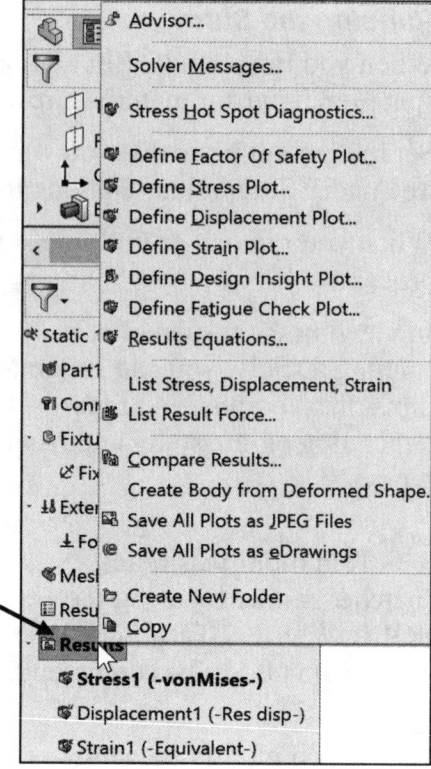

Adaptive Methods for Static Studies

Adaptive methods help you obtain an accurate solution for static studies. There are two types of adaptive methods: h-adaptive and p-adaptive method.

The concept of the h-method (available for solid part and assembly documents) is to use smaller elements (increase the number of elements) in regions with high relative errors to improve accuracy of the results. After running the study and estimating errors, the software automatically refines the mesh where needed to improve results.

The p-adaptive method (available for solid part and assembly documents) increases the polynomial order of elements with high relative errors. The p-method does not change the mesh. It changes the order of the polynomials used to approximate the displacement field using a unified polynomial order for all elements. See SOLIDWORKS Help for additional information.

A complete understanding of p-adaptive and h-adaptive methods require advanced study; for the CSWSA-FEA exam, general knowledge is required of these two different methods.

Sample Exam Questions

These questions are examples of what to expect on the certification exam. The multiple choice questions should serve as a check for your knowledge of the exam materials.

1. What is the Modulus of Elasticity?

- The slope of the Deflection-Stress curve.

- The slope of the Stress-Strain curve in its linear section.

- The slope of the Force-Deflection curve in its linear section.

- The first inflection point of a Strain curve.

2. What is Stress?

- A measure of power

- A measure of strain

- A measure of material strength

- A measure of the average amount of force exerted per unit area

3. Which of the following assumptions are true for a static analysis in SOLIDWORKS Simulation with small displacements?

- Inertia effects are negligible and loads are applied slowly.

- The model is not fully elastic. If loads are removed, the model will not return to its original position.

- Results are proportional to loads.

- All the displacements are small relative to the model geometry.

4. What is Yield Stress?

- The stress level beyond which the material becomes plastic.

- The stress level beyond which the material breaks.

- The strain level above the stress level which the material breaks.

- The stress level beyond the melting point of the material.

5. A high quality Shell element has _____ nodes.

- 4
- 5
- 6
- 8

6. Stress σ is proportional to _____ in a Linear Elastic Material.

- Strain
- Stress
- Force
- Pressure

7. The Elastic Modulus (Young's Modulus) is the slope defined as _____ divided by
_____.

- Strain, Stress
- Stress, Strain
- Stress, Force
- Force, Area

8. Linear static analysis assumes that the relationship between loads and the induced
response is _____.

- Flat
- Linear
- Doubles per area
- Translational

9. In SOLIDWORKS Simulation, the Factor of Safety (FOS) calculations are based on
one of the following failure criterion.

- Maximum von Mises Stress
- Maximum shear stress (Tresca)
- Mohr-Coulomb stress
- Maximum Normal stress

10. The Yield point is the point where the material begins to deform at a faster rate than at the elastic limit. The material behaves _____ in the Plastic Range.

- Flatly

- Linearly

- Non-Linearly

- Like a liquid

11. What are the Degrees of Freedom (DOFs) restrained for a Solid?

- None

- 3 Translations

- 3 Translations and 3 Rotations

- 3 Rotations

12. What are the Degrees of Freedom (DOFs) restrained for Truss joints?

- None

- 3 Translations

- 3 Translations and 3 Rotations

- 3 Rotations

13. What are the Degrees of Freedom (DOFs) restrained for Shells and Beams?

- None

- 3 Translations

- 3 Translations and 3 Rotations

- 3 Rotations

14. Which statements are true for Material Properties using SOLIDWORKS Simulation?

- For solid assemblies, each component can have a different material.

- For shell models, each shell cannot have a different material and thickness.

- For shell models, the material of the part is used for all shells.

- For beam models, each beam cannot have a different material.

15. A Beam element has _____ nodes (one at each end) with _____ degrees of freedom per node plus _____ node to define the orientation of the beam cross section.

- 6, 3, 1

- 3, 3, 1

- 3, 6, 1

- None of the above

16. A Truss element has _____ nodes with _____ translational degrees of freedom per node.

- 2, 3

- 3, 3

- 6, 6

- 2, 2

17. In general, the finer the mesh the better the accuracy of the results.

- True

- False

18. How does SOLIDWORKS Simulation automatically treat a Sheet metal part with uniform thickness?

- Shell

- Solid

- Beam

- Mixed Mesh

19. Use the mesh and displacement plots to calculate the distance between two _____ using SOLIDWORKS Simulation.

- Nodes

- Elements

- Bodies

- Surfaces

20. Surface models can only be meshed with _____ elements.

- Shell
- Beam
- Mixed Mesh
- Solid

21. The shell mesh is generated on the surface (located at the mid-surface of the shell).

- True
- False

22. In general, use Thin shells when the thickness-to-span ratio is less than _____.

- 0.05
- 0.5
- 1
- 2

23. The model (a rectangular plate) has a length to thickness ratio of less than 5. You extracted its mid-surface to use it in SOLIDWORKS Simulation. You should use a _____.

- Thin Shell element formulation
- Thick Shell element formulation
- Thick or Thin Shell element formulation, it does not matter
- Beam Shell element formulation

24. The model, a rectangular sheet metal part, uses SOLIDWORKS Simulation. You should use a:

- Thin Shell element formulation
- Thick Shell element formulation
- Thick or Thin Shell element formulation, it does not matter
- Beam Shell element formulation

25. The Global element size parameter provides the ability to set the global average element size. SOLIDWORKS Simulation suggests a default value based on the model volume and _____ area. This option is only available for a standard mesh.

- Force
- Pressure
- Surface
- None of the above

26. A remote load applied on a face with a Force component and no Moment can result in: Note: Remember (DOFs restrain).

- A Force and Moment of the face
- A Force on the face only
- A Moment on the face only
- A Pressure and Force on the face

27. There are _____ DOFs restrain for a Solid element.

- 3
- 1
- 6
- None

28. There are _____ DOFs restrain for a Beam element.

- 3
- 1
- 6
- None

29. What best describes the difference(s) between a Fixed and Immovable (No translation) boundary condition in SOLIDWORKS Simulation?

- There are no differences.
- There are no difference(s) for Shells but it is different for Solids.
- There is no difference(s) for Solids, but it is different for Shells and Beams.
- There are only differences(s) for a Static Study.

30. Can a non-uniform pressure of force be applied on a face using SOLIDWORKS Simulation?

- No.

- Yes, but the variation must be along a single direction only.

- Yes. The non-uniform pressure distribution is defined by a reference coordinate system and the associated coefficients of a second order polynomial.

- Yes, but the variation must be linear.

31. You are performing an analysis on your model. You select five faces, 3 edges and 2 vertices and apply a force of 20lbf. What is the total force applied to the model using SOLIDWORKS Simulation?

- 100lbf

- 1600lbf

- 180lbf

- 200lbf

32. Yield strength is typically determined at _____ strain.
- 0.1%

- 0.2%

- 0.02%

- 0.002%

33. There are four key assumptions made in Linear Static Analysis: 1. Effects of inertia and damping are neglected, 2. The response of the system is directly proportional to the applied loads, 3. Loads are applied slowly and gradually, and_____.

- Displacements are very small. The highest stress is in the linear range of the stress-strain curve.

- There are no loads

- Material is not elastic

- Loads are applied quickly

34. How many degrees of freedom does a physical structure have?

- Zero

- Three - Rotations only

- Three - Translations only

- Six - Three translations and three rotational

35. Brittle materials have little tendency to deform (or strain) before fracture and do not have a specific yield point. It is not recommended to apply the yield strength analysis as a failure criterion on brittle material. Which of the following failure theories is appropriate for brittle materials?

- Mohr-Coulomb stress criterion

- Maximum shear stress criterion

- Maximum von Mises stress criterion

- Minimum shear stress criterion

36. You are performing an analysis on your model. You select three faces and apply a force of 40lbf. What is the total force applied to the model using SOLIDWORKS Simulation?

- 40lbf

- 20lbf

- 120lbf

- Additional information is required

37. A material is orthotropic if its mechanical or thermal properties are not unique and independent in three mutually perpendicular directions.

- True

- False

38. An increase in the number of elements in a mesh for a part will:

- Decrease calculation accuracy and time

- Increase calculation accuracy and time

- Have no effect on the calculation

- Change the FOS below 1

39. SOLIDWORKS Simulation uses the von Mises Yield Criterion to calculate the Factor of Safety of many ductile materials. According to the criterion:

- Material yields when the von Mises stress in the model equals the yield strength of the material.

- Material yields when the von Mises stress in the model is 5 times greater than the minimum tensile strength of the material.

- Material yields when the von Mises stress in the model is 3 times greater than the FOS of the material.

- None of the above.

40. SOLIDWORKS Simulation calculates structural failure on:

- Buckling

- Fatigue

- Creep

- Material yield

41. Apply a uniform total force of 200lbf on two faces of a model. The two faces have different areas. How do you apply the load using SOLIDWORKS Simulation for a Linear Static Study?

- Select the two faces and input a normal to direction force of 200lbf on each face.

- Select the two faces and a reference plane. Apply 100lbf on each face.

- Apply equal force to the two faces. The force on each face is the total force divided by the total area of the two faces.

- None of the above.

42. Maximum and Minimum value indicators are displayed on Stress and Displacement plots in SOLIDWORKS Simulation for a Linear Static Study.

- True

- False

43. What SOLIDWORKS Simulation tool should you use to determine the result values at specific locations (nodes) in a model using SOLIDWORKS Simulation?

- Section tool

- Probe tool

- Clipping tool

- Surface tool

44. What criteria are best suited to check the failure of ductile materials in SOLIDWORKS Simulation?

- Maximum von Mises Strain and Maximum Shear Strain criterion

- Maximum von Misses Stress and Maximum Shear Stress criterion

- Maximum Mohr-Coulomb Stress and Maximum Mohr-Coulomb Shear Strain criterion

- Mohr-Coulomb Stress and Maximum Normal Stress criterion.

45. Set the scale factor for plots_____ to avoid any misinterpretation of the results, after performing a Static analysis with gap/contact elements.

- Equal to 0

- Equal to 1

- Less than 1

- To the Maximum displacement value for the model

46. It is possible to mesh _____ with a combination of Solids, Shells and Beam elements in SOLIDWORKS Simulation.

- Parts and Assemblies

- Only Parts

- Only Assemblies

- None of the above

47. SOLIDWORKS Simulation supports multi-body parts. Which of the following is a true statement?

- You can employ different mesh controls to each Solid body

- You can classify Contact conditions between multiple Solid bodies

- You can classify a different material for each Solid body

- All of the above are correct

48. Which statement best describes a Compatible mesh?

- A mesh where only one type of element is used

- A mesh where elements on touching bodies have overlaying nodes

- A mesh where only a Shell or Solid element is used

- A mesh where only a single Solid element is used

49. The Ratio value in Mesh Control provides the geometric growth ratio from one layer of elements to the next.

- True

- False

50. The structures displayed in the following illustration are best analyzed using:

- Shell elements

- Solid elements

- Beam elements

- A mixture of Beam and Shell elements

51. The structure displayed in the following illustration is best analyzed using:

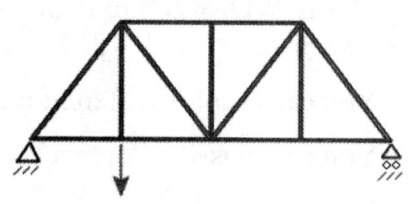

- Shell elements

- Solid elements

- Beam elements

- A mixture of Beam and Shell elements

52. The structure displayed in the following illustration is best analyzed using:

- Shell elements

- Solid elements

- Beam elements

- A mixture of Beam and Shell elements

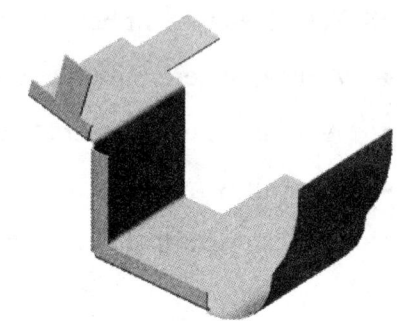

Sheet metal model

53. The structure displayed in the following illustration is best analyzed using:

- Shell elements

- Solid elements

- Beam elements

- A mixture of Beam and Shell elements

54. Surface models can only be meshed with _____ elements.

- Shell elements

- Solid elements

- Beam elements

- A mixture of Beam and Shell elements

55. Use the _____ and _____ plots to calculate the distance between two nodes using SOLIDWORKS Simulation.

- Mesh and Displacement

- Displacement and FOS

- Resultant Displacement and FOS

- None of the above

56. You can simplify a large assembly in a Static Study by using the _____ or _____ options in your study.

- Make Rigid, Fix

- Shell element, Solid element

- Shell element, Compound element

- Make Rigid, Load element

57. A force "F" applied in a static analysis produces a resultant displacement URES. If the force is now 2x F and the mesh is not changed, then URES will:

- Double if there is no contact specified and there are large displacements in the structure

- Be divided by 2 if contacts are specified

- The analysis must be run again to find out

- Double if there is no source of nonlinearity in the study (like contacts or large displacement options)

58. To compute thermal stresses on a model with a uniform temperature distribution, what type/types of study/studies are required?

- Static only

- Thermal only

- Both Static and Thermal

- None of these answers is correct

59. In an h-adaptive method, use smaller elements in mesh regions with high errors to improve the accuracy of results.

- True

- False

60. In a p-adaptive method, use elements with a higher order polynomial in mesh regions with high errors to improve the accuracy of results.

- True

- False

61. Where will the maximum stress be in the illustration?

- A

- B

- C

- D

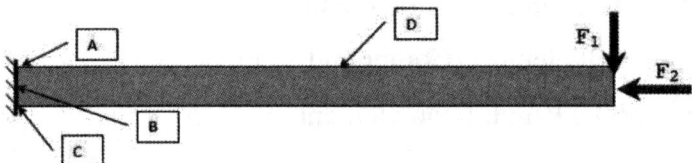

 The purpose of this chapter is not to educate a new or intermediate user on SOLIDWORKS Simulation, but to cover and to inform you on the types of questions, layout and what to expect when taking the CSWSA-FEA exam.

 The CSWSA-FEA only covers Linear Static analysis.

FEA Modeling Section

Tutorial FEA Model 7-1

An exam question in this category could read:

In the figure displayed, what is the vertical displacement in the Global Y direction in (inches) at the location of the dot? Calculate the answer to 3 decimal places.

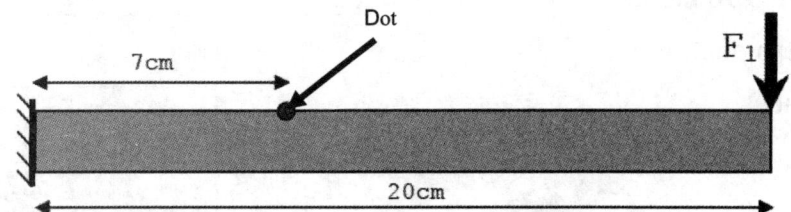
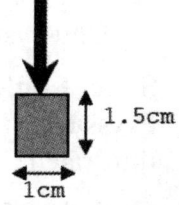

Given Information:

Material: Alloy Steel (SS) from the SOLIDWORKS Simulation Library.

Elastic modulus = $2.1e11$ N/m^2

Poisson's ratio = 0.28

$F_1 = 200$lbf

Use the default high quality element size to mesh.

Let's start.

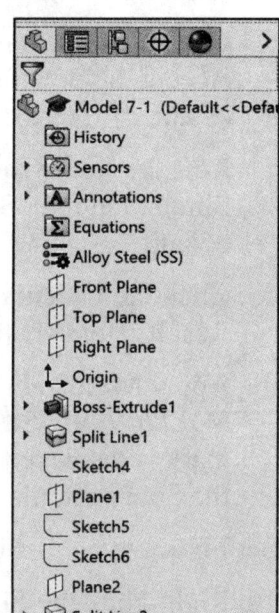

1. **Open** Model 7-1 from the CSWSA-FEA Model folder.

Think about the problem. Think about the model.

The bar which you opened was created on the Front Plane.

The upper left corner of the rectangle is located at the origin. This simplifies the actual deformation of the part. The height dimension references zero in the Global Y direction.

Split Lines were created to provide the ability to locate the needed Joints in this problem. To add the force at the center of the beam, a split line in the shape of a small circle on the top face of the right end of the beam is used.

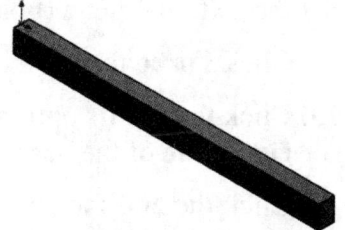

The proper model setup is very important to obtain the correct mesh and to obtain the correct final results.

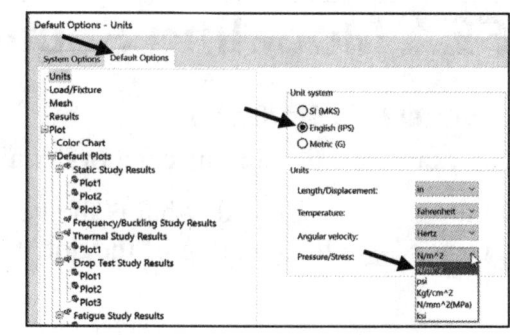

Set Simulation Options and start a Static SOLIDWORKS Simulation Study.

2. **Add-In** SOLIDWORKS Simulation.

3. Click **Simulation**, **Options** from the Main menu. Click the **Default Options** tab.

Set the Unit system and Mesh quality.

4. Select **English (IPS)** and **Pressure/Stress (N/m²)** as illustrated.

5. Click the **Mesh folder**. Select **High** for Mesh quality.

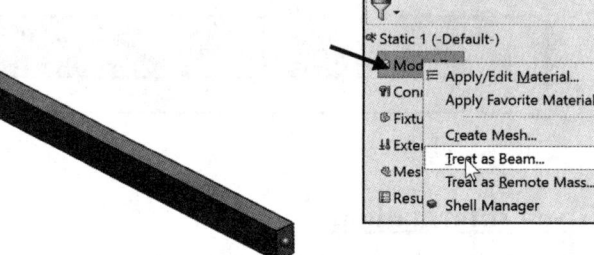

6. **Create** a new Static Study. Accept the default name (Static #). Treat the model as a **Beam**.

7. **Edit** the Joint groups folder from the Study Simulation tree. Split Line 2 is selected by default.

8. Click the **Calculate** button and accept the Results: Joint 1, Joint 2.

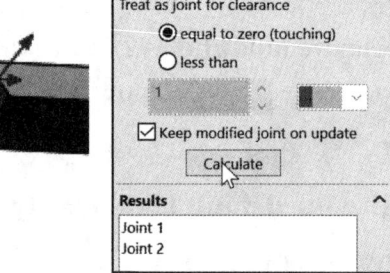

9. Apply **Material** - Alloy Steel (SS) from the SOLIDWORKS Simulation Library. A check mark is displayed next to the model name in the Study Simulation tree.

Set Fixture type. Set Fixed Geometry.

10. Right-click the **Fixtures** folder.

11. Click **Fixed Geometry**. The Fixture PropertyManager is displayed. Select the **joint on the left side** of the beam.

Set the External Load (Force) at the end of the beam.

12. Click **Force** for the External load.

13. Click the **Joints** option. Click the **joint on the right side** of the beam.

14. Click the **end face** of the beam as the plane for direction. Enter **200**lbf Along Plane Direction1. The arrow is displayed downwards; reverse the direction if needed.

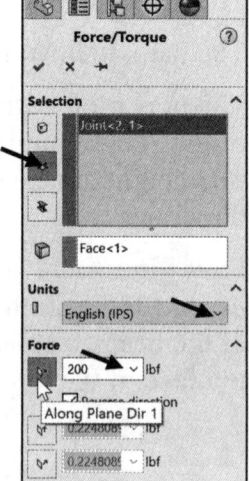

Mesh and Run the model.

15. **Mesh and Run** the model. Use the standard default setting for the mesh.

16. Double-click the **Stress1** folder. View the results.

17. Double-click the **Displacement1** folder. View the results. If needed, Right-click the Displacment1 folder, click Edit Definition. Set Chart Options to floating.

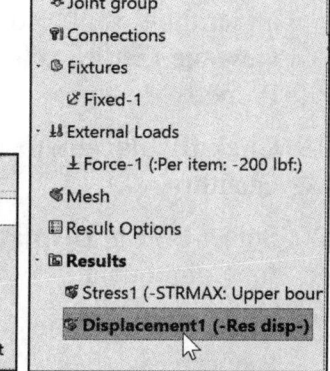

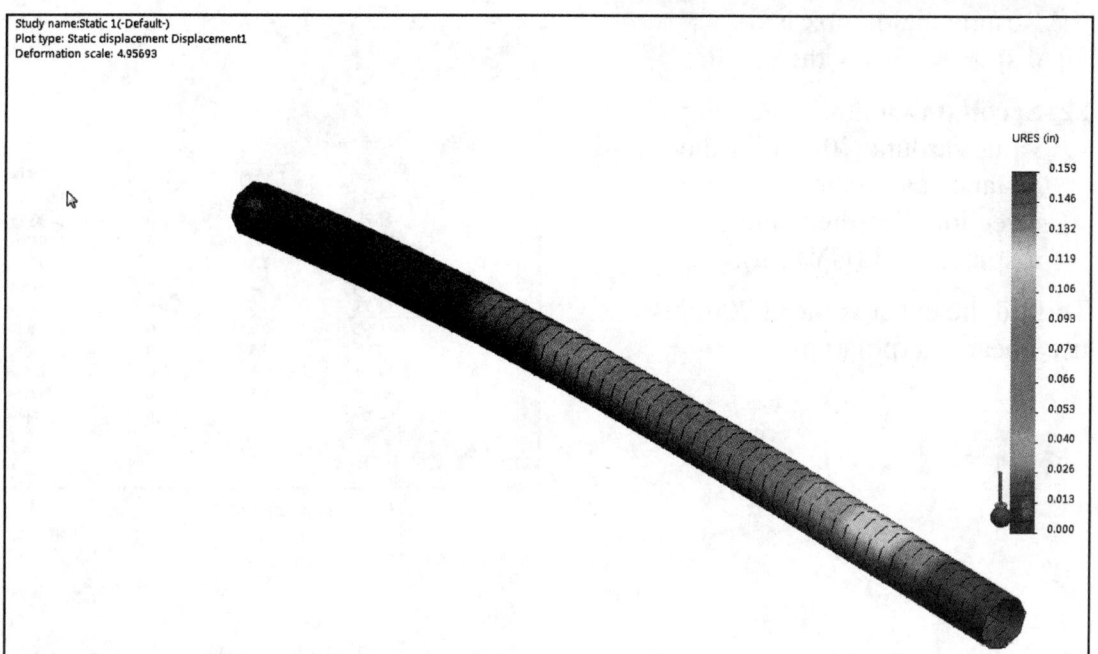

Illustrations may vary slightly depending on your SOLIDWORKS version.

Locate the displacement at 7cm.

18. Click **List Stress, Displacement and Strain** under the Results Advisor to view the List Results PropertyManager.

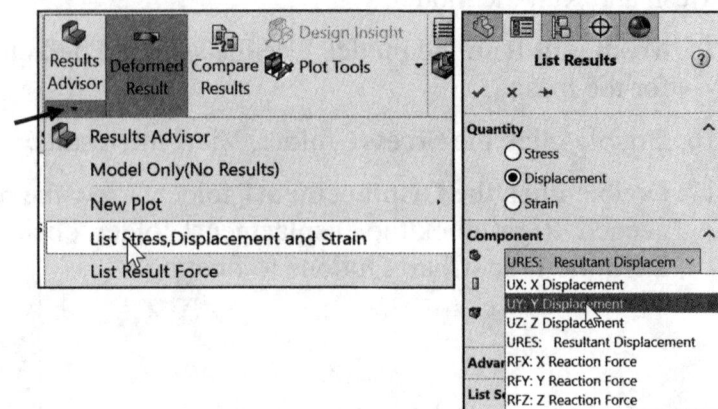

19. Click **Displacement** for Quantity.

20. Select **UY: Y Displacement** for Component.

21. Click **OK** from the PropertyManager. The List Results dialog box is displayed. View the results.

22. **Scroll down** until you see values around 70mm for the distance alone the X direction. See the value of displacement (UY) (in).

To find the exact value at 70mm, use linear interpolation.

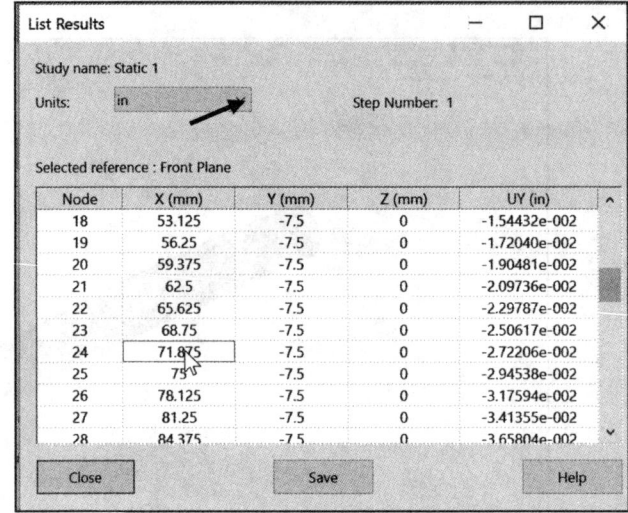

Node	X (mm)	Y (mm)	Z (mm)	UY (in)
18	53.125	-7.5	0	-1.54432e-002
19	56.25	-7.5	0	-1.72040e-002
20	59.375	-7.5	0	-1.90481e-002
21	62.5	-7.5	0	-2.09736e-002
22	65.625	-7.5	0	-2.29787e-002
23	68.75	-7.5	0	-2.50617e-002
24	71.875	-7.5	0	-2.72206e-002
25	75	-7.5	0	-2.94538e-002
26	78.125	-7.5	0	-3.17594e-002
27	81.25	-7.5	0	-3.41355e-002
28	84.375	-7.5	0	-3.65804e-002

This method is shown below and uses the values greater and less than the optimal one to find the actual displacement.

$$\frac{X_U - X_L}{UY_U - UY_L} = \frac{X_U - X_O}{UY_U - UY_O}$$

$$\frac{71.875 - 68.75}{-0.0272206 - -0.0250617} = \frac{71.875 - 70}{-0.02718 - UY_O}$$

$$UY_o = 0.0258$$

At the distance of 7cm (70mm) the displacement is found to be approximately 0.026in.

The correct answer is **B**.

A = 0.034in

B = 0.026in

C = 0.043in

D = 0.021in

Tutorial FEA Model 7-2

Below is a second way to address the first problem (Tutorial FEA Model 7-1) with a different model, without using Split lines, using the Study Advisor and the Probe tool.

In the figure displayed, what is the vertical displacement in the Global Y direction in (inches) at the location of the red dot? Calculate the answer to 3 decimal places.

Given Information:

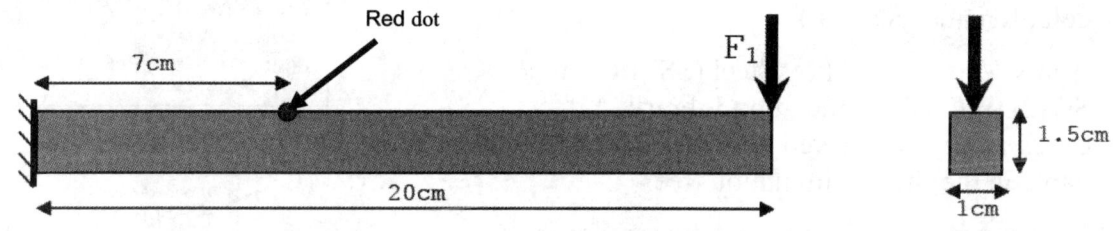

Material: Alloy Steel (SS) from the SOLIDWORKS Simulation Library.

Elastic modulus = 2.1e11 N/m^2

Poisson's ratio = 0.28

F$_1$ = 200lbf

Use the default high quality element size to mesh.

Let's start.

1. **Open** Model 7-2 from the CSWSA-FEA Model folder.

Think about the problem. Think about the model. The bar that you opened is created on the Front Plane.

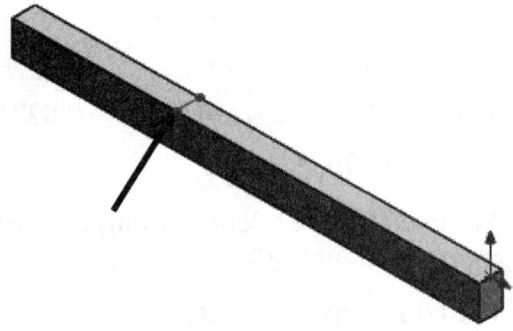

The bar was created so that the origin is the point at which the force is applied. A construction line is created across the part at a distance of 7cm from the end that is to be fixed.

Set Simulation Options and start a Static SOLIDWORKS Simulation Study.

2. **Add-In** SOLIDWORKS Simulation.

3. Click **Simulation**, **Options** from the Main menu.

4. Click the **Default Options** tab.

Set the Unit system and Mesh quality.

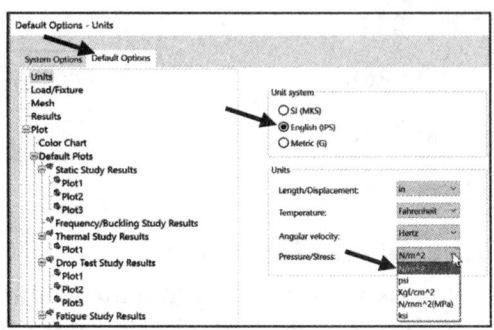

5. Select **English (IPS)** and **Pressure/Stress (N/m²)** as illustrated.

6. Click the **Mesh folder**. Select **High** for Mesh quality.

7. **Create** a new Static Study. Accept the default name (Static #).

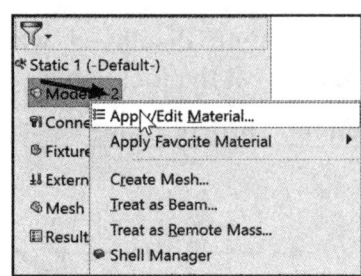

8. Apply **Material** - Alloy Steel (SS) from the SOLIDWORKS Simulation Library. A check mark is displayed next to the model name in the Study Simulation tree.

Set Fixture type. Use the Study Advisor. Set as Fixed Geometry.

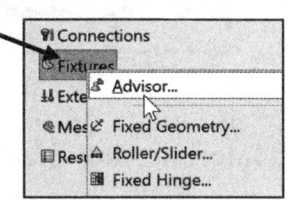

9. Right-click the **Fixtures** folder from the Simulation study tree.

10. Click **Advisor**.

11. Click **Add a fixture**.

12. Select the **proper face (left end)** as illustrated.

13. Set as **Fixed Geometry**.

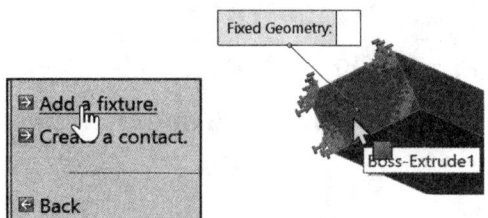

Set the Force.

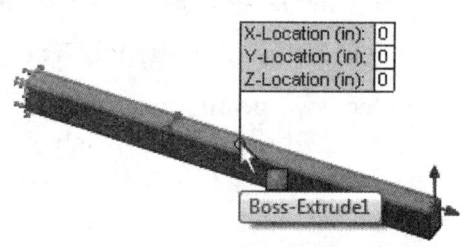

14. Right-click the **External Loads** folder from the Simulation study tree. Select **Remote Load/Mass**. The Remote Loads/Mass PropertyManager is displayed.

15. Click **Load (Direct transfer)** for Type.

16. Select the **top face of the part** - for Faces for Remote Load.

17. Set the Reference Coordinate system to **Global**.

18. Leave all of the location boxes at **zero** value.

19. Select the **Force** check box.

20. Click the **Y-Direction** box.

21. Enter **200lbf**. Use the X-, Y-, and Z-direction boxes to direct the load; reverse direction as necessary.

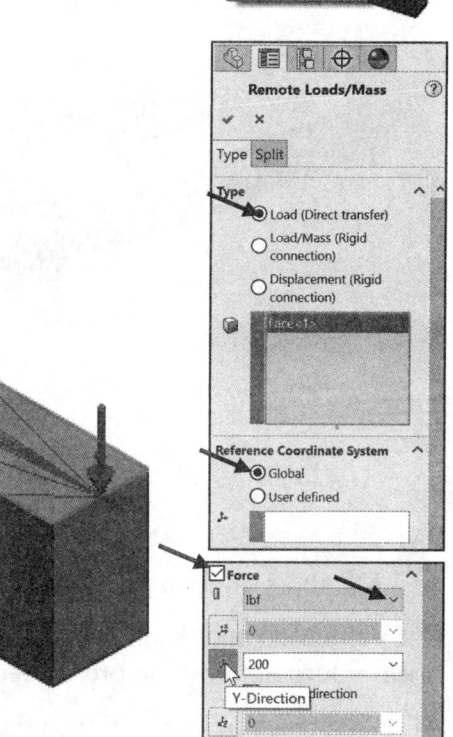

Mesh and Run the model.

22. **Mesh and Run** the model. Use the standard default setting for the mesh.

23. Double-click the **Stress1** folder.

24. **View** the results.

25. Double-click the **Displacement1** folder.

26. **View** the results. If needed, Right-click the Displacment1 folder, click Edit Definition. Set Chart Options to floating.

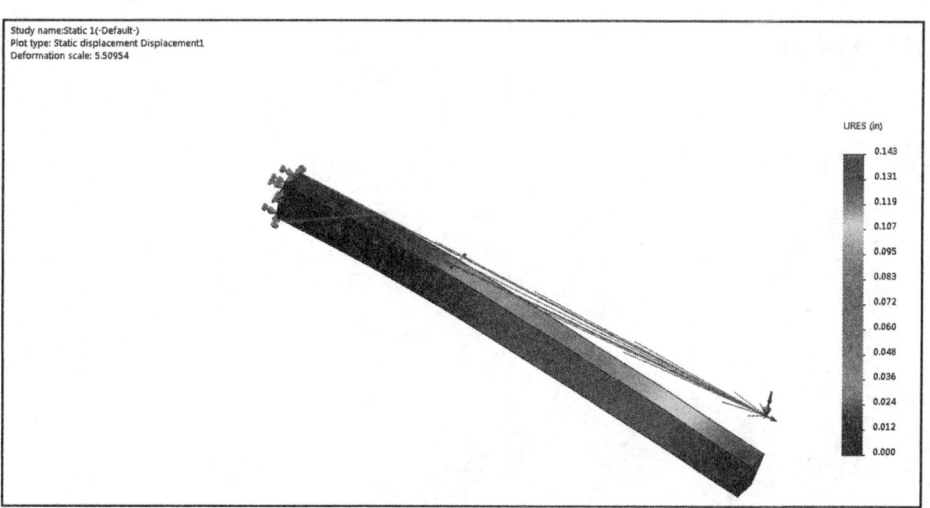

Locate the displacement at 7cm using the Probe tool.

27. Click the **Displacement1** Results folder if needed.

28. Click **Probe** from the Plot Tools drop-down menu.

29. Select **two points**: one on each side of the construction line as illustrated in the Results table.

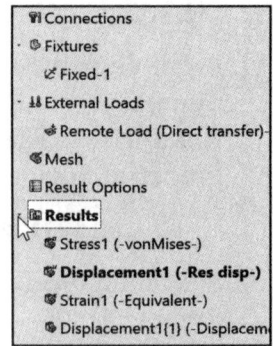

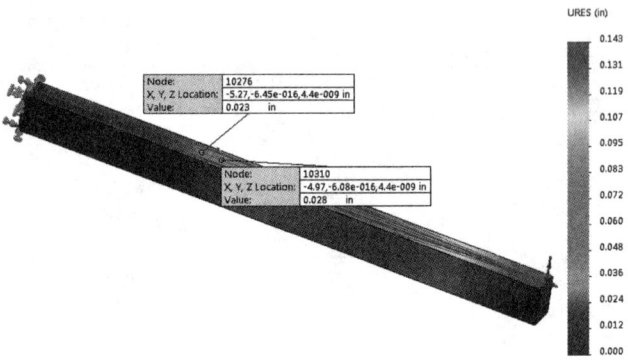

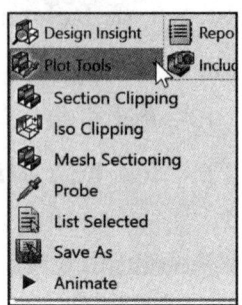

 Numbers will vary depending on the selection location.

Use the length and displacement values of the selected points to find the answer through linear interpolation. The prescribed distance of 7cm is equal to 2.755in.

At the distance of 7cm (70mm) the displacement is found to be approximately 0.026in.

The correct answer is **B**.

A = 0.034in

B = 0.026in

C = 0.043in

D = 0.021in

Tutorial FEA Model 7-3

Proper model setup is very important to obtain the correct mesh and to obtain the correct final results. In the last two examples, you needed to manually apply linear interpolation to locate your final answer.

How can you eliminate the need to manually apply linear interpolation for your final answer? Create a Sensor or use Split Lines at the 7cm point.

Below is the Tutorial FEA Model 7-2 problem. Let's use the same model, but apply a Split line at the 7cm point before we begin the Linear Static study.

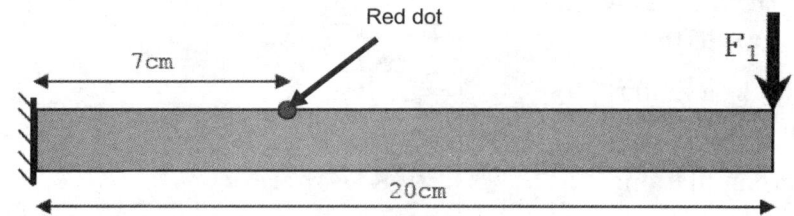
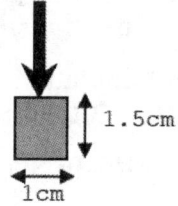

In the figure displayed, what is the vertical displacement in the Global Y direction (in inches) at the location of the red dot? Calculate the answer to 3 decimal places.

Given Information:

Material: Alloy Steel (SS) from the SOLIDWORKS Simulation Library.

Elastic modulus = $2.1\text{e}11 \ \text{N/m}^2$

Poisson's ratio = 0.28

F₁ = 200lbf

Use the default high quality element size to mesh.

Let's start.

1. **Open** Model 7-3 from the CSWSA-FEA Model Folder.

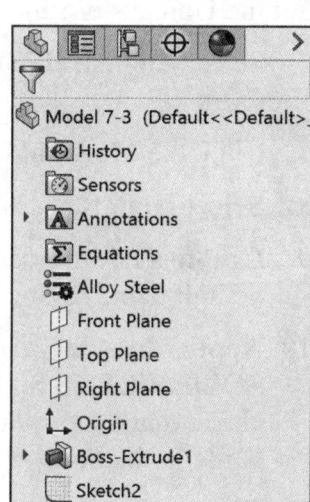

Think about the problem. This is the same model that you opened in the second example.

How can you eliminate the need to manually apply linear interpolation for your final answer?

Address this in the initial setup of the provided model.

Create a Split line at 70mm.

Apply the Probe tool and select the Split Line for the exact point.

2. Create a **Split line feature** with a new sketch **(Insert, Curve, Split Line)** at 70mm.

Set Simulation Options and start a Static SOLIDWORKS Simulation Study.

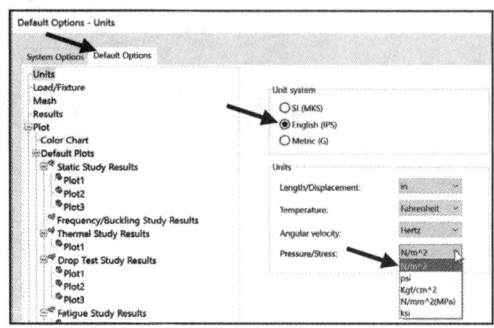

3. **Add-In** SOLIDWORKS Simulation.

4. Click **Simulation**, **Options** from the Main menu.

5. Click the **Default Options** tab.

Set the Unit system and Mesh quality.

6. Select **English (IPS)** and **Pressure/Stress (N/m²)**.

7. Click the **Mesh folder**.

8. Select **High** for Mesh quality.

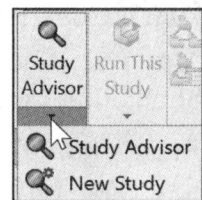

9. **Create** a new Static Study. Accept the default name (Static #).

10. Apply **Material** - Alloy Steel (SS) from the SOLIDWORKS Simulation Library. A check mark is displayed next to the model name in the Study Simulation tree.

Set Fixture type. Set as Fixed Geometry.

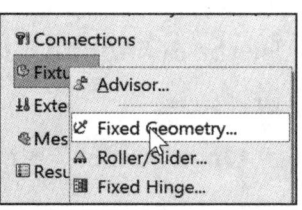

11. Right-click **Fixtures** folder from the Simulation study tree.

12. Click **Fixed Geometry**.

13. Select the **proper face (left end)** as illustrated.

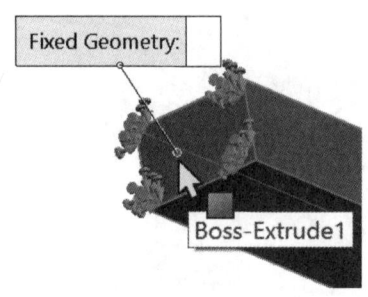

Set the External Load.

14. Right-click the **External Loads** folder from the Simulation study tree.

15. Click **Remote Load/Mass**. The Remote Loads/Mass PropertyManager is displayed.

16. Click **Load (Direct transfer)** for Type.

17. Select the **top face of the part** - for Faces for Remote Load. Note: Click **on both sides** of the Split line.

18. Set the Reference Coordinate system to **Global**.

19. Leave all of the location boxes at **zero** value.

20. Select the **Force** check box. Click the **Y-Direction** box.

21. Enter **200lb**. Use the X-, Y- and Z-direction boxes to direct the load; reverse the direction as necessary.

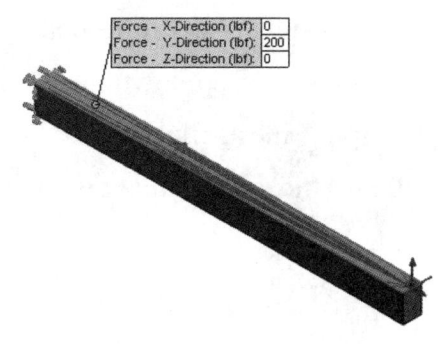

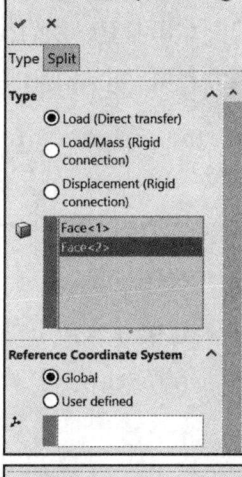

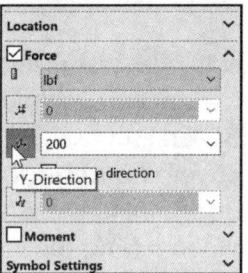

Mesh and Run the model.

22. **Mesh and Run** the model. Use the standard default setting for the mesh.

23. Double-click the **Stress1** folder. View the results.

24. Double-click the **Displacement1** folder. View the results.

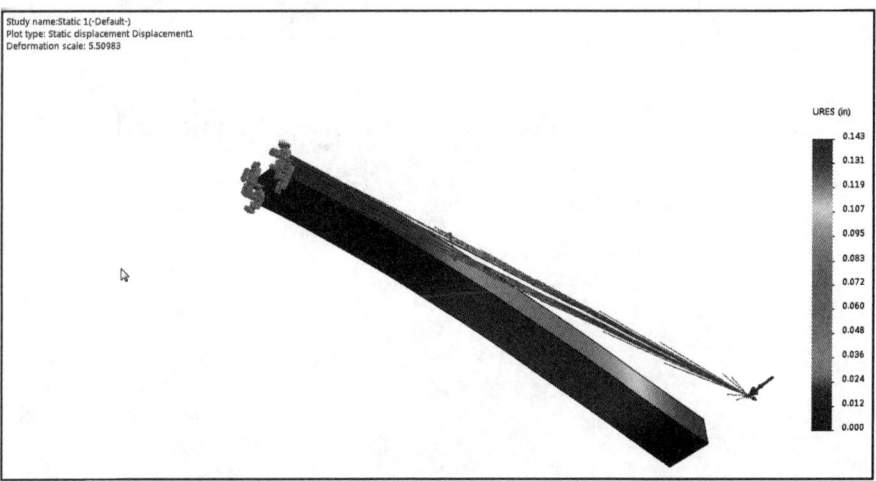

Locate the displacement at 7cm using the Probe tool.

25. Click the **Displacement1** Results folder if needed.

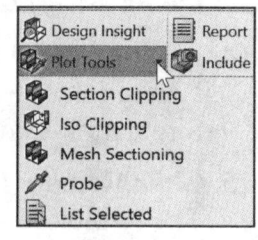

26. Click **Probe** from the Plot Tools drop-down menu.

27. Click a **position** on the Split Line as illustrated. View the results.

At the distance of 7cm (70mm) the displacement is found to be 0.026in.

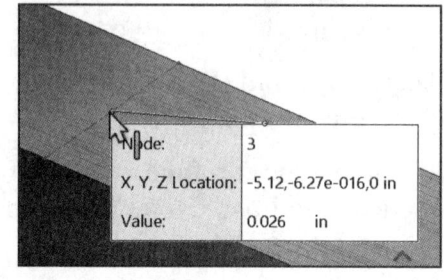

The correct answer is **B**.

A = 0.034in

B = 0.026in

C = 0.043in

D = 0.021in

The purpose of this chapter is not to educate a new or intermediate user on SOLIDWORKS Simulation, but to cover and to inform you on the types of questions, layout and what to expect when taking the CSWSA-FEA exam.

The CSWSA-FEA exam requires that you work quickly. You can modify the units in the Plot menu. Right-click on the required Plot, and select Edit Definition.

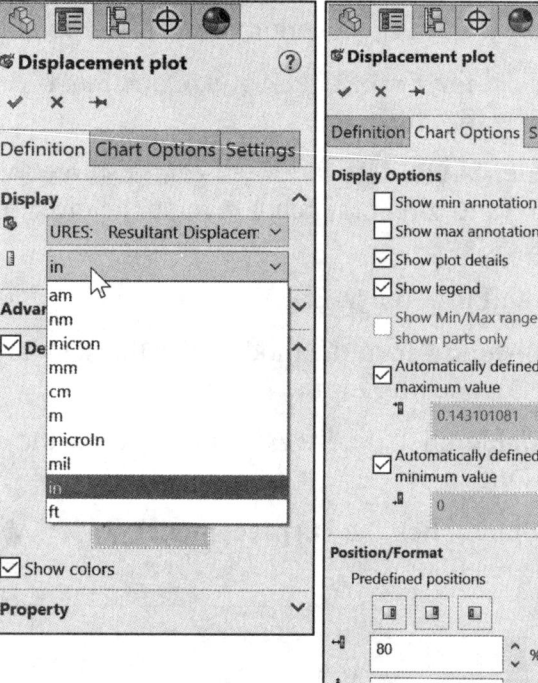

Each hands-on problem in the CSWSA-FEA exam requires a single answer. To save time, set the Chart value to floating and the number of decimal places required. Right-click on the required Plot, and select Chart Options.

Decimal places require change often. Verify units and decimal places.

Tutorial FEA Model 7-4

An exam question in the Solid category could read:

In the figure displayed, what is the maximum resultant displacement in millimeters on the annular face of the model? The three holes are fixed.

Calculate the answer to 3 decimal places.

Given Information:

Material: Alloy Steel (SS).

A normal force, F_1 is applied to the annular face. $F_1 = 3000$lbf.

The three holes are **fixed**.

Use the default high quality element size to mesh.

Let's start.

1. **Open** Model 7-4 from the CSWSA-FEA Model folder. Think about the problem. Think about the model.

Set Simulation Options and start a Static SOLIDWORKS Simulation Study.

2. **Add-In** SOLIDWORKS Simulation.

3. Click **Simulation**, **Options** from the Main menu.

4. Click the **Default Options** tab.

Set the Unit system and Mesh quality.

5. Select **English (IPS)** and **Pressure/Stress (psi)**.

6. Click the **Mesh folder**.

7. Select **High** for Mesh quality.

8. **Create** a new Static Study. Accept the default name (Static #).

9. Apply **Material** - Alloy Steel (SS) from the SOLIDWORKS Simulation Library. A check mark is displayed next to the model name in the Study Simulation tree.

10. Apply Fixed Geometry **Fixtures**. Select the three cylindrical faces of the hole pattern as illustrated.

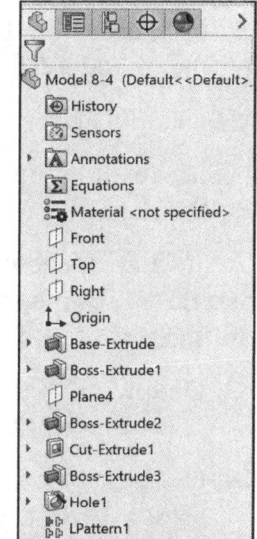

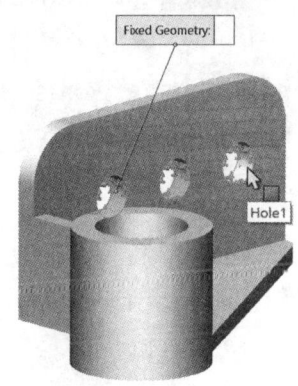

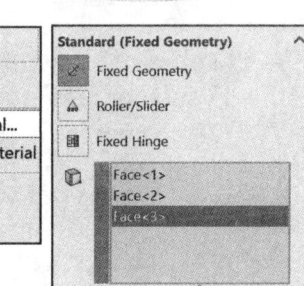

11. Apply an External Load (Force) of **3000lbf** on the annular face of the model as illustrated.

Mesh and Run the model.

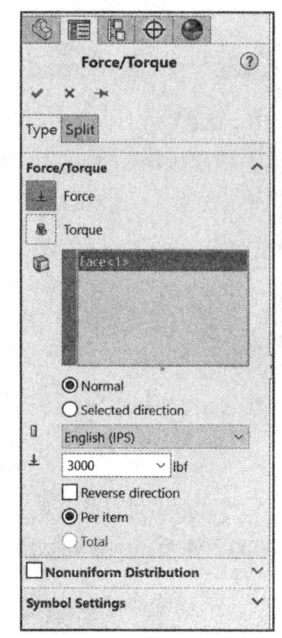

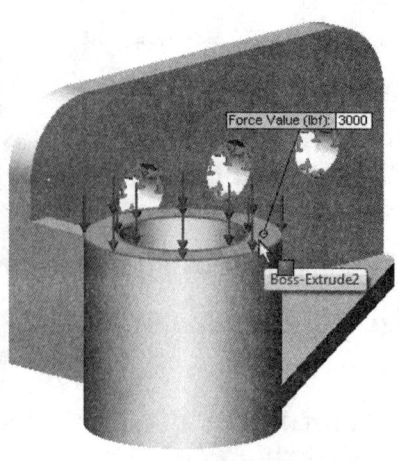

12. **Mesh** and **Run** the model. Use the default setting for the mesh.

Create a Displacement Plot for the maximum resultant displacement in millimeters.

13. Double-click the **Stress1** folder. View the results.

14. Double-click the **Displacement1** folder. View the results.

15. Right-click **Edit Definition** from the Displacement folder.

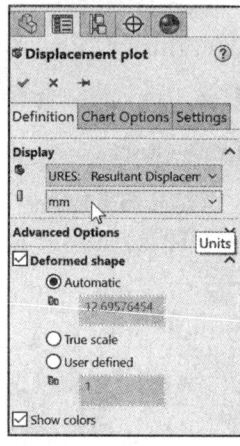

16. Select **URES, Resultant Displacement**.

17. Select **mm** for units.

18. Click the **Chart Options** tab.

19. Select **Show max annotation**. The maximum displacement is displayed: 1.655mm.

The correct answer is **±1%** of this value.

The correct answer is **C**.

A = 1.112mm

B = 1.014mm

C = 1.655mm

D = 1.734mm

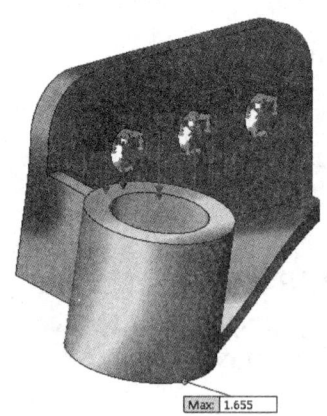

Displacement components are:
UX = Displacement in the X-direction,
UY = Displacement in the Y-direction,
UZ = Displacement in the Z-direction,
URES = Resultant displacement.

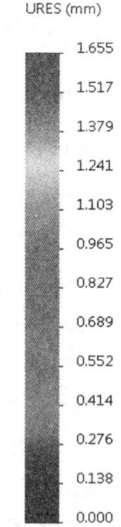

After you calculate displacement or other parameters in a Simulation Study, the CSWSA-FEA exam will also deliver a series of successive questions to test the understanding of the results.

In the first question you calculate Displacement; in the second question you calculate Resultant Force. Do not re-mesh and re-run. Create the required parameter in the Results folder.

In the third question, you are asked to determine if the results are valid or invalid. If the materials yield strength was passed, then the results are invalid.

Use the Define Factor of Safety Plot to determine if your results are valid or invalid. The CSWSA-FEA exam requires you to apply Finite Element Method theory and review displacement values, factory of safety, mesh refinement, and material properties such as yield strength.

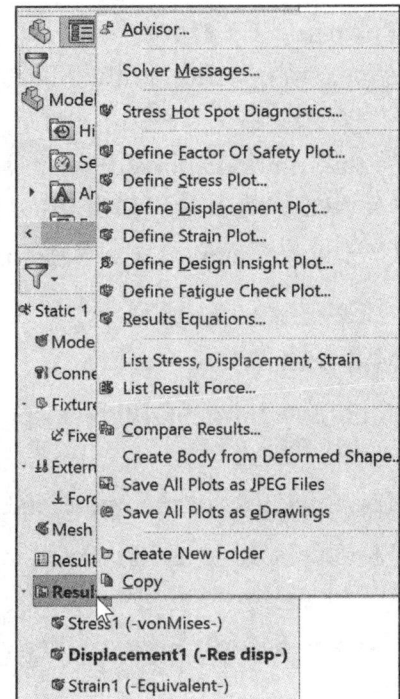

The following are some statements you will encounter in the CSWSA-FEA exam:

- The results are invalid because the material's yield strength was passed.

- The results area is invalid because the displacement is more than half the plate's thickness.

- The results are valid as they are, even if mesh refinement was better.

- The results are invalid because a dynamic study is required.

☀ In general use Thin Shells when thickness to span ratio < 0.05.

☀ Displacement components are UX = Displacement in the X-direction, UY = Displacement in the Y-direction, UZ = Displacement in the Z-direction, URES = Resultant displacement.

Tutorial FEA Model 7-5

An exam question in the Sheet Metal category could read:

In the figure displayed, what is the maximum *UX* displacement in millimeters?

Calculate the answer to 4 decimal places.

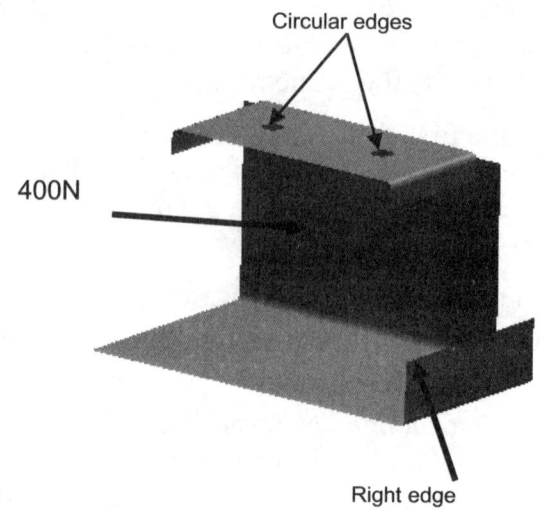

Circular edges

400N

Right edge

Given Information:

Material: Alloy Steel (SS).

A normal **force of 400N** is applied to the **inside** face.

The thickness of the materials is **0.15in**.

The Right edge as illustrated and circular edges are **immovable**.

Use the default high quality element size to mesh.

Let's start.

You need to define the thickness. The Fixture option Immovable is added for shell models. Thin models created with no Sheet Metal feature require you to define the use of Shell elements in SOLIDWORKS Simulation.

Use the models from the CSWSA-FEA Model folder for this section. Models created with the Sheet Metal feature automatically create Shell elements in SOLIDWORKS Simulation.

1. **Open** Model 7-5 from the CSWSA-FEA Model folder.

Set Simulation Options and start a Static SOLIDWORKS Simulation Study.

2. **Add-In** SOLIDWORKS Simulation.

3. Click **Simulation, Options** from the Main menu. Click the Default Options tab.

Set the Unit system and Mesh quality.

4. Select **SI (MKS)** and **Pressure/Stress (N/m²)**.

5. Click the **Mesh folder**.

6. Select **High** for Mesh quality.

7. **Create** a new Static Study. Accept the default name (Static #).

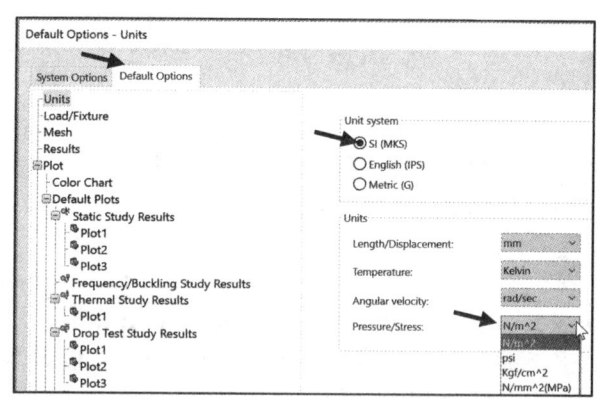

8. Apply **Material** - Alloy Steel (SS) from the SOLIDWORKS Simulation Library. A check mark is displayed next to the model name in the Study Simulation tree.

Define the Shell thickness.

9. Right-click **Model 8-5** in the Study tree.

10. Click **Edit Definition** from the drop-down menu.

11. Enter **0.15in** for **Thin** Type.

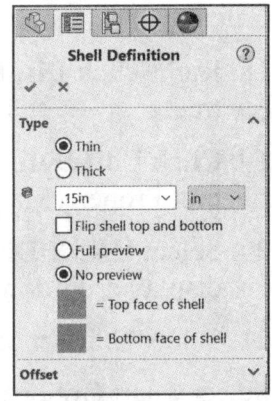

In general use Thin Shells when thickness to span ratio < 0.05.

Apply Fixed Geometry Fixtures.

12. Click the **Immovable (No translation)** option.

13. Select the **edge** and the **two circular edges** of the model as illustrated.

Apply an External Load (Force) of 400N.

14. Apply an **External Load** of **400N** normal to the inside face as illustrated.

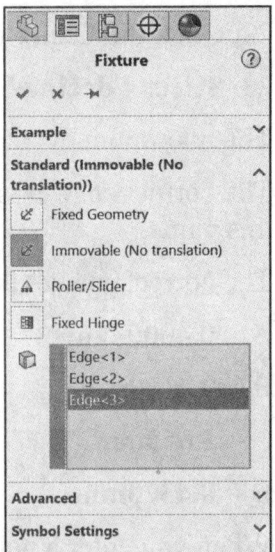

Mesh and Run the model.

15. **Mesh** and **Run** the model. Use the standard default setting for the mesh. Review the Results.

View the Results.

16. Double-click the **Stress1** folder. View the results.

17. Double-click the **Displacement1** folder. View the results.

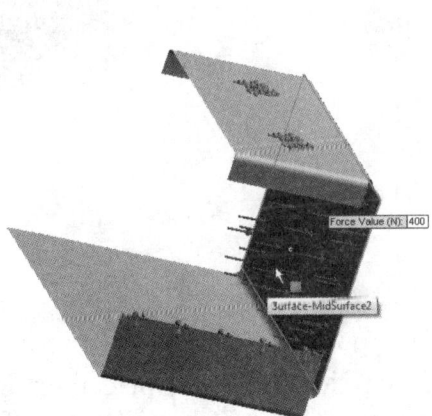

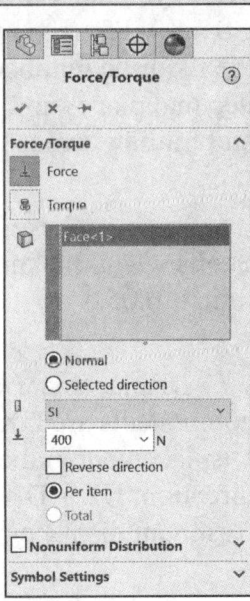

Calculate Displacement in X.

18. Right-click **Displacement1** from the study tree.

19. Click **Edit Definition**. The Displacement plot PropertyManager is displayed.

20. Select **UX: X Displacement** from the display drop-down menu.

21. Select Units in **mm**.

Select Chart Options.

22. Click the **Chart Options** tab.

23. Select **4 decimal places**, millimeter display and floating.

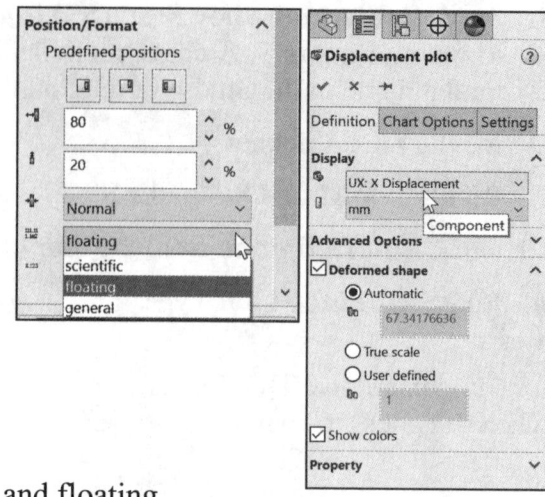

The maximum displacement in X, UX = 0.4370mm.

The correct answer is ±**1%** of this value.

The correct answer is **D**.

A = 0.4000mm

B = 0.4120mm

C = 1.655mm

D = 0.4370mm

When you enter a value in the CSWSA-FEA exam, include the required number of decimal places and leading and trailing zeroes.

🔅 In general use Thin Shells when thickness to span ratio < 0.05.

🔅 Displacement components are UX = Displacement in the X-direction, UY = Displacement in the Y-direction, UZ = Displacement in the Z-direction, URES = Resultant displacement.

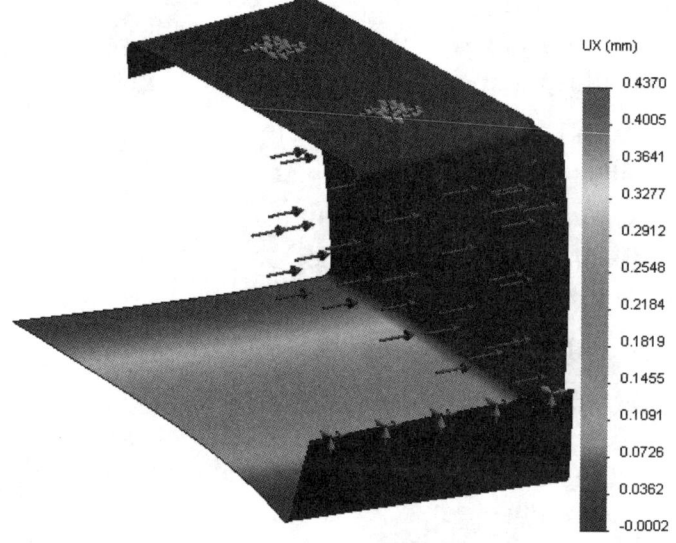

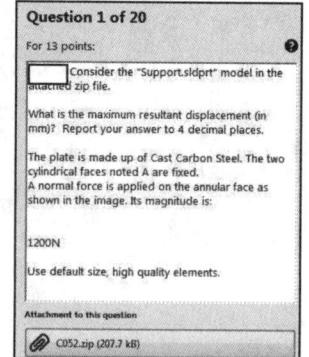

Screen shot from the exam

Tutorial FEA Model 7-5 Part 2

An exam question in the Understanding your Knowledge category could read:

Given Information:

From the study you just completed, can you modify the applied force from **400N** to **4000N** without creating a new mesh and still calculate the maximum von Mises stress?

Think about the problem. Think about the model.

Answer: In SOLIDWORKS Simulation you need to only select Run.

In a Yes/No question, the answer would be: **Yes**.

Screen shot from the exam

Tutorial FEA Model 7-5 Part 3

An exam question in the Understanding your Knowledge category could read:

Given Information:

From the study you just completed with a force of 4000N applied, are the results for the maximum von Mises stress valid?

Think about the problem. Think about the model.

Answer: The results are not valid because the maximum von Mises stress (968 MPa) is greater than the Yield strength (620 MPa) of the material.

In a Yes/No question, the answer would be: **No**.

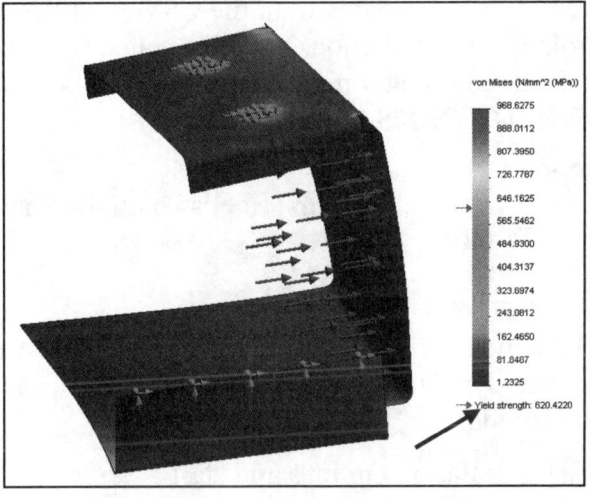

Tutorial FEA Model 7-6 Part 1

An exam question in the Connections category could read:

What is the resultant displacement of the plate in millimeters to four decimal places?

Given Information:

Two cylindrical tubes, with a **thickness of 0.9mm** and one rectangular tube with a **thickness of 1.0mm** are **fixed** to the rectangular plate.

The tubes are manufactured from **Cast Alloy Steel**.

The top of **each tube is fixed**.

The bottom plate is manufactured from **Carbon Sheet Steel**.

A load of **800N** is applied to the circular face at the bottom of the rectangular plate.

Use the default high quality element size to mesh.

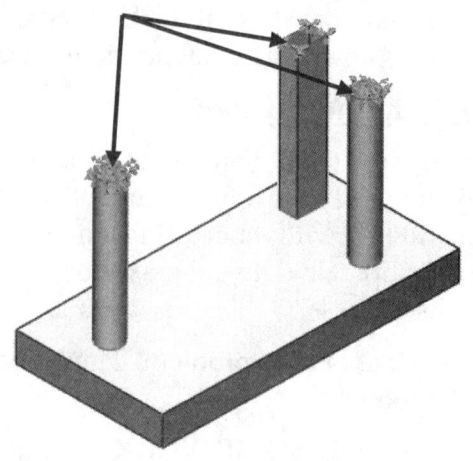

Use the models from the CSWSA-FEA Model folder for this section. Models created with the Sheet Metal feature automatically create Shell elements in SOLIDWORKS Simulation.

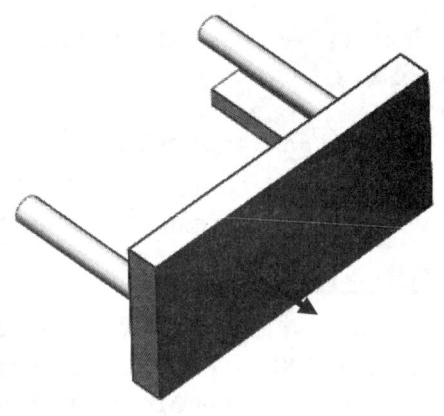

In general use Thin Shells when thickness to span ratio < 0.05.

Let's start.

1. **Open** Model 7-6 from the CSWSA-FEA model folder. Think about the problem. Think about the model.

Set Simulation Options and start a Static SOLIDWORKS Simulation Study.

2. **Add-In** SOLIDWORKS Simulation. **Create** a Static Study. Accept the default name (Static #).

Set the Unit system and Mesh quality.

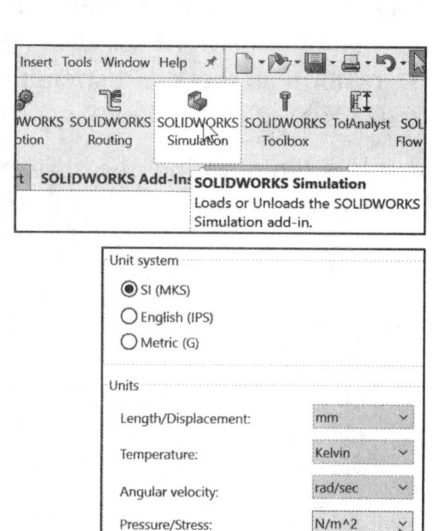

3. Click **Simulation, Options** from the Main menu. Set the Unit system. Select **SI (MKS)** and **Pressure/Stress (N/m²)**.

4. Click the **Mesh folder**. Select **High** for Mesh quality.

5. Apply **Material**. The tubes are manufactured from Cast Alloy Steel. A check mark is displayed next to the SurfaceBody.

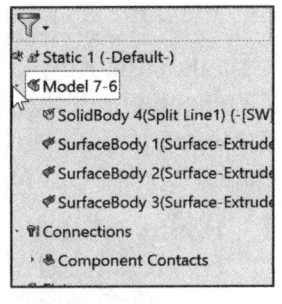

Define the Shell thickness for each SurfaceBody.

6. Select **Edit Definition** for each SurfaceBody. Type: **Thin**. Enter **0.9mm** for the two cylinders thickness. Enter **1.0mm** for the rectangle thickness.

Create three Bonded Type Connections.

7. Right-click the **Connections** folder from the study tree. Click **Contact Set**.

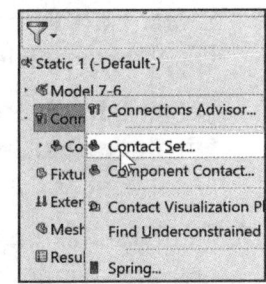

8. Create a Bonded Content Set 1 between the **bottom 4 edges** of the rectangle and the **top face** of the plate.

9. **Repeat** for the two bottom circular edges.

Apply Fixtures.

10. Select the **Immovable** option.

11. Select the **top rectangular edges** and **two circular edges**. The top of each tube is fixed.

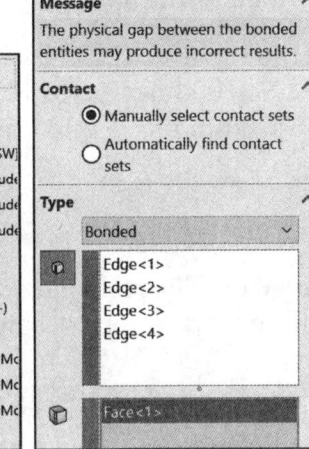

Apply an External Load.

12. Apply an External Load of **800N** normal to the bottom circular face of the model. The direction point outward.

Mesh and Run the model.

13. **Mesh** and **Run** the model. Use the standard default setting for the mesh.

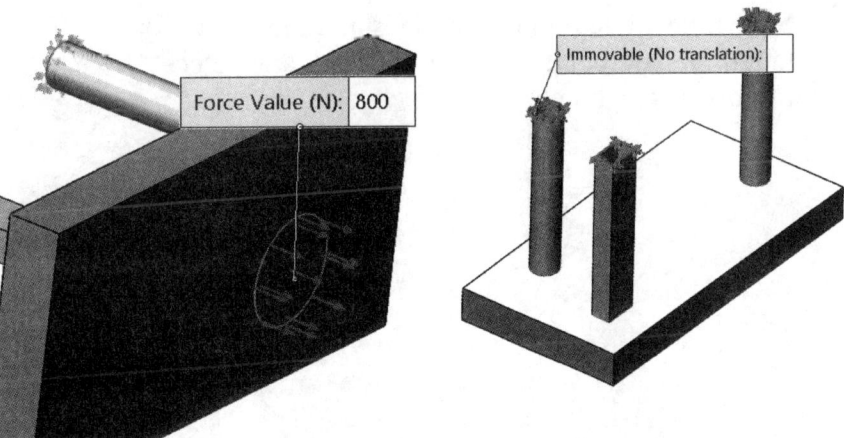

14. **View** the Results.

Calculate the Resultant displacement of the plate in millimeters to four decimal places. Select Chart Options.

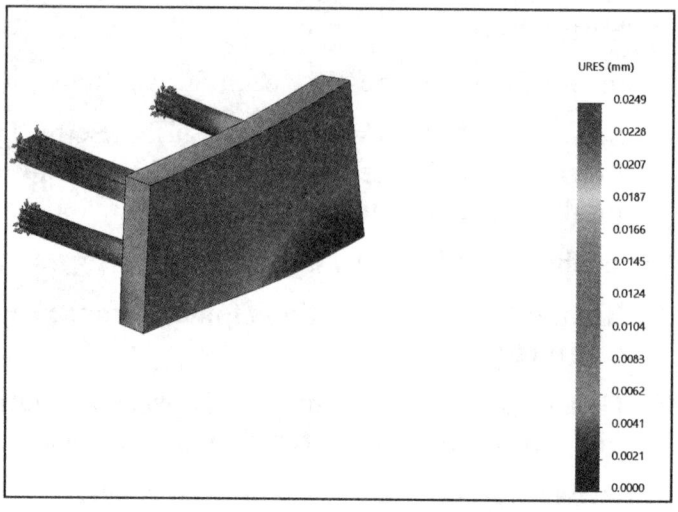

15. **Double-click the** Displacement1 folder from the Results section.

16. Select **Edit Definition** from the Displacement1 folder.

17. Select **URES: Resultant Displacement** from the Displacment Plot. Units in **mm**.

18. Double-click on the **chart** in the graphics window. The Chart Options PropertyManager is displayed.

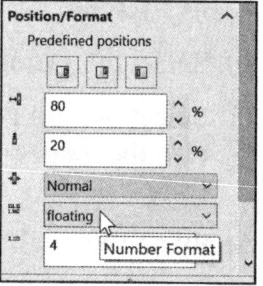

19. Select **4 decimal places**, **millimeter** display and **floating**.

20. **View** the results.

The correct answer is ±**1%** of this value.

Answer: The resultant displacement of the plate in millimeters to four decimal places = **0.0249mm**.

Note, you need to input the trailing zeroes for four decimal places in the exam.

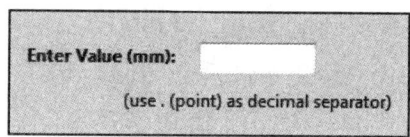

Screen shot from the exam

Save time. When selecting edges in a loop, such as a rectangle, select the first edge, right-click and select Open Loop to select the remaining edges.

Tutorial FEA Model 7-6 Part 2

An exam question in the Understanding your Knowledge category could read:

Given Information:

Without rerunning the study, what is the Resultant Force of the **left most, top circular edge** of the tube?

Think about the problem. Think about the model.

Answer: Resultant Force = **571N**.

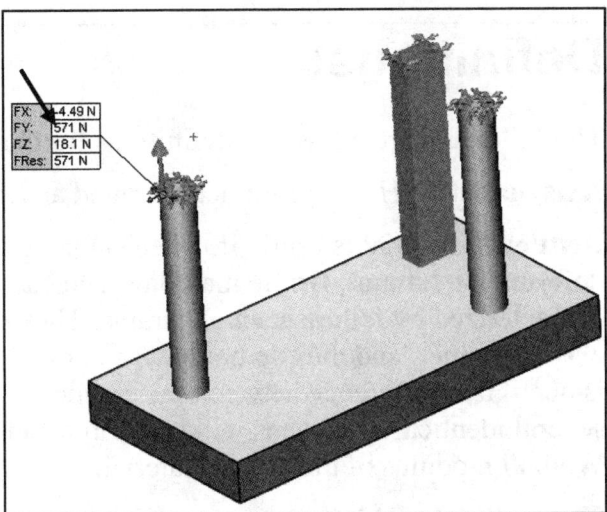

Tutorial FEA Model 7-6 Part 3

An exam question in the Understanding your Knowledge category could read:

Given Information:

What force component, Fx, Fy or Fz contributes the most to the overall Resultant Force?

Think about the problem. Think about the model.

Answer: **Fy**. The y component of the resultant force contributes the most.

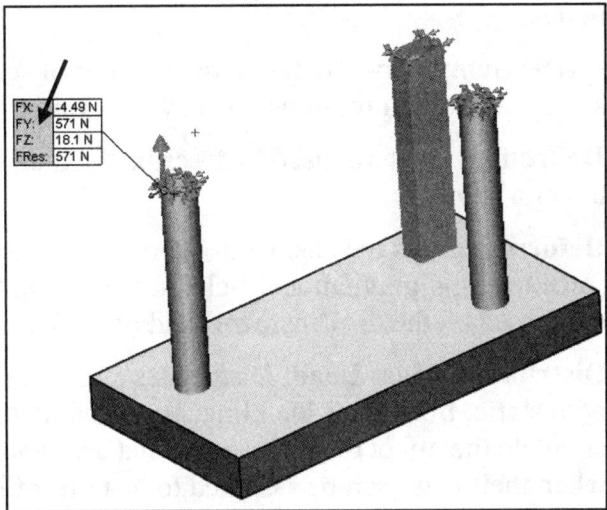

Definitions:

The following are a few key definitions for the exam:

Axisymmetry: Having symmetry around an axis.

Brittle: A material is brittle if, when subjected to stress, it breaks without significant deformation (strain). Brittle materials, such as concrete and carbon fiber, are characterized by failure at small strains. They often fail while still behaving in a linear elastic manner, and thus do not have a defined yield point. Because strains are low, there is negligible difference between the engineering stress and the true stress. Testing of several identical specimens will result in different failure stresses; this is due to the Weibull modulus of the brittle material.

Compatible meshing: A mesh where elements on touching bodies have overlaying nodes.

Cyclic Symmetry: To define the number of sectors and the axis of symmetry in a cyclic symmetric structure for use in a cyclic symmetry calculation.

Deflection: is a term used to describe the magnitude to which a structural element bends under a load.

Deformation: is the change in geometry created when stress is applied (in the form of force loading, gravitational field, acceleration, thermal expansion, etc.). Deformation is expressed by the displacement field of the material.

Distributed Mass Load: Distributes a specified mass value on the selected faces for use with static, frequency, buckling, and linear dynamic studies. Use this functionality to simulate the effect of components that are suppressed or not included in the modeling when their mass can be assumed to be uniformly distributed on the specified faces. The distributed mass is assumed to lie directly on the selected faces, so rotational effects are not considered.

Ductile Material: In materials science, ductility is a solid material's ability to deform under tensile stress; this is often characterized by the material's ability to be stretched into a wire. Stress vs. Strain curve typical of aluminum.

Maximum Normal Stress criterion: The maximum normal stress criterion also known as Coulomb's criterion is based on the Maximum normal stress theory. According to this theory, failure occurs when the maximum principal stress reaches the ultimate strength of the material for simple tension.

This criterion is used for brittle materials. It assumes that the ultimate strength of the material in tension and compression is the same. This assumption is not valid in all cases. For example, cracks decrease the strength of the material in tension considerably while their effect is far less small in compression because the cracks tend to close.

Brittle materials do not have a specific yield point, and hence it is not recommended to use the yield strength to define the limit stress for this criterion.

This theory predicts failure to occur when:

$$\sigma_1 \geq \sigma_{limit}$$

where σ_1 is the maximum principal stress.

Hence:

Factor of safety $= \sigma_{limit} / \sigma_1$

Maximum Shear Stress criterion: The maximum shear stress criterion, also known as Tresca yield criterion, is based on the Maximum Shear stress theory.

This theory predicts failure of a material to occur when the absolute maximum shear stress (τ_{max}) reaches the stress that causes the material to yield in a simple tension test. The Maximum shear stress criterion is used for ductile materials.

$$\tau_{max} \geq \sigma_{limit} / 2$$

τ_{max} is the greatest of τ_{12}, τ_{23} and τ_{13}

Where:

$$\tau_{12} = (\sigma_1 - \sigma_2)/2; \ \tau_{23} = (\sigma_2 - \sigma_3)/2; \ \tau_{13} = (\sigma_1 - \sigma_3)/2$$

Hence:

Factor of safety (FOS) $= \sigma_{limit} / (2 * \tau_{max})$

Maximum von Mises Stress criterion: The maximum von Mises stress criterion is based on the von Mises-Hencky theory, also known as the Shear-energy theory or the Maximum distortion energy theory.

In terms of the principal stresses s1, s2, and s3, the von Mises stress is expressed as:

$$\sigma_{vonMises} = \{[(s1 - s2)2 + (s2 - s3)2 + (s1 - s3)2]/2\}(1/2)$$

The theory states that a ductile material starts to yield at a location when the von Mises stress becomes equal to the stress limit. In most cases, the yield strength is used as the stress limit. However, the software allows you to use the ultimate tensile or set your own stress limit.

$$\sigma_{vonMises} \geq \sigma_{limit}$$

Yield strength is a temperature-dependent property. This specified value of the yield strength should consider the temperature of the component. The factor of safety at a location is calculated from:

Factor of Safety (FOS) $= \sigma_{limit} / \sigma_{vonMises}$

Modulus of Elasticity or Young's Modulus: The Elastic Modulus (Young's Modulus) is the slope defined as stress divided by strain. E = modulus of elasticity (Pa (N/m²), N/mm², psi). The Modulus of Elasticity can be used to determine the stress-strain relationship in the linear-elastic portion of the stress-strain curve. The linear-elastic region is either below the yield point, or if a yield point is not easily identified on the stress-strain plot it is defined to be between 0 and 0.2% strain, and is defined as the region of strain in which no yielding (permanent deformation) occurs.

Force is the action of one body on another. A force tends to move a body in the direction of its action.

Mohr-Coulomb: The Mohr-Coulomb stress criterion is based on the Mohr-Coulomb theory, also known as the Internal Friction theory. This criterion is used for brittle materials with different tensile and compressive properties. Brittle materials do not have a specific yield point, and hence it is not recommended to use the yield strength to define the limit stress for this criterion.

Mohr-Coulomb Stress criterion: The Mohr-Coulomb stress criterion is based on the Mohr-Coulomb theory, also known as the Internal Friction theory. This criterion is used for brittle materials with different tensile and compressive properties. Brittle materials do not have a specific yield point and hence it is not recommended to use the yield strength to define the limit stress for this criterion.

This theory predicts failure to occur when:

$$\sigma_1 \geq \sigma_{TensileLimit} \quad \text{if } \sigma_1 > 0 \text{ and } \sigma_3 > 0$$

$$\sigma_3 \geq -\sigma_{CompressiveLimit} \quad \text{if } \sigma_1 < 0 \text{ and } \sigma_3 < 0$$

$$\sigma_1 / \sigma_{TensileLimit} + \sigma_3 / -\sigma_{CompressiveLimit} \geq 1 \quad \text{if } \sigma_1 \geq 0 \text{ and } \sigma_3 \leq 0$$

The factor of safety is given by:

$$\text{Factor of Safety (FOS)} = \{\sigma_1 / \sigma_{TensileLimit} + \sigma_3 / -\sigma_{CompressiveLimit}\}^{(-1)}$$

Stress: Stress is defined in terms of Force per unit Area:

$$Stress = \frac{f}{A}.$$

Stress vs. Strain diagram: Many materials display linear elastic behavior, defined by a linear stress-strain relationship, as shown in the figure up to point 2, in which deformations are completely recoverable upon removal of the load; that is, a specimen loaded elastically in tension will elongate but will return to its original shape and size when unloaded. Beyond this linear region, for ductile materials, such as steel, deformations are plastic. A plastically deformed specimen will not return to its original size and shape

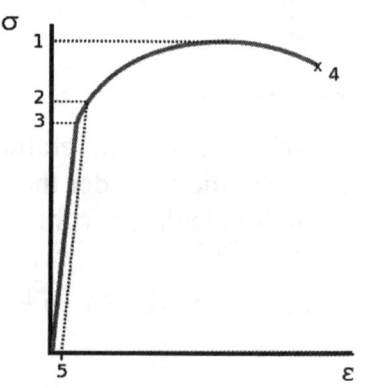

Stress vs. Strain curve typical of aluminum

when unloaded. Note that there will be elastic recovery of a portion of the deformation. For many applications, plastic deformation is unacceptable and is used as the design limitation.

1 - Ultimate Strength

2 - Yield Strength

3 - Proportional Limit Stress

4 - Rupture

5 - Offset Strain (usually 0.002)

Tensile strength: Ultimate tensile strength (UTS), often shortened to tensile strength (TS) or ultimate strength, is the maximum stress that a material can withstand while being stretched or pulled before necking, which is when the specimen's cross-section starts to significantly contract. Tensile strength is the opposite of compressive strength and the values can be quite different.

Yield Stress: The stress level beyond which the material becomes plastic.

Yield Strength: is the lowest stress that produces a permanent deformation in a material. In some materials, like aluminum alloys, the point of yielding is difficult to identify, thus it is usually defined as the stress required to cause 0.2% plastic strain. This is called a 0.2% proof stress.

Young's Modulus, or the "Modulus of Elasticity": The Elastic Modulus (Young's Modulus) is the slope defined as stress divided by strain. E = modulus of elasticity (Pa (N/m2), N/mm2, psi). The Modulus of Elasticity can be used to determine the stress-strain relationship in the linear-elastic portion of the stress-strain curve. The linear-elastic region is either below the yield point, or if a yield point is not easily identified on the stress-strain plot it is defined to be between 0 and 0.2% strain, and is defined as the region of strain in which no yielding (permanent deformation) occurs.

Thermal Expansion: The change in length per unit length per one degree change in temperature (change in normal strain per unit temperature) (K).

Specific Heat: Quantity of heat needed to raise the temperature of a unit mass of the material by one degree of temperature (J/kg K).

Density: Mass per unit volume (kg/m^3).

Elastic Modulus (Young's Modulus): Ratio between the stress and the associated strain in a specified direction (N/m^2).

Shear Modulus (Modulus of Rigidity): Ratio between the shearing stress in a plane divided by the associated shearing strain (N/m^2).

Thermal Conductivity: Rate of heat transfer through a unit thickness of the material per unit temperature difference (W/m K).

Poisson's Ratio: Ratio between the contraction (traverse strain), normal to the applied load to the extension (axial strain), in the direction of the applied load. Poisson's ratio is a dimensionless quantity.

Tensile Strength: The maximum amount of tensile stress that a material can be subjected to before failure (N/m^2).

Yield Strength: Stress at which the material becomes permanently deformed (N/m^2).

Appendix

SOLIDWORKS Keyboard Shortcuts

Listed below are some of the pre-defined keyboard shortcuts in SOLIDWORKS:

Action:	Key Combination:
Model Views	
Rotate the model horizontally or vertically	**Arrow** keys
Rotate the model horizontally or vertically 90 degrees	**Shift** + **Arrow** keys
Rotate the model clockwise or counterclockwise	**Alt** + left of right **Arrow** keys
Pan the model	**Ctrl** + **Arrow** keys
Magnifying glass	**g**
Zoom in	**Shift + z**
Zoom out	**z**
Zoom to fit	**f**
Previous view	**Ctrl + Shift + z**
View Orientation	
View Orientation menu	**Spacebar**
Front view	**Ctrl + 1**
Back view	**Ctrl + 2**
Left view	**Ctrl + 3**
Right view	**Ctrl + 4**
Top view	**Ctrl + 5**
Bottom view	**Ctrl + 6**
Isometric view	**Ctrl + 7**
Normal To view	**Ctrl + 8**
Selection Filters	
Filter edges	**e**
Filter vertices	**v**
Filter faces	**x**
Toggle Selection Filter toolbar	**F5**
Toggle selection filters on/off	**F6**
File menu items	
New SOLIDWORKS document	**Ctrl + n**
Open document	**Ctrl + o**
Open From Web Folder	**Ctrl + w**
Make Drawing from Part	**Ctrl + d**
Make Assembly from Part	**Ctrl + a**
Save	**Ctrl +s**
Print	**Ctrl + p**
Additional shortcuts	
Access online help inside of PropertyManager or dialog box	**F1**
Rename an item in the FeatureManager design tree	**F2**

Rebuild the model	**Ctrl + b**
Force rebuild – Rebuild the model and all its features	**Ctrl + q**
Redraw the screen	**Ctrl + r**
Cycle between open SOLIDWORKS documents	**Ctrl + Tab**
Line to arc/arc to line in the Sketch	**a**
Undo	**Ctrl + z**
Redo	**Ctrl + y**
Cut	**Ctrl + x**
Copy	**Ctrl + c**
Additional shortcuts	
Paste	**Ctrl + v**
Delete	**Delete**
Next window	**Ctrl + F6**
Close window	**Ctrl + F4**
View previous tools	**s**
Selects all text inside an Annotations text box	**Ctrl + a**

🔅 In a sketch, the **Esc** key un-selects geometry items currently selected in the Properties box and Add Relations box. In the model, the **Esc** key closes the PropertyManager and cancels the selections.

🔅 Use the **g** key to activate the Magnifying glass tool. Use the Magnifying glass tool to inspect a model and make selections without changing the overall view.

🔅 Use the **s** key to view/access previous command tools in the Graphics window.

Windows Shortcuts

Listed below are some of the pre-defined keyboard shortcuts in Microsoft Windows:

Action:	Keyboard Combination:
Open the Start menu	Windows Logo key
Open Windows Explorer	Windows Logo key + E
Minimize all open windows	Windows Logo key + M
Open a Search window	Windows Logo key + F
Open Windows Help	Windows Logo key + F1
Select multiple geometry items in a SOLIDWORKS document	Ctrl key (Hold the Ctrl key down. Select items.) Release the Ctrl key.

Helpful Online Information

The SOLIDWORKS URL:
http://www.SOLIDWORKS.com contains
information on Local Resellers, Solution Partners,
Certifications, SOLIDWORKS users groups and
more.

Access 3D ContentCentral using the Task Pane to
obtain engineering electronic catalog model and
part information.

Use the SOLIDWORKS Resources tab in the
Task Pane to obtain access to Customer Portals,
Discussion Forums, User Groups, Manufacturers,
Solution Partners, Labs and more.

Helpful on-line SOLIDWORKS information is
available from the following URLs:

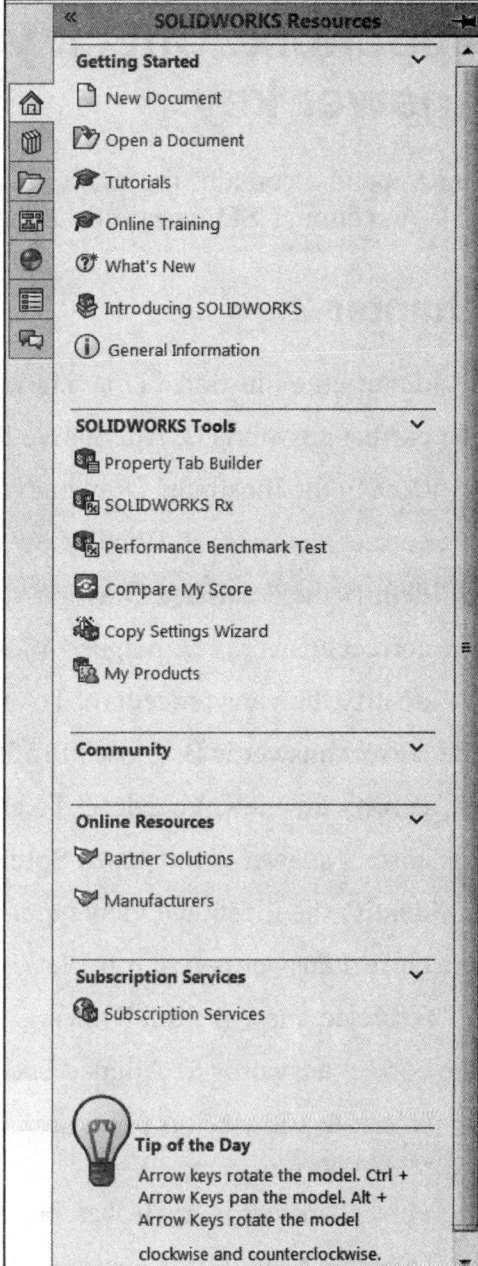

- http://www.mechengineer.com/snug/.

  News group access and local user group
  information.

- http://www.swugn.org/.

  List of all SOLIDWORKS User groups.

- http://www.caddedge.com/SOLIDWORKS-
  user-group-calendar-for-CT-MA-ME-NH-NJ-
  NY-PA-RI-VT/.

  Updated SOLIDWORKS information and
  user group calendar for New England and
  surrounding areas.

- http://www.SOLIDWORKS.com/sw/engineer
  ing-education-software.htm.

  SOLIDWORKS in Academia. Information on
  software, support, tutorials, blog and more.

*Online tutorials are for educational purposes only.
Tutorials are copyrighted by their respective owners.

Appendix: Check your understanding Answer key

The Appendix contains the answers to the questions at the end of the chapter in the CSWA section, CSDA section and the CSWSA-FEA section.

Chapter 2

1. Identify the illustrated Drawing view.

The correct answer is B: Alternative Position View

2. Identify the illustrated Drawing view.

The correct answer is B: Break View.

3. Identify the illustrated Drawing view.

The correct answer is D: Aligned View.

4. Identify the view procedure. To create the following view, you need to insert a:

The correct answer is B: Closed Profile: Spline.

5. Identify the view procedure. To create the following view, you need to insert a:

The correct answer is B: Closed Spline .

6. Identify the illustrated view type.

The correct answer is A: Crop View.

7. To create View B from Drawing View A insert which View Type?

The correct answer is C: Aligned Section View.

8. To create View B it is necessary to sketch a closed spline on View A and insert which View type?

The correct answer is A: Broken out Section View.

9. To create View B it is necessary to sketch a closed spline on View A and insert which View type?

The correct answer is A: Horizontal Break View.

Chapter 3

1. Calculate the overall mass of the part, volume, and locate the Center of mass with the provided information using the provided Option 1 FeatureManager.

   - Overall mass of the part = 1105.00 grams

- Volume of the part = 130000.00 cubic millimeters

- Center of Mass Location: X = 43.46 millimeters, Y = 15.00 millimeters, Z = -37.69 millimeters

2. Calculate the overall mass of the part, volume, and locate the Center of mass with the provided information using the provided Option 3 FeatureManager.

   - Overall mass of the part = 269.50 grams

   - Volume of the part = 192500.00 cubic millimeters

   - Center of Mass Location: X = 35.70 millimeters, Y = 27.91 millimeters, Z = -1.46 millimeters

3. Calculate the overall mass of the part, volume, and locate the Center of mass with the provided information.

   - Overall mass of the part = 1.76 pounds

   - Volume of the part = 17.99 cubic inches

   - Center of Mass Location: X = 0.04 inches, Y = 0.72 inches, Z = 0.00 inches

4. Calculate the overall mass of the part, volume, and locate the Center of mass with the provided illustrated information.

   - Overall mass of the part = 1280.91 grams

   - Volume of the part = 474411.54 cubic millimeters

   - Center of Mass Location: X = 0.00 millimeters, Y = -29.17 millimeters, Z = 3.18 millimeters

5. Calculate the overall mass of the part, volume, and locate the Center of mass with the provided information.

   - Overall mass of the part = 248.04 grams

   - Volume of the part = 91868.29 cubic millimeters

   - Center of Mass Location: X = -51.88 millimeters, Y = 24.70 millimeters, Z = 29.47 millimeters

6. Calculate the overall mass of the part with the provided information.

   - Overall mass of the part = 3015.53 grams

7. Calculate the overall mass of the part with the provided information.

   - Overall mass of the part = 319.13 grams

8. Calculate the overall mass of the part, volume, and locate the Center of mass with the provided information.

   - Overall mass of the part = 0.45 pounds. Volume of the part = 4.60 cubic inches. Center of Mass Location: X = 0.17 inches, Y = 0.39 inches, Z = 0.00 inches

9. Calculate the overall mass of the part, volume, and locate the Center of mass with the provided information.

    - Overall mass of the part = 0.28 pounds. Volume of the part = 2.86 cubic inches. Center of Mass Location: X = 0.70 inches, Y = 0.06 inches, Z = 0.00 inches

Chapter 4

1. Calculate the overall mass of the part, volume, and locate the Center of mass with the provided information.

    - Overall mass of the part = 1.99 pounds

    - Volume of the part = 6.47 cubic inches

    - Center of Mass Location: X = 0.00 inches, Y = 0.00 inches, Z = 1.49 inches

2. Calculate the overall mass of the part, volume, and locate the Center of mass with the provided information.

    - Overall mass of the part = 279.00 grams

    - Volume of the part = 103333.73 cubic millimeters

    - Center of Mass Location: X = 0.00 millimeters, Y = 0.00 millimeters, Z = 21.75 millimeters

3. Calculate the overall mass of the part, volume, and locate the Center of mass with the provided information.

    - Overall mass of the part = 1087.56 grams

    - Volume of the part = 122198.22 cubic millimeters

    - Center of Mass Location: X = 44.81 millimeters, Y = 21.02 millimeters, Z = -41.04 millimeters

4. Calculate the overall mass of the part, volume and locate the Center of mass with the provided information.

    - Overall mass of the part = 2040.57 grams

    - Volume of the part = 755765.04 cubic millimeters

    - Center of Mass Location: X = -0.71 millimeters, Y = 16.66 millimeters, Z = -9.31 millimeters

5. Calculate the overall mass of the part, volume and locate the Center of mass with the provided information. Create Coordinate System1 to locate the Center of mass for the model.

    - Overall mass of the part = 2040.57 grams

    - Volume of the part = 755765.04 cubic millimeters

- Center of Mass Location: X = 49.29 millimeters, Y = 16.66 millimeters, Z = -109.31 millimeters

6. Calculate the overall mass of the part, volume and locate the Center of mass with the provided information.

   - Overall mass of the part = 37021.48 grams

   - Volume of the part = 13711657.53 cubic millimeters

   - Center of Mass Location: X = 0.00 millimeters, Y = 0.11 millimeters, Z = 0.00 millimeters

7. Calculate the overall mass of the part, volume and locate the Center of mass with the provided information.

   - Overall mass of the part = 37021.48 grams

   - Volume of the part = 13711657.53 cubic millimeters

   - Center of Mass Location: X = 225.00 millimeters, Y = 70.11 millimeters, Z = -150.00 millimeters

Chapter 5

1. Calculate the overall mass and volume of the assembly. Locate the Center of mass using the illustrated coordinate system.

   - Overall mass of the assembly = 843.22 grams

   - Volume of the assembly = 312304.62 cubic millimeters

   - Center of Mass Location: X = 30.00 millimeters, Y = 40.16 millimeters, Z = -53.82 millimeters

2. Calculate the overall mass and volume of the assembly. Locate the Center of mass using the illustrated coordinate system.

   1. Overall mass of the assembly = 19.24 grams

   2. Volume of the assembly = 6574.76 cubic millimeters

   3. Center of Mass Location: X = 40.24, Y = 24.33, Z = 20.75

3. Calculate the overall mass and volume of the assembly. Locate the Center of mass using the illustrated coordinate system.

   4. Overall mass of the assembly = 19.24 grams

   5. Volume of the assembly = 6574.76 cubic millimeters

   6. Center of Mass Location: X = 40.24, Y = -20.75, Z = 24.33

Chapter 6

1. Environmental Product Declarations, or EPDs, are an increasingly used method for communicating sustainability results with:

A. **Suppliers and Customers**

B. Engineers

C. Managers

D. None of the Above

2. The commonly referenced definition of sustainable development put forth by the Brundtland Commission reads as follows:

A. "Sustainability requires closed material loops and energy independence"

B. **"Sustainable development is development that meets the needs of the present without compromising the ability of future generations to meet their own needs"**

C. "Sustainable development is the use of environmental claims in marketing"

D. None of the above

3. The study of sustainable development broadly covers these three elements:

A. Land, air, and water

B. Natural, man-made, hybrid

C. **Environment, social equity, economics**

D. Animal, vegetable, mineral

4. This answer choice is NOT part of a long-term, working definition of a "sustainable company" ideal:

A. Generates wastes that are useful as inputs by industry or nature

B. Sources recycled waste material and minimal virgin resources

C. **Follows all current environmental regulations**

D. Uses minimal energy that is ultimately from renewable sources

5. "The intelligent application of the principles of sustainability to the realm of engineering and design" is a working definition for the following concept:

A. **Sustainable design**

B. Sustainable business

C. Life cycle assessment

D. SOLIDWORKS Sustainability

6. A focus on product design that ensures the ultimate recyclability of a product you're developing is a sustainable design technique most specifically called:

A. Design for Environment (DfE)

B. **Design for Disassembly (DfD)**

C. Life Cycle Assessment (LCA)

D. Design for Total Life Assessment (TLA)

7. The sustainable design technique that promotes systematically using natural inspiration and technologies found in nature to design products is known as:

A. **Biomimicry**

B. Cradle to Cradle

C. Environmental Management System (EMS)

D. Intelligent Design

8. The sustainable design technique that can most simply be characterized by the concept that the waste from one entity equals the food of another is:

A. **Cradle to Cradle**

B. Design for Disassembly (DfD)

C. Life Cycle Assessment (LCA)

D. Intelligent Design

9. The sustainable design technique that focuses on re-formulating the raw materials we use to design out their toxicity and environmental impacts is known as:

A. **Green chemistry**

B. Design for Environment (DfE)

C. Life cycle assessment (LCA)

D. Cradle to cradle

10. The following is an example of green marketing:

A. A brochure of a product painted green, printed on 100% post-consumer recycled paper

B. An ad touting the cost savings you can get from driving an efficient vehicle

C. **A label that indicates how many trees will be saved by purchasing this product**

D. None of the above

11. A green product is defined as one that:

A. Is made of 100% recycled content, and is itself recyclable

B. Uses no energy or only renewable energy

C. Has been designed using SOLIDWORKS Sustainability

D. **There is no such thing as a green product - the only "green" product is the one that's never made**

12. LCA stands for:

A. Life Cycle Analysis, because LCA is an exact science, similar to Finite Element Analysis (FEA)

B. **Life Cycle Assessment, because LCA is an approximate and pragmatic method, like medicine**

C. Left Cymbal Assassination, because LCA practitioners rove the world destroying half of all percussion equipment

D. None of the above

13. Photochemical oxidation (smog) and ozone layer depletion are examples of environmental impacts that fall into the following domain:

A. **Air impacts**

B. Terrestrial & aquatic impacts

C. Natural resource depletion

D. Climate effects

14. The "global warming potential" (GWP) from greenhouse gases emitted throughout a product's lifecycle, such as carbon dioxide and methane, is a measure of the product's tendency to affect:

A. Human toxicity

B. **Climate change**

C. Ionizing radiation

D. Air acidification

15. The following: "(1) raw material extraction, (2) material processing, (3) part manufacturing, (4) assembly, (5) transportation, (6) product use, and (7) end of life" describes a product's:

A. Environmental indicators

B. Metrics

C. **Lifecycle stages**

D. Good times

Chapter 7

1. What is the Modulus of Elasticity?

- The slope of the Deflection-Stress curve
- **The slope of the Stress-Strain curve in its linear section**
- The slope of the Force-Deflection curve in its linear section
- The first inflection point of a Strain curve

2. What is Stress?

- A measure of power
- A measure of strain
- A measure of material strength
- **A measure of the average amount of force exerted per unit area**

3. Which of the following assumptions are true for a static analysis in SOLIDWORKS Simulation with small displacements?

- **Inertia effects are negligible and loads are applied slowly**
- The model is not fully elastic. If loads are removed, the model will not return to its original position
- **Results are proportional to loads**
- **All the displacements are small relative to the model geometry**

4. What is Yield Stress?

- **The stress level beyond which the material becomes plastic**
- The stress level beyond which the material breaks
- The strain level above the stress level which the material breaks
- The stress level beyond the melting point of the material

5. A high quality Shell element has _____ nodes.

- 4
- 5
- **6**
- 8

6. Stress σ is proportional to _____ in a Linear Elastic Material.

- **Strain**
- Stress
- Force
- Pressure

7. The Elastic Modulus (Young's Modulus) is the slope defined as _____ divided by _____.

- Strain, Stress
- **Stress, Strain**
- Stress, Force
- Force, Area

8. Linear static analysis assumes that the relationship between loads and the induced response is _____.

- Flat
- **Linear**
- Doubles per area
- Translational

9. In SOLIDWORKS Simulation, the Factor of Safety (FOS) calculations are based on one of the following failure criterion.

- **Maximum von Mises Stress**
- **Maximum shear stress (Tresca)**
- **Mohr-Coulomb stress**
- **Maximum Normal stress**

10. The Yield point is the point where the material begins to deform at a faster rate than at the elastic limit. The material behaves _____ in the Plastic Range.

- Flatly
- Linearly
- **Non-Linearly**
- Like a liquid

11. What are the Degrees of Freedom (DOFs) restrained for a Solid?

- None
- **3 Translations**
- 3 Translations and 3 Rotations
- 3 Rotations

12. What are the Degrees of Freedom (DOFs) restrained for Truss joints?

- None
- **3 Translations**
- 3 Translations and 3 Rotations
- 3 Rotations

13. What are the Degrees of Freedom (DOFs) restrained for Shells and Beams?

- None
- 3 Translations
- **3 Translations and 3 Rotations**
- 3 Rotations

14. Which statements are true for Material Properties using SOLIDWORKS Simulation?

- **For solid assemblies, each component can have a different material**
- For shell models, each shell cannot have a different material and thickness
- **For shell models, the material of the part is used for all shells**
- For beam models, each beam cannot have a different material

15. A Beam element has _____nodes (one at each end) with _____degrees of freedom per node plus_____ node to define the orientation of the beam cross section.

- 6, 3, 1
- 3, 3, 1
- **3, 6, 1**
- None of the above

16. A Truss element has _____ nodes with _____ translational degrees of freedom per node.

- **2, 3**
- 3, 3
- 6, 6
- 2, 2

17. In general, the finer the mesh the better the accuracy of the results.

- **True**
- False

18. How does SOLIDWORKS Simulation automatically treat a Sheet metal part with uniform thickness?

- **Shell**
- Solid
- Beam
- Mixed Mesh

19. Use the mesh and displacement plots to calculate the distance between two _____ using SOLIDWORKS Simulation.

- **Nodes**
- Elements
- Bodies
- Surfaces

20. Surface models can only be meshed with _____ elements.

- **Shell**
- Beam
- Mixed Mesh
- Solid

21. The shell mesh is generated on the surface (located at the mid-surface of the shell).

- **True**
- False

22. In general, use Thin shells when the thickness-to-span ratio is less than _____.

- **0.05**
- .5
- 1
- 2

23. The model (a rectangular plate) has a length to thickness ratio of less than 5. You extracted its mid-surface to use it in SOLIDWORKS Simulation. You should use a _____.

- Thin Shell element formulation
- **Thick Shell element formulation**
- Thick or Thin Shell element formulation, it does not matter
- Beam Shell element formulation

24. The model, a rectangular sheet metal part, uses SOLIDWORKS Simulation. You should use a:

- **Thin Shell element formulation**
- Thick Shell element formulation
- Thick or Thin Shell element formulation, it does not matter
- Beam Shell element formulation

25. The Global element size parameter provides the ability to set the global average element size. SOLIDWORKS Simulation suggests a default value based on the model volume and _____ area. This option is only available for a standard mesh.

- Force

- Pressure

- **Surface**

- None of the above

26. A remote load applied on a face with a Force component and no Moment can result in: Note: Remember (DOFs restrain).

- **A Force and Moment of the face**

- A Force on the face only

- A Moment on the face only

- A Pressure and Force on the face

27. There are _____ DOFs restrain for a Solid element.

- **3**

- 1

- 6

- None

28. There are _____ DOFs restrain for a Beam element.

- 3

- 1

- **6**

- None

29. What best describes the difference(s) between a Fixed and Immovable (No translation) boundary condition in SOLIDWORKS Simulation?

- There are no differences

- There are no difference(s) for Shells but it is different for Solids

- **There is no difference(s) for Solids but it is different for Shells and Beams**

- There are only differences(s) for a Static Study

30. Can a non-uniform pressure of force be applied on a face using SOLIDWORKS Simulation?

- No

- Yes, but the variation must be along a single direction only

- **Yes. The non-uniform pressure distribution is defined by a reference coordinate system and the associated coefficients of a second order polynomial**

- Yes, but the variation must be linear

31. You are performing an analysis on your model. You select five faces, 3 edges and 2 vertices and apply a force of 20lbf. What is the total force applied to the model using SOLIDWORKS Simulation?

- 100lbf

- 1600lbf

- 180lbf

- **200lbf**

32. Yield strength is typically determined at _____ strain.
- 0.1%

- **0.2%**

- 0.02%

- 0.002%

33. There are four key assumptions made in Linear Static Analysis: 1. Effects of inertia and damping are neglected, 2. The response of the system is directly proportional to the applied loads, 3. Loads are applied slowly and gradually, and_____ .

- **Displacements are very small. The highest stress is in the linear range of the stress-strain curve**

- There are no loads

- Material is not elastic

- Loads are applied quickly

34. How many degrees of freedom does a physical structure have?

- Zero

- Three - Rotations only

- Three - Translations only

- **Six - Three translations and three rotational**

35. Brittle material has little tendency to deform (or strain) before fracture and does not have a specific yield point. It is not recommended to apply the yield strength analysis as a failure criterion on brittle material. Which of the following failure theories is appropriate for brittle materials?

- **Mohr-Columb stress criterion**

- Maximum shear stress criterion

- Maximum von Mises stress criterion

- Minimum shear stress criterion

36. You are performing an analysis on your model. You select three faces and apply a force of 40lb. What is the total force applied to the model using SOLIDWORKS Simulation?

- 40lb

- 20lb

- **120lb**

- Additional information is required

37. A material is orthotropic if its mechanical or thermal properties are not unique and independent in three mutually perpendicular directions.

- True

- **False**

38. An increase in the number of elements in a mesh for a part will:

- Decrease calculation accuracy and time

- **Increase calculation accuracy and time**

- Have no effect on the calculation

- Change the FOS below 1

39. SOLIDWORKS Simulation uses the von Mises Yield Criterion to calculate the Factor of Safety of many ductile materials. According to the criterion:

- **Material yields when the von Mises stress in the model equals the yield strength of the material**

- Material yields when the von Mises stress in the model is 5 times greater than the minimum tensile strength of the material

- Material yields when the von Mises stress in the model is 3 times greater than the FOS of the material

- None of the above

40. SOLIDWORKS Simulation calculates structural failure on:

- Buckling

- Fatigue

- Creep

- **Material yield**

41. Apply a uniform total force of 200lb on two faces of a model. The two faces have different areas. How do you apply the load using SOLIDWORKS Simulation for a Linear Static Study?

- Select the two faces and input a normal to direction force of 200lb on each face

- Select the two faces and a reference plane. Apply 100lb on each face

- **Apply equal force to the two faces. The force on each face is the total force divided by the total area of the two faces**.

- None of the above

42. Maximum and Minimum value indicators are displayed on Stress and Displacement plots in SOLIDWORKS Simulation for a Linear Static Study.

- **True**

- False

43. What SOLIDWORKS Simulation tool should you use to determine the result values at specific locations (nodes) in a model using SOLIDWORKS Simulation?

- Section tool
- **Probe tool**
- Clipping tool
- Surface tool

44. What criteria are best suited to check the failure of ductile materials in SOLIDWORKS Simulation?

- Maximum von Mises Strain and Maximum Shear Strain criterion
- **Maximum von Misses Stress and Maximum Shear Stress criterion**
- Maximum Mohr-Coulomb Stress and Maximum Mohr-Coulomb Shear Strain criterion
- Mohr-Coulomb Stress and Maximum Normal Stress criterion

45. Set the scale factor for plots_____ to avoid any misinterpretation of the results, after performing a Static analysis with gap/contact elements.

- Equal to 0
- **Equal to 1**
- Less than 1
- To the Maximum displacement value for the model

46. It is possible to mesh _____ with a combination of Solids, Shells and Beam elements in SOLIDWORKS Simulation.

- **Parts and Assemblies**
- Only Parts
- Only Assemblies
- None of the above

47. SOLIDWORKS Simulation supports multi-body parts. Which of the following is a true statement?

- You can employ different mesh controls to each Solid body
- You can classify Contact conditions between multiple Solid bodies
- You can classify a different material for each Solid body
- **All of the above are correct**

48. Which statement best describes a Compatible mesh?

- A mesh where only one type of element is used
- **A mesh where elements on touching bodies have overlaying nodes**
- A mesh where only a Shell or Solid element is used
- A mesh where only a single Solid element is used

49. The Ratio value in Mesh Control provides the geometric growth ratio from one layer of elements to the next.

- **True**
- False

50. The structures displayed in the following illustration are best analyzed using:

- Shell elements
- Solid elements
- **Beam elements**
- A mixture of Beam and Shell elements

51. The structure displayed in the following illustration is best analyzed using:

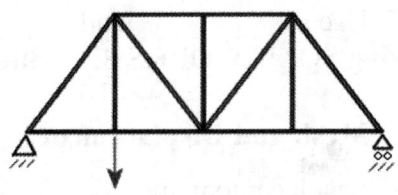

- Shell elements
- Solid elements
- **Beam elements**
- A mixture of Beam and Shell elements

52. The structure displayed in the following illustration is best analyzed using:

- **Shell elements**
- Solid elements
- Beam elements
- A mixture of Beam and Shell elements

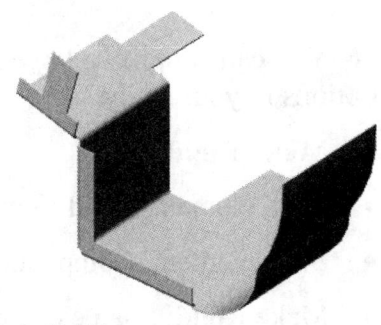

Sheet metal model

53. The structure displayed in the following illustration is best analyzed using:

- Shell elements
- **Solid elements**
- Beam elements
- A mixture of Beam and Shell elements

54. Surface models can only be meshed with _____ elements.

- **Shell elements**
- Solid elements
- Beam elements
- A mixture of Beam and Shell elements

55. Use the _____ and _____ plots to calculate the distance between two nodes using SOLIDWORKS Simulation.

- **Mesh and Displacement**
- Displacement and FOS
- Resultant Displacement and FOS
- None of the above

56. You can simplify a large assembly in a Static Study by using the _____ or _____ options in your study.

- **Make Rigid, Fix**
- Shell element, Solid element
- Shell element, Compound element
- Make Rigid, Load element

57. A force "F" applied in a static analysis produces a resultant displacement URES. If the force is now 2x F and the mesh is not changed, then URES will:

- Double if there is no contact specified and there are large displacements in the structure
- Be divided by 2 if contacts are specified
- The analysis must be run again to find out
- **Double if there is no source of nonlinearity in the study (like contacts or large displacement options)**

58. To compute thermal stresses on a model with a uniform temperature distribution, what type/types of study/studies are required?

- **Static only**
- Thermal only
- Both Static and Thermal
- None of these answers is correct

59. In an h-adaptive method, use smaller elements in mesh regions with high errors to improve the accuracy of results.

- **True**
- False

60. In a p-adaptive method, use elements with a higher order polynomial in mesh regions with high errors to improve the accuracy of results.

- **True**
- False

61. Where will the maximum stress be in the illustration?

- A
- B
- C
- D

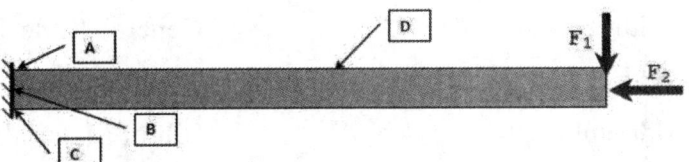

SOLIDWORKS DOCUMENT TYPES

SOLIDWORKS has three main document file types: Part, Assembly and Drawing, but there are many additional supporting types that you may want to know. Below is a brief list of these supporting file types:

Design Documents	Description
.sldprt	SOLIDWORKS Part document
.slddrw	SOLIDWORKS Drawing document
.sldasm	SOLIDWORKS Assembly document

Templates and Formats	Description
.asmdot	Assembly Template
.asmprp	Assembly Template Custom Properties tab
.drwdot	Drawing Template
.drwprp	Drawing Template Custom Properties tab
.prtdot	Part Template
.prtprp	Part Template Custom Properties tab
.sldtbt	General Table Template
.slddrt	Drawing Sheet Template
.sldbombt	Bill of Materials Template (Table-based)
.sldholtbt	Hole Table Template
.sldrevbt	Revision Table Template
.sldwldbt	Weldment Cutlist Template
.xls	Bill of Materials Template (Excel-based)

Library Files	Description
.sldlfp	Library Part file
.sldblk	Blocks

Other	Description
.sldstd	Drafting standard
.sldmat	Material Database
.sldclr	Color Palette File
.xls	Sheet metal gauge table

Index

Index

Index